Hidden Texts, Hidden Nation
(Re)Discoveries of Wales in Travel Writing
in French and German (1780–2018)

KATHRYN N. JONES,
CAROL TULLY,
HEATHER WILLIAMS

Hidden Texts, Hidden Nation

(Re)Discoveries of Wales in Travel Writing
in French and German (1780–2018)

LIVERPOOL UNIVERSITY PRESS

First published 2020 by
Liverpool University Press
4 Cambridge Street
Liverpool
L69 7ZU

British Library Cataloguing-in-Publication data
A British Library CIP record is available

ISBN 978-1-78962-143-3 cased

Typeset by Carnegie Book Production, Lancaster
Printed and bound by CPI Group (UK) Ltd, Croydon CR0 4YY

Contents

Acknowledgements

This book was made possible by the generous funding of the Arts and Humanities Research Council which has supported the *European Travellers to Wales 1750–2010* project since 2013. The project has been a collaboration between Bangor University, Swansea University and the University of Wales Centre for Advanced Welsh and Celtic Studies, based in Aberystwyth. The fact that this is a co-authored book speaks to the overall collaborative nature of the whole project and the authors would like to thank a range of individuals and organizations who have helped along the way.

We would like to thank our Research Assistant, Rita Singer, who has been central to the success of the project, in particular in terms of the archival work undertaken to locate the primary sources which surface, many for the first time, in this book. We would also like to thank our two doctoral students, Anna-Lou Dijkstra (Swansea) and Christina Les (Bangor), both of whom have now successfully defended their theses.

We are indebted also to the project's Advisory Board: Mary-Ann Constantine, Robert Evans, Charles Forsdick, Michael Freeman, Katie Gramich, Dafydd Johnston and Alison Martin. Their support and advice have been invaluable.

The staff at various organizations have been hugely helpful, especially those at the National Library of Wales, the Royal Commission on the Ancient and Historical Monuments of Wales, Aberdeen University Library, the Bodleian Library, Ceredigion Museum, Swansea Museum, Storiel (Bangor) and the Centre de recherche bretonne et celtique at the Université de Bretagne Occidentale in Brest, in particular Fañch Postic, Nelly Blanchard and Ronan Calvez.

We are also extremely grateful to colleagues at our own institutions for their support. Nia Davies and Angharad Elias (CAWCS) and Heather Roberts (Bangor) have been hugely helpful behind the scenes. Particular thanks should go to Sam Foster from Bangor University IT Services for his hard work in building our website and database (http://etw.bangor. ac.uk/about-database).

We would also like to thank the following people for sending us valuable references and information that has been used in our database: Gwen Awbery, Wendy Bracewell, Stephen Briggs, Ann Corkett, Adam N. Coward, Alex Drace-Francis, Robert Evans, Michael Freeman, Gábor Gelléri, Bruce Griffiths, Heini Gruffudd, Bethan Jenkins, Marion Löffler, Peter Lord, Gerald Morgan, Ann Parry Owen, Charles Parry, Fañch Postic, Elmar Schenkel, Joachim Schwend, Elizabeth Siberry, Richard Tholoniat, Peter Ward Jones, C.J. Woods and Anthony Zielonka.

We would also like to thank Liverpool University Press, especially Chloé Johnson, for their support in seeing this book through to publication.

Finally, a word of thanks should go to our respective families and friends who, as ever, have been there to lend encouragement throughout. *Diolch o galon.*

Introduction

Hidden Texts, Hidden Nation

Wales is a nation whose identity has long been compromised by its relationship with its globally dominant neighbour. The infamous entry in the index of the 1888 *Encyclopaedia Britannica* which read 'For Wales, see England' remains a significant frame of reference for contemporary scholars, journalists, writers, artists and other social commentators seeking to tease apart Wales and its identities in order to place Welsh culture on an equal footing. The persistence of the tendency to see Wales as a part of England has been further complicated in the years since devolution which have seen Welsh difference expand to fields beyond those of language and culture to legislation, education and the broader political and social landscape. This tension is reflected in the nation's profile within the travel writing genre. From the mid-eighteenth century, which saw the emergence of the travel narrative as a popular source of information and entertainment, writing about Wales has often been embedded in accounts of travel to 'England' or overlooked because it served as a transit zone for travellers on their way to Ireland.

This reflects a broader issue in relation to the cultural 'invisibility' of Wales as a minoritized nation. Even where there is interest in 'Celtic' nations, Wales has often been overlooked in both the artistic and critical imaginations in favour of Scotland and Ireland.[1] In the section on the Celtic lands in his 1999 anthology of French travel writing on the British Isles, Jacques Gury explicitly treats Wales as a forgotten place, described as the 'Cendrillon des îles Britanniques' [Cinderella of the British Isles] for French travellers, with Wales featuring for all of twenty pages in

---

1   See, for example, Damian Walford Davies and Lynda Pratt (eds), *Wales and the Romantic Imagination* (Cardiff: University of Wales Press, 2007), p. 2.

a volume numbering over twelve hundred.[2] The resultant invisibility in the broader European cultural context and in travel writing in particular leaves Wales as something of an elided nation; hidden, as nineteenth-century German traveller Hermann von Pückler-Muskau puts it, between England and Ireland.

The complex relationship with England has not only led to minoritization and elision in relation to Wales's place in the travel writing canon but also to a skewing of focus in the field of travel writing studies which, prior to this volume, had almost exclusively centred on English writing about Wales. Even here, Welsh tours remain under-researched in travel writing studies as a whole when compared to tours of Scotland and Ireland; as Elizabeth Edwards claims, these texts have been neglected because they are positioned 'on the fringes of our field via geography and genre – an outlying location compounded by travel writing's status as a category that defies easy definition'.[3] While prominent Welsh historians and sociopolitical commentators have probed the temporality of Wales and its nationhood, asking *When Was Wales?*[4] and *Why Wales Never Was*,[5] external observers have remained focused on its topography and geopolitical location, more likely to ask, 'Where is Wales'?

That is not to say, however, that travel writing on Wales has been entirely ignored. The argument that perceptions of Wales begin to shift dramatically in the last decades of the eighteenth century is certainly well rehearsed in scholarship on English writing about Wales. According to Malcolm Andrews, by the 1780s 'the Welsh tour could no longer be considered [neglected]'.[6] Similarly Hywel Davies asserts that 'accounts of Wales were so numerous during the last two decades of the eighteenth century that "Welsh Tours" constituted a

2   Jacques Gury, 'Le Pays de Galles oublié', in *Le Voyage Outre-Manche. Anthologie de voyageurs français de Voltaire à Mac Orlan du XVIIIe au XXe siècle* (Paris: Robert Laffont, 1999), pp. 565–85 (p. 565).

3   Elizabeth Edwards, '"A Kind of Geological Novel": Wales and Travel Writing, 1783–1819', *Romanticism*, 24:2 (2018), pp. 134–47 (p. 135).

4   Gwyn Alf Williams, *When Was Wales?* (Harmondsworth: Penguin, 1985).

5   Simon Brooks, *Pam na fu Cymru: Methiant Cenedlaetholdeb Cymraeg* (Cardiff: University of Wales Press, 2015), subsequently published in English as *Why Wales Never Was: The Failure of Welsh Nationalism* (Cardiff: University of Wales Press, 2017).

6   Malcolm Andrews, *The Search for the Picturesque* (Aldershot: Scholar Press, 1989), p. 114.

literary type'.[7] The shift they both refer to was from overwhelmingly negative connotations of Wales's backwardness and barrenness for English observers to broadly positive associations, including cultural authenticity and pleasing aesthetics. In the words of historian Prys Morgan, this was a 'period of one of the greatest shifts in the stereotyping of Wild Wales, away from the hostile image of incivility to one of admiration'.[8] Capturing the exotic yet familiar appeal of Wales, Katie Gramich observes that increasing numbers of travellers from the nineteenth century onwards became keen to take advantage of what she has termed Wales's 'accessible otherness'.[9]

Numerous explanations for this growth in travel narratives on Wales have been offered by scholars of travel writing. For instance, Mary-Ann Constantine states that the hundreds of surviving travelogues to Romantic-era Wales are 'testimony to a seismic shift in aesthetics and the magnetic pull of a nascent tourist industry'.[10] On the literary front, the publication of Thomas Pennant's *A Tour in Wales* (1778–1781) is widely considered to have been key in encouraging visitors and writers alike.[11]

7   Hywel M. Davies, 'Wales in English Travel Writing 1791–8: The Welsh Critique of Theophilus Jones', *Welsh History Review*, 23:3 (2007), pp. 65–93 (p. 65).

8   Prys Morgan, 'Wild Wales: Civilizing the Welsh from the Sixteenth to the Nineteenth Centuries', in Peter Burke, Brian Harrison and Paul Slack (eds), *Civil Histories: Essays in Honour of Keith Thomas* (Oxford: Oxford University Press, 2000), pp. 265–83 (p. 274). This shift is also traced in W.J. Hughes, *Wales and the Welsh in English Literature from Shakespeare to Scott* (Wrexham: Hughes and Son, 1924), pp. 84–107; Jane Zaring, 'The Romantic Face of Wales', *Annals of the Association of American Geographers*, 67:3 (1977), pp. 397–418; and Shannon L. Rogers, 'From Wasteland to Wonderland: Wales in the Imagination of the English Traveller, 1720–1895', *North American Journal of Welsh Studies*, 2:2 (2002), pp. 15–26. Beyond travel writing, this shift in perception is traced in R.R. Davies, *The First English Empire: Power and Identities in the British Isles, 1093–1343* (Oxford: Oxford University Press, 2000).

9   Katie Gramich, '"Every Hill Has its History, Every Region its Romance": Travellers' Constructions of Wales, 1844–1913', in Benjamin Colbert (ed.), *Travel Writing and Tourism in Britain and Ireland* (Basingstoke: Palgrave Macmillan, 2012), pp. 147–63 (p. 147).

10   Mary-Ann Constantine, 'Beauty Spot, Blind Spot: Romantic Wales', *Literature Compass*, 5:3 (2008), pp. 577–90 (p. 577).

11   See Alex Deans and Nigel Leask, 'Curious Travellers: Thomas Pennant and the Welsh and Scottish Tour (1760–1820)', *Studies in Scottish Literature*, 42:2

Long hailed as the 'father of Cambrian tourists',[12] more recent commentators have argued that he 'commodified' Welsh culture and history,[13] but all agree that he 'effectively set tourist itineraries for the future', and made an imprint on subsequent texts.[14] Equally important in the popularization of Wales as a picturesque travel destination was William Gilpin's *Observations on the River Wye, and Several Parts of South Wales* (1772). Held to have 'unleashed hordes of tourists' in the Wye Valley in south Wales, Gilpin's ideas certainly influenced French travellers, in part via Blumenstein's 1800 translation, and also indirectly through their early adaptations in illustrated travel accounts between 1786 and 1811.[15]

Other studies have drawn attention to the role of various literary sources in bringing about the shift in perception, citing the hugely influential ode 'The Bard' (1757) by Thomas Gray (1716–1771), which helped to popularize the Welsh sublime, and *Ossian*, the spurious epic published by James MacPherson (1736–1796), which played its part in luring to Wales travellers who hoped to find scenery similar to that described in the poetry.[16] The cultural revival in Welsh textual

(2016), pp. 164–72; Pennant's significance and influence on later travellers and writers are currently being reassessed in the context of a major AHRC-funded research project entitled 'Curious Travellers'.

12   This claim was first made in 1851, and is reevaluated in R. Paul Evans, 'Thomas Pennant (1726–1798): The Father of Cambrian Tourists', *Welsh History Review*, 13:4 (1987), pp. 395–417.

13   Shawna Lichtenwalner, *Claiming Cambria* (Newark: University of Delaware Press, 2008), p. 168.

14   Mary-Ann Constantine, '"To trace thy country's glories to their source": Dangerous History in Thomas Pennant's *Tour in Wales*', in Porscha Fermanis and John Regan (eds), *Rethinking British Romantic History 1770–1845* (Oxford: Oxford University Press, 2014), pp. 121–43 (p. 123).

15   Lynne Withey, *Grand Tours and Cook's Tours: A History of Leisure Travel, 1750–1915* (London: Aurum Press, 1997), p. 37; William Gilpin, *Observations pittoresques sur le cours de la Wye et sur différentes parties du pays de Galles, par M. William Gilpin*, translated by Baron de B*** [Blumenstein] (Breslau: G.T. Korn, 1800). For an overview of Gilpin's ideas and influence on English travelogues to Wales, see Miriam Griffiths, 'Wider Empire for the Sight: Picturesque Scenery and the First Tourists', in William Tudeman (ed.), *The Welsh Connection* (Llandysul: Gomer, 1986), pp. 67–98; and for a French perspective, see Rita Singer, 'Through Wales in the Footsteps of William Gilpin: Illustrated Travel Accounts by Early French Tourists, 1768–1810', *European Romantic Review*, 30:2 (2019), pp. 127–47.

16   Richard Morris wrote to his brother Lewis in 1763: 'Macpherson with his Galic poetry has set all the English antiquarians agog after the Welsh, in the hopes

scholarship and the interest in antiquarianism among the London Welsh in the late eighteenth century has been described as an 'outburst of interest in things Welsh'.[17] Still others have suggested that the newfound popularity of Wales was a response to social disturbances in England; according to Andrews, 'the idealisation of a remote, peaceful rural existence intensified at a time when there was conspicuous social unrest in the English counties'.[18] In similar vein, David Solkin has memorably described Welsh scenery as a 'landscape of reaction',[19] and Romantic-era scholars have argued that Wales provided not only a political utopia but also a refuge for radicalism during the French Revolution.[20]

What all these studies have in common, however, is a reliance on English-language source texts. According to Hywel Davies, in his study of travelogues to Wales in the 1790s: 'It was the English, by and large, who were the authors of Welsh Tours'.[21] Prys Morgan has described the second half of the eighteenth century as a time 'when English sympathy for things Welsh rose to a high point'.[22] One of the aims of this book is to locate the change in perceptions of Wales on the part of observers from further afield, and to show how many European exceptions there are to this assumption. This book seeks to broaden perspectives outwards to encompass Continental perceptions, investigating the works of European travellers to Wales writing in languages other than English. While it does

to find something equal to it'; J.H. Davies (ed.), *The Letters of Lewis, Richard, William and John Morris, of Anglesey, (Morrisiaid Mon)*, 1728–1765, 2 vols, (Aberystwyth: Published privately by the editor and printed for him by Fox, Jones & Co., Oxford, 1907–1909), 2: p. 537., cited in Constantine, 'Beauty Spot', p. 578. On the role of Gray, see Sarah Prescott, *Eighteenth-Century Writing from Wales: Bards and Britons* (Cardiff: University of Wales Press, 2008).

17   Prys Morgan, 'From a Death to a View: The Hunt for the Welsh Past in the Romantic Period', in Eric Hobsbawm and Terence Ranger (eds), *The Invention of Tradition* (Cambridge: Cambridge University Press, 1992), pp. 43–100 (p. 43). See also his *The Eighteenth-Century Renaissance* (Swansea: Christopher Davies, 1981).

18   Andrews, *The Search for the Picturesque*, p. 111.

19   David H. Solkin, *Richard Wilson: The Landscape of Reaction* (London: Tate Gallery Publications Department, 1982).

20   Damian Walford Davies, following Alan Liu, asserts that Wales at this time can be seen 'as a mirror of, and substitute for, radical France', *Presences that Disturb: Models of Romantic Identity in the Literature and Culture of the 1790s* (Cardiff: University of Wales Press, 2002), p. 65.

21   Davies, 'Wales in English Travel Writing', p. 65.

22   Morgan, 'Wild Wales', p. 265.

not encompass detailed discussion of accounts in English by travellers from Ireland, Scotland and England, writing within the confines of the British (imperial) framework, it does note the presence of specific texts in English which had a strong influence on the reception of Wales by European travellers.

Despite the generally deficient appraisal of European travel writing on Wales highlighted above, there are, in fact, a great many travel accounts in existence. They are simply much harder to find, partly due to the obscurity of their publication, but chiefly because the default for most European languages and travellers to the British Isles has been to define the entire archipelago as 'England' – a tendency which continues to this day among some travellers despite the greater visibility of Wales as an entity and travel destination in its own right. The large degree of overlap between the names 'England', 'Angleterre', 'Grande Bretagne', 'Pays de Galles' and 'Wales' in the titles of travel works, as well as incorrect labelling in archives and databases, means that Wales has often found itself subsumed into narratives on England; these are, put simply, hidden texts on a hidden nation.

Works studied for the present volume include travelogues, private correspondences, diaries, periodical contributions and blogs which have Wales or Welsh culture as their focus. The definition of 'traveller' includes people from contrasting socioeconomic backgrounds, travelling for the purpose of leisure, scholarship or commerce. It also encompasses the textual responses of those travellers who as exiles and refugees found themselves in Wales as a result of sociopolitical events rather than of their own volition. These involuntary travellers undertake travel as a negotiation of displacement which allows for observation, self-development and understanding of new environments.[23] The (hi)stories of travellers or migrants who did not leave textual traces of their time in Wales fall outside the scope of this project. Therefore, to take perhaps the most prominent example, the voices of the many twentieth-century Breton onion sellers who came to Wales remain silent. Conversely, advances in the digitization of texts and catalogues such as the Gallica digital library at the *Bibliothèque nationale de France* [National Library of France] have facilitated much greater access to previously concealed works on Wales written in languages other than English, which has allowed a far wider range of viewpoints to be studied.

23   See Carol Tully, 'Out of Europe: Travel and Exile in Mid-Twentieth-Century Wales', *Studies in Travel Writing*, 18:2 (2016), pp. 174–86 (p. 184).

This volume recognizes the mutability and fluidity involved in any definition of 'Europe' or 'European' and subscribes to Wendy Bracewell's view that, 'like all imaginative geographies, Europe's symbolic maps are highly contingent, varying according to perspective and purpose as well as changing over time. There is no one unified mental map of Europe, nor are its cultural coordinates – North, South, East, and West – fixed and immutable'.[24] The travellers under discussion in this volume are northern and western Europeans who are interpreting the unknown and unfamiliar destination of Wales for the readership at home.[25] The vast majority of European accounts dealing with Wales since the mid-eighteenth century have been written by French- and German-speaking travellers, which thus constitute the main focus of this study. The final chapter also analyses texts written in Breton in the twentieth and twenty-first centuries. The high proportion of texts uncovered in these areas would appear to reflect the greater mobility of travellers from France and Germany as Britain's nearest trading partners during the nineteenth century in particular.

Texts written in French come primarily from France itself. However, while France remained a stable geopolitical entity during the period of study, it is acknowledged that the notion of 'Germany' is rather more fluid and encompasses numerous states and political alliances over time. The term 'German' is used throughout to denote the language used while the nationality of individual writers is noted. The complexity of authorial identity is underlined by the fact that, while the vast majority of texts written in German are authored by travellers from Germany, Austria and Switzerland, this is not exclusively the case. In his *Aus dem Tagebuche eines in Grossbritannien reisenden Ungarn* (1837) [From the Diary of a Hungarian Travelling in Great Britain], Hungarian cultural tourist Ferenc A. Pulszky (1814–1897), writing in German, places Wales within a more familiar European frame of reference, deeming that the melancholy of the overgrown Tintern Abbey surpasses that of ancient Greek and Roman architecture, and comparing the coast between the

---

24 Wendy Bracewell, 'Europe', in Carl Thompson (ed.), *The Routledge Companion to Travel Writing* (New York: Routledge, 2015), pp. 341–50 (p. 341).

25 On eastern European travel writing on Europe, see Wendy Bracewell and Alex Drace-Francis (eds), *Under Eastern Eyes: A Comparative Introduction to East European Travel Writing on Europe* (Budapest: CEU Press, 2008), and *A Bibliography of East European Travel Writing on Europe* (Budapest: CEU Press, 2008).

Great Orme and Bangor with that of the Gulf of Naples.[26] Furthermore, an anonymous account of holidaying in Aberystwyth, admiring the Welsh cultural revival and linguistic vitality, was published in German in the Latvian capital of Riga at the onset of the First World War in the summer of 1914.[27] While the vast majority of French-language travellers came from France, others also originated from Belgium, Switzerland and Romania. To take one example, Romanian mathematician, engineer and inventor of the fountain pen Petrache Poenaru (1799–1875) came to study industrial production in south Wales in 1831, and he compared the Welsh landscape with that of France.[28]

While this study examines the evolving perceptions and representations of Wales in texts written in French, German and Breton, travel accounts in other languages do exist from other parts of Europe, including Imperial Russia, Hungary, Poland, Czechoslovakia, Norway and Iceland. Dutch-language travelogues constitute the largest number in this category, ranging from a governess's views of north Wales's stately homes in 1849[29] to a 1908 exploration of railway networks and steamboat lines,[30] and numerous accounts of the 1930 Labour Party conference in Llandudno.[31] In the case of Sweden, there is a cluster of mid-eighteenth-century travel texts by metallurgists and mineralogists who came to Wales to study its industry and geology.[32] These accounts

---

26   Ferenc A. Pulszky, *Aus dem Tagebuche eines in Grossbritannien reisenden Ungarn* (Pesth: Gustav Heckenast, 1837), pp. 95–98, 108–17.

27   'Aus dem Land der Barden und Druiden', *Rigasche Rundschau*, 20 August 1914, pp. 1–2.

28   Petrache Poenaru, 'Voyage en Angleterre', in N. Iorga (ed.), 'Contributii la istoria literaturii romane in veacul al XVIII-lea si al XIX-lea', *Analele Academiei Romane. Memoriile sectiunii literare*, 2nd series, 28 (1905–1906), pp. 255–57.

29   M.M. Chr., 'Schetsen uit Noord-Wales: Uit de Reis-herinneringen eener jeugdige Hollandsche', *Het Leeskabinet*, 36:1 (1869), pp. 134–51.

30   Gos[ewinus] de Voogt, 'Per Grimsbylijn: Great-Central Ry. naar Wales', *Eigen Haard*, 34:34 (22 August 1908), pp. 534–38.

31   See for example J.J. de R., 'Naar Llandudno', *Voorwaarts: sociaal-democratisch dagblad*, 9 October 1930, unpaginated.

32   For example, Swedish industrial spy Bengt Ferner came to Wales in May 1760 to inspect spelter works in Holywell and lead mines near Flint. See his *Resa in Europa, en astronom, industriespion och teaterhabitue genom Denmark, Tyskland, Holland, England och Italien – 1758–1762*, ed. Sten G. Lindberg (Uppsala: Swedish Society for the History of Science, 1956), pp. 258–60. See also William Linnard, 'A Swedish visitor to Flintshire in 1760', *Flintshire Historical Society Journal*, 30 (1981–1982), pp. 145–49.

from more distant countries can offer unusual perspectives on Wales; for example, the tremendous heat experienced by Kór Söngskolans from Reykjavik during the Llangollen International Eisteddfod in 1977 made the members of the choir wish for a spot of Icelandic rain to cool them in their traditional costumes.[33] While Wales was a destination to be visited for trade or leisure for northern, western and eastern Europeans, significant blank spots exist with regard to travellers from southern Europe. A short travelogue in Galician published in 2010 by Claudio Rodríguez Fer (1956–), entitled 'Que verde era o meu Gales' [How Green Was My Wales],[34] is one of the very few textual traces left by travellers from Spain or Portugal.

One of the major objectives of this study is to explore how the main body of travel narratives emerges and how it engages with Wales as an entity to be disentangled from its relationship to both England and the rest of the European Celtic periphery. Analysis of the texts will centre on the representation of Wales and 'Welshness' and focus on key points in the period of Welsh modernization from the Industrial Revolution to the post-devolution era, in order to chart how European perceptions of Wales have developed and evolved since the 1780s. Wales will be positioned as a case study, an exemplar of a particular type of relationship between peripheral and hegemonic culture(s). This volume goes beyond the centre-periphery relationships and major-minor dichotomies found in many studies of travel writing to also analyse periphery-periphery relations, notably through the significant role played by Breton travellers to Wales.[35] Exploration of the texts reveals some overlap in terms of foci and themes with the English-language tours and there are also a number of key themes shared between French- and German-speaking travellers. However, even when dealing with similar topics, the two traditions often treat these very differently and approach them from very diverse perspectives, dictated in large part by the circumstances of their native lands, illustrating the notion that travel writing is, as Patrick Holland and Graham Huggan put

---

33 'Minningar úr ferð Söngskólakórsins til Wales í byrjun julí', *Alþýðublaðið Sunnudagsblað*, 146 (24 July 1977), pp. 3, 8.

34 Claudio Rodríguez Fer, 'Que verde era o meu Gales', *Unión libre*, 15, 'Meus amores celtas' (2010), pp. 75–80.

35 Breton is understood here as an identifier of origin; it was only from the middle of the twentieth century that several travellers to Wales also began to publish accounts written in Breton.

it, a 'useful vehicle of cultural self-perception' and critique.[36] In the latter part of the twentieth century, differences between French- and German-language cultural representations of Wales receded markedly, something which allows for comparative analysis of their similar loci of interest and new interpretative frameworks for envisioning the nation.

In the past decade, interest in Wales's Europeanism has grown once more, having been rather neglected since the heady days of Saunders Lewis's 'European' literary criticism and R.T. Jenkins's Continental historical perspective. Recent work in Welsh studies displays an impatience with a reliance on England as sole point of comparison. This includes a study of cultural nationalism by Simon Brooks, who berates scholars for confining the horizon of Welsh studies to England, while himself including discussion of German views of Wales in a resolutely comparatist approach.[37] Michael Maurer's anthology, *Wales: Die Entdeckung einer Landschaft und eines Volkes durch deutsche Reisende (1780–1860)* (2014) [Wales: The Discovery of a Landscape and People through German Travellers (1780–1860)] provides an introduction to the writing of a number of German travellers.[38] Angharad Price has recently discussed the life of Welsh poet T.H. Parry Williams in a European context that encompasses his own travels but also the flow of Celtic scholars who arrived in Rhyd-ddu in Wales from the Continent.[39] Mererid Puw Davies has advocated a 'non-metropolitan reading' of German fiction about Wales in her study of W.G. Sebald's *Austerlitz*.[40] Christina Les has explored the representation of Wales in European fiction in geocritical terms, identifying a trend in reception towards a reading of Wales as a blank 'space' rather than a defined 'place'.[41]

---

36   Patrick Holland and Graham Huggan, *Tourists with Typewriters: Critical Reflections on Contemporary Travel Writing* (Ann Arbor: University of Michigan Press, 1998), pp. xiii, 48.

37   Brooks claims that anglophone British culture is 'unig gwmpawd diwylliannol y drafodaeth' [the only cultural compass of the debate]. Brooks, *Pam na fu Cymru*, p. 4, see also pp. 32–33, 39.

38   Michael Maurer (ed.), *Wales: Die Entdeckung einer Landschaft und eines Volkes durch deutsche Reisende (1780–1860)*, Quellen und Forschungen zur europäischen Kulturgeschichte 3 (Frankfurt am Main: Peter Lang, 2014).

39   Angharad Price, *Ffarwél i Freiburg: Crwydriadau Cynnar T.H. Parry-Williams* (Llandysul: Gomer, 2013), pp. 20–21, 134, 229.

40   Mererid Puw Davies, 'On (Not) Reading Wales in W.G. Sebald's *Austerlitz* (2001)', *Oxford German Studies*, 47:1 (2018), pp. 84–102 (p. 87).

41   Christina Les, 'Space beyond Place: Welsh Settings in European Fiction,

Further work that seeks to study Wales from new international perspectives in this vein include Daniel Williams's *Black Skin, Blue Books* (2012), whose exemplary comparative approach to Wales and Black American culture seeks to avoid the binary of the virtuous periphery that resists the homogenizing, dominating centre,[42] and M. Wynn Thomas, who recently argued for the 'micro-cosmopolitanism' of Wales. 'Micro-cosmopolitanism', a term coined by Michael Cronin, counters the idea that only large politico-cultural units can nurture tolerance and pluralism, and is thus a way of saying that Wales need not be narrow simply because it is small.[43] This book will demonstrate Wales's micro-cosmopolitanism, as well as responding to Thomas's call for 'a comprehensive study of Wales's relations with Europe'.[44]

In seeking to understand how these complex interdependencies might work, our understanding of travellers' perceptions of Wales draws on John Urry's concept of the socially constructed 'tourist gaze', created through notions of difference.[45] Urry and Jonas Larsen emphasize the importance of specific filters of perception: 'People gaze upon the world through a particular filter of ideas, skills, desires and expectations, framed by social class, gender, nationality, age and education. Gazing is a performance that orders, shapes and classifies, rather than reflects the world'.[46] Travel therefore plays a significant role in the formation and ordering of national and cultural identities,

1900–2010' (unpublished doctoral thesis, Bangor University, 2019).

42 Daniel Williams, *Black Skin, Blue Books: African Americans and Wales, 1845–1945* (Cardiff: University of Wales Press, 2012), p. 8.

43 See Michael Cronin, 'Global Questions and Local Visions: A Microcosmopolitan Perspective', in Alyce von Rothkirch and Daniel Williams (eds), *Beyond the Difference* (University of Wales Press, 2004), pp. 186–202, and also M. Wynn Thomas, 'Studying Wales Today: A Microcosmopolitan Approach', http://www.cymmrodorion.org/wp-content/uploads/2017/01/STUDYING-WALES-TODAY-M-W-THOMAS-6-DECEMBER-2016-compressed.pdf [accessed 27 January 2019]; M. Wynn Thomas, 'Introduction: Microcosmopolitan Wales', in *All That Is Wales: The Collected Essays of M. Wynn Thomas* (Cardiff: University of Wales Press, 2017), pp. 1–29.

44 M. Wynn Thomas, *The Nations of Wales: 1890–1914* (Cardiff: University of Wales Press, 2016), p. 296, n. 17.

45 John Urry, *The Tourist Gaze: Leisure and Travel in Contemporary Societies* (London: Sage, 1990), p. 1. Similarly, Caren Kaplan has described tourism as a 'structuring gaze' in *Questions of Travel: Postmodern Discourses of Displacement* (Durham, NC: Duke University, 1996), p. 79.

46 John Urry and Jonas Larsen, *The Tourist Gaze 3.0* (London: Sage, 2011), p. 2.

for both the 'home' and 'foreign' contexts. As Chris Rojek and John Urry have argued: 'All cultures get remade as a result of the flows of peoples, objects and images across national borders, whether these involve colonialism, work-based migration, individual travel or mass tourism'.[47] Michael Cronin, following Dean MacCannell, highlights the way in which contemporary travellers, in particular travellers from urban centres in developed countries, are typically in pursuit of authenticity and 'authentic experiences' in order to escape from the perceived 'inauthentic, alienating reality of their modernity'.[48] In the Welsh context, the argument might just as easily apply to travellers in earlier periods, and this dynamic can be seen to evolve over time as what might be termed the paraphernalia of tourism gradually becomes more evident. Cronin's observation of 'the use of staged authenticity, providing the tourist with a carefully constructed and managed illusion of authentic experience' (p. 94), is especially pertinent regarding the presentation of the Welsh language and cultures to overseas visitors. The Wales Tourist Board (known since 2006 as Visit Wales) has repeatedly used Wales's language and cultural uniqueness as marketing tools in order to attract overseas visitors, which can be seen to reflect the increased profile of Welsh national identity in the post-devolutionary age. In respect to tourist marketing, Nigel Morgan and Annette Pritchard have observed that while distinctive features of Welshness are generally evaluated negatively within the UK, overseas they are regarded as positive additions to the tourist experience.[49]

While the role of travellers and in particular travel writers in the process of identity formation has not yet been explored, Susan Pitchford's study *Identity Tourism: Imaging and Imagining the Nation* (2008) investigates tourism's potential for (re)shaping images and identities in the Welsh context. She contends that tourism, especially identity tourism, can help protect marginalized cultures as it depends on the notion of difference: cultural idiosyncrasies become tourist

47 Chris Rojek and John Urry, 'Introduction', in *Touring Cultures: Transformations of Travel and Theory* (London: Routledge, 1997), pp. 1–19 (p. 11).
48 Michael Cronin, *Across the Lines: Travel, Language, Translation* (Cork: Cork University Press, 2000), p. 94.
49 Nigel Morgan and Annette Pritchard, 'Culture, Identity and Tourism Representation: Marketing Cymru or Wales?', *Tourism Management*, 22 (2001), pp. 167–79 (p. 174).

commodities and therefore valuable and worth preserving. Pitchford argues that 'tourism can give the state an incentive to preserve the distinctiveness of minority cultures, which may outweigh the benefits of homogeneity'; moreover 'the growth of ethnic tourism can offer an economic rationale for the preservation of ethnic diversity'.[50] Instead of pursuing a policy of cultural and linguistic standardization, tourism serves in these cases as an incentive to preserve the distinctiveness of lesser-known cultures.[51]

In approaching the texts on Wales to be explored in this volume, it is useful to consider the parallel discussion of European travel writing about the rest of the world put forward in Mary Louise Pratt's *Imperial Eyes: Travel Writing and Transculturation* (1992).[52] Pratt's focus on the far-flung reaches of European empire can fruitfully be turned back in on itself, to foster an understanding of the representation of the related dynamics of power and appropriation of what could in a global context be termed rather perversely as Europe's internal periphery.[53] Her seminal study of the way 'travel books written by Europeans about non-European parts of the world created the imperial order for Europeans "at home" and gave them their place in it' (p. 3) centres on writing about spaces and places far removed from the European centre. These were places defined by their position on the periphery of modern geographical and cultural understanding, visited by few and studied by even fewer. The increasing number of travel accounts which emerged over the eighteenth and nineteenth centuries

50 Susan Pitchford, *Identity Tourism: Imaging and Imagining the Nation*, Tourism Social Science Series 10 (Bingley: Emerald, 2008), pp. 80–81.

51 Pitchford, *Identity Tourism*, pp. 80–81.

52 Mary Louise Pratt, *Imperial Eyes: Travel Writing and Transculturation*, 2nd ed. (London and New York: Routledge, 2008 [1992]). Pratt's understanding of 'European' in this context as primarily northern/western European travellers is close to our own.

53 There is a large and respected body of scholarship within Welsh history and Welsh literary studies that accepts the characterization of Wales as 'postcolonial'. Perceptions of Wales from beyond the British Isles are often mediated through Great Britain/England and, as such, can be said to parallel those of a colonized nation defined in relation to a dominant power. On Wales and postcolonialism, see in particular: Kirsti Bohata, *Postcolonialism Revisited* (Cardiff: University of Wales Press, 2004); Jane Aaron and Chris Williams, *Postcolonial Wales* (Cardiff: University of Wales, 2005). On postcolonialism in relation to other Celtic nations, see: Heather Williams, *Postcolonial Brittany: Literature Between Languages* (Bern: Peter Lang, 2007); Clare Carroll and Patricia King (eds), *Ireland and Postcolonial Theory* (Notre Dame: University of Notre Dame Press, 2003).

were part of the process of assimilation, bringing these lands into view by describing and explaining their differences and, often more importantly, their value to the European mission. Pratt highlights this (imperial) instrumentalization of travel narratives in her introduction:

> Travel books, I argue, gave European reading publics a sense of ownership, entitlement and familiarity with respect to the distant parts of the world that were being explored, invaded, invested in, and colonized. Travel books were very popular. They created a sense of curiosity, excitement, adventure, and even moral fervor about European expansionism. They were, I argue, one of the key instruments that made people 'at home' in Europe feel part of a planetary project; a key instrument, in other words, creating a 'domestic subject' of empire. (p. 3)

Many of the questions set out by Pratt in her introduction mirror those which are at the heart of this book, in particular those which relate to the way in which travel writing encapsulates a binary relationship between centre and periphery:

> With what codes has travel and exploration writing *produced* 'the rest of the world' for European readerships at particular points in Europe's expansionist process? How has it produced Europe's evolving conceptions of itself in relation to something it became possible to call 'the rest of the world'? How do the signifying practices of travel writing encode and legitimate the aspirations of economic expansion and empire? At what points do they undermine those aspirations? What did writers on the receiving end of European intervention do with those European codifications of their reality? How did they claim, revise and transcend them? How have Europe's subordinated others shaped Europeans' constructions of them and the places they inhabit? Or Europe's understanding of itself? (p. 4)

This last question is central to this book too: how does the depiction of a nation by a visiting traveller in fact reflect the issues, concerns and reality of that traveller's home environment? Those travellers are, of course, in the main what Pratt terms 'the "seeing man" [...] he whose imperial eyes passively look out and possess' (p. 9), but do they respond differently when travelling in Europe itself? This highlights one of the key aspects of the current study: how does European travel writing deal with the unknown on its doorstep? In the case of Wales, the answer is often 'with surprise'.

The intellectual European mission of the eighteenth and nineteenth centuries was to systematize and understand the world through exploration, scholarship and text, the natural extension of which is the internet-driven world of knowledge today. As Pratt argues, the 'systematizing of nature' had implications at home and abroad, as it was 'projected within European borders as well as beyond them' (p. 34). The Linnean systematization of the natural world was soon extended to the political, economic, industrial and cultural practices of every nation, which could again be applied at home or further afield. Pratt observes: 'As differences between urban and rural lifeways widened, European peasantry came to appear only somewhat less primitive than the inhabitants of the Amazon' (p. 35). As Pratt notes, this has a sentimental parallel where the traveller uses the 'contact zone' as an area for reflection, cultural recasting and appreciation.[54] In both cases, intellectual possession is central to the appropriation of the 'foreign' in the service of the imperial eye. That might include the fate of any number of smaller nations whose presence is clouded by an inequitable relationship with a hegemonic governing state or nation: Catalans, Basques, Lombards, to name but a few. Their treatment in travel writing fits with the broader trend towards a systematized knowledge of the world which emerged from the Enlightenment, but they can be seen to wrong-foot the traveller, arriving often in a place deemed to be known within the broader system, only to find it is in fact very different – not what the traveller was expecting. This is undoubtedly and consistently the case with Wales.

In a recent essay, Michael Cronin, following Jonathan Culler, observes that 'one of the paradoxes of contemporary travel is that travellers often want to see what they already know'.[55] That 'knowing' is created through exposure to written and oral accounts, visual images and education. It relies on these sources for accuracy. This knowledge is then reaffirmed or destabilized by the empirical experience gained by travel to the destination. How the individual travel writer chooses to approach that negotiation is at the very heart of the travel writing genre. In all of this, there is a fundamental choice to be made, conscious or otherwise, as to whether to reaffirm the expectations

---

54 Mary Louise Pratt's highly influential concept of the 'contact zone' is an 'attempt to invoke the spatial and temporal copresence of subjects previously separated by geographic and historical disjunctures, and whose trajectories now intersect'. This approach 'foregrounds the interactive, improvisational dimensions of colonial encounter'. Pratt, *Imperial Eyes*, p. 8.

55 Michael Cronin, 'Home Truths: Language, Slowness, and Microspection', in Colbert (ed.), *Travel Writing and Tourism*, pp. 219–35 (p. 219).

created by pre-travel knowledge or to destabilize those expectations by foregrounding differences encountered in actual contact with the destination, its culture and inhabitants. There is, of course, a range of options between these two poles. The writer positions themself within this spectrum according to their own circumstances, agenda and world view. As that positioning develops, the place visited becomes the place the writer wants it to be.

This shift can be understood in terms of Jean-Didier Urbain's notions of endotic and exotic travel.[56] Exotic travel is understood as travel away from the familiar, whereas endotic travel centres on re-engaging with the purportedly known, the local. The scope of what might be considered the 'local' is expanding exponentially in an increasingly globalized world with once-exotic places now – it is assumed – utterly familiar and underpinned accordingly by certain expectations. Indeed, the more established pre-travel expectations become, the less exotic and more endotic travel becomes – what is physically far becomes virtually near. Thus, the possibility of exotic travel is lessened by access to ever more information as the virtual world simultaneously informs the traveller's expectations and exposes the 'contact zone' to growing levels of scrutiny. It is increasingly hard to experience 'newness'; for many, in fact, the shock of the new is deadened. The traveller expects to know where they are going. As a result, to experience the once-characteristic novelty of the 'contact zone' requires ever more effort.

Benjamin Colbert argues that travellers are subject to what Germaine de Staël (1766–1817) was already calling 'a necessary alienation', 'the state of mind in which incomprehension dulls the gloss of preconceived familiarity, that textual legacy of accumulated travel writings'.[57] That state of incomprehension, arguably once a natural by-product of experiencing new locations and cultures with which one could only be marginally familiar, is increasingly conscious. This poses a problem for the travel writer in negotiating their own stance in relation to a given place: how to respond creatively to or distance oneself from an increasingly fixed set of notions of place? Cronin identifies endotic travel as a series of 'strategies of defamiliarization' which 'compel the reader to

---

56   Jean-Didier Urbain, *Secrets de voyage: menteurs, imposteurs et autres voyageurs immédiats* (Paris: Payot, 1998), pp. 217–32.

57   Benjamin Colbert, 'Britain through Foreign Eyes: Early Nineteenth-Century Home Tourism in Translation', in Colbert (ed.), *Travel Writing and Tourism*, pp. 68–84 (p. 68).

look afresh, to call into question the taken for granted, to take on board the infinitely receding complexity of the putatively routine or prosaic'.[58] As knowledge of places intensifies, the question arises as to how to travel 'endotically' in a destination rendered utterly familiar; how to establish 'strategies of defamiliarization' in a global-local context.

As Colbert's reference to Stäel makes clear, this is not a new phenomenon. The plethora of travel accounts found in today's globalized virtual world finds its historical equivalent in the rapid layering of accounts emerging from the publishing boom of the early to mid-nineteenth century. The effect today is probably more acute in terms of sheer volume but the impact on the reading public of the ever-expanding access to travel accounts in the early nineteenth century would have been similar in its ironically disorienting effect. The 'strategies of defamiliarization' identified by Cronin were soon required to enable travel writers to take a fresh look at places which were becoming increasingly familiar to a reading and, as tourism steadily developed, a travelling public.

What happens, however, when the weight of expectation is destabilized, either by some conscious strategy deployed by the travel writer or by the place itself? If travellers are used to expecting what they already know, what happens when that knowledge is either challenged or simply flawed, when they find they are not where they expected to be? This is particularly interesting in relation to travellers' responses to the unexpected aspect of peripheral places, places which are near and therefore thought to be familiar but which, in fact, turn out to be thoroughly unfamiliar: the bit of 'England' called Wales, for example. The issue of (often misleading) nomenclature regarding Wales is clearly connected to that of travellers' expectations of what they think they are seeing. There is an assumed endotic approach to travel to peripheral areas which is then undermined when the reality of their 'otherness' – effectively their exotic nature – becomes apparent.

In the case of Wales, notions of difference and peripherality are, perhaps inevitably, allied to the Celtic. The discussion of Wales as a Celtic nation, a major theme throughout the periods under discussion, is central to this volume. For the French-speaking travellers, this can be a matter of internal politics and cultural understanding with a propensity to view Wales through the prism of their own Celtic periphery, namely Brittany. For the German-speaking travellers, the

58   Cronin, 'Home Truths', p. 230.

issues centre more on the tense relationship between England and Wales and its subsequent impact on the survival of the Welsh language and culture. This differing approach is testament in itself to the complexity of the Celtic context. This book uses the terms 'Celt' and its derivatives 'Celtic', 'Celticity'/'Celticness', 'Celticist' and even 'Celtomania' in full awareness of the fact that they had become 'a battleground' in the 1990s.[59] Though the terms are much older, Malcolm Chapman's *The Celts: The Construction of a Myth* (1992) and Simon James's *The Atlantic Celts: Ancient People or Modern Invention?* (1999) ignited this debate in modern scholarship. Chapman's study demythologized the Celts as a category, and James highlighted doubts about the unreliability and selectivity of Celtic studies.[60] Amongst the most influential responses to this debate from within the discipline of Celtic studies was the collection of essays *Celticism* (1996), which developed the idea of a discourse about the Celts that might be considered as a parallel to Orientalism. It contained a key intervention by Patrick Sims-Williams that contributed to the deconstruction of the discipline's roots, but did so with characteristic erudition and patience, by exposing exaggerations and half-truths in the seminal texts of, among others, Ernest Renan (1823–1892) and Matthew Arnold (1822–1888).[61]

Renan's 'Celt' has been summed up by Malcolm Chapman as: 'A conflation of the domesticity and femininity of Renan's childhood; of the emotionality that he felt his intellectuality had lost him; all the supposed characteristics of primitive literature, *naïveté*, spontaneity,

59   On these problematic terms and the controversy, see Patrick Sims-Williams, 'Celtomania and Celtoscepticism', *Cambrian Medieval Celtic Studies*, 36 (1998), pp. 1–34 (p. 1); D. Ellis Evans, 'Celticity, Celtic Awareness and Celtic Studies', *Zeitschrift für celtische Philologie*, 49–50 (1997), pp. 1–27, where he claims that 'Celtomania' plagued the nineteenth century (p. 17).

60   An overview of the debate is available in Amy Hale and Philip Payton, 'Introduction', in Amy Hale and Philip Payton (eds), *New Directions in Celtic Studies* (Exeter: University of Exeter Press, 2000), pp. 1–14.

61   Ernest Renan, 'La Poésie des races celtiques', *Revue des Deux Mondes*, n.s. 5 (1854), pp. 473–506, reprinted in *Essais de morale et de critique* (Paris: Calmann-Lévy, 1928), pp. 375–456; Matthew Arnold, *On the Study of Celtic Literature* (London: Smith, Elder & Co., 1867); Patrick Sims-Williams, 'The Invention of Celtic Nature Poetry', in Terence Brown (ed.), *Celticism* (Amsterdam: Rodopi, 1996), pp. 97–124. See also Patrick Sims-Williams, 'The Visionary Celt: The Construction of an Ethnic Preconception', *Cambrian Medieval Celtic Studies*, 11 (1986), pp. 71–96.

and simple unaffected truth'.[62] Arnold's work, in embellishing and interpreting Renan, has in turn been described as 'arguably the most influential piece ever written in the field of Celtic studies'.[63] Together these are considered a watershed in perceptions of all things Celtic, and also to have inaugurated a discourse known as 'Celticism', formed by analogy with 'Orientalism'.[64] Just as 'Orientalism' describes a discourse composed of blanket statements about other cultures classed as 'Oriental', so 'Celticism' is composed of blanket statements about Celts made from a particular point of view.

Of course Renan's essay did not come out of the blue; rather it is a crystallization of themes that had been developing since Romanticism and can be seen as very much the product of its time, representing, as Chapman notes, a 'meeting point between the high sophistication of comparative philology as developed in Germany, France, and Britain from the initiative of Herder, and the popular perception of a Celtic fringe as an aesthetic survival in the industrial age'.[65] The overwhelming sentiment expressed is one of sadness and melancholia proposed as a context for the Celtic predilection for the spiritual or the otherworldly, or what Arnold, borrowing from the French historian Henri Martin (1810–1883), famously described as the Celts' resistance to 'the despotism of fact'.[66] This was an ostensibly pro-Celtic reaction to the positivist view that the Celtic languages, though noble, were not compatible with

62   Malcolm Chapman, *The Gaelic Vision in Scottish Culture* (London: Croom Helm, 1978), p. 84.

63   Malcolm Chapman, *The Celts: The Construction of a Myth* (London: Macmillan, 1992), p. 215. For a recent discussion of Arnold's text, see Daniel Williams, *Wales Unchained: Literature, Politics and Identity in the American Century* (Cardiff: University of Wales Press, 2015), especially p. 53, as well as his earlier 'Pan-Celticism and the Limits of Post-Colonialism: W.B. Yeats, Ernest Rhys and Williams Sharp in the 1890s', in Tony Brown and Russell Stephens (eds), *Nations and Relations: Writing across the British Isles* (Cardiff: New Welsh Review, 2000), pp. 1–29.

64   Edward W. Said, *Orientalism* (London: Penguin, 1995 [1978]). W. J. McCormack was the first to deliberately model 'Celticism' on 'Orientalism' in order to describe the discourse inaugurated by Renan and Arnold in his *Ascendancy and Tradition in Anglo-Irish Literary History from 1789 to 1939* (Oxford: Clarendon Press, 1985); see especially p. 220. For a sustained discussion of the term, see Brown (ed.), *Celticism* and the chapter 'Oriental Brittany' in Sharif Gemie, *Brittany, 1750–1950: The Invisible Nation* (Cardiff: University of Wales Press, 2007).

65   Chapman, *The Gaelic Vision*, p. 224.

66   Arnold, *Celtic Literature*, p. 102.

modern life and would eventually die. The analyses of travel narratives in French, Breton and German will question to what extent Wales becomes subsumed under the 'Celtic' label, and whether comparisons between Wales and other 'Celtic' nations such as Scotland, Ireland and perhaps most notably Brittany serve to illuminate or to obscure.

The identification of prevalent similarities between hegemonic European accounts of imperial expansionism and those directed internally towards depictions of the 'Celtic' nations, the Alps or the Mediterranean, for instance, does not take account of the way in which minoritized nations are treated within accounts of hegemonic nation states. That they require attention seems clear. As Charles Forsdick, Ludmilla Kostova and Corinne Fowler argue in relation to travel writing and ethics, within today's discipline of travel writing studies, there is an 'ethical imperative to challenge dominant voices and explore alternative means of intercultural contact and communication'.[67] As an 'inherently transcultural' and hybrid genre, travel writing 'permits critical dialogues that are themselves often powerfully comparative and cross-cultural'.[68] Nevertheless, this volume questions to what extent it is possible for travellers to encounter a minoritized culture without reference to the relationship of that culture with its hegemonic neighbours and the dominant critical discourse.

Michael Cronin is one of the few critics to have problematized the relationship between travel and so-called minority cultures and lesser-used languages. In *Across the Lines* (2000), his influential study of travel, language and translation, he addresses a number of the issues pertinent to the case of Wales in European travel writing. Cronin depicts the complex, labyrinthine dilemma faced by anglophone travellers in the British Isles who encounter 'pockets of translation resistance' in areas with strong accents or dialects.[69] The thwarted promise of monoglossia is amplified for non-anglophone travellers visiting an assumed English-speaking country, for which they are prepared, but who then discover that there is in fact another language at play, in this case Welsh. Cronin interrogates the issue of minority languages by examining anglophone writers' responses to Irish and Welsh. He notes how, for some writers, the

---

67   Charles Forsdick, Corinne Fowler and Ludmilla Kostova, 'Introduction: Ethics on the Move', in Corinne Fowler, Charles Forsdick and Ludmilla Kostova (eds), *Travel and Ethics* (New York: Routledge, 2014), pp. 1–15 (p. 3).

68   Forsdick, Fowler and Kostova, 'Ethics on the Move', p. 1.

69   Cronin, *Across the Lines*, p. 14.

presence of Irish is a sign of the 'implied pre-modern backwardness' of the nation, rather than evidence of the 'linguistic ineptness' of the writer concerned (p. 27). Similar attitudes are identified in Bill Bryson's 'vignette of comic condescension in his description of a Welsh soap-opera' (*Pobl y Cwm* [The People of the Valley]) in his *Notes from a Small Island* (1996) and Paul Theroux's *The Kingdom by the Sea* (1984) which views 'bilingualism not as an asset but as a congenital problem' (p. 27). Building on Johannes Fabian's notion of the 'denial of coevalness',[70] Cronin argues:

> The Western traveller represents the here and now, the trajectory of the modern while the country s/he visits is frozen in time. The response may either be to condemn this time-lag as further evidence of the feckless backwardness of the natives or to sentimentalise the glories of past greatness and adopt an elegiac salvage mode. Either way, the Western traveller is confirmed in his/her ready identification with modernity. (p. 27)

The minority-language speaker thereby inhabits a pre-modern and pre-technical 'world of quaint moral propriety and irredentist crankiness' (p. 27). In the Welsh context, this attitude is complicated by a third stance which is found in relation to the first half of the nineteenth century (when industrial expansion was a source of interest and wonder to travelling Europeans in search of ideas to transfer home), the early twentieth century (when the events of the Welsh Revival saw Wales emerge as a model of piety) and in the twenty-first century (specifically in relation to the social-political developments around devolution which have seen Wales foregrounded as a paradigm).

Observing the closely intertwined relationship between travel and translation, Cronin asserts that 'travel accounts themselves are active interpreters of the cultures through which they travel. They are in this respect translations of a culture into a language and like all translations they are productions in time' (p. 23). Nevertheless, the language of the place visited tends to be masked through some form of translation and rendered in the language of the published account. In the case of Welsh, this masking is often dual, the original speaker's words mediated via a local translator who is in turn then translated into the language of the travel writer. Thus, one of the main 'exotic' elements of the 'foreign' is ironically subverted in order to make it more accessible, a tendency

---

70 Johannes Fabian, *Time and the Other: How Anthropology Makes its Object* (New York: Columbia University Press, 1983), p. 36.

which often leads to the objectification of the 'travellees', the term coined by Pratt for those who populate the traveller's destination and inhabit the 'contact zone', defined as 'persons traveled to (or on) by a traveler, receptors of travel' (p. 258, n. 42). While acknowledging the risk of othering and denial of agency inherent in the binary suffixes of the terms traveller/travellee,[71] this volume advocates a fluid and active relationship between visitor and inhabitant described in terms of 'copresence' (Pratt, p. 8). This book explores to what extent Welsh inhabitants are present in these travel accounts and in which guise, for example as hosts, guides and servants. It considers whether their experiences, voices and viewpoints are represented directly or indirectly in the travel narratives, or whether their presence is obscured and silenced. Furthermore, it questions to what extent the travellee is able to 'write back' when the travel texts are unpublished and untranslated and therefore not received in the travellee culture.

The myriad motivations for travel to Wales considered here encompass Romantic appreciation of sublime landscapes, observation of industrial prowess and architectural feats, and participation in a religious revival and cultural festivals. The book adapts the concept of the long nineteenth century pioneered by historian Eric Hobsbawm, which here encompasses travel works written between 1784 and 1907, the period during which a narrative of Wales emerges in texts by travellers from Continental Europe. Following this Introduction, four chapters are devoted to the long nineteenth century which saw the zenith of western European travel writing on Wales, examining specific historical flashpoints, and significant cultural and religious movements, in first the French-language and then the German-language contexts. Having been thus 'discovered' by Continental travellers in the nineteenth century, in the years following the First World War it would appear that Wales became lost once more, remaining largely hidden until a new wave of interest emerged towards the end of the twentieth century. In the final

71 See, for example, Claire Lindsay's 'Beyond *Imperial Eyes*', in Justin D. Edwards and Rune Graulund (eds), *Postcolonial Travel Writing: Critical Explorations* (London: Palgrave Macmillan, 2011), pp. 17–35, which explores criticisms of Pratt's *Imperial Eyes*. Alex Drace-Francis underlines that 'travelees are often excluded from the group of recipients of the message. Whether they are excluded from speaking, Pratt doesn't say'. Alex Drace-Francis, *The Traditions of Invention: Romanian Ethnic and Social Stereotypes in Historical Context* (Leiden and Boston: Brill, 2013), p. 118.

chapter, which focuses primarily on the late twentieth and early twenty-first century, travel accounts from both linguistic contexts are examined together. As noted above, their modes of perceiving Welsh landscapes and cultures have become less disparate, allowing for a comparative analysis of their interpretative frameworks.

The first chapter, 'Landscape, Industry, Piety: Wales as a Site of Inspiration in Travel Writing in French from 1780 to 1905', sketches French attitudes to Wales prior to the French Revolution before discussing French travelogues written during the Revolution and the period of rapid industrialization that followed it and ends with a discussion of travel accounts of the 1904–1905 Welsh Revival. These are shown to reflect concerns in France: following the Revolution the young Republic was grappling with the reinvention of its own past, and both the Gauls and Celts came into vogue. This is reflected in the development of travelogues to Wales, in which Switzerland, the dominant Romantic point of comparison, slowly gives way to a concern with Celticness, and Brittany becomes the preferred prism through which to view Wales. A wish to view industrial progress and feats of engineering first-hand is the other factor responsible for the huge increase in French-language travelogues to Wales during the course of the nineteenth century, even if these attractions are viewed as part of a British success story. By the end of the century, however, the industrial communities of south Wales are the setting for a religious revival, and travelogues from this period interpret the Revival as a specifically Welsh phenomenon. The chapter concludes that the Revival narratives constitute a paradigmatic shift as Continental travellers begin to view Wales on its own terms, rather than through the filters of Switzerland, Brittany or England.

The second chapter, 'Patriotism, Pan-Celticism and the Welsh Cultural Paradigm in Travel Writing in French from 1830 to 1900', covers the period when Wales's Celticness dominated French views. It contrasts travelogues by 'Celtomaniac' visitors with those by travellers with other agendas, such as social justice. While industrial locations in south Wales continued to attract French interest, discussion of the Welsh language and culture is now often inseparable from the descriptions of the changing landscape and workforce. A number of these texts describe *eisteddfodau*, and the discussion of a cluster of travelogues prompted by the visit of a Breton delegation to the Cardiff National Eisteddfod of 1899 considers to what extent these travellers' idealized expectations of Wales as a role model, in terms of its ability to adapt to modernity while preserving its traditions, are met. Nevertheless, this episode also suggests the extent to which encounters between peripheries remain within and become subsumed by the mediating framework of the relationship with the centre, as Bretons and Welsh negate their reciprocal cultural identities by designating the other as English and French. Both French chapters show Wales going from a little-known quantity to being considered an intriguing Celtic 'other'.

The third chapter, 'Periphery, Modernity and the Discovery of Wales in Travel Writing in German from 1790 to 1850', traces the first encounters of German-speaking travellers with Wales. This is very much a period of discovery, many German writers exploring the notion of Wales and Welsh culture from a position of ignorance. Consequently, Wales is framed as a peripheral 'other' throughout, but nevertheless gradually establishes a presence in the German understanding of the British Isles. This is underpinned by a deeply conflicted reading. Some writers focus on an exoticized, romanticized Wales which is also seen to be colonized and threatened by its dominant neighbour. Other works highlight the impact, but also the desirability, of encroaching modernity in the shape of industry and tourism. The majority of travellers make their way to north Wales, drawn by the sublime landscape and ancient ruins, as well as the developments in mining and infrastructure. Writers adopt different prisms through which to observe Wales but, as time goes on, these begin to merge as the beginnings of a recognizable tourist trail develop. Central throughout, however, is an ongoing critique of the English domination of Wales and its culture, often described explicitly in colonial terms. This serves to undermine the image of England (as a cipher for Great Britain) as a paradigmatic locus of progressive ideals for the German-speaking lands in the aftermath of the Napoleonic Wars and on the brink of industrial revolution.

The fourth chapter, 'Identity, Celtomania and the Narrative of Wales in Travel Writing in German from 1850 to 1900', sees a continued focus on the north and its striking landscape, but with a shift in emphasis away from the industrial to the cultural. Earlier writers had certainly taken note of and commented on Welsh culture and language, but by the later nineteenth century the advance of Celtic studies on the Continent meant that the engagement of individual travellers with the indigenous culture was far deeper. This heightened appreciation leads many writers to view the development of tourism, of which they are of course a symptom, as a palpable threat to the survival of Welsh culture. The impact of this on Welsh identity is a common theme throughout and reflects concerns about the situation closer to home as the German states moved towards unification in 1871 and the realization of a political underpinning to the long-held sense of a common 'national' German identity. The image of Wales which emerges by the end of the nineteenth century is a distillation of cultural elements – bards, princes, legends – which can to some extent be seen as an attempt to preserve the cultural alterity deemed to be under threat. This marks the culmination of a century of germanophone writing about Wales, which sees the consolidation of a narrative of Wales and a layering of textual influences which, while sharing numerous themes with francophone writers, nevertheless addresses over time a number of key German concerns around national identity, the advance of modernity and the place of ancient cultures in the modern world.

The fifth chapter, 'Safe Haven, Literary Paradise and Present-Day Adventureland: Wales in Travel Writing in Breton, French and German from 1945 to 2018', analyses the new interpretative frameworks offered by travel narratives published between the late 1980s and the present day. As a prelude, the chapter offers a snapshot of the 'lost decades' of the interwar and post-war years, when travel accounts on Wales were far less frequent than before the First World War. The chapter explores how the trope of a hidden, undiscovered and unknown Wales has proven to be surprisingly persistent, with the continued common portrayal of Wales as a quasi-invisible unknown quantity, a peripheral site of inspiration and alterity. When Wales resurfaced in mainstream Continental travel writing in the 1980s, it was viewed on its own terms by travellers writing in French, Breton and German, as an entity and often a country in its own right.[72] Yet, paradoxically, Wales's increasing accessibility, through the proliferation of dedicated guidebooks and travel websites as well as improvements to its travel infrastructure, also led to the atomization and fragmentation of visions of Wales and modes of experiencing the nation. These include a sensory or physical 'consumption' of Wales, the 'internationalization' of Wales for a global visitor and a shift away from

---

72   As significant numbers of Breton-language travel accounts of Wales appeared in journals such as *Al Liamm* and *Breizh* from 1970 onwards, they are discussed in this fifth chapter. Three notable and exceptional predecessors were François Jaffrennou (Taldir), *Eur wech e oa* (Morlaix: Armorica, 1944), and Roparz Hemon and Frañsez Vallée, whose Breton travelogues on Wales in 1899, 1901, 1907 and 1920 were serialized in the journals *Gwalarn* (1926–1930) and *Sterenn* (1941). See Gilles Siche, 'Trois écrivains bretonnants au Pays de Galles: Taldir Jaffrennou, Frañsez Vallée et Roparz Hemon', in *Parcours Pays de Galles–Bretagne* (Brest: CRBC, 1995), pp. 33–46.

engagement with the Welsh language and its cultures, leading to their neutralization and dilution.

The conclusion, 'The Narrative of Wales: From Blind Spot to Blank Canvas', draws together the key themes discussed in the preceding chapters with a focus on the various prisms – Celtic, Breton, English, sublime, Romantic, industrial, modern, touristic, colonial – through which Wales has been viewed in travel writing in French and German since 1750. The narratives are placed in the context of the 'Home Tour' and English-language writing on Wales, patterns of travel and the broader notion of 'where' Wales is perceived to be. There is a concluding emphasis, drawing on Cronin's concept of micro-cosmopolitanism, on the value of travel writing as a means to interrogate centre-periphery and, importantly, periphery-periphery relations which points to potential new areas of research based on multilingual resources.

CHAPTER ONE

Landscape, Industry, Piety

Wales as a Site of Inspiration in Travel Writing in French from 1780 to 1905

For the French-speaking traveller embarking on a trip to the British Isles in the years before the French Revolution, Wales would have been something of an enigma. The vague notion of Welshness which existed in France at the time was inconsistent and largely ill-informed. In Paris in 1764, for example, a key text of the Welsh cultural revival, the recently published *Some Specimens of the Poetry of the Antient Welsh Bards* by Evan Evans (1731–1788),[1] was given short shrift by the editor of the *Gazette Littéraire* [Literary Gazette], who took the opportunity to compare Welsh poets unfavourably with Scotland's Ossian.[2] His reviewer, John Wilkes (1725–1797), found the Welsh to be 'une nation guerrière, mais féroce et superstitieuse' [a warrior nation, but fierce and superstitious], their poets 'dépravés par la superstition et la pédanterie

---

[1] For a recent reappraisal of the Welsh cultural revival in which Evan Evans features prominently, see Bethan M. Jenkins, *Between Wales and England: Anglophone Welsh Writing of the Eighteenth Century* (Cardiff: University of Wales Press, 2017).

[2] On the influence of Ossian in France, from the beginnings in the 1760s via Suard, Turgot and Diderot through to Chateaubriand, Lamartine and La Villemarqué, see Paul van Tieghem, *Ossian en France*, 2 vols (Geneva: Slatkine, 1967), first published 1917, and for a more recent survey of the importance of these poems that purported to be translated from the Gaelic of a third-century bard, see Howard Gaskill, *The Reception of Ossian in Europe* (London: Thoemmes Continuum, 2004).

monacales qui régnaient de leur temps' [corrupted by the superstition and monastic pedantry that reigned in their day].[3] This was hardly a view likely to foster a desire to read more about Welsh culture, let alone encourage anyone to venture to Wales itself. Yet there were some with a more favourable view, perhaps most notably Swiss writer and thinker Jean-Jacques Rousseau (1712–1778), who was enthusiastic about the idea of travelling to Wales in 1766 to escape persecution. He found, however, that the majority of his network of correspondents were firmly against his proposed destination.[4] Indeed, Rousseau's correspondence, reflecting the views of an international network of people, is something of a compendium of the largely negative associations that Wales held in the mid-eighteenth century. Friends, both in Britain and abroad, cited the constant rain, the fact that he would 'see nothing but mountains & wild goats' and find nothing but further suffering there as reasons against his plan, which did indeed founder.[5]

There was, however, one lone positive voice in Rousseau's network: Chevalier Charles-Geneviève-Louis-Auguste-André-Timothée d'Eon de Beaumont (1728–1810), famous as a French spy who dressed as a woman, whose suitably ambiguous portrait now hangs in the National Portrait Gallery in London. Beaumont cannot recommend Wales highly enough and informs Rousseau that it is 'la Suisse de l'Angleterre' [the Switzerland of England]. He offers to put him in touch with friends there, and even to come and visit him, noting that 'Si vous aimez la Chasse & la pêche, vous pourriés [*sic*] vivre lá, Sans le Secours de personne, avec la même liberté & innocence que nos premiers peres' [If you like hunting and fishing you could live there without being a burden on anybody, with

3   Jean-Baptiste-Antoine Suard translating John Wilkes, *Gazette Littéraire*, October 1764, cited in Van Tieghem, *Ossian en France*, I, p. 168.

4   For a more detailed discussion of Rousseau and Wales, see Heather Williams, 'Rousseau and Wales', in Mary-Ann Constantine and Dafydd Johnston (eds), *'Footsteps of Liberty and Revolt': Essays on Wales and the French Revolution in Wales* (Cardiff: University of Wales, 2013), pp. 35–51; Heather Williams, 'Cymru trwy lygaid Rousseau (ac eraill)', Y *Traethodydd*, CLXVIII (2013), pp. 241–54; and Heather Williams, 'Rousseau and Romanticism in Wales', in Russell Goulbourne and David Higgins (eds), *Jean-Jacques Rousseau and British Romanticism* (London: Bloomsbury Academic, 2017), pp. 75–90.

5   R.A. Leigh (ed.), *Correspondance complète de Jean-Jacques Rousseau*, 52 vols (Geneva: Institut et musée Voltaire, 1965–1998), Sarah Bunbury, née Lennox, to Susan O'Brien, née Fox Strangeways, 5 February 1766, letter 5034bis, Vol. 28, p. 273.

the same freedom and innocence as our first fathers].[6] Beaumont's more positive view is an early indication of an attempt to position Wales in the European context which, in the years spanning the long nineteenth century, would see the nation and its culture emerge from the shadows of French understanding of the British Isles.

This chapter and that following will trace Wales's fortunes in the French imagination from the 1780s to the first decade of the twentieth century. Discussing a selection of travel texts written in French, or by French authors, it begins in the pre-Revolutionary period, when Wales was little known and still less liked, considered at best remote and exotic, at worst backward and wild, and ends at the dawn of the twentieth century, when Welsh industry led the world. The present chapter will first sketch French perceptions of Wales prior to the revolutionary decade of the 1790s, a period when overwhelmingly negative connotations were still attached to Wales in both French and British high society. In those travelogues that do mention Wales at this time, Switzerland is the most frequent point of comparison, and concern with Wales's 'Celticness', which would come to dominate nineteenth-century descriptions, is shown to be only just emerging. Then a discussion of texts written by French exiles during the Revolution of 1789 contrasts writing by Bretons, who viewed Wales primarily through the prism of their native Brittany, with texts by a French prisoner of war and a noblewoman from Burgundy, which display either indifference or confusion about Celticness. After 1815, although landscape lovers continued to produce travelogues that focused exclusively on the natural wonders of Wales, with any human figures or human-made edifices subsumed into aesthetically driven projects, industrial travellers come to the fore in a new era of travel freedom following the Napoleonic Wars. This era saw exchanges of workforces and students, accompanied by a sense of anxious competition between France and Britain for intellectual property and economic advantage. For the travelogue this meant a huge increase in numbers, as well as new developments both generic and thematic. Some of the accounts written by those on professional visits to Welsh sites of industry are purely technical, and contain little more than facts, figures and measurements crucial for the advancement of French industry. Though important historically, and also responsible for encouraging other travellers, these reports are less interesting than what might be termed the 'hybrid' texts that begin to emerge from 1815 onwards. In the middle section of this

---

6   Leigh, *Correspondance de Rousseau*, Letter 5062, Vol. 28, p. 313.

chapter, industry is shown to play a role rather different from the one it had played in pre-1815 texts, reflecting a new political and economic situation. The focus here is on 'hybrid' travel texts that borrow lexical fields and tropes from earlier rural, natural descriptions, and use these to convey the brand new industrial spectacles. This is self-conscious writing where industrial visitors claim to lack the literary skills required to do justice to these new sights, and declare themselves 'lost for words'. The communities that grew up around these industrial sites in south Wales were to attract French observers for a novel reason in 1904–1905, when visitors came to see first-hand the religious revival that was taking place there, and this chapter ends with analysis of a selection of these Nonconformist revival narratives. Over time, Wales emerges as a paradigm, initially in relation to landscape and industry, and later in the context of religion via the French reception of the great Welsh Revival of 1904–1905. This chapter will explore this nascent reading of Wales as a site of inspiration, one which is informed by the Romantic aesthetic, an emerging understanding of the Celtic in the French context, often via the Breton prism, and the sociopolitical upheavals of the nineteenth century which so frequently saw writers reaching out for alternative paradigms of stability and social order.

In all of this, Wales is consistently positioned as somewhere apart. The concept of Wales as a site of alterity emerges early on, teased out in the context of a series of comparisons which focus primarily on Switzerland and, more vaguely, the European Celtic periphery. Key is the appreciation of the Welsh landscape which centres on the sublime. The works of Rousseau himself were of course instrumental in revolutionizing attitudes towards nature and the natural, and in making places such as Wales attractive to painters and travellers from afar in entirely new ways. As Beaumont's comments show, Rousseau's native Switzerland was a favoured point of comparison for Wales from an early stage, and indeed part of Wales's appeal for Rousseau himself was its similarity with his homeland. A common motif in English tours of Wales as well, comparison with Switzerland is also found in one of the earliest French travel accounts of Wales, the diary of Marc de Bombelles (1744–1822), *Journal de voyage en Grande Bretagne et en Irlande 1784* [Diary of a Journey through Great Britain and Ireland in 1784].[7] Bombelles was a reluctant traveller to Britain, he only went because he

7 Marc de Bombelles, *Journal de voyage en Grande Bretagne et en Irlande 1784*, ed. Jacques Grury (Oxford: Voltaire Foundation, 1989).

had been persuaded that a knowledge of Britain was essential for the advancement of his career as diplomat. He enters Wales via a crossing from Waterford to Haverfordwest, and travels to Carmarthen and then Brecon, Chepstow and Bristol. He sees Wales partly through the eyes of an official visitor from a rival country, noting the quality of the housing, and partly through landscape painting, when he imagines the influential Italian landscape artist Salvator Rosa (1615–1673) painting Canaston Bridge near Narberth. When at Brecon he conveys the extreme prettiness of the area – 'plus joli petit Pays qu'il y ait peut-être sur la surface du globe' (p. 282) [the prettiest little land that there is, perhaps on the surface of the globe] – by stating that it is unsurpassed even by Swiss valleys. His use of the diminutive 'petit Pays' [little land] sets Wales apart from its near neighbour, England, and frames the landscape as different. The other emergent cornerstone of Welsh alterity, its Celticness, is also touched on in his account, but only through a brief discussion of the Welsh language, which Bombelles maintains is the same 'Celtique' as that spoken by the Scottish and the Irish, though the Bretons (whose language is in fact far more closely related to Welsh) are notably absent from the discussion. The term 'Celtic' is used in a purely linguistic sense here, without cultural or religious meaning. Indeed, the fact that Bombelles omits Brittany shows that he is not searching for any particular Celtic affinity: the only reason he compares Wales with Ireland and Scotland is because these three together form part of 'les trois royaumes de Georges III' [the three kingdoms of George III], thus placing Wales firmly in its British context. This travel account clearly predates French anxieties about Britain's industrial progress, as well as the French interest in Celticness, both of which will grow only after the French Revolution. Arguably, only the Breton visitors discussed below seem sure about what they see in Wales, and understand that Wales is related to Brittany both linguistically and culturally.

More detailed acknowledgement of the Celtic aspect of Welsh culture features in the work of Charles Étienne Coquebert de Montbret (1755–1831), who travelled through Wales with his son and his Irish secretary during the Revolution in September 1789 on his way to a new diplomatic post in Dublin. This account is encyclopedic in scope, since Coquebert is gathering in his notebooks all manner of information that may be of use to himself or to the state at a later date. Indeed, over the years he returned to these notebooks, adding details here and there.[8]

8 Charles Étienne Coquebert de Montbret, *Voyage de Paris à Dublin à travers*

Coquebert's writing is typical of the age, displaying something of the commonplace book, and evidence of the author's scholarly knowledge of geology and geography. His account reads at times like an inventory, with the emphasis firmly on facts and figures (numbers of hectares, varieties of tree, numbers of lead mines) rather than the aesthetic effect of the landscape, but the text also contains personal opinion and intertextuality, and pits lists of facts against personal anecdotes. The latter include an account of a disappointing visit to Thomas Pennant at his home in Downing Hall in Flintshire, where the reception Coquebert receives is described as 'à l'anglaise, c'est-à-dire passablement froide' (p. 169) [in the English style, that is rather frosty]. Nevertheless Coquebert continues to quote Pennant as an authority throughout the rest of this text, and also played his part in ensuring the dissemination of the latter's ideas in France, through publishing a translation of his description of the Anglesey copper mines in the *Journal des mines* [Mining Journal].[9]

Besides his enthusiasm for industry, the Welsh-language culture which Coquebert encounters in north Wales is also of great interest to him. His library included some twenty-six books relating to Wales (of 632 titles on Britain), including a Bible in Welsh from 1769, two Welsh dictionaries, a number of travelogues and some poetry: *The Heroic elegies and other pieces of Llywarç Hen, translated by M. Owen* (1792). He pursues this interest in a meeting in Abergele, where the local schoolmaster and cobbler is delighted to talk poetry and to tell the travellers all about the London-based Gwyneddigion Society's efforts to revive the eisteddfodic culture of Wales.[10] This conversation leads Coquebert to explain that the English government aims to eradicate

la Normandie et l'Angleterre en 1789 (Lyon: Université Saint-Étienne, 1995). For a discussion of his text, see Jane Conroy, 'Time and the Traveller: The Case of Coquebert de Montbret', in Eamon Maher and Catherine Maingant (eds), *Franco-British Connections in Space and Time* (Oxford: Peter Lang, 2013), pp. 29–52.

9   See 'Description des mines de cuivre de l'île d'Anglesey, dans le pays de Galles: extraite et traduite du voyage de M. Pennant, intitulé: Tour in Wales. Londres, 1781, tome II, pag. 265', *Journal des mines*, Nivôse, of year four, in the Revolutionary calendar (or Dec.–Jan. 1795). There is no translator named, but it seems likely that this was Coquebert, as he was the editor of the journal from September 1793 to April 1795.

10   The Gwyneddigion Society was one of several London-based Welsh literary and cultural societies founded by expatriate Welsh during the late eighteenth century. The Gwyneddigion was active from 1770 to 1843.

the Welsh language by establishing free English-medium schools throughout the area (p. 173). Coquebert clearly regrets the decline of Welsh, because he considers ancient languages a valuable conduit to knowledge about the past. Though Coquebert, en route for Ireland in the company of his Irish secretary, is naturally curious about the similarities between Welsh, Irish and Scots Gaelic, this curiosity, as his editor explains, is typical of linguistic thinking about the origins of and connections between different languages at the time. In fact, Coquebert seems just as interested in the comparison of Welsh with Hebrew that he read about in Y *Ffydd Ddiffuant, sef hanes y ffydd Gristionogol* (1677) [Sincere Faith, the History of Christianity][11] as the comparison between Welsh and the other languages spoken in the British Isles. What is significantly absent from his discussion, however, is mention of the Breton language or use of the word 'Celtic'. Nevertheless, like Bombelles, Coquebert displays an awareness of Wales and its culture which sets it apart in his reading of the British Isles. In these earlier eighteenth-century travelogues, then, it is possible to see French-speaking travellers attempting to position Wales in their understanding of the aesthetic, industrial and Celtic contexts at a time of great change. This effectively establishes the key themes which will feature in French-language travel writing into and throughout the nineteenth century as Wales begins to emerge as a site of inspiration, initially in particular through the twin foci of landscape and industry.

In the wake of the French Revolution, however, the decision by some travellers to visit Wales was driven less by the quest for new paradigms and more by survival itself as France descended into the chaos of the Terror. It is widely accepted that around 120,000 people left France between 1789 and 1802, with some 25,000 exiles choosing Britain.[12] The vast majority of these revolutionary exiles settled in the London area, but some found themselves visiting Wales. Of these, some painted the landscape, while others left written accounts of their travel. The imprint of the Revolution is clear in many of their texts, even

11   See Coquebert de Montbret, 'A la fin du catéchisme il y a une comparaison de l'hébreu et du gallois', in *Voyage de Paris à Dublin*, p. 172.

12   William Doyle, *The Oxford History of the French Revolution* (Oxford: Oxford University Press, 2002), p. 395; Rosena Davison, 'Friend or Foe? French Émigrés Discover Britain', in Kathleen Doig and Dorothy Medlin (eds), *British-French Exchanges in the Eighteenth Century* (Newcastle: Cambridge Scholars Publishing, 2007), pp. 131–48.

when they neglect to name the cause of their exile. One of the most prolific artists to travel to Wales was Philippe-Jacques de Loutherbourg (1740–1812). He originally came to London for professional reasons in 1771, and made tours to Wales in the summer of 1786 and again in 1800.[13] Sixty-nine of his sketches, the majority of which show Welsh ruins,[14] accompanied by a bilingual text, *Romantic and Picturesque Scenery of England and Wales / Scènes romantiques et pittoresques, de l'Angleterre et du pays de Galles* (1805), were published in book form.[15] In Wales Loutherbourg is remembered for the image of Gray's bard that he created for the second edition of *Musical and Poetical Relicks of the Welsh Bards* (1784) by Edward Jones (1761–1836), which served as a model for the anonymous artist who painted the bard on Swansea ceramics in the early nineteenth century.[16] In addition, Loutherbourg is believed to be the first to represent Tintern Abbey in paint.[17] Another artist, Amélie de Suffren (1765–1817), was also fleeing the Revolution. Her volume *Voyage pittoresque dans le midi et le nord du pays de Galles* [Picturesque Tour of South and North Wales] was published in 1805,[18] although the plates had been published in batches prior to this, and her tour must have happened a few years before 1805, certainly before May 1802 (the earliest date on a plate). For her, Wales offers everything that a modern artist could wish for; she finds the sublime at Devil's Bridge, 'lieu sauvage [...] où la nature a déployé sa terrifique grandeur' [a wild place (...) where nature is displayed in all her terrifying glory], and

13   See Rüdiger Joppien, *Philippe Jacques de Loutherbourg, RA 1740–1812* (London: Greater London Council, 1973); Rüdiger Joppien, 'A Visitor to a Ruined Churchyard: A Newly Discovered Painting by P.J. De Loutherbourg', *The Burlington Magazine*, 118:878 (1976), pp. 294–301.

14   Philippe-Jacques de Loutherbourg, *Sketches*, W6 DV 61 (4to), National Library of Wales, Aberystwyth. MS.

15   Philippe-Jacques de Loutherbourg, *Romantic and Picturesque Scenery of England and Wales: From Drawings Made Expressly for this Undertaking by P.J. de Loutherbourg, Esq. R.A. with Historical and Descriptive Accounts of the Several Places of which Views are Given / Scènes romantiques et pittoresques, de l'Angleterre et du pays de Galles* (London: T. Bensley, 1805).

16   See the image in Peter Lord, 'Y Bardd: Celtiaeth a chelfyddyd', *Cof Cenedl*, 7 (1992), pp. 99–131 (p. 113).

17   Joppien, 'A Visitor to a Ruined Churchyard', p. 295.

18   Amélie de Suffren, *Voyage pittoresque dans le midi et le nord du pays de Galles, ou suite de 48 vues déssinées sur les lieux* (Paris: Gille, 1805). The text is unpaginated.

describes the road northwards from Aberystwyth to Cadair Idris as beautiful: rich, picturesque, gay, charming, terrifying, wild and varied. A third artist, Louis-Antoine-Philippe d'Orléans, duc de Montpensier (1775–1807)[19] was drawn to Wales for personal rather than professional reasons. Living in exile in Twickenham with his family from February 1800, and eager to learn about Britain, Montpensier was an amateur artist, and made tours of south Wales in 1805, and possibly 1803, sketching waterfalls at 'Mellincourt in Glamorganshire', on the Hafod Uchdryd estate in upland Ceredigion, and Cilgerran Castle in Pembrokeshire.[20] This was followed by a sketching tour of parts of north Wales in summer 1806.

While the artists focus perhaps predictably on the sublime landscape, finding in Wales a new source of grandeur to rival other European locations, those who recorded their impressions of Wales in textual form begin to shift their attention, explicitly and implicitly, to the restorative character of the landscape and the sociopolitical potential of Wales as a paradigm of stability to counter the chaos of upheaval from which they have recently fled. This is often quite subtle, as in the work of renowned Enlightenment educationalist and writer Stéphanie-Félicité du Crest de Saint-Aubin, comtesse de Genlis (1746–1830). In Britain from October 1791 to November 1792,[21] Genlis did not come to Wales because she had heard that it was 'another Switzerland', but rather to satisfy her curiosity

19   Younger brother of Louis-Philippe, who became king in 1830, and son of Louis-Philippe, known as Philippe Égalité.

20   These pictures are listed in the catalogue by J. Vatout, *Notices historiques sur les tableaux de la Galerie de SAR, Mgr le Duc d'Orléans* (Paris: n.p., 1826). However, they have since disappeared, and were probably destroyed when the Palais-Royal was sacked in 1848. This is discussed in Malcolm Hay, *Prince in Captivity: Based on the Memoirs and Unpublished Letters of Antoine Philippe d'Orléans Duc de Montpensier, 1775–1807* (London: Eyre & Spottiswoode, 1960), pp. 165–66.

21   The best account of her visit is in Jacques Bertaud, 'Madame de Genlis et l'Angleterre: la femme et l'œuvre de 1779 à 1792' (unpublished doctoral thesis, Paris III-Sorbonne, 1974). See also Magdi Wahba, 'Mme de Genlis in England', *Comparative Literature*, 13:3 (1961), pp. 221–38; Gillian Dow, 'Stéphanie-Félicité de Genlis and the French Historical Novel in Romantic Britain', *Women's Writing*, 19:3 (2012), pp. 273–92. Genlis's visit to Wales specifically has not received much critical attention, though in a recent discussion of her memoirs, Gábor Gelléri identifies the passage treating insomnia in Llangollen as a turning point in her description of her travels in Britain, in *Philosophies du voyage: visiter l'Angleterre aux 17e–18e siècles* (Oxford: Voltaire Foundation, 2016), p. 435 ff.

about female friendship by paying a visit to Sarah Ponsonby (1755–1831) and Eleanor Butler (1739–1829). Known as the 'ladies of Llangollen', this pair had run away from Ireland together to escape marriage and make their home in a cottage they named 'Plas Newydd' just outside Llangollen in north Wales. Genlis's visit is described in her *Mémoires*, written over a quarter of a century later.[22]

Her text demonstrates the difficulty some travellers had in positioning Wales at this time, as it is not clear where she thought she was; though she does at one point actually refer to it as the 'principauté de Galles' [principality of Wales], elsewhere she thinks that she is in 'Angleterre'. She explains the workings of the wind harp, 'que l'on appelle en Angleterre une harpe éolienne' (p. 351) [which is known as an Aeolian harp in England], and speaks of its appropriateness to a stormy island, which is a reference to the whole of Britain, rather than just Wales. Although it is not perhaps surprising that she should think of Wales as part of 'Angleterre', as administratively it was, she does seem more confused than most about its identity. This becomes apparent in her references to the British Celtic nations in general. On a morning walk around the area with the ladies, for example, she sees goats everywhere, and notices goatherds peppering the landscape, seated on rocks playing harps that she describes as 'Irish'. The text moves swiftly to another 'Celtic' location, with the description of the seat where the ladies inform her that they often come to reread Ossian. This set of references is an early example of the relative positioning of the British Celtic nations which tends to place Wales at the bottom of the Celtic hierarchy as a lesser-known quantity. It is Ireland (via the harps) and Scotland (via Ossian) that are called upon to help situate and convey her impression of this Welsh landscape, as though these two names had some currency in the French language, which the word *gallois* [Welsh], or even *celtique* lacked.

The main focus of Genlis's Welsh passage is an extraordinary description of the effect of music and landscape on her psyche. Harp music was something of a cliché in the Welsh tour, especially in north Wales,[23] and as Andrews remarks: 'Many a tourist delightedly remarked

---

22 Stéphanie-Félicité du Crest de Saint-Aubin, comtesse de Genlis, *Mémoires inédits de Madame la comtesse de Genlis, sur le dix-huitième siècle et la révolution française, depuis 1756 jusqu'à nos jours*, 8 vols (Paris: Ladvocat, 1825), III, pp. 344–56.

23 For a detailed discussion of harps, see Morgan, *The Eighteenth-Century Renaissance*, pp. 124–32.

on the correspondence between their music and their native landscape'.[24]
It is an Aeolian harp that makes the Welsh landscape encroach on
Genlis's mental space, as it transforms a stormy night into a celestial
concert. First of all she is unable to sleep because her head feels so full of
everything that she has seen and heard (p. 350). She finally gets to sleep,
only to be awoken by:

> Une mélodie vague et céleste qui pénétroit jusqu'au fond de l'âme. A force
> d'attention, je connus qu'un vent assez violent, qui venoit de s'élever, la
> produisoit. Mon oreille distinguoit dans le lointain le bruit et le sifflement
> ordinaires causés par un orage; mais les vents, changeant de nature en
> approchant de cet asile de la paix et de l'amitié ne formoient plus, lorsqu'ils
> frappoient ses arbres et ses murs qu'une harmonie enchanteresse.

> [A vague and celestial melody that penetrated to the depths of the soul.
> Straining to hear, I realized that a quite violent wind that had just got
> up was producing it. My ear distinguished in the distance the noise and
> whistling normally caused by a storm, but the winds, on approaching
> this sanctuary of peace and friendship, were changed and transformed,
> as they hit its trees and walls, into nothing more than an enchanting
> harmony]

Genlis presents this experience as otherworldly: all earthly music is
outshone, redundant. However, the text moves swiftly to temper this
and explain that the incident was merely the result of an Aeolian
harp. So now that the otherworldly music has been demystified and
explained, in theory everything has come back down to earth, with a
morning walk in the ladies' company. Yet there is something not quite
literal about the landscape that she records the following morning.
What she sees is all beauty, symmetry and order reflected in pleasing,
balanced syntax:

> Langollen, entouré d'ombrages et de prairies délicieuses, par la fraîcheur
> de leur verdure, est situé au pied de la montagne des deux amies, qui
> forme là une majestueuse pyramide couverte d'arbres et de fleurs. (p. 347)

> [Llangollen, surrounded by shade and delicious meadows, and the
> freshness of their greenery, is situated at the foot of the two friends'
> mountain, which forms a majestic pyramid covered in trees and flowers]

Psychological turmoil ends in harmony and order, the very landscape
envisioned as a geometrical shape. Genlis seems to take comfort from

---

24   Andrews, *The Search for the Picturesque*, p. 129.

the fact that the 'ladies' appear to be 'souveraines' of the area. She is dreaming of order, resolution and perfect cadence; and perhaps hinting at the old order, or the *ancien régime*, whose erstwhile stability she finds reflected in the existence of her hosts in their Welsh idyll.

More explicit longing for the old order is found in the narrative by Jacques-Louis de La Tocnaye (1767–1832),[25] a Breton royalist refugee from Nantes, who published *Promenade autour de la Grande-Bretagne* (1795) [Wanderings around Great Britain], based on travel undertaken in 1793.[26] This text marks a shift away from the predominence of Switzerland as a broad geographical comparator towards a more specific, culturally informed comparison with Brittany. Bored with London, La Tocnaye travels on foot, and uses travel writing for psychological and financial survival: it banished his depression and he hoped to make money, although admittedly his work was published at his own expense. However, such was its success that La Tocnaye was able to launch a subscription, and translations into English and German followed shortly. In his narrative he describes Welsh mountains as seen from the English side of the border, where the Avon meets the Severn. Later in the same text he visits the Shrewsbury area where again he imagines peering over the border into Wales, overcome by a sense of longing for the past and a need to connect more deeply with his own native culture. The people and language remind him of his native Brittany, and the spectacle makes him wish that he could wander in the hills, and that he was able to speak Breton:

> Combien j'ai regretté ici, de ne pas savoir le bas-breton. Quel plaisir n'eût-ce pas été pour moi de m'égarer dans les montagnes de ce pays? En voyant ces hommes agrestes, si semblables à ceux de Bretagne dans leurs manières, faire encore usage du même langage, je me serais cru avec des compatriotes. (p. 73)

> [How I regretted, here, not knowing the Breton language. What pleasure it would have been for me to wander in the mountains of this country. Seeing these rustic men, so similar to those of Brittany in their manners,

25   See Gábor Gelléri, 'Les "promenades" de La Tocnaye: exil, voyage, survie, transfert', in Augustin Lefebvre and Judit Maar (eds), *Exils et transfers culturels dans l'Europe moderne* (Paris: L'Harmattan, 2015), pp. 277–87.

26   Jacques-Louis de La Tocnaye, *Promenade autour de la Grande Bretagne; précédé de quelques détails sur la campagne du duc de Brunswick, par un officier français émigré* (Edinburgh: Jean Paterson, 1795), revised as *Promenade d'un Français dans la Grande-Bretagne* (Brunswick: P.F. Fauche et Compagnie, 1801). Quotations are taken from the revised edition.

still using the same language, I would have believed myself with my compatriots]

His longing here conjures up fellow countrymen in the Welsh hills, the conditional verbs exposing the tension between actual travel experience and the journey of the mind. Later, in his volume on Ireland, *Promenade d'un Français dans l'Irlande* (1797) [Wanderings of a Frenchman in Ireland],[27] he is initially horrified when he arrives at Milford Haven, although he proceeds to note local customs and material culture, commenting on women's clothes and hats, and the coracles that are used for salmon fishing which double up as cradles for children. In particular he comments that the flowers and plants found in graveyards make them more like gardens than places of death, and once again he imagines himself in Wales: he wishes he could spend some time here, as people with such funerary customs must be 'douce' [gentle]. The fact that these peasants have a 'Celtic' language that is specific to them, but related to Breton, makes him imagine himself not only back in his own past, at home in pre-revolutionary Brittany, but also speaking Breton (p. 11). Thus Wales creates for him an alternative version of his own past and culture, one embedded in the security of the old order and a heightened sense of identity.

Another Breton émigré, Armand-Louis-Bon Maudet de Penhouët (1764–1839), wrote a book-length epistolary travelogue, *Letters Describing a Tour through Part of South Wales*,[28] describing a walking tour undertaken in June 1796. The text was published on his return to London in 1797, unusually in English (with the exception of quotations of French verse). This is a highly scholarly and literary travelogue, revealing the author's classical education and previous travels. The intended readership is British, and there are many features in his text that are familiar from English-language tours. For instance the opening sentence of his preface – 'the whole [of Wales] is properly termed another Switzerland' (p. i) – was by now a topos of Welsh tours. He views the country predominantly through landscape painting and scenery, and the whole tour is framed as a series of letters – not intended for publication until his friends persuaded him otherwise – to an unnamed woman, calling to mind Saint-Preux writing

---

27 Jacques-Louis de La Tocnaye, *Promenade d'un Français dans l'Irlande* (Dublin: Graisberry, 1797).

28 Armand-Louis-Bon Maudet de Penhouët, *Letters Describing a Tour through Part of South Wales: By a Pedestrian Traveller. With Views, Designed and Etched by the Author* (London: T. Baylis, Greville-Street, 1797). Penhouët wrote his text in English, presumably with a view to publication in his adopted homeland.

to Julie in Rousseau's *La Nouvelle Héloïse* (1761) [The New Heloise]. The underlying context, however, is undoubtedly one of revolution. The Brittany Penhouët has left behind is one that is resisting France, through its *chouannerie* or counter-Revolution (Brittany, along with the Vendée, was considered the most 'loyal' province) and comments like 'my unfortunate King' (p. 22) and 'a brave Chief of the Chouans' (p. 74) point to his reasons for being abroad, although he shies away from being explicit. What makes this tour stand out, however, is Penhouët's Breton perspective on Welsh culture, as his description of similarities linguistic and cultural goes beyond factual reporting. Like La Tocnaye, the striking similarity fires his imagination to the point of altering his own identity, making him perceive Wales as offering a new and comforting self, or a home, at a time of trauma. In his imagination Penhouët is no longer a foreigner; he is transported back to his native Brittany:

> Half a dozen Welch [*sic*] peasants were settling the affairs of their country over a pot of ale. Their language, which, for the first time struck my ear so freely, the conformity of manners between these good people and those of Lower Brittany, all increased the illusion – and I believed myself for a moment in my own country. (pp. 29–30)

He further explores the similarities between Wales and Brittany in a long concluding letter to the volume that sets out to explain the origins and history of the Breton people in relation to the Welsh. His comparison of each country's loss of independence and union with a larger neighbour suggest that, for Penhouët, Wales is another Brittany, not only in linguistic terms, but crucially in political terms too; in this he is unique in the period. Much of his writing appears idyllic on the surface, with Wales seemingly offering comfort and reassurance. However the Terror is present, too, and the psychological responses he describes betray his inner trauma. There is a glimpse of danger, in the form of a reminder of France, specifically Paris, rather than of Brittany in his description of wretched female workers at Neath: 'an innumerable gang of mendicants, whose figures are hideous beyond all that can be imagined [...] the tone of voice in which they begged of us could be compared only to that of those women who headed the rebels at Paris' (p. 38). Where the vision of Brittany had reaffirmed his sense of identity, the spectre of France here looms large, and a 'nightmare of France'[29]

29   Elizabeth Edwards, 'Iniquity, Terror and Survival: Welsh Gothic, 1789–1804', *Journal for Eighteenth-Century Studies*, 35:1 (2012), pp. 119–33 (pp. 121–22).

erupts into the comforting vision of Brittany that Wales had initially conjured. At a time when picturesque tour texts tended to edit out such details, the fact that Penhouët mentions poor workers at all is worthy of note.[30] Penhouët's unnamed crisis of identity makes of Wales another Brittany, an idyll punctured by the horror of the French Revolution. This text, in which the experience of being in Wales connects a Breton with his cultural identity, foreshadows many twentieth- and twenty-first-century Breton travel accounts to Wales. Along with La Tocnaye, Penhouët's case also demonstrates that peripheral cultures can and do interact with other peripheral cultures at an early date, offering a corrective to the model that has been dominant in Enlightenment studies: that of a francophone beacon shining out towards the vernaculars of Europe.

Although the theme of exile reappears later in the century, notably with socialist idealist Alphonse Esquiros (1812–1876), who lived by his pen in Britain in the aftermath of the 1848 Revolution, after the Napoleonic Wars a new chapter opened in travel writing in French, as 'the atmosphere lightened' and 'travel became identified with freedom'.[31] It was a time of change in both France and Wales, the former looking to prove its place on the world stage, the latter undergoing rapid industrial transformation. Indeed, it was industry which drew many French travellers to Wales and this gives an added dimension to their travel accounts. While descriptions of rural idylls or sublime mountain-scapes in Wales written by the French bear close resemblance to those penned by the English, their respective views of industry in Wales are necessarily distinct. Where English visitors, living under the same government as the Welsh people they are observing, view Wales as part of a burgeoning industrial 'Britain', French travellers view this same process of change through the eyes of Britain's competitor. Many travellers felt a sense of mission, and formal industrial and educational connections were forged between experts in France and Britain, including Wales.[32] British industrialists were certainly used to this kind of attention. There had been a tradition of receiving and welcoming foreign scientists that extended back beyond the French

30 Peter Lord, *The Visual Culture of Wales: Industrial Society* (Cardiff: University of Wales Press, 1998), p. 129 ff.

31 C.W. Thompson, *French Romantic Travel Writing: Chateaubriand to Nerval* (Oxford: Oxford University Press, 2012), p. 17.

32 Peter Stearns, 'British Industry through the Eyes of French Industrialists (1820–1848)', *The Journal of Modern History*, 37:1 (1965), pp. 50–61 (p. 50).

Revolution.[33] However, the openness of British industrialists towards these visitors from abroad varied as international relations fluctuated and there is, perhaps inevitably, evidence of friction and even paranoia in many travel texts that reveals French travellers anxiously assessing the opposition, constantly comparing notes with French industry and in some cases undoubtedly sending secrets home. In an era when Wales was a scene of advancement that afforded a glimpse of the industrial future over and above panoramas of natural beauty, a 'weary and humiliated' France was only too aware of British progress.[34] In all of this, however, the extent to which these travellers explicitly see Wales as an entity in itself varies, with a large degree of overlap between the names 'Angleterre', 'Grande Bretagne' and 'Pays de Galles', and it is perhaps fair to say that the real focus of their narratives is the industrialization of the mines and factories which happened to be located in Wales, rather than Wales itself.

An early industrial observer was Pierre-Armand Dufrénoy (1792–1857), who was sent to south Wales in 1823 by the director of the Paris *École des Ponts et Chaussées et des Mines* [School of Bridges, Highways and Mines] to inspect industrial furnaces in various metallurgical factories. The visit resulted in a highly technical travel account which set the tone for future ventures.[35] The *École* would regularly send students to Wales to observe best practice as part of their studies from the 1830s to the 1860s; some of the students' work was published in the school's journal, the *Annales des Mines* [Annals of Mining], and many of the reports that remained in manuscript form have been preserved by the school's library in the collection 'Journaux et mémoires de voyage de MM. les Élèves' [Travel Journals and Recollections of the Students].[36] Other

33   John R. Harris, *Industrial Espionage and Technology Transfer: Britain and France in the Eighteenth Century* (Farnham: Ashgate, 1998).
34   Margaret Bradley and Fernand Perrin, 'Charles Dupin's Study Visits to the British Isles, 1816–1824', *Technology and Culture*, 32:1 (1991), pp. 47–68 (p. 47). For a general discussion of the context, see Chris Evans and Göran Rydén (eds), *The Industrial Revolution in Iron: The Impact of British Coal Technology in Nineteenth-Century Europe* (Farnham: Ashgate, 2005).
35   Pierre-Armand Dufrénoy and Léonce Élie de Beaumont, *Voyage Métallurgique en Angleterre: ou Recueil des Mémoires sur le gisement, l'exploitation et le traitement des Minerais d'étain, de cuivre, de plomb, de zinc et de fer, dans la Grande-Bretagne* (Paris: Bachelier, Libraire pour les sciences, 1827), pp. 429–38. The book reproduces extracts from the *Annales des Mines*, 1824–1827.
36   The journals are available digitally at *Bibliothèque patrimoniale numérique*

students made models of architectural feats seen in Wales, such as the model of the Menai Suspension Bridge that is conserved in the *Musée des Arts et Métiers* [Museum of Industrial Design] in Paris. Similar educational connections led to the exchange of workers, and during the Bourbon Restoration (1814–1830) it is estimated that between 15,000 and 20,000 British workers were employed in France. Welsh workers from the Merthyr area migrated to Decazeville (Aveyron), and also Imphy and Garchizy (both in the Nièvre) around 1830, staying there until about 1847–1848.[37] This is partly explained by the intermarriage over two generations between the Crawshays, the family who owned Cyfarthfa ironworks in Merthyr Tydfil, and the Dufauds, owners of the Fourchambault works in the Nièvre area, to the west of Burgundy in France.

Georges Dufaud (1777–1852), a graduate of the *École Polythechnique* [Polytechnic School], first travelled to Wales in 1817 to observe Cyfarthfa, which was probably the most advanced ironworks in Britain, in order to perfect his own ironmaking procedures. Then in 1819 his daughter Louise (dates unknown) was married to George Crawshay (1821–1896), second son of the ironmaster William Crawshay (1764–1834). His son Achille Dufaud (1796–1856) left a written account of visiting the ironworks, in the form of a series of letters.[38] The Dufaud family certainly saw Merthyr as a world leader: 'Le pays de Galles et Cyfarthfa surtout a et conserve les meilleurs puddleurs du monde, un puddleur ordinaire et non soigneux n'est pas admis' [Wales and Cyfarthfa in particular has and retains the best puddlers in the world, an ordinary, careless puddler is not admitted].[39] Impressed by what he saw, Achille Dufaud makes detailed enquiries, taking notes and precise measurements. Despite the close family ties, however, fear of industrial espionage is never far beneath the surface. In a letter to his father on 8 July 1823 Achille Dufaud describes a deterioration in relations with the Crawshays, implying

de l'*École nationale supérieure des mines de Paris*: https://patrimoine.mines-paristech.fr/Journaux_de_voyage.

37 See Brian Wagstaffe, 'Welsh Ironworkers in France', *Glamorgan Family History Society*, 51 (1998), pp. 14–15.

38 See 'Achille Dufaud en Angleterre', in Guy Thuillier, *Georges Dufaud et les débuts du grand capitalisme dans la métallurgie, en Nivernais, au XIXe siècle* (Paris: SEVPEN, 1959), pp. 225–32. A later descendent also recorded the period in novel form: Denise Le Mallier, *Le Roman des Dufaud* (La Charité-sur-Loire: Imprimerie Delayance, 1971).

39 Cited in Thuillier, *Georges Dufaud*, p. 225.

that they have accused him of coming to England – the nomenclature eliding Wales once more – with the sole purpose of taking notes in their factories.[40] Claiming that British industrialists are particularly wary of French visitors, refusing them entry, he urges his father to reciprocate:

> La plus grande prévention existe contre les étrangers, surtout contre les Français pour lesquels toutes les usines sont fermées. Aucun Français ne peut maintenant aller puiser à la source, et je t'engage à refuser la porte à tous [...] Il faut aussi supprimer toutes entrées pour les fils, cousins d'ouvriers.[41]

> [The greatest prejudice exists against foreigners, especially against the French, for whom all the factories are closed. No Frenchman can now get to the source, and I urge you to close your door to all [...] You must also refuse entry to all sons and cousins of workmen]

This palpable tension heightens a sense of national pride and, for some French observers, praising the technological advances of a rival clearly goes against the grain; Pierre Trabaud (dates unknown), who travelled in summer 1846, freely admits his own *parti pris*:

> Il est impossible de ne pas songer à la belle France, quand on est français et qu'on voudrait donner à sa patrie tout ce qui lui manque, tout ce que possèdent les autres nations et les nations voisines et puissantes avant toutes les autres. Tout ici respire le succès.[42]

> [It is impossible not to think of fair France, when you are French and you would like to give your fatherland all that it lacks, all that which other nations, and particularly neighbouring powerful nations have. Everything here radiates success]

Of course the success that these commentators describe is not perceived by them as specifically Welsh but, as Dufaud's reference to England shows, rather as part of an English, that is to say British, success story.

Although the main focus of many texts in the restoration period is industrial, the tradition of travellers interested exclusively in landscape persists. This is particularly the case of those who confine themselves to north Wales, such as Adolphe Thiébault (1797–c. 1875), an artist from a Franco-British family who toured in 1827 with the main aim

---

40   Thuillier, *Georges Dufaud*, p. 228.
41   Thuillier, *Georges Dufaud*, p. 228.
42   Pierre Trabaud, 'Pays de Galles', in *D'Inverness à Brighton: notes et sentiments sur les Îles Britanniques* (London: Baillière, 1853), p. 377.

of sketching waterfalls.[43] Even here, however, the impact of industry is never far from travellers' minds. Some are explicit about the Welsh landscape providing a refuge from industrialized parts of England. Others even seem to want to have it both ways, like Basile-Joseph Ducos (1767–1836), who came to north Wales in 1826 and published his *Itinéraire et souvenirs d'Angleterre et d'Ecosse 1814–1826* [Itinerary and Memories of England and Scotland 1814–1826] in 1834. He sees poetic possibilities everywhere in the Welsh landscape, noting harpists and heroes from Welsh history, but nevertheless complains that Wales needs to modernize, both generally: 'Le commerce, l'industrie, l'agriculture y ont fait peu de progrès' (p. 158) [business, industry and agriculture have made little progress here], and, especially, for the benefit of travellers: 'Les confortabilités anglaises ne peuvent manquer de s'établir ici prochainement; mais malheur aux voyageurs qui, comme nous, les auront devancées' (p. 182) [English comforts cannot fail to establish themselves here soon; but woe betide the travellers who, like us, will have preceded them]. Ducos is travelling at the height of the development of the road infrastructure in north Wales under the auspices of the Scottish engineer Thomas Telford (1757–1834) who, following the Acts of Union in 1800, was tasked with improving the transport links between London, Holyhead and, ultimately, Ireland. Alluding to the need for such developments, Ducos's views echo those of many German travellers in this period, who see in Wales a land of engineering and technological opportunity.

The most interesting texts of the early nineteenth century, however, are arguably those in which the cultural and aesthetic sit alongside the industrial. A passage from a travelogue by Charles Dupin (1784–1873) shows that the relationship between the aesthetic and the technical is a close one. This young French naval engineer, who had graduated from the *École Polytechnique* in 1803, made a series of journeys around Britain between about 1816 and 1820 to survey modern bridges, ports and other feats of engineering.[44] Dupin published multiple multivolume works in which he systematically surveys Britain. His work remained authoritative for some time, despite him falling out of favour because, it seems,

---

43   Adolphe Thiébault, *Voyage à pied dans le nord du pays de Galles*, Books 14.1–2 (1827), Thiébault Family mss., 1733–1872, bulk 1793–1872, Lilly Library, Indiana University Bloomington. See Phyllis Guskin, 'A French Tourist in Wales', *The Bulletin* (1995), pp. 3–4.

44   See Bradley and Perrin, 'Charles Dupin', pp. 47–68.

the French government thought that his writing was too pro-English.[45]
His description of a scene of landscape and industry at Pontcysyllte in
north Wales, published in 1818 in his *Mémoires sur la marine et les
ponts et chaussées de France et d'Angleterre* [Recollections of the Navy,
the Bridges and the Highways of France and England],[46] is an early
example of seeing perfect harmony in Wales's industrial architecture.
The description here is remarkably literary, despite this being a professional report aimed at fellow scientists and engineers and the aim being
technology transfer. The reader is informed that the great engineer
Telford, described as Dupin's 'friend',[47] had given him the plans for the
aqueduct and arranged for him to visit the foundry:

> Jamais spectacle plus imposant n'a frappé mes regards. Au milieu d'une
> végétation vigoureuse, et conservant encore toute sa fraîcheur, les feux
> des forges, des fours à chaux et des charbons réduits en *coaks*, élevant
> leurs tourbillons de flamme en fumée. Des villages, des fabriques, des
> maisons de plaisance se déployant en amphithéâtre sur les flancs de la
> vallée. Dans le fond, un rapide torrent; par-dessus, le canal aquéduc
> offrant son enveloppe de fer, posée comme par enchantement sur les hauts
> et minces piliers de brique; et ce magnifique ouvrage, fruit de l'heureuse
> audace d'un de mes amis! Perdu dans la contemplation de ces beautés
> de l'art et de la nature, qui, par dégradations d'une lumière mourante,
> variaient à chaque instant leur aspect, je suis resté comme en extase,
> jusqu'à ce que la fin du crépuscule me forçat à m'éloigner pour chercher
> un asile à quelques milles de distance. Voilà ce que j'ai vu, ce que je ne
> puis rendre sans le dépouiller des charmes de la réalité et qui, pourtant,
> fait encore battre mon cœur au souvenir des émotions que produisit en
> moi cet admirable paysage. (pp. 81–82)

> [Never have I been struck by a more impressive spectacle. In the midst of
> vigorous vegetation, that retains all its freshness, the ironwork fires, lime
> kilns and coal reduced to *coke,* each offer up swirls of flame and smoke.
> Villages, factories, country residences arranged like an amphitheatre

---

45   Ethel Jones, *Les Voyageurs français en Angleterre de 1815 à 1830* (Paris:
Boccard, 1930), p. 140.

46   Charles Dupin, *Mémoires sur la marine et les ponts et chaussées de France
et d'Angleterre* (Paris: Bachelier, 1818), pp. 81–82. This is based on travel in 1816.
Dupin then quotes this passage (with some changes) in his own *Voyages dans la
Grande-Bretagne V*, which is part of volume one of his *Force Commerciale de la
Grande-Bretagne* (Paris: Bachelier, 1824), pp. 192–93.

47   Joseph-Michel Dutens, *Mémoires sur les travaux publics de l'Angleterre*
(Paris: Imprimerie royale, 1819), p. 60.

on the sides of the valley. At the far end, a rapid torrent; up above, the
aqueduct canal offers its envelope of iron, placed there as if by magic on
the high and slender brick pillars; and this magnificent work, the fruit of
the fortunate audacity of one of my friends! Lost in the contemplation of
these beauties of art and nature, that looked different every minute with
the dissipation of the dying light, I stayed there as if in ecstasy, until the
end of the twilight forced me to leave and seek shelter a few miles away.
That is what I saw, and though I cannot describe it without divesting it
of the charm of its reality, the memory of the emotion that this admirable
landscape caused me still makes my heart beat faster]

The writing is in superlative mode, the passage opening with 'jamais'
[never] and conveying a liminal setting of autumnal, dying light, almost
at the moment of sunset. Industry, represented by 'des tourbillons
de flamme et de fumée' [swirls of flame and smoke], is pitted against
'végétation vigoureuse' [vigorous vegetation] and 'fraîcheur' [freshness],
but only so as to stress order and harmony. Symmetry and balance
are conveyed in the patient listing of the diverse elements (ranging
from the industrial to the bucolic) that unite in the pleasing form
of an amphitheatre. The scene shows careful textual composition.
Rhetorically, nature and artifice are made equal in the coupling, 'beautés
de l'art et de la nature' [beauties of art and nature], and there is careful
attention to lighting in this autumn setting: 'lumière mourante' [dying
light]. Indeed this is a rather visual piece, with an emphasis on light as
well as on sight – 'mes regards' [my sight] – and the writer's status as
eyewitness – 'Voilà ce que j'ai vu' [That is what I saw]. This is not a
cool, scientific observation, rather the description mounts to a magical
climax with the words 'enchantement' [enchantment] and 'magnifique'
[magnificent], and the effect spreads beyond the visual to a full physical
and emotional reaction on the part of the traveller, who is 'perdu dans
la contemplation' [lost in contemplation] and 'resté comme en extase'
[stayed there as if in ecstasy], before a scene which 'fait encore battre
mon cœur' [makes my heart beat faster]. In fact, so overwhelming is the
experience of this scene that Dupin claims (despite all evidence to the
contrary) that he is lost for words: 'je ne puis rendre' [I cannot describe
it]. Overall, this industrialization of the landscape is experienced as
an emotional encounter to be enjoyed after physical effort: 'Après une
marche longue et pénible, je suis entré dans cette vallée' (p. 192) [After a
long and arduous walk, I entered this valley].

This is in stark contrast to earlier travellers such as compatriot
Amélie de Suffren, who complains at Briton Ferry that her painter's eye

is tired by industry and longs to rest on nature, and again, at Clydach brick kiln, that the sound of hammers makes her want to retreat beneath an ash tree.[48] For her, industry is a distraction from the quasi-sublime surroundings; thus the location of the brick kiln is described as 'sauvage' [wild] and 'entouré de rochers, et coupés par des précipices et par des torrents' [surrounded by rocks and cut through by precipices and torrents]. For Suffren the Welsh landscape is inspiring and worth painting in spite of the nascent industrial scenery, whereas for Dupin, the scene is inspiring because of this innovation in the landscape.

Other writers develop the aestheticization of the industrial landscape a step further. For Pierre-Étienne-Denis Saint-Germain-Leduc (1799–date unknown), Wales is the scene of a harmonious combination of industry and nature where manufacturing towns blend seamlessly into a landscape of gothic ruins: 'les sommets sont couronnés tantôt d'une ruine gothique, tantôt d'une délicieuse habitation de plaisance ou d'une petite ville manufacturière, tantôt enfin de masses de rochers nus et sauvages' (p. 2) [the summits are crowned now with a Gothic ruin, now with a delightful country residence or a little manufacturing town, or now with a mass of bare and savage rocks]. His own text, in *L'Angleterre, l'Ecosse et l'Irlande: relation d'un voyage récent dans les trois royaumes* (1838) [England, Scotland and Ireland: An Account of a Recent Tour of the Three Kingdoms],[49] is something of a generic balancing act, reminiscent of the eclectic eighteenth-century travelogues. It combines technical detail about processes (copper mining, fishing) with long digressions into legends (such as that of Saint Winifred), while providing rather predictable Romanticized descriptions of landscapes. The text also switches unexpectedly in and out of the Romantic vein, such as when a technical history of bridge building is given, including a long comparison between the Menai Suspension Bridge and that in Fribourg in Switzerland, that functions as a prelude to a paean to the Welsh bridge: 'On dirait un merveilleux bijou en filigrane, qu'une fée se serait amusée à jeter dans les airs' (p. 21) [It looks just like a marvellous jewel of metal wires, that a fairy might have thrown into the air].

By the mid-century, then, it appears that the aesthetic impact of the emerging industrial landscape is such that even those charged with

---

48   Suffren, *Voyage pittoresque*, unpaginated.
49   Pierre-Etienne-Denis Saint-Germain-Leduc, *L'Angleterre, l'Ecosse et l'Irlande: relation d'un voyage récent dans les trois royaumes*, 4 vols (Paris: Levrault, 1838), III, pp. 1–46.

producing more technical accounts find themselves frustrated by their inability to do the scenes they encounter true justice. Of the more professional, technical travel accounts, that on the north Wales slate industry by L. Smyers (dates unknown) stands out, partly because the author was unusual in speaking to individuals and was even invited into the homes of workers, but also because he reflects on his inablility to adequately render the industrial scenes before him. In his *Essai sur l'état actuel de l'industrie ardoisière en France et en Angleterre* (1858) [Essay on the Current State of the Slate Industry in France and England],[50] Penrhyn quarry is presented as a northern equivalent to Merthyr, in other words a world leader 'qui n'a pas son pareil dans le monde' (p. 8) [unparalled in the world]. Overall, the text reflects industrial concerns. Smyers works in the industry himself and has been sent on this study trip by a French company. The great questions of the day revolve around economy of time versus money rather than safety or conditions. Technology transfer is clearly one of the main aims of the trip, and Smyers states that he has already fed information back to French slate experts on the specific matter of using explosives. In his constant comparisons with the industry in France and Belgium, French national pride is evident and when he reports that Welsh slate is even exported to France, he cannot but express his regret and suggests that French exploitations could change this (p. 12). Although this is, like many others, a rather practical and technical text, it also stands out because of the author's attempts to position his responses and, indeed, the text itself in relation to more literary travel accounts through Smyers's periodic expressions of frustration at his own lack of literary skill. The spectacle of Penrhyn, he claims, is unique: 'je n'ai jamais rien vu qui puisse lui être comparé' (p. 27) [I have never seen anything that could be compared to it]. Moreover, the traveller would need the skills of a poet to do justice to the sudden and complete silence between the lighting and an explosion at the slate quarry, for the experience has 'quelque chose que j'ai ressenti, mais qu'il ne m'est pas donné de décrire; je ne suis ni poète ni écrivain' (p. 26) [something that I felt but that I am incapable of describing; I am neither poet nor writer]. Similarly, when underground, he is lost for words:

> Il m'est presqu'impossible de décrire d'une manière palpable ces effrayants souterrains. Mon imagination se les rappelle très-bien, mais je ne trouve

50 L. Smyers, *Essai sur l'état actuel de l'industrie ardoisière en France et en Angleterre, suivi de quelques observations pratiques sur la formation du schiste ardoisier* (Paris: Poulet-Malassis, 1858).

pas de mots pour rendre les sensations diverses qu'elle y a ressenties. (p. 35)

[I find it almost impossible to describe in a palpable way these frightening underground places. My imagination remembers them well, but I cannot find the words to convey the different sensations that it felt there]

His skills as a writer, he complains, cannot measure up to these new scenes: 'Ce chemin de fer mériterait d'être décrit aussi bien que les ardoisières par un homme plus lettré que moi' (p. 39) [This railway line and these slate quarries deserve to be described by somebody who is more of a man of letters than I am].

Smyers's text also gives insight into the lives of travellees and these in turn are contextualized in relation to the awe-inspiring industrial landscape. He claims that he probably would not have believed an account of Penrhyn had he not been an eyewitness (p. 18), as the spectacle is on such an overwhelming scale. Although the workers are 'eclipsed' by the vast scale of the works: 'mille ouvriers [...] éclipsés aux yeux du visiteur par l'immensité du spectacle qu'il a devant lui' (p. 9) [a thousand workers [...] eclipsed in the eyes of the visitor by the immensity of the spectacle in front of him], Smyers goes out of his way to talk to and even to eat with travellees, despite the probable language barriers. He refers to conversations with masters (pp. 15, 17), and recommends talking to the workers as the best way of becoming well-informed about the industry (p. 25). Their houses are approved of, and found to be aesthetically pleasing, too, having something of the 'Swiss village' about them, and he assures the reader that the surroundings of Penrhyn Castle are as good as the best views in France. Despite his own perceived shortcomings, Smyers views the industrial landscape and the society within it aesthetically as well as technically. Landscape and industry are fused inextricably in a process of aesthetization which draws Wales into the broader phenomenon of the industrial sublime.

Smyers's text is also invaluable in drawing attention to the social changes at work in Wales in the mid-nineteenth century. Despite claiming that 'Quand on a vu Penrhyn, on se demande si on n'a pas tout vu, et s'il est utile d'aller ailleurs' (p. 28) [Once you have seen Penrhyn, you wonder if you have not seen everything, if there is any point in going elsewhere], he feels that he must visit Ffestiniog too, and reports that the workers there receive a good salary, live well (p. 44) and benefit from good order and temperance. Smyers is invited into the house of a 'contre-maître surveillant' [supervisor] and he accepts enthusiastically, as he is keen to ask him questions. The Welsh family fuss around the French visitor who is served bread that is very white, but not very leavened (like all British bread, he remarks), along with butter, cheese and a jug of milk. When Smyers asks for a different drink he is surprised to be brought water. Having thus inadvertently discovered the temperance movement, he wishes that Wales would export this idea rather than its many slate products.

By the 1850s, Wales had established a reputation amongst many French travellers as a site of inspiration. Its sublime landscape and industrial innovation fused in the minds of some to create an impression of grandeur and majesty to which numerous French writers felt their own nation should seek to aspire. For many, the Celtic culture of Wales remained a side issue or was simply ignored in the quest for technological advancement. After the 1860s, as France itself developed economically, interest in Wales as a site of advancement diminished. There was, however, a further development in Wales during the long nineteenth century which would once again shift the nation from the periphery to centre stage. Smyers's text already alludes to the temperate lifestyle of the north Walian community and in so doing draws attention to an aspect of Welsh life largely absent from French narratives in the early to mid-nineteenth century: the impact of the spread of Nonconformism. Although present in Welsh society throughout the long nineteenth century, it was from November 1904 onwards that a transformation truly occurred across Wales and its southern valleys in particular which drew global attention to the nation. This time, however, Wales was perceived as world-leading in religious rather than industrial terms.[51] The 1904–1905 Revival (in Welsh *diwygiad*, meaning 'reform'), with its emphasis on democratic audience participation, reportedly led to the conversion of one hundred thousand people to Christianity.[52] The Revival's influence was seen in countries in every part of the world,

---

51   Gitre views the Revival not as an isolated religious movement but very much a part of Britain's modernization. See Edward J. Gitre, 'The 1904–05 Welsh Revival: Modernization, Technologies, and Techniques of the Self', *Church History*, 73:4 (2004), pp. 792–827.

52   The most succinct introduction to the Welsh Revival of 1904–1905 is provided by Noel Gibbard, *Fire on the Altar: A History and Evaluation of the 1904–05 Welsh Revival* (Pen-y-bont ar Ogwr: Gwasg Bryntirion, 2005). For the wider historical context of the Revival, including the development of Welsh Nonconformism and the 1902 Education Act, see John Davies, *A History of Wales* (London: Penguin, 1997).

including France, Germany, Denmark, the Netherlands, the United States, India, Russia, China and Madagascar, bringing Wales new international renown. Believers and atheists, ministers of all confessions and professional observers rushed to Wales to study the historical, psychological and mystical causes and social effects of the movement. R. Tudur Jones notes that one of the most prominent features of the Revival was the fact that other countries took such an interest in it, and none more so than France.[53] Indeed, Pamela Atzori asserts that 'In many ways, it was the French correspondents, along with other foreign visitors, that made the 1904 Revival "Great"'.[54] Some French newspapers, including *L'Européen* [The European], *Le Temps* [Time], *Le Christianisme* [Christianity] and *L'Eglise Libre* [The Free Church], published detailed descriptions of meetings held by Revival leader Evan Roberts (1878–1951), as well as special Revival supplements which told his life story. From January 1905 onwards, French-language newspapers frequently discussed the possibility of a French Revival,[55] and numerous visitors from France came to Wales in 1905 with the express purpose of seeing the Revival for themselves.

The situation in France at the beginning of the twentieth century was such, however, that the events in Wales took on a particular relevance. The French reception of the Revival can be placed in the context of the heated debates in French public spheres in the period leading up to the passing of the law on the Separation of the Churches and State on 9 December 1905, thereby establishing state secularism in France. The law was based on the principles of the freedom of religious exercise, the neutrality of the state and public powers related to the church. Harshly condemned by the Roman Catholic Church, the law elicited a range of responses amongst French Protestants, and it was in France that the Welsh Revival was received most enthusiastically. As well as many shorter accounts in periodicals, three lengthy travelogues were produced

53   See, for example, the article 'Foreigners and the Revival', *The Western Mail*, 6 February 1905, p. 6, cited in R. Tudur Jones, *Faith and the Crisis of a Nation: Wales, 1890–1914*, ed. Robert Pope, trans. Sylvia Prys Jones (Cardiff: University of Wales Press, 2004), p. 345. See also Noel Gibbard, *On the Wings of the Dove: The International Effects of the 1904–05 Revival* (Pen-y-bont ar Ogwr: Gwasg Bryntirion, 2002), pp. 23–35.

54   Pamela Atzori, 'The International Effects of the Welsh Revival 1904–5: The Case of France' (unpublished master's thesis, Aberystwyth University, 2005), p. 1.

55   The first article on this theme was printed on 20 January 1905 in *L'Eglise Libre*. See Atzori, p. 62.

in this period by both Christian and atheist travellers who paint detailed and contrasting portraits of the Revival and its effects.

The first of these is by Jeanne Saillens (née Crétan, 1856–1941), who travelled to Wales in February 1905 at the zenith of the Revival, visiting Cardiff, Nantymoel, Ogmore and Maesteg with her Baptist minister husband Rev. Reuben Saillens (1855–1942), with whom she would later found the first Bible school in France. She published her account of the visit as well as editing those of a number of other leading Protestant ministers from France and Switzerland who had also witnessed the Welsh revival first-hand, namely Rev. S. Lombard, Rev. E. Lenoir, Rev. D. Lortsch (President of the French Free Church synod) and Rev. Ulysse Emery in the compendium *Le Réveil du Pays de Galles* (1905) [The Welsh Revival].[56] Penned by fervent admirers of the Revival, the accounts edited by Saillens are marked by an absence of descriptions of travel to and within Wales as well as specific Welsh sites or geographical features, focusing instead on the interiors of chapels and a coal mine in Pontypridd, where the visitors participated in a prayer meeting on 8 February 1905. Such deterritorialized accounts would have made it easier for contemporary French readers to transport the revivalist scenes back to France, echoing the technology transfer of the previous century in continuing the elision of Wales as a place, centring on it instead as a site of inspiration.

Saillens presents pre-Revival Wales as a society in decline, typified by drunkenness, swearing and blasphemy by miners, and rugby fields filling up while churches were emptying. This negative portrayal of waning Welsh piety is fundamental to the author's missionary zeal and the text's overarching narrative of redemption, something from which the Welsh are well-placed to benefit as the Revival takes effect. The reading of Wales as a Celtic nation resurfaces here. Saillens deems the Welsh to be typical of the Celtic race as a whole, possessing 'le caractère vif, ardent, démonstratif' (p. 21) [a lively, intense, demonstrative character]. She praises the welcome she received, noting that 'l'hospitalité de ces gens simples est proverbiale en Angleterre et ailleurs' (p. 7) [the hospitality of this simple people is proverbial in England and elsewhere]. This example presents one of numerous instances of slippage between England and Wales in the account, with Wales also providing England with many bards, for example (p. 6). Conversely, the 'profondément religieux' [deeply religious] Welsh are also constructed as superior to 'nos Bretons'

---

56   Jeanne Saillens, *Le Réveil du Pays de Galles* (Valance: Ducros, 1905).

[our Bretons] as, unlike the mainly Catholic 'pauvres compatriotes' [poor compatriots] of Brittany, the predominantly Protestant Welsh are ranked as world-leading in terms of their 'véritable civilisation' (p. 6) [true civilization]. Rather than predicating Wales's pioneering status on its industrial prowess as previous travellers had done, for this set of visitors Wales's exemplary nature lies in its religious fervour.

Sensory descriptions abound in Saillens's representation of her experience of attending revivalist meetings, thereby reinforcing her eyewitness status. She affirms that the chapels are overflowing on every day of the week, and experiences for the first time the creation of unending sequences of song and prayer at revivalist meetings (p. 39). When she sees revivalist leader Evan Roberts in the flesh, she thanks God for being able to witness the events of the Revival with her own eyes and '[les] toucher du doigt' (p. 51) [be within touching distance (of them)]. In contrast to other outsider accounts of the Revival, Saillens's portrayal of an overwhelming, immersive, emotional encounter means that the Welsh language is not experienced as a barrier to participation or understanding: 'On sentait une force invisible vous étreindre le cœur, et même sans rien comprendre, on était pris' (p. 50) [You could feel an invisible power seize your heart, and even without understanding anything you were caught up in it]. The locations of these revivalist meetings are anonymized, which creates an impression of their ubiquity in southern, industrialized Wales. While noting that the first sparks of the Revival were lit in New Quay in February 1904 under the leadership of Calvinist minister Joseph Jenkins (1861–1929) (p. 9), much of Jeanne Saillens's account is devoted to descriptions of Evan Roberts and her experience of listening to him preach. Attesting to his popularity and renown, she notes that it was impossible to enter the overflowing chapel, and that she was only able to enter the meeting with the help of a policeman (p. 46). Roberts's voice and physical appearance are described as both imposing and approachable, authoritative and tender, and reinforce the image of the evangelist as a prophet and charismatic leader of the movement:

> Il est grand, et largement bâti; le front haut, l'air intellectuel, d'un abord extrêmement aimable, avec un sourire rayonnant qui illumine tous ceux qui l'approchent. Quand il parle en public, son geste a quelque chose de prophétique, qui marque l'autorité et la douceur; c'est un geste noble et harmonieux. Sa voix est un peu rude, très claire. Autant il a d'autorité et de sévérité en public, autant, en particulier, il est doux et simple comme un enfant. (p. 21)

[He is tall and broadly built; he has a high forehead, an intellectual look and an extremely pleasant manner, with a beaming smile which lights up all those who approach him. When he speaks in public his gestures have something prophetic about them which show authority and gentleness; his gestures are noble and harmonious. His voice is a little gruff and very clear. As much as he is authoritative and serious in public, he is especially gentle and as simple as a child]

Despite Roberts's 'tempérament celtique' [Celtic temperament] and related 'facultés mystiques' [mystical faculties] (p. 19), Saillens asserts that the veracity of his supernatural visions cannot be doubted, and her text incorporates numerous testimonial accounts to validate his position as a visionary and success in producing conversions to Christianity.

While Evan Roberts epitomizes the force of the Welsh Revival in Saillens's account, her fellow travellers are more impressed by the newfound piety of the converts to the revivalist cause. In his letter to 'M.D.' dated 14 April 1905, Swiss pastor Rev. Ulysse Emery (dates unknown) notes that the most striking event of his journey to Wales occurred underground, when he joined over two hundred miners in a prayer meeting in a mine near Pontypridd. In Emery's sonorous description, the reverberation of a hymn sung far beneath the earth's surface implies that the Revival has reached significant depths in Wales, both literal and figurative. The letter depicts the collective religious, moral and social transformation and redemption of an anonymous and depersonalized mass of over two hundred miners singing praises to God in a corner of the mine where they used to meet to drink, swear, blaspheme and fight (p. 69). The Protestant evangelists return to France and Switzerland satisfied that their journeys to Wales have allowed them to affirm the strength, vitality and significance of the Welsh Revival. Having been taught a 'grande leçon de foi en la prière' (p. 65) [great lesson of faith in prayer] by the Welsh movement, the travellers are renewed in their desire to see the spread of the Revival to France and beyond. Nevertheless, it could be argued that their textual visions and hopes of a revival for France obscure the travellers' visions of Wales to a certain extent; their gaze is fixed on the question of whether the Revival can 'travel' to France and beyond, and as such the Welsh context of the Revival is diminished.

Theologian Henri Bois (1862–1924) arrived in Wales two months after Saillens and her party and, indeed, his account begins by stating his fervent hope that he has not arrived too late in order to witness the Revival first-hand (pp. 94–95). His *Le Réveil au Pays de Galles* (1906) [The Revival in Wales] is an extensive study of over six hundred pages analyzing diverse aspects of the Welsh Revival, including a diarised travelogue detailing his journey to Wales between 10 and 27 April 1905.[57] Bois was professor of theology at the University of Montpellier when he travelled to Wales, and was also an ordained minister of the Reformed Church in France. He attempts to measure the strength and reach of the movement throughout, and verify the rumour that in many places in Wales only a maximum of four people remained who had not yet been converted (p. 98). Like Saillens and her fellow travellers, Bois was active in his promotion of the revivalist cause in France, organizing and speaking at a revivalist meeting in L'Oratoire, the main Presbyterian church in Paris, in April 1905 immediately following his return from Wales.[58] Although the main focus of Bois's account is also on his experience of attending revivalist meetings, a much wider vision of Wales is offered than in Saillens's work, and he is relatively unusual amongst Revival visitors and correspondents in travelling to north Wales (Wrexham, Trefor and Rhosllanerchrugog) as well as the main strongholds of the south. Moreover, Bois underlines the working-class basis of the revivalist movement, and nowhere is this more evident than in the chapter devoted to his experience of attending a prayer meeting underground in Penrhiw mine.

For the majority of his stay, Bois is reluctantly based in a noisy Cardiff hotel while commuting by train to meetings in the south Wales mining valleys, though on one occasion he is delighted to discover a temperance hotel in Aberdare, where he stays overnight (p. 118). While in Cardiff, he is able to draw on the advice of the Principal of the Baptist College and a *Western Mail* journalist in order to locate the 'special services' held by itinerant young revivalists (pp. 106–07). Bois is at pains to underline that he is not in Wales as a tourist (p. 118), and generally avoids sightseeing, with the exception of Wrexham's Catholic Cathedral, although this does not merit a description in his travelogue (p. 128). Yet the narrator does engage in some aesthetic evaluation. His first glimpse of Aberdare on 13 April 1905 provides an occasion to reassure the reader of the veracity of Reclus's *Nouvelle géographie universelle* (1879) [New Universal Geography]:

Je constate l'exactitude du jugement de Reclus: 'Aberdare, les villes avoisinantes et les villages d'usines qui se succèdent dans la vallée de

---

57   Henri Bois, *Le Réveil au Pays de Galles* (Toulouse: Société des publications morales et religieuses, 1906).

58   See Gibbard, *On the Wings of the Dove*, p. 31; Atzori, p. 67.

la Taff jusqu'à Cardiff, sont de celles que leur laideur et leur vulgarité rendent le[s] plus déplaisantes à voir'. (pp. 117–18)[59]

[I can confirm that Reclus's judgement is accurate: 'Aberdare, the neighbouring towns and the factory villages which come one after the other all the way down the Taff Valley to Cardiff, are amongst those places whose ugliness and tawdriness make them the most unpleasant to see']

As well as ascertaining the unpleasant ugliness of Aberdare, Bois is also disappointed by the Anglicization of Cardiff, described in racial terms as multi-ethnic and cosmopolitan, 'pas une ville purement galloise' (p. 107) [not a purely Welsh town]. He affirms his (unnamed) guidebook's view that Anglicized Wrexham is 'quoique située dans le Pays de Galles, une ville anglaise. Pas moyen de rentrer en contact avec les Gallois! Où sont les Gallois?' (pp. 126–27) [although situated in Wales, an English town. No means of coming into contact with the Welsh! Where are the Welsh?]. There are numerous descriptions of the narrator spending a long time searching for the locations of revival meetings in the south Wales valleys, and this confusing geography adds to the sense of mysticism that surrounds the Revival (pp. 109, 119, 126). Bois maintains that the Revival's influence is such that its traces can be found in Wales's visual landscape, and he is very impressed when he sees pious phrases on posters displayed in Aberaman railway station, something that would be unthinkable in soon-to-be secular France (p. 109).

As was the case with Saillens, Bois was keen to meet revivalist leader Evan Roberts in the flesh, making a special trip to Liverpool, where Roberts was preaching at the time of his stay. He also provides details of his encounters with other famous figures from the movement, such as Miss S.A. Jones and Dan Roberts (Evan's brother), and is moved to tears by a hymn sung by Miss Maggie Davies in an Aberaman chapel. He devotes a separate 50-page chapter to his meeting with the visionary and preacher Mrs Mary Jones, whose sermons in Egryn in north-west Wales were said to be accompanied by mysterious balls of light in the sky.[60] In addition to underlining the traveller-narrator's eyewitness status,

---

59   Élisée Reclus, *Nouvelle géographie universelle: la terre et les hommes*, Vol. 4 (Paris: Hachette, 1879), p. 402.

60   While he does underline that Miss (S.A.) Jones (a south Wales revivalist from Nantymoel who was one of Evan Roberts's most prominent assistants) and north Wales revivalist Mrs Mary Jones are different people (see p. 345), Bois nevertheless does not provide a first name for the former in his account.

such encounters are afforded a deeper significance, as Bois's presence as a foreigner is on several occasions perceived as an affirmation of the revivalist cause. Conversely, Bois does express scepticism about the cult of personality surrounding Evan Roberts and the commodification of the Revival, which he sees while wandering through Cardiff's shopping arcades:

> Je me promène dans les arcades qui servent de passages entre les rues; je vois aux devantures des magasins de petites broches de 10 centimes, 20 centimes, où figure le portrait d'Evan Roberts – dans le genre de certaines petites broches que vendent les camelots de Buffalo Bill's. (p. 104)

> [I go for a walk in the arcades which serve as passages between the streets; in the shops' front windows I see small brooches costing 10 or 20 centimes which feature a portrait of Evan Roberts, in the style of those small brooches sold by Buffalo Bill's street peddlers]

This evocation of vulgarity diminishes the seriousness of the visionary's portrayal to some extent and chimes with M. Wynn Thomas's assessment of Evan Roberts as 'one of the people; a hero for a new age; a revelation of the potential of the ordinary [...] like Jesse James and other characters of the Wild West, partly a product of the popular press'.[61] Nevertheless, Bois's travelogue does contain eulogistic descriptions of revivalist meetings, such as one evening meeting held in Aberdare in an overflowing chapel. As a foreign visitor, Bois is offered an excellent place in the *set fawr*,[62] and only leaves after four hours, when the meeting is still in full flow, exclaiming enthusiastically: 'Ce meeting de quatre heures n'a pas été fatigant. Il y a tant d'imprévu, tant de variété, tant de vie, de spontanéité, de ferveur!' (p. 118) [This four-hour meeting has not been tiring. There is so much that is unexpected, so much variety, so much life, spontaneity, fervour!]. Considerable attention is paid to him by ministers and members of the congregation; Bois becomes an object of curiosity, an exotic figure of the travellees' interest, a visitor from afar who is prayed for during the meetings he attends. The minister of Saron Chapel in Aberaman first regards him with astonishment and suspicion, questioning his motives. This suspicion can be seen as echoing the Welsh inhabitants' earlier fears

---

61   M. Wynn Thomas, *In the Shadow of the Pulpit: Literature and Non-Conformist Wales* (Cardiff: University of Wales Press, 2010), p. 13.

62   In English, 'the great pew'. The *set fawr* or *sedd fawr* is a key feature of Nonconformist chapels in Wales, placed immediately in front of the pulpit, and occupied by the elders or deacons elected by the members.

of industrial spies: 'Il me regarde d'un œil scrutateur, étonné évidemment de me voir là, se demandant si je suis sérieux ou si je suis un curieux, un dilettante, un critique' (p. 109) [He gives me a searching look, clearly astonished to see me there, asking himself if I am serious or if I am a curious onlooker, an amateur, a critic]. On several occasions Bois is taken aback when he is put on the spot and asked to address the congregation, to prove the nobility of his intention and desire not just to 'see' the Revival, but to 'feel' it (p. 110). The congregation respond warmly to his efforts to pray and testify in halting English, which leads to a feeling of communion: 'C'est une sensation toute particulière que de prier en étant interrompu tout le temps ou plutôt accompagné par des: Amen! Bravo! Ah! Oui! etc. On se sent tellement encouragé, soutenu' (p. 111) [It is a very special feeling to pray while being continually interrupted or rather being accompanied by cries of 'Amen!', 'Bravo!', 'Ah!', 'Yes!' You feel so encouraged, supported]. Indeed, such scenes represent a highly unusual dynamic in travel literature, where the encounters are framed by the wishes and needs of the travellee, and not the traveller. As Catharine Mee has noted: 'Travellers are accustomed to being spectators, absorbing the sight of travellees in their landscapes and cityscapes with an all-encompassing gaze'.[63] Here the traveller's controlling gaze and itinerary are secondary to the religious fervour of the revivalists, whose meetings often endured long into the night.

Nevertheless, in spite of Bois's enthusiasm for the revivalists' cause, a dissonant note is sounded in relation to the Welsh language, which is experienced as a barrier. When listening to the 'remarkable' prayer of a young girl, Bois regrets: 'Malheureusement, c'est en gallois, et je ne puis juger que de la longueur, de l'abondance et de la facilité' (p. 111) [Unfortunately it is in Welsh, and I can only judge its length, abundance and ease]. Language issues surface regularly in this travelogue as an obstacle to a fuller appreciation of the Revival, although on one occasion a young man tries to serve as an interpreter into French. A comic incident of linguistic misunderstanding occurs when Dan Roberts bids the narrator good night ('nos da' in Welsh) at the end of a meeting:

A une bifurcation, nous nous séparons, Dan Roberts me disant quelque chose qui ressemble à no star. Je lève les yeux, le ciel est très pur et très étoilé. Je confesse que je ne comprends pas. Mais il m'explique qu'il n'a

---

63 Catharine Mee, *Interpersonal Encounters in Contemporary Travel Writing: French and Italian Perspectives* (London and New York: Anthem Press, 2014), p. 84.

voulu faire aucune allusion aux étoiles, et que les mots qu'il a prononcés sont gallois et signifient: bonne nuit! (p. 124)

[We go our separate ways at a fork in the road, Dan Roberts saying something to me which sounded like 'no star'. I raise my eyes, the sky is very clear and very starry. I confess that I do not understand. But he explains that he did not mean to refer to the stars at all, and that the words he said are Welsh and mean 'good night'!]

Although Bois's expectations of the Revival are fulfilled by his experiences in Wales, in places he adopts a more critical view than that expressed in Saillens's work. Bois asserts that the Revival was still at its height while he was in Cardiff, Rhosllanerchrugog and Trefor and that he witnessed numerous conversions with his own eyes (p. 101). However, he also admits that there was a large degree of regional variation, and that the Revival had already peaked in some areas of Wales. Bois's status as an English-speaking minister and theologian meant that he was afforded privileged access to and opportunities to participate in revivalist meetings, and as a result far greater attention is given to Welsh travellees in his work than in most travelogues on Wales from this period.

Another extensive travelogue of the period filters its viewpoint on Wales from an atheist and scientific perspective. The renowned psychoanalyst Joseph Rogues de Fursac (1872–1942), who was the chief psychiatrist at the Ville-Évrard asylum in Paris, travelled to Wales in 1906 in an official capacity. Fursac had been commissioned by the French Interior Ministry in the spring of that year to study the influence of mysticism on the development of mental illnesses (p. 6).[64] Fursac adopts a non-religious, detached stance as a 'visiteur curieux et indépendant' (p. 95) [curious and independent visitor] as he travels to Cardiff, Pontypridd, Merthyr Tydfil, Neath, Swansea, Loughor (where he is welcomed by Evan Roberts's mother), Bridgend, the Rhondda Valley and Treorchy. His long weeks spent in south Wales, 'le berceau et la terre promise' (p. 5) [the cradle and promised land] of the Revival, led to the publication in 1907 of *Un mouvement mystique contemporain. Le réveil religieux du Pays de Galles (1904–1905)* [A Contemporary Mystical Movement: The Religious Revival in Wales (1904–1905)],[65] a hybrid text

---

64   Fursac was well-placed to carry out such a study, having published the highly influential *Manuel de Psychiatrie* in 1903.

65   Joseph Rogues de Fursac, *Un mouvement mystique contemporain. Le réveil religieux du Pays de Galles (1904–1905)* (Paris: Alcan, 1907).

which combines a lengthy travelogue of over two hundred pages with psychological observations about the revivalist movement. Throughout his work Fursac takes a keen interest in Evan Roberts, undertaking a detailed psychological assessment of the revivalist leader and making several diagnoses, such as 'l'hyperesthésie moral' [moral hyperesthesia] and 'émotivité morbide' [morbid emotiveness] (p. 166).

Fursac's presence is not always welcome when he reveals the true nature of his 'mission'. In Pontypridd, for example, his revivalist hostess asks suspiciously: 'Vous n'allez pas trouver de la folie dans le Réveil, j'imagine?' (p. 49) [I presume that you are not going to find madness in the Revival?]. The work is part scientific study; Fursac interviews the director of Bridgend Mental Hospital and the Glamorganshire chief of police, and obtains statistics relating to admissions to the institution, and cases of intoxication and delinquency before and after the Revival. Fursac concludes that the Revival did lead to a significant rise in religion-induced psychoses (p. 124), but that the evidence relating to a decline in drunkenness was inconclusive (p. 127). As a result of his professed atheism and determination to base his analysis of the Revival on natural rather than supernatural causes, Fursac's account has been praised by numerous subsequent historians and critics of the movement. To take one example, Gareth Miles hails it as the 'best work' he has read on the Revival, commending Fursac's objectivity in juxtaposition with the 'inflammatory' coverage by the British press.[66]

In contrast to the other travellers examined here, Fursac came to Wales the year after the peak of the Revival. While he expresses the desire 'de voir soi-même le sol où la fleur mystique s'est épanouie avec tant de magnificence' (p. 5) [to see for oneself the land where the mystical flower has flourished so magnificently] in appreciative terms, his main concern is with its after-effects, questioning what had become of the claimed 100,000 people who converted in 1904–1905. Fursac is an especially sharp observer who focuses his gaze on social rather than spiritual after-effects. His sociological observations range from

---

66 Gareth Miles, 'Y Diwygiad trwy lygad Ffrancwr', *Taliesin*, 124 (2005), pp. 22–26 (p. 22). Miles also translated extracts from the work and its key findings into Welsh as part of this article. Conversely, Gaius Davies argues that Fursac's atheism makes it impossible for him to evaluate the facts properly, as he discounts the spiritual and divine. Gaius Davies, 'Evan Roberts: wedi ei ddifa gan y tân?', in Noel Gibbard (ed.), *Nefol Dân: Agweddau ar Ddiwygiad 1904–05* (Pen-y-bont ar Ogwr: Gwasg Bryntirion, 2004), pp. 157–67 (p. 167).

discussing urban planning in Cardiff to sporting activities such as rugby and cricket. He keeps a keen professional eye out for signs of degeneracy and delinquency, and in many respects Anglicized Cardiff is portrayed as a den of vice, especially alcohol and prostitution. Fursac emphasizes the educational rather than solely the aesthetic value of sights, such as in this desolate description of the Rhondda Valley:

> J'ai promené mes regards sur les collines nues et désolées qui, de chaque côté, ferment l'horizon; j'ai respiré l'atmosphère épaisse et comme saturée de charbon qui enveloppe les villages. Ce n'est pas gai, mais c'est instructif. (p. 176)

> [I turned my eyes to the bare, desolate hills which block off the horizon on each side; I inhaled the thick coal-saturated atmosphere that shrouds the villages. It is not cheerful but it is instructive]

Nevertheless, his visit to Merthyr Tydfil and the Dowlais Forge is portrayed as a transformational experience. His initial negative impression of Merthyr Tydfil focuses on the environmental destruction caused by industrial development. Yet inside Dowlais Forge, Fursac has a powerful, quasi-religious emotional response to visiting 'hell', and his adulation of the industrial sublime is tempered by his appreciation of the immense human effort it entailed:

> On s'en va à regret. Cet enfer a son charme, avec son vacarme et sa prodigieuse activité. Ces affreuses bâtisses avec leurs forêts de cheminées si peu sympathiques vues du dehors, vous émotionnent vues du dedans, par le déploiement colossal de force docile qu'elles mettent sous vos yeux. Cette émotion a quelque chose de religieux; elle évoque la toute-puissance de l'homme, et, comme tout sentiment religieux, fait naître l'idée de quelque chose de vague et de sublime: l'idée du progrès indéfini et éternel. (p. 86)

> [We leave reluctantly. This hell has its charm, with its din and prodigious activity. These frightful buildings with their forests of chimneys, so unpleasant from the outside, thrill you when viewed from within, through the colossal deployment of docile force which lies before you. This emotion has something religious about it; it evokes the omnipotence of man and, like all religious sentiment, gives birth to the idea of something vague and sublime: the idea of indefinite and eternal progress]

Fursac is also profoundly moved by his visit to a prayer meeting in a mine near Pontypridd, and his account is sympathetic towards the workers, highlighting the dangers they face underground more than their piety. He is particularly affected by one elderly miner's prayer: 'Il demande à Dieu de protéger les mineurs, d'éloigner les fléaux de la mine, l'inondation et le terrible grisou. Ces simples mots donnent à la scène un caractère poignant' (p. 82) [He asks God to protect the miners, to keep away the plagues of the mines, the flooding and terrible methane. These simple words give the scene a poignant character]. Unusually, his account also portrays these same miners as relatively well-off. In the Rhondda Valley, as he observes miners and their families in their Sunday best, he comments: 'Cette population, les femmes et les enfants, comme les hommes, sent l'aisance. Et, de fait, la situation économique dans ces vallées minières est tolérable' (p. 138) [This population, women and children, like the men, suggests affluence. And, in fact, the economic situation in these mining valleys is tolerable].

When Fursac finally attends a revivalist meeting, he deems the chapel to be cheerful and engaging (p. 138). In their dissociation from Anglo-Saxon reserve and reverence, the narrator maintains that these lively, talkative congregations are much closer to the Catholic churches of Italy or Spain than Protestant England (pp. 138–39). Fursac's scepticism and detachment is sometimes overtaken by an emotional response during the revivalist meetings he attends; for instance, when he listens to a young girl pray in a chapel in Porth, he is deeply moved in spite of the linguistic barrier. The psychiatrist diagnoses many of the causes of the Revival as being distinctively Welsh, as Thomas notes, 'the unique product of a specific people moulded by a singular religious culture'.[67] These included geographical and (Welsh-language) intellectual isolation, formative Welsh-language religious education, an innate Welsh religious temperament and emotionality, the strong presence of the supernatural and the working-class and rural basis of the Revival. Welsh alterity is fully foregrounded here as Fursac argues that Wales's geographical remoteness and insurmountable linguistic barrier has protected its religiosity, making the Welsh people the most religious in the 'monde civilisé' (p. 181) [civilized world]. Fursac also underlines the significance of Welsh musicality as an integral part of the Revival. When he hears Welsh choral singing in Pontypridd, he believes this to be the first time he has heard truly religious music. Moreover, he draws attention to the key role played by female revivalists and preachers in Wales, and hails this progressive example as a 'type d'humanité nouveau' (p. 144) [new type of humanity] and a sign of the future. Such a positive view of their

67 Thomas, *In the Shadow of the Pulpit*, p. 95.

subversion of traditional gender roles was out of step with most contemporary observers and historians of the Revival, as Deirdre Beddoe has noted: 'Eight of Roberts' team of ten followers on his first missionary journey were women who, far from being besotted religious "groupies", as male versions of history frequently depict them, in fact, played a key part in organizing meetings and preaching'.[68]

Fursac concludes his account by praising, yet also infantilizing 'ce petit peuple gallois si confiant dans l'avenir de sa race, si sincère dans ses croyances, si ardents à les manifester' [this little Welsh people so confident in the future of its race, so sincere in its beliefs, so passionate to express them], and stating his respect for their 'fond de vitalité' (p. 183) [depths of vitality]. However, while on the one hand he expresses admiration for the salutary effects of the Revival as a unifying force which has spread a spirit of tolerance, and for its numerous concrete social benefits, such as a reduction of intoxication leading to improved family lives (p. 183); on the other, the Revival is also equated with Welsh backwardness and a lack of modernity, and viewed as 'the last gasp of a vanishing, primitive, pre-rational civilization'.[69] He concludes that it would be puerile to attempt a revival elsewhere, especially in France, which in his view has long since left behind the conditions necessary for a religious revival and has progressed too far to turn back (p. 185).

As noted, the French travellers who witnessed the Revival first-hand have been valorized not only for the significance of their mere presence, but also due to the original perspectives offered by their rigorous analyses. With reference to both the theologian Bois and the psychiatrist Fursac, R. Tudur Jones concludes that 'these French scholars made a substantial contribution to the debate', that 'their emphasis on Welsh Christian culture as a creative contribution to the revival is valuable and their belief that the revival indicated a crisis of Welsh identity is striking'.[70] The Revival texts by Bois and Fursac echo the concern voiced in earlier accounts for the social welfare and culture of the people in

---

68   Deirdre Beddoe, *Out of the Shadows: A History of Women in Twentieth-Century Wales* (Cardiff: University of Wales Press, 2000), pp. 11–12. For a discussion of Welsh women writers' responses to the Revival in fiction, see Katie Gramich, 'Dehongli'r Dywygiad: Ymateb Awduron Cymreig i Ddiwygiad 1904–05', *Taliesin*, 128 (Summer 2006), pp. 12–28.

69   Thomas, *In the Shadow of the Pulpit*, p. 95.

70   Jones, *Faith and the Crisis of the Nation*, p. 354.

these industrial areas of south Wales. The perceived peripherality of Wales becomes a positive force in terms of its ability to sustain the effects of the Revival. Rather than being marginalized, Wales becomes an exemplar, seen as more authentically Celtic and more advanced in its piety: a true site of cultural and spiritual inspiration.

Throughout the late eighteenth and nineteenth centuries, the perception of Wales in the French-speaking world develops from an unknown entity to a site of inspiration for key groups of travellers. The initial focus on the landscape, via comparisons with Switzerland, gradually shifts to take into account notions of the Celtic via the Breton prism. As interest centres primarily on the industrial development of Wales, in many texts the aestheticization of the industrial landscape permeates the more economically driven exploration of Welsh industry as a paradigm of industrial expansion and technological advance. Writers are not oblivious to the social implications of this, however, and for many the spread of Nonconformism offers an antidote to societal decline in both Wales and potentially France as the twentieth century dawns. Increasingly visible is the notion of Wales as a Celtic nation, though the connections between Celtic languages seem only to be properly understood initially by visitors from Brittany in whose writing attention to Celticness seems to be part of a nostalgia and longing, not just for their home country, but also arguably for the *ancien régime*. Celticness becomes the key focus for many nineteenth-century travellers. Their narratives, which tackle Celticness alongside industrialization, are the focus of the following chapter.

CHAPTER TWO

Patriotism, Pan-Celticism
and the Welsh Cultural Paradigm
in Travel Writing in French
from 1830 to 1900

In the broader context of French culture, the nineteenth century was very much the century of the Celt. In France, as well as in the German-speaking lands, social upheaval led to a revaluation of national pasts and cultural paradigms as Herderian cultural ideals became inextricably linked to developments following the French Revolution, which brought about the need to reframe the past for the newly forged French nation. Within the Romantic project of creating a history of and for the Republic, 'nos ancêtres les Gaulois' [our ancestors the Gauls] came to be favoured over the Franks, who were too closely associated with the Germanic tribes to offer national comfort. The Franks were, furthermore, considered the ancestors of the aristocracy. The Gauls, however, were seen as the ancestors of the people, and were also perceived as Celts. Indeed, the terms were often used interchangeably at this time, as 'the Celts became topical within mainstream French historiography' for the first time.[1] The founding of the *Académie celtique* [Celtic Academy] in 1805 shows how valorized Celts were in France at the beginning of the nineteenth century, as its purpose was to study the past of the whole of France, and not only Celtic Brittany. The term 'Celtomaniac' has most often been used by those critical of the *Académie*'s excessive claims to Celtic virtues and superiority. Indeed the demise of the *Académie* is explained

---

1 Ann Rigney, 'Immemorial Routines: The Celts and their Resistance to History', in Brown (ed.), *Celticism*, pp. 159–82 (p. 163).

by the fact that its members were so pro-Celtic that they manipulated or exaggerated evidence, to construct a 'système plus séduisant que solide' [a system more seductive than solid].[2] The term continues to be used by scholars to refer to the overenthusiasm for things Celtic displayed by the likes of La Villemarqué.[3] There is also a clear link to the ongoing enthusiasm for MacPherson's notorious epic, *Ossian*. Though Ossian was an eighteenth-century phenomenon that spread across Europe, the Gaelic bard was still enjoying fresh incarnations in nineteenth-century France, having been Napoleon's favourite poet and a notable influence on Chateaubriand.

Despite this essentially national enterprise, the impact was most profoundly felt in the Breton context as the status of Brittany rose in the consciousness of the reading public. By the 1830s, as a result of the Bretons being seen as the living link to the Gaulois, and thus perceived as Celtic, Brittany was a rather fashionable topic in French literature, providing material for novels and poetry as well as travelogues.[4] This trend is reflected in travel writing in French on Wales. As has already been shown, ideas of the Celtic permeated a diverse range of foci throughout the long nineteenth century with notions of Celticness featuring to varying degrees in appraisals of landscape, industry and religion. For many travellers, some of whom were themselves of Breton extraction, however, the Celtic aspect of Wales was at the heart of their reading of the Welsh nation and its culture. Before the Revolution, Wales's Celticness was certainly noticed by travellers, particularly by French exiles, but the real connections between Celtic languages seem only to be properly understood by those travellers who were from Brittany. Beyond this group of travellers Celticness seems to be a rather vague notion that owes rather a lot to Ossian; indeed, it has been argued that Ernest Renan 'probably did most to Ossianize the landscape of Brittany'.[5] This was all

2   Phrase used by the society that replaced it in volume 1 of *Mémoires de la Société Royale des Antiquaires de France* (1817), cited in Bernard Tanguy, *Aux origines du nationalisme breton*, 2 vols (Paris: Union générale d'éditions, 1977), II, p. 275.

3   See Patrick Sims-Williams, 'Celtomania and Celtoscepticism', pp. 1–35; Heather Williams, 'Celtomania', in *Celtic Culture: A Historical Encyclopedia*, 5 vols, ed. John T. Koch (Santa Barbara: ABC-CLIO, 2006), V, pp. 391–92.

4   For an overview of representations of Brittany in French literature, see Heather Williams, *Postcolonial Brittany*.

5   Mary-Ann Constantine, 'Ossian in Wales and Brittany', in Gaskill (ed.), *The Reception of Ossian in Europe*, p. 88.

set to change by the second half of the century, when Celtomania spread beyond Brittany to become a France-wide phenomenon. This chapter will explore this very particular theme which in some respects represents the pinnacle of Wales's discovery as a site of inspiration in travel writing in French. It considers three significant cultural-historical episodes, namely La Villemarqué's visit to the Abergavenny Cymreigyddion Society *eisteddfod* in 1838, tours of Wales by Celtic enthusiasts Alfred Erny and Henri Martin in the 1860s and the 1899 pan-Celtic *eisteddfod* in Cardiff, where a number of Breton-speaking delegates were invested as bards.

First, however, the chapter will explore the emergence of an evolving dialogue with the notion of Wales as a Celtic nation through the work of prominent French historian Jules Michelet (1798–1874), who engaged critically with the Celtic debate, albeit in his private journal. During a month-long stay in Britain (or 'Angleterre' as he calls it) in summer 1834, he passed through Wales, recording his impressions in his travel journal. According to his editor, Paul Viallaneix, he was in Britain 'pour voir de plus près le pays ennemi du sien' [to take a closer look at the country that was an enemy of his own][6] as he prepared to write the section on the Hundred Years War for his multivolume *Histoire de France* (1833–1841) [History of France]. Michelet was no Celtomaniac, and his view of the Celtic heritage of the French was more measured than those of fellow historians the Thierry brothers and Henri Martin.[7] Michelet thought of the French as a successful blend of the raw ingredients of Romans, Germans and Celts;[8] in his view, 'the meaning of France coincided neither with the Gauls nor with the Franks', but resided rather in the fact that France had made and remade itself out of diversity.[9] In other words, it was not the elements that made up France that mattered so much as the success of their fusion. Each had had their time, then faded to allow

6   Jules Michelet, *Journal*, ed. Paul Viallaneix, 4 vols (Paris: Gallimard, 1959); I: (1828–1848), Introduction, p. 746; Welsh passage, pp. 134–35.

7   Augustin Thierry (1795–1856) and Amédée Thierry (1797–1873) discuss Welsh history in some detail in Augustin Thierry, *Histoire de la conquête de l'Angleterre par les Normands*, 3 vols (Paris: Firmin Didot, 1825), and Amédée Thierry, *Histoire des Gaulois*, 3 vols (Paris: Hachette, Hetzel, 1828–1845). Henri Martin, author of *Histoire de France*, 19 vols (Paris: Furne, Jouvet, 1833–1854), is discussed below. These books went through several editions.

8   Jules Michelet, *Histoire de France*, 18 vols (Paris: A. Lacroix et Compagnie, 1880), I: pp. i–xliv (p. vii).

9   Ceri Crossley, *French Historians: Thierry, Guizot, the Saint-Simonians, Quinet, Michelet* (London: Routledge, 1993), p. 203.

another to shine. Indeed, for Michelet, the Celts, as he saw them in his day, had failed and were weak, and though he calls the Bretons a 'peuple de granit' [people of granite], he considered them now the detritus of history, and ultimately doomed.[10] Unchanged, the most they could offer modern France was a connection to its past. This colours Michelet's reading of Wales, which he views through the prism of Brittany, or rather through French hopes that Brittany will provide a living connection to the Gaulish past of the people, while simultaneously modernizing and abandoning its language. This drive for modernity underpins his narrative and, in particular, his description of north Wales which views the country through a dual Celtic/industrializing filter. Indeed, from Michelet's account onwards the search for Celticness, or even Bretonness, in Wales is inseparable from an investigation of industrialization.

Michelet was influenced by ideas found in *Voyage dans le Finistère* (1799) [A Tour in Finistère] by founder of the *Académie celtique* and native of Brittany, Jacques Cambry (1749–1807), which he read in preparation for his tour of Brittany, and which was popular among Romantic historians. The clearest illustration of Cambry's influence is the episode where Michelet hopes that the Welsh farmer who joins him in his stagecoach will regale him with some songs from the past. Michelet's concept of history was one that rejected the chronological or dynastic perspective in favour of seeing races, people and nations as agents of historical change.[11] He valued the collective consciousness, seeing it as a repository of wisdom, and myths, legends and epic poetry as 'phenomena deserving serious study'.[12] The idea, influenced by Herder and current among French Romantic historians, that the songs of peasants gave access to an authentic past, was soon to culminate in Brittany in La Villemarqué's *Barzaz Breiz* (1839) [Breton Ballads]. Notably, Michelet's narrative predates La Villemarqué's 1838 visit to Wales but he shared the latter's view that 'the true national history of a people' was to be found in myth and popular poetry,[13] and that the

10   Rigney, 'Immemorial Routines', p. 175.
11   Crossley, *French Historians*, p. 44.
12   Crossley, *French Historians*, pp. 193–97.
13   Crossley, *French Historians*, p. 194. Just as he did not subscribe to Celtomania, his views were more measured than those of, say La Villemarqué, on this matter too. Michelet was always for progress, and though he believed that popular poetry contained truth, he did not think that the past provided a 'workable blueprint for the social organization of the future'. Crossley, *French Historians*, p. 197.

stories found in these were even more important than the facts because they are true to the character of the people who created them. Indeed, around 1828, he had even planned to write an encyclopaedia of popular song, modelled on Herder.[14] Sadly the Welsh farmer who joins him in the stagecoach is a disappointment to Michelet. He does sing, but in the text he has no voice of his own because Michelet is presumably trying to elicit responses in English (or perhaps in French?) from a man who is probably a monoglot Welsh speaker. The Romantic idea that poetry originates in the primitive cries of man in nature is behind this, but Michelet cannot access this primitive wisdom, or the travellee's view: 'j'essayais de le mettre sur la voie de leur ancienne poésie. A toute chose, il répondait: *Yes*' (pp. 134–35) [I tried to get him onto the topic of their ancient poetry. To everything he answered, 'Yes'].

Despite this positive if frustrating engagement with Welsh culture, Michelet's narrative describing his visit to Wales ends in sadness: 'la triste petite île d'Anglesey. C'était la tristesse du soir, la tristesse des bruyères, la tristesse de la mer, dont nous nous sentions environnés' (p. 135) [the sad little island of Anglesey. It was the sadness of the evening, the sadness of the heath, the sadness of the sea that seemed to surround us]. It seems odd that this passage should end with such an emphasis on sadness, despite stating that Wales is better off than Brittany in terms of industry, natural resources and infrastructure. Once again, the Breton prism is key. In the *carnet* of his tour of Brittany in 1831, Michelet says that peasant and nature are in harmony, and that a certain sadness comes from the land itself: 'La beauté triste des bruyères roses mêlées de plantes jaunes' [The sad beauty of pink heather mixed with yellow plants].[15] Elsewhere, on travelling westwards, further into Brittany, he writes: 'Le pays est sérieux, il va devenir triste et sauvage' [The land is solemn, it will become sad and wild],[16] and goes as far as to present the landscape as one of death: 'toute cette côte est un cimetière' [this whole coast is a cemetery].[17] This 'sadness' is something that came to Brittany with Romanticism, and would culminate in Renan's 'La poésie

14 Paul Bénichou, *Nerval et la chanson folklorique* (Paris: José Corti, 1970), p. 51.

15 Jules Michelet, *Carnet de Bretagne: Journal de Michelet en Bretagne (1831) suivi de la Bretagne dans 'Le Tableau de la France' (1833)* (Rennes: Terre de Brume, 1997), p. 36.

16 Michelet, *Carnet de Bretagne*, p. 49.

17 Michelet, *Carnet de Bretagne*, p. 54.

des races celtiques'. It is therefore striking that the sadness seems more pronounced in French-language travel texts on Brittany than in those on Wales. It is so prominent in Michelet's passage because of the distorting influence of the Breton prism which means that he is seeing, or rather not seeing, Wales for Brittany. Attention will return to Michelet's Welsh narrative later in this chapter as the impact of Pan-Celticism on the published version, edited by his widow Athénaïs in 1893, highlights the extent to which the Breton reading of Wales is consolidated in the intervening years as the periphery-periphery dialogue first hinted at by La Tocnaye and Penhouët becomes central to travel writing on Wales in French.

In the years following Michelet's trip, interest in Welsh culture was precipitated by developments in Wales itself. Between 1834 and 1853 the Cymreigyddion Society of Abergavenny[18] held a series of *eisteddfodau* under the patronage of Augusta Hall née Waddington, or Lady Llanover (1802–1896), also known as Gwenynen Gwent.[19] Hers was an international vision, with visitors coming to the *eisteddfod* from Europe and beyond, and scholars from France and Germany competing in the essay competitions. The emphasis of the Cymreigyddion Society was always on reconciliation between the native Welsh culture and that of the powerful neighbour to the east, as reflected in the fact that the ceremonial procession contained a six-foot leek alongside Union Jacks. Moreover, many of the Cymreigyddion's supporters did not speak Welsh, and many of the prizewinning compositions were not written in Welsh, a fact which perturbed some observers. Nevertheless, events in Abergavenny were key to the development of travel writing on Wales in French as a delegation of Bretons, including Hersart de la Villemarqué (1815–1895), were invited to attend the town's 1838 *eisteddfod*,[20] marking a turning point in inter-Celtic relations, seen by many as the beginning of the modern era of inter-Celtic connections. The story of Celtomania, which dominates French views of the Celtic 'other' that is to be found in Wales,

---

18   The Cymdeithas Cymreigyddion y Fenni [Abergavenny Welsh Society] was founded in 1833 to promote Welsh language and culture.

19   Her bardic name is literally 'Gwent's bee'. For more information on her, see Prys Morgan, 'Lady Llanover (1802–1896), "Gwenynen Gwent"', *Transactions of the Honourable Society of Cymmrodorion*, new series 13 (2007), pp. 94–106.

20   Among those travelling with La Villemarqué were Jules, vicomte de Francheville (c. 1810–1866), Louis Jacquelot du Boisouvray (date unknown–1881), Auguste-Félix du Marchallac'h (1808–1873), Alexis-François Rio (1797–1874) and Joseph de Maudit (dates unknown).

must be traced back to the founding figure of La Villemarqué, and what became his iconic visit to a Welsh *eisteddfod* in 1838. Henri Martin and Alfred Erny, who wrote travelogues in the 1860s, consciously travelled in his footsteps, as did the Breton delegation to the Cardiff *eisteddfod* of 1899.[21]

The 1838 visit has received more attention than most visits to Wales by travellers from France, both in terms of press coverage at the time and in more recent scholarship, perhaps only exceeded by the interest shown in those visiting the 1904–1905 Revival.[22] This can be attributed to the ambition and enthusiasm of the young La Villemarqué and to the accusations of forgery that dogged his collection of Breton ballads, the *Barzaz Breiz*. The Bretons' visit received coverage in the French press at the time,[23] and travel accounts and reports by less famous members of

21   Henri Martin asks La Villemarqué for directions to Wales in a letter of 18 July 1861, document digitized by the CRBC (LV21.034) and kept at the *Archives départementales du Finistère*. Fonds Théodore Hersart de la Villemarqué. 263 J. Fonds en cours de classement [collection currently being catalogued].

22   Modern scholarship on both sides of the Channel has discussed the significance of La Villemarqué's visit for inter-Celtic relations. See Pierre de la Villemarqué, *La Villemarqué, sa vie et ses œuvres* (Paris: Champion, 1926); Francis Gourvil, *Un Centenaire: l'Eisteddfod d'Abergavenny (Septembre 1838) et les relations spirituelles Bretagne-Galles* (Morlaix: Imprimerie nouvelle, 1938), and his *Théodore-Claude-Henri Hersart de la Villemarqué (1815–1895) et le 'Barzaz-Breiz'* (Rennes: Oberthur, 1960); Fañch Postic, 'La Villemarqué et le pays de Galles (1837–1838)', *Triade I, Galles, Ecosse, Irlande* (Brest: CRBC, 1995), pp. 15–30; Fañch Postic, 'Le voyage de La Villemarqué au pays de Galles en 1838. Les premières relations interceltiques', *Ar Men*, 125 (November 2001), pp. 34–43. On the Welsh side, the most comprehensive discussion is in Mair Elvet Thomas, *Afiaith yng Ngwent* (Cardiff: University of Wales Press, 1978). And most recently Mary-Ann Constantine has drawn a fascinating parallel between La Villemarqué's attitude towards medievalism in architecture and interior design in some of the grand houses of south Wales, and his project for reviving Breton culture, which would soon be launched with the publication of the *Barzaz Breiz* in 1839. See Mary-Ann Constantine, '"Impertinent structures": A Breton's Adventures in Neo-Gothic Wales', *Studies in Travel Writing*, 18:2 (2014), pp. 134–47; Mary-Ann Constantine, 'La "sainte terre de Cambrie": La Villemarqué et le romantisme gallois', in Nelly Blanchard and Fañch Postic (eds), *Au-delà du Barzaz Breiz: Théodore Hersart de la Villemarqué* (Brest: CRBC, 2016), pp. 209–26.

23   For example, the *Gazette de France* of 22 October 1838 featured a piece, and the *Journal des débats politiques et littéraires* of 19 October 1838 printed a short press report by Auguste François Félix du Marhallac'h. 'Fête galloise d'Abergavenny'. In the British press the *Hereford Times* published a supplement on the *eisteddfod*

the delegation have also been published.[24] La Villemarqué's own official report for the French Minister of Public Instruction, who part-funded his visit, was published in the *Feuilles d'Annonce* [The Gazette] of Morlaix on 1 January and 5 February 1842, and was even translated into Welsh, in slightly shortened form, by the Rev. J. Jenkins, published in *Y Gwir Feddyliwr* [The True Thinker] on 20 May 1842.[25] This proliferation of contemporary texts in various different voices and languages describing the same trip allows for an unusually full view of the visit, but undoubtedly the most fascinating are the lengthy letters that La Villemarqué wrote to his family back in Brittany.[26] These are bristling with information, descriptions and opinions. If he was officially in Britain to study the Welsh language and literature and their relation with the Breton language and literature and to consult the Welsh manuscripts in the library of Jesus College Oxford,[27] in reality the pinnacle of the trip for him was the ceremony at Abergavenny in which he was made a bard by William Ellis Jones, 'Cawrdaf' (1795–1848). La Villemarqué was particularly taken by the *gorsedd* ceremony itself,[28] and he enthusiastically describes the unsheathed sword, the blue ribbon on his arm, the circle of stones on a mountaintop and the gift of a ceremonial cup. He wrote ecstatically to his father: 'Je suis barde maintenant, vraiment barde! Barde titré et j'ai été reçu selon les anciens rites des V et VI siècles, qui se sont transmis jusqu'à nous' [I am a bard now, a real bard! An

on 20 October 1838 which included a translation into English of a speech by La Villemarqué, which was also translated into Welsh in 'Cofnodau Cymdeithas Cymmreigyddion y Fenni', National Library of Wales MS 13858E, p. 105.

24   For example, Rio's account was published by L. Gougaud as 'La Société lettrée de Londres observée par un écrivain français en 1839. Journal inédit de François Rio', *Revue d'histoire ecclésiastique*, 30:2 (1934), p. 297. See also L. Gougaud, 'Alexis-François Rio et la Bretagne', *Annales de Bretagne*, 29:3 (1913), pp. 439–63, and Sister Mary Camille Bowe, *François Rio: sa place dans le renouveau catholique en Europe (1797–1874)* (Paris: Boivin, 1938).

25   Cited in John Watkins, 'Wales and France', *Transactions of the Honourable Society of Cymmrodorion*, 2 (1967), pp. 179–202 (p. 193).

26   A number of these were published in a biography by his son Pierre de la Villemarqué, *La Villemarqué*. All are now available online: Mary-Ann Constantine and Fañch Postic, 'C'est mon journal de voyage': La Villemarqué's Letters from Wales, 1838–1839', (2019), <https://hal.univ-brest.fr/hal-02350747/document>.

27   See Pierre de la Villemarqué, *La Villemarqué*, p. 40.

28   The Gorsedd of the Bards of the Island of Britain, founded by Iolo Morganwg in 1792, leads the ceremonial aspects of the *eisteddfod*.

official bard and I was received following the ancient rites of the fifth and sixth centuries that have been handed down to us].[29]

When most of the Bretons left Wales at the end of the *eisteddfod*, La Villemarqué stayed on, until March 1839, visiting the homes of culturally influential hosts Lady Llanover, Lady Charlotte Guest (1812–1895) at Dowlais and John Henry Vivian (1785–1855) and his wife Sarah at Singleton. La Villemarqué had a particular interest in Lady Charlotte Guest, not least on account of her translations of medieval Welsh tales, as he himself had hopes of putting his own name to a translation of the medieval Welsh prose tale *Iarlles y Ffynnon* [The Lady of the Fountain]. Alas he found her 'froide et réservée' [cold and reserved] and felt that 'toutes mes peines furent perdues' [all my efforts were in vain], and they became engaged in a translation race.[30] Through his work, La Villemarqué wanted to draw on the Welsh example in order to revive Brittany's cultural awareness, and so he overstressed the similarities and closeness between the languages, notably the myth of mutual comprehension (which becomes something of a leitmotif in travel accounts). La Villemarqué is at pains to convince both sides that Breton and Welsh are mutually comprehensible, and so claims in his letters home that 'mon breton est entendu de tout le monde' [my Breton is understood by all].[31] With the same aim, he composed a song for the occasion – 'Kan Aouen Eistezvod' [Song of the *Eisteddfod* Muse] – in a rather opportunistic hybrid language that struck a perfect balance between Breton and Welsh, which was published a few days later as a trilingual 'feuille volante' [broadsheet], with translations into Welsh and English arranged by Thomas Price (1787–1848).[32] The poem was the product of linguistic wishful thinking, however, and commentators

29   Letter from La Villemarqué to his father, Llanarth Court, 5 November 1838, letter 8, Constantine and Postic, 'C'est mon journal de voyage', p. 59.

30   Letter from La Villemarqué to his sister Camille du Laz, 12 February 1839, letter 29, Constantine and Postic, 'C'est mon journal de voyage', p. 146. On the strained relationship between Guest and La Villemarqué, see Revel Guest and Angela V. John, *Lady Charlotte Guest: An Extraordinary Life* (Stroud: Tempus, 2007), pp. 109–10.

31   Letter from La Villemarqué to his father, 5 November 1838, letter 8, Constantine and Postic, 'C'est mon journal de voyage', p. 60.

32   A number have survived in the National Library of Wales and in the La Villemarqué family archives kept at Kernault, Finistère. In due course La Villemarqué's French translation was published in the *Gazette de France*.

agree that it is a fabrication.[33] Nevertheless, La Villemarqué had a huge influence on scholars and poets alike back in France. What he actually saw in Wales and described in his letters corresponds to the utopic vision he had for Brittany.

The Wales that La Villemarqué depicts fits with a specifically cultural reading of the Welsh as a Celtic nation. He was not oblivious to other aspects of Wales, such as encroaching modernity and industrialization, but he seemed to shy away from any detailed engagement. On the surface of it, the letters that chronicle his time in Wales show him mostly filtering out the industrial, ignoring the fact that he is visiting one of the industrial powerhouses of Europe. Constantine has recently noted that La Villemarqué is blind to the revolt stirring among the workers, which was preoccupying his hosts, the Guests, and would lead to some 5,000 Chartists marching on Newport a few months after his visit in 1838.[34] Yet even La Villemarqué reveals something about industry as the industrial becomes part of the spectacle of Wales for the young Breton and, despite being absolutely appalled by industrial pollution in Merthyr Tydfil, he is enthralled by the sight of

> épouvantables montagnes de charbon et de cendre [...] l'air est chargé de brouillards et de nuages de fumées [...] La nuit toutes ces fournaises allumées à la ronde sont du plus magnifique effet; on dirait quatorze maisons en flammes. J'ai passé, hier soir, une heure à ma fenêtre, jouissant de ce spectacle extraordinaire [...] Au bruit sourd et grinçant des machines, qui par moment semble s'éloigner et s'éteindre, puis se rapproche, gronde et mugit dans le flanc des montagnes, vous croiriez entendre les flots de la mer.[35]

> [terrible mountains of coal and ash (...) the air is heavy with fog and clouds of smoke (...) At night all these furnaces blazing for miles around make the most magnificent impression, like fourteen houses in flames. Last night I spent an hour at my window, rejoicing in this

33   See Gourvil, *Un Centenaire*, p. 10; Ambrose Bebb, *Pererindodau* (Llandysul: Clwb Llyfrau Cymreig, 1941). The various contemporary reactions to this have been analysed by Constantine, who concludes that much multilingual work remains to be done on these texts. 'La "sainte terre de Cambrie"', p. 226.

34   Constantine concludes that his letters 'reveal little real awareness of the industrial world, or understanding of the tense social relations at this time'. 'Impertinent Structures', p. 135.

35   Letter from La Villemarqué to his father, from Dowlais, 22 December 1838, letter 20, Constantine and Postic, 'C'est mon journal de voyage', p. 111.

extraordinary sight (...) The dull, grating noise of the machines that seems now to retreat and fade, and now to return, rumbling and roaring on the mountainside, makes you think you can hear the waves of the sea]

Here, the awe-inspiring industrial landscape is a spectacle to enjoy, just like that of the bardic costumes at the Abergavenny *eisteddfod*, evoked using the language of landscape. Less prevalent is any sense or evaluation of encroaching progress.

This relative lack of interest in the modernization of Wales to some extent sets La Villemarqué's account apart. Many French-language travelogues on Wales in the nineteenth century, like Michelet's, are concerned with the balance between industrial progress, or modernization, and the preservation of the traditional landscape and Celtic culture, conceived primarily as one shared with the Bretons. Four travelogues that explore this question in the context of the south Wales industrial communities in the 1860s are illustrative of this trend. The first two, texts by Alfred Erny (1838–date unknown) and historian Henri Martin (1810–1883), are considered together as they are closely intertwined. Erny and Martin travelled together in Wales in August 1862. Erny went on to publish his essay, 'Voyage dans le pays de Galles' [Travels in Wales], in 1867[36] and Martin published his *Études d'archéologie celtique: notes de voyages dans les pays celtiques et scandinaves* [Studies on Celtic Archaeology: Notes from a Journey through the Celtic and Scandinavian Lands] in 1872.[37] Erny's text negotiates a path between travelogue and Celtic scholarship and makes frequent references to Martin in erudite footnotes. Martin is also referred to frequently in the body of the text as an authority (e.g. 'as Mr H. Martin tells me'), though Erny also made use of other sources, including La Villemarqué and some in English, such as *A Walk through Wales in August 1797* (1798) by Rev. Richard Warner (1763–1857). Unlike the majority of the eighteenth- and nineteenth-century travel writers discussed in this book, Erny and Martin

36   Alfred Erny, 'Voyage dans le pays de Galles', *Le Tour du Monde*, 15:1 (1867), pp. 257–88. Very little is known about Erny; for a discussion of his use of medieval Welsh poetry in this travelogue, see Heather Williams, 'La construction du Moyen Âge dans les récits de voyage français portant sur le pays de Galles', *Actes du colloque de Brest*, ed. Hélène Bouget and Magali Coumert (Brest: CRBC, 2019), pp. 65–81.

37   Henri Martin, *Études d'archéologie celtique: notes de voyages dans les pays celtiques et scandinaves* (Paris: Didier, 1872).

explore both north and south Wales, moving westwards from Newport and Caerleon to Llanover, Neath, Dowlais and Llandovery, eventually making their way north through Aberystwyth, which is described by Erny as 'the Dieppe of Wales', and the Cadair Idris Pass, which puts him in mind of the Pyrénées, before entering north Wales proper. Erny's response to the landscape mirrors that of earlier travellers as he identifies a certain spirituality or otherworldliness that recalls Renan's text. He is searching for the past, as well as something beyond the material or natural world. On one level he is like so many other picturesque travellers; for instance, he regrets the lack of ivy on Caernarfon Castle and compares the Llanberis Pass to Glencoe in Scotland (p. 286), or to Switzerland, in this case declaring Wales superior as it does not suffer from the thick mists that obscure the mountains there (p. 267). The language Erny uses in a description of industry as some kind of idyll betrays the fact that he is searching for the 'sauvage' and the supernatural in the landscape, despite travelling through one of the most industrialized regions of Europe. When he describes crossing into the industrial zone of Wales, at Neath, he describes a rural scene in which the factories are only hinted at through the 'white clouds' with which they grace the sky: 'collines arides, à moitié ensevelies dans les vapeurs grises du ciel et les nuages blancs des fabriques' (p. 263) [arid hills, half hidden by the sky's grey fumes and the white clouds of the factories].

The influence of Renan is not limited to Erny's appreciation of the landscape, however. It is clear from the depth of his erudition, as well as an admiring description of 'Welsh rebels' who have been nurtured by the rugged northern terrain, that Erny is a pro-Celtic travel writer. His referencing and intertextuality show a keen interest in Celtic studies and his exclamations betray a real enthusiasm for what he sees in Wales. However, close analysis of his text raises the question of precisely what kind of 'Celt' he thinks is fit for the modern world that he observes, as his understanding of the Celts as one race, à la Renan, leads him first to view Wales through comparison with Brittany, as many of his predecessors had done, and then to envisage a French-Welsh Celtic pact of the type advocated also by Martin, as well as later Breton visitors to the Cardiff *eisteddfod* of 1899. In this context, the influence of La Villemarqué, Martin and Renan is evident from the outset. He quotes all three writers early in the travelogue in his retelling of the story of Arthur, the narrative seen as a means to unite the various branches of Celticness which becomes something of a motif in his travelogue. Erny stops at Newport, as he wishes to visit Arthur's ancient home at Caerleon; later he seeks Arthur again at Craig-y-Ddinas and then at Carmarthen, where he quotes La Villemarqué's version of Merlin and Vivian's story (p. 265). He follows Renan in thinking of the Celts as one unified people – 'Toutes les nations celtiques se ressemblent de goût et de sentiments' (p. 283) [All the Celtic nations share similar tastes and feelings] – and adds that their music is also very similar. It is in describing the vestiges of the Roman site at Caerleon that the word 'celtique' gains entry into the text, as the tumulus has an 'aspect celtique' [Celtic aspect], and some of the objects that Erny sees in the museum there are described as 'Celtic'. It is in this context that the first comparison with Brittany is made (p. 258). This underpins the whole of the travelogue, surfacing in discussions of bidding customs (p. 265), linguistic similarities (p. 262), peasant interiors (p. 267), church architecture (p. 275) and terrain (p. 264). Once Erny has left Monmouthshire behind, and feels that he has really entered Wales, he repeats the myth of mutual understanding between Breton sailors and south Walians. Later, in his description of Llanover Hall, he is delighted to provide evidence that the Welsh are just as aware of their connection with Brittany as the French. In relating a guided tour of Llanover, Erny, who is impressed by the interiors of the farms that he sees (furniture and floors all polished, grates made of iron), remarks to Martin that these are quite different from Breton interiors, which prompts Lady Llanover to object: 'Ne dites pas de mal des Bretons, ce sont nos frères!' (p. 267) [Do not speak ill of the Bretons, they are our brothers!]. Erny seizes the opportunity to explain that the Welsh call the Bretons their Gaulish brothers, and consider Brittany their sister-motherland (p. 267) ['sœur patrie']. As a result of his pro-Celtic and thus pro-Welsh agenda, Erny makes huge efforts to find harmony and balance in all that he sees in Wales, to the extent that his text displays some rather telling blind spots. At Swansea, there is no doubting how bad and poisonous industry is. The air is 'vicié' [polluted] with arsenic and sulphur fumes, and the ground is barren. Yet Erny contends that these conditions pose no threat to the workforce. Indeed, the labourers seem to do well on it, with many living to a ripe old age. His description of Merthyr Tydfil betrays a similar bias. The iron capital of the world is presented as a Celtic paragon of progress where industry and Welsh culture coexist in happy harmony (p. 270). Projecting back to the time of La Villemarqué's by now legendary visit, Erny's portrait presents Guest's Dowlais works as leading the world in iron, while his wife, Lady Charlotte, is at the forefront of Celtic philology, translating the *Mabinogi*, it is suggested, by the light of the forges.

Extending Celticness beyond Brittany to the whole of France, Erny proposes an affinity between the Welsh and the French people. The Welsh, he claims, are more like the French than they are like their English neighbours: 'rien n'est plus différent d'un Anglais qu'un Gallois' (p. 267) [nothing is more different from an Englishman than a Welshman] and he goes on to refer to their 'vieux sang indompté des Kymris' (p. 267) [old untamed Cymric blood]. He cites Martin in noting as they enter Dowlais that the children there have a 'Gaulish' air about them (p. 271). Throughout, he tends to refer to Gaul rather than France, in order to stress that the French are all quite Celtic, and therefore natural allies of the Welsh. This idea of a special affinity will be further developed by the Breton delegation who visit the Cardiff *eisteddfod* in 1899.

Erny's claim that the Welsh are similar to the French is bolstered by the suggestion that the Welsh had sympathized with the French Revolution. He is attracted by the idea that in 1796 Iolo Morganwg (bardic name of Edward Williams, 1747–1826), the self-taught stonemason, poet, antiquarian, notorious literary forger and known radical, had displayed the tricolour along with his sympathy for the French Revolution, thus annoying the authorities (p. 279). However, Erny is disappointed to find, when he and Martin meet M.E. Williams, Iolo's grandson, that the family papers are in chaos, leaving them guessing as to the details that may be in Iolo's letters from the time of the French Revolution (p. 271).[38] However, this lack of evidence in no way prevents him from seeing in an *eisteddfod* trophy, the 'ariandlws' [silver prize medal], an echo of French Republican values: 'la devise se rapproche de celle de la République française: c'est *liberté, force et fraternité*' (p. 282) [the motto is similar to that of the French Republic: it's *liberty, strength and fraternity*]. Not far beneath the pro-Celtic surface lies an anti-English bias. Erny blames the English for attacking the Welsh language and Welsh customs, using the language of battle to describe how Lady Llanover, his host for a few days, 'defends' 'la langue et les coutumes galloises battues en brèche par le mauvais vouloir des Anglais' (p. 267) [the Welsh language and customs, menaced by the ill will of the English]. This is followed by an uncompromising description of English aims: 'le même travail d'absorption qui a

38   See Geraint H. Jenkins, Ffion Mair Jones and David Ceri Jones, *The Correspondence of Iolo Morganwg*, 3 vols (Cardiff: University of Wales Press, 2007). The question of Iolo's radicalism is most comprehensively treated in Geraint H. Jenkins, *Bard of Liberty: The Political Radicalism of Iolo Morganwg* (Cardiff: University of Wales Press, 2012).

si bien réussi en Écosse et en Cornouailles' (p. 267) [the same process of absorption that has been so successful in Scotland and Cornwall]. This parallels the views of numerous German travellers who read the English domination of the British Isles as a process of colonization. For Erny, however, the main objective seems to be to tease out a positive reading of Wales to bolster the Gaulish aspect of France. It is possible, in his eyes, to be both Celtic and modern but it is a delicate balance to strike. The 1862 Caernarfon *eisteddfod* is presented as further evidence of just such a harmonious balance of traditional culture and industry, its display of 'vivacité' [liveliness] and 'véritable talent d'improvisation' [real talent for improvisation] giving cause for optimism about the future of Welsh culture.

More negatively, however, the event in Caernarfon, in the heart of Welsh-speaking Wales, also provides Erny with an opportunity to discuss the relationship between Celtic and Anglo-Saxon cultures. He begins with a history of the *eisteddfod* (p. 278), backed up by quotations from La Villemarqué and a 'M. Ampère', presumably the historian Jean-Jacques Ampère (1800–1864). He then expresses regret at seeing the English language gaining ground at the *eisteddfod* when orators urge participants to learn English. He is far from impressed when he hears more speeches in English than in Welsh, and seems disappointed by what he terms a 'reconciliation' speech that claims that the old days of enmity between Wales and England have gone forever. According to the speech, Wales is now at one with England, and anyone who incites hatred of the English in the Welsh is not only an enemy of the *eisteddfod*, but also an enemy to himself and to his own country (p. 282). This is followed by a second speech in similar vein, which prompts Erny to comment that it marks something of a break with *eisteddfod* tradition: 'Ce discours anglo-gallois était peu conforme aux traditions des anciens *Eisteddfods*' (p. 282) [This Anglo-Welsh speech was not in keeping with the tradition of the ancient *eisteddfod*s]. Though he refrains from expressing his own opinion here, his rather conciliatory view is hinted at later, in a discussion of Bretons in France (p. 283), where he approves of those Bretons who consider themselves Breton when in France but French when abroad, and likens this to the attitude that he encounters at the *eisteddfod*. Erny's description of the chairing of the bard shows that the violence of the past has been drained from the relationship between Welsh and English: 'au-dessus de sa tête l'un d'eux étendit l'épée nue, figurant la lance sanglante, sur laquelle les initiés juraient autrefois la guerre éternelle aux envahisseurs Germains et Saxons' (p. 284) [above his head one of them brandished an unsheathed sword, representing the bloody spear upon which the initiated used to swear eternal war on Germanic and Saxon invaders]. Where once there was eternal war, today there is symbolic ceremony. Reconciliation of this type is what Erny wants for France and Brittany: a harmonious relationship between the 'petite patrie' or province and the 'grande patrie' or France. Thus, despite his pro-Celtic agenda, Erny is a 'petite patrie' nationalist of the variety that will be rejected by twentieth-century Breton activists.

Erny's travel companion, the historian and Celtic scholar Henri Martin, is remembered today as the 'sole author of a mediocre history of France',[39] though his work was rather popular in his day. If his Celtic scholarship is dismissed today as overenthusiastic and biased, he nevertheless played an important part in the founding of Celtic studies as a discipline, not least through his work in establishing the Chair of Celtic in 1882 at the *Collège de France*. Martin had previously visited Wales in August 1861, and returned a year later, this time accompanied by Erny. His account of the first trip was published initially in the journal *Le Siècle* [The Century], and then a decade later together with an account of the second trip, as part of his book *Études d'archéologie celtique* in 1872.[40] Martin, who described himself as an 'incorrigible Celt',[41] had scholarly reasons for visiting Wales, as he intended to publish a book on Iolo Morganwg. He was able to make contact with the Welsh intelligentsia in 1861, thanks to La Villemarqué's letter of recommendation to Thomas Stephens (1821–1875), 'le docte écrivain gallois' [the learned Welsh writer] and author of *The Literature of the Kymry* (1849).[42] He then travelled to north Wales in 1862 for discussions with John Williams ab Ithel (1811–1862), the cleric and

---

39 *The Oxford Companion to French Literature*, ed. Paul Harvey and J.E. Heseltine (Oxford: Oxford University Press, 1959), p. 458. For an assessment, see Charles Rearick, 'Henri Martin: From Druidic Traditions to Republican Politics', *Journal of Contemporary History*, 7:3 (1972), pp. 53–64. Rearick explains how Martin was overshadowed by the great historian Jules Michelet.

40 'Le Pays de Galles: notes de voyage', in *Le Siècle*, 17 December 1861, 27 December 1861 and 9 January 1862, later collected and supplemented with an account of his 1862 visit, 'Les antiquités irlandaises', in *Études d'archéologie celtique*, pp. 25–158. Martin also describes his time in Wales in his correspondence.

41 Cited in Rearick, 'Henri Martin', p. 55.

42 NLW MS 964E, no. 308, Hersart de la Villemarqué to Thomas Stephens, 29 July 1861, in *Knowledge Transfer and Social Networks Transcript*, https://archives. library.wales/index.php/letters-534. Further references to this correspondence are

antiquary who, despite being taken in by Iolo's ingenious forgeries, was widely regarded as the principal Welsh scholar of his day. These encounters were critical to his endeavours. Close observation of living Welsh culture, conceived of as essentially Celtic, was to bolster Martin's case that the best of France was its Celtic inheritance, and enrich his reimagining of the druid's role along the lines of modern intellectual leaders in the fields of history, science and philosophy.[43]

Martin's decision to visit the 1861 Aberdare *eisteddfod* was based on two factors. Firstly, he claimed a feeling of Celtic solidarity, as might be expected of a Celtic scholar, and secondly, a sense of duty as French historian: 'Mes devoirs d'historien français et ma sympathie fraternelle pour un peuple si fidèle aux souvenirs de nos communs ancêtres' (p. 33) [my duties as a historian of France and my fraternal fondness for a people who are so faithful to the memory of our shared ancestors]. This second assertion is striking, and shows that, like his travel companion Erny, he believed that the Gauls and the Welsh were the same people. If the whole of France has an affinity with the Welsh, it is no wonder that the Bretons are described here as 'leurs frères' (p. 37) [their brothers], and that the music he hears reminds him of the airs of 'notre Bretagne' (p. 58) [our Brittany]. Like Erny, Martin states that Wales today has more in common with France than with England. Doubtless speaking for himself, he states that the French feel at home in Wales: 'malgré la différence de langue qui élève d'ordinaire une si forte barrière, il ne tient qu'au Français de se croire chez lui' (p. 41) [despite the language difference that usually presents such a big barrier, the Frenchman need only believe himself at home]. For him, the Celtic connection has the power to break down language barriers and to dissolve differences. Speaking on behalf of the Welsh, he claims that the Celts are fond of all French people, and not just the Bretons (p. 59). Like Erny, Martin sees a tricolour at the *eisteddfod* in Conwy, as well as in Aberdare, and enthusiastically evokes Welsh radicalism's solidarity with the French:

> C'était celle d'une des sociétés populaires galloises, et peut-être remontait-elle jusqu'au temps où les patriotes gallois, Iolo Morganwg en tête, témoignaient pour la Révolution française une sympathie fort désagréable à M Pitt. (p. 49)

from this source. Martin had asked La Villemarqué to put them in contact in a letter of 24 July 1861.

43   Rearick, 'Henri Martin', p. 57.

[It belonged to one of those popular Welsh societies, and maybe dated back to the time when Welsh patriots, led by Iolo Morganwg, felt a sympathy with the French Revolution that was rather irritating to Mr Pitt]

Martin's decision to attend the Aberdare *eisteddfod* was certainly fruitful. Not only did the Welsh bards make the Frenchman an honorary Breton, or ancient Briton (the same word, *Breton*, is used for both in French), but he was also afforded the opportunity to address the crowds and to set forth his Celtic pact formally. In a letter to Thomas Stephens written in rather broken English from the Royal Victoria Hotel in Llanberis shortly before the *eisteddfod*, he discusses his planned speech, thanking Stephens for offering to translate it from French into Welsh: 'Since you are so generous so at me to offer to translate in Welsh any words of a French and Gaul traveller at his brothers of Cymru',[44] though it seems that Stephens was the facilitator of the translation rather than the translator, as the manuscript states clearly 'translated by Mr. James'.[45] Martin was acutely conscious of the language barrier, and expressed his regret in the speech, as well as in a letter, that he was not able to speak in one of the Celtic languages that united the two peoples, as La Villemarqué had done in 1838: 'if I speak with a foreign tongue I do not speak to you with a foreign heart, nor have I foreign blood'.[46] His peroration provides a concise account of the pro-Celtic sentiment found already in texts by La Villemarqué and Erny:

Cymric people! As our France becomes better acquainted with its past and its origins, she feels more and more that she is not the daughter of the Germans or of the Romans. She understands that she must react against [?all] excessive centralisation, the tradition of which has been left her by the Romans, to return to the old Keltic spirit, to the ancient and yet always young spirit of liberty. She feels, and will feel more and more her ties with you people of Cymry [*sic*] and England too, is she not the daughter of the Gauls? Had she but saxon blood in her veins, would she be the great nation which she is? Her indefatigable activity, her clear and practical spirit, does she not hold it from our Keltic race? The labouring classes of England, are they not, for the most part, descendants of the

44   NLW MS 964E, no. 189, Henri Martin to Thomas Stephens, 18 August 1861, in *Knowledge Transfer and Social Networks Transcript*, https://archives.library. wales/index.php/letters-534.
45   NLW MS 947A, unpaginated.
46   NLW MS 947A, unpaginated.

ancient Britons? As England too, shall better understand her Keltic origin, England and France will draw nearer and nearer to each other; and the alliance of the two [?great] people of the West, often shaken, never broken, yet please God, will at last repose upon sympathy, and not upon mere interest. Roman France, and Saxon England, might be enemies; Gallic France and British England, will, and must be Friends. Ancient Gaul and Ancient Albion were nursed in the same cradle.[47]

This was the most rousing call for Celtic solidarity since the heady days of the 1838 Abergavenny *eisteddfod*, and this visitor from France certainly made an impression on Henry Bruce, first Lord Aberdare (1815–1895) who, almost a quarter of a century later on the occasion of the 1885 *eisteddfod* remembered how 'my friend' was an 'ardent lover of everything Celtic' who was 'of the opinion that you could not have too much of the Celtic element in the national character'.[48] However, in 1861 the Welsh were too busy balancing out their relationship with England, and making themselves look 'progressive' and loyal, to be receptive to Martin's rhetoric. As Hywel Teifi Edwards has explained, the inferiority complex born of the Blue Books betrayal in 1847,[49] compounded by the hostility of the English press, led in the 1860s to what he terms 'the English chapter' which saw a refashioning of the *eisteddfod* as a shop window on a modernizing and progressive Welsh culture.[50] The consequences of this drive were a lessening of the role of

47   NLW MS 947A, unpaginated.

48   See E. Vincent Evans (ed.), *Cofnodion a Chyfansoddiadau Buddugol Eisteddfod Aberdar, 1885 / Transactions of the National Eisteddfod of Wales, Aberdare, 1885* (Cardiff: Duncan and Sons, 1887), p. civ. The speech was also reported, and the English version reproduced in the press, *The Cardiff Times*, 23 August 1861, p. 8.

49   The 'Blue Books' was the name given to the three-volume *Reports of the commissioners of enquiry into the state of education in Wales* which appeared in 1847. The reports were highly critical of the Welsh language, Nonconformism and the culture and habits of the Welsh people in general. For a discussion of their impact and context, see Prys Morgan, 'From Long Knives to Blue Books', in R.R. Davies, Ralph A. Griffiths, Ieuan Gwynedd Jones and Kenneth O. Morgan (eds), *Welsh Society and Nationhood: Historical Essays Presented to Glanmor Williams* (Cardiff: University of Wales Press, 1984), pp. 199–215; and Gwyneth Tyson Roberts, *The Language of the Blue Books: Wales and Colonial Prejudice* (Cardiff: University of Wales Press, 1998).

50   Hywel Teifi Edwards, 'Eisteddfodau'r Cyngor 1858–1868', *Taliesin*, 14 (1967), pp. 82–93 (p. 83). See also his *Gŵyl Gwalia: Yr Eisteddfod Genedlaethol yn Oes Aur Victoria 1858–1868* (Llandysul: Gomer, 1980) and 'The Welsh Language in

druids and the promotion of English as the language for getting on in life, while venerating Welsh as the language of poetry and religion. The Aberdare *eisteddfod* was the first in this series. There were tensions within the movement, and needless to say this Anglicization happened against a backdrop of protests,[51] for instance an *eisteddfod* with stricter Welsh-language rules was held in Rhyl in 1863 as a protest against the Englishness of the official National Eisteddfod. Historians agree that the *eisteddfod* worked to appease Britishness for the best part of a century,[52] because 'Celt' was a dangerous label to choose in Britain at a time when Ireland was considered a threat to the Union.

There is little doubt as to what side of the Celtic debate Martin would have found himself on. Like Erny, Martin's Welsh blind spots also relate to the impact of industry on people and places, as he insists that the balance of industry to culture found here is just right: 'La poésie et la tradition venaient s'installer au cœur de l'industrie moderne' (p. 49) [Poetry and tradition came to take their place at the heart of modern industry]. Through his eyes the man-made slag heaps are happily reabsorbed into nature. Indeed, initially, when travelling up the picturesque Taff Valley, he mistakes such slag heaps for natural phenomena (p. 35). He affirms that the area is not 'triste' [sad], and he delights in the contrast between industry and productivity on the one hand and the 'nature presque sauvage' [almost wild nature], complete with medieval ruins on the other (p. 36). Martin is also more supportive of the Welsh language than Erny, pointing out that it survives even in the most industrial areas, and insisting that the Welsh language is capable of everything. He seems surprised when presidents of the *eisteddfod* who invite people to learn English are welcomed to the event despite expressing this pro-English view. For him, the Welsh are to be lauded for their proud but non-hostile attitude towards England: 'Il y a ici, vis-à-vis de l'Angleterre, réserve, distinction, pour éviter l'absorption; il n'y a point hostilité' (p. 54) [There is, with regard to England, reserve and distinction, in order to avoid absorption: there is no hostility]. Martin seeks to highlight the international validity of Welsh culture. At the *eisteddfod* he hears music reminiscent of Jean-Baptiste Lulli (1632–1687)

the *Eisteddfod*', in Geraint H. Jenkins (ed.), *The Welsh Language and its Social Domains 1830–1911* (Cardiff: University of Wales Press, 2000), pp. 293–316.

51 Hywel Teifi Edwards, 'Eisteddfodau Cenedlaethol Chwe-degau'r ganrif ddiwethaf a'r wasg Saesneg', *Ysgrifau Beirniadol*, 8 (1974), pp. 205–25 (p. 206).

52 Edwards, *Gŵyl Gwalia*, p. 300.

and Jean-Phillipe Rameau (1683–1764), and is delighted to be told that these are not imitations of classical eighteenth-century French pieces, but rather based on much older Welsh melodies (p. 58).

Martin's discussion of the originality of Welsh culture then switches abruptly to the theme of a funeral that he witnesses. The description of the doleful but heroic funerary music and evocation of a horizon of mountains betrays a general feeling of decline and melancholia (p. 58), which might seem to call into question the kind of forward-looking, modern Celticness that Martin claims he was seeking in Wales. Instead, it suggests an emotive depth which underpins this Celtic culture. In line with Renan's thinking, Martin contrasts the materiality of England with the 'imagination' and 'idealism' of Wales's 'poésie, de musique d'œuvres, de l'intelligence désintéressée' (p. 52) [poetry, music, works of pure intelligence]. Similarly, when in north Wales Martin seems to be searching for something beyond the material landscape, and in a passage where he is chased off Snowdon by an awful storm (p. 47), his travelogue takes a literary turn. In the rich tradition of Snowdonia literature, the all too frequent Celtic mists and storms are often experienced as straightforward disappointment, but sometimes, as here, it is claimed that a storm somehow enhances the experience. Elsewhere mists hanging over the Welsh landscape are described as imparting a particular sweetness and are not the same as mists in England (p. 68). The travelogue continues in this vein, with the description of Holyhead a few paragraphs later betraying something of a Celtic confusion.

Holyhead often features in texts of this period as a place of transit, and here too it is portrayed as a liminal place both culturally and geographically, both as a border between thriving industrial Britain and problematic Ireland, as evoked when Martin notes a ship waiting to take Queen Victoria to Dublin, and a portal to a more Anglicized version of Celtic culture. As a specifically inter-Celtic gateway, Holyhead occupies a climactic point in Martin's text, representing his departure from Wales, precipitated by the death of Williams ab Ithel, which marked the end of his planned book on Iolo Morganwg. Holyhead's Celticness is stressed when Martin calls on Brittany for comparison; he describes a promontory with rocks worthy of Breton ones: 'J'arrivai à un promentoire dont les rochers abruptes et déchirées dominent d'aussi loin le vaste Océan que les plus fiers de nos caps de Bretagne' (p. 48) [I arrived at a promontory whose abrupt and rugged rocks dominate the ocean as far out as our proudest Breton headlands]. This comparison then leads into a description of Holyhead as a fantastical place when the movement of birds sets the whole landscape spinning: 'la masse entière du cap semble tourbillonner avec eux et en reçoit un aspect fantastique' (p. 48) [the whole mass of the headland seems to whirl around with them, giving it a fantastical look]. His dizziness may be read as excitement at his impending travel, or perhaps more likely excitement about his own scholarly plans. On a textual level the dizziness seems to result from the encroachment of clichés of the Breton landscape into his description of Wales: 'En côtoyant durant quelques milles des collines couvertes d'ajoncs dorés et de bruyères roses' (p. 48) [Following the coast for a few miles along hills covered in golden gorse and pink heather].

This conclusion to Martin's travelogue on Wales seems to mark a surrender to the clichés about Celtic lands as having fantastic, mysterious qualities. For all that he marvels at successful modernization, he leaves the land on a backward-looking high, his text in the grip of ideas of Celticness that crystallized in Renan's notorious essay. The real aim of Martin's version of Celtomania, which was at the heart of his peroration at Aberdare, was not to incite revolt in solidarity with other peripheral Celts, but rather to unite Frenchmen, through a better understanding of their Celtic heritage, in devotion to their new Republic: 'la Patrie' was always paramount, and was the guarantor of France's strength in the world. He differs from Michelet in that, for the latter, the Celts existed outside history – they were a crucial repository of knowledge about the past, but they could not develop, whereas for Martin they could become the core of a new, unified Frenchness.

It should not be assumed, however, that appraisal of Wales as a Celtic nation was purely the domain of Celtomaniacs like Erny and Martin. Other travellers who found themselves in south Wales for different reasons (either professional or political) provide an instructive contrast to the work of these two Celtic enthusiasts. Alphonse Esquiros (1812–1876) and Louis Simonin (1830–1886) had no Celtic agenda per se, yet they nevertheless provided comment on matters of Welsh culture, and the Welsh language in particular is integral to their discussions. Again, their work is closely related. Esquiros wrote a substantial article on Wales, 'Le Sud du pays de Galles et l'industrie du fer. Carmarthen, les Eisteddfodau et les Iron-Works de Merthyr Tydfil' (1865) [South Wales and the Iron Industry: Carmarthen, *Eisteddfodau* and the Merthyr Tydfil Ironworks],[53] along with a *Guide Joanne*

---

53   Alphonse Esquiros, 'Le Sud du pays de Galles et l'industrie du fer. Carmarthen, les Eisteddfodau et les Iron-Works de Merthyr Tydfil', *Revue des Deux Mondes*, 55 (1865), pp. 801–43.

guidebook to Britain and Ireland that devotes significant attention to Wales – *Itinéraire descriptif et historique de la Grande-Bretagne et de l'Irlande* (1865) [Descriptive and Historical Itinerary in Great Britain and Ireland];[54] Simonin's article 'Une Visite aux grandes usines du pays de Galles' [A Visit to the Great Factories of Wales], published in *Le Tour du Monde* [The World Tour] in 1865,[55] is indebted to Esquiros's work, and even quotes him at length in one passage that discusses the *eisteddfod* (p. 332). Simonin and Esquiros are also united by a perspective on Wales and the Celtic that is very different from that of the Celtic enthusiasts discussed above. However, the absence of a pro-Celtic agenda, and of the consequent blind spots, does not necessarily result in a more authentic picture of nineteenth-century Wales, as other prejudices and factors come into play.

As a political exile, Esquiros had a rather different agenda from that of the scholar-travellers, though Welsh culture and the Welsh language receive ample attention in his travelogue.[56] An idealistic social republican from Paris, he had been engaged in journalism in the run-up to the 1848 Revolution, and escaped France in the wake of Louis-Napoléon's coup d'état in 1851.[57] Writing, for Esquiros, was a way of making ends meet, which may explain the fact that he seems to have plagiarized some of his material.[58] His interest is in the growth of industry and its effect on society, and the representation of Wales in

---

54   Alphonse Esquiros, *Itinéraire descriptif et historique de la Grande Bretagne et de l'Irlande* (Paris: Hachette, 1865). This, along with other guidebooks, is discussed in Anna-Lou Dijkstra, 'Wales in Continental Guidebooks (1850–2013): A Country on the Imaginative Periphery' (unpublished doctoral thesis, Swansea University, 2017), especially pp. 117–60.

55   Louis Simonin, 'Une Visite aux grandes usines du pays de Galles', *Le Tour du Monde*, 11 (1865), pp. 321–52.

56   On his time in Wales, see S. Beynon John, 'Alphonse Esquiros: A French Political Exile in Merthyr and Dowlais in 1864', *Merthyr Historian*, 3 (1980), pp. 12–23. For a general study of his work, see Anthony Zielonka, *Alphonse Esquiros (1812–76): A Study of his Works* (Paris: Champion, 1985).

57   On this particular wave of French exiles in Britain see I.C. Jones and R. Tombs, 'The French Left in Exile: *Quarante-huitards* and Communards in London, 1848–80', in Debra Kelly and Martyn Cornick (eds), *A History of the French in London: Liberty, Equality, Opportunity* (London: Institute of Historical Research, 2013), pp. 165–91.

58   The description of Aberystwyth in his account is strikingly close to that contained in the popular English guidebook *Black's Picturesque Tourist of England and Wales*, which appeared in several editions from the 1840s onwards; see

his article 'Le Sud du pays de Galles et l'industrie de fer' shows south Wales to be an excellent case study in this respect. He has no hesitation in condemning what he sees (for instance, the conditions of the workers in Merthyr Tydfil, discussed below), but he is full of admiration for Britain because, he claims, it has worked hard at industry. Prosperity, Esquiros argues, is not something that is attributable to luck alone; rather he argues that 'Les grandes industries ne naissent point avec les nations; elles *deviennent*, elles se développent' (p. 801) [Great industries are not born with nations, but rather they *become*, they are developed]. When describing south Wales to his French readership he stresses that its Celticness, or what he calls the Ancient Brythonic setting, demands attention first, perhaps to demonstrate how modernity can be built on ancient foundations:

> C'est dans le sud du pays de Galles qu'il faut se placer de préférence pour l'étudier. Les mœurs des anciens Bretons donnent ici au travail industriel un cadre pittoresque, et c'est sur ce cadre même que l'attention doit se porter d'abord. (p. 805)

> [The best place to go to study (modern industry) is south Wales. The customs of the ancient Britons provide the industrial work here with a picturesque setting, and it is on this setting itself that our attention must first focus]

Unusually among these nineteenth-century texts in French, this article displays a concern for the effects of industry on nature. In describing his journey to Merthyr Tydfil, Esquiros uses the language of injury and violence to convey the effects of industry on the natural environment that he sees from the window of the train:

> Le spectacle extérieur se modifie: l'agriculture et l'industrie semblent se disputer le terrain. De petits moutons welshes, à la laine noircie par le brouillard et par la fumée des usines, errant encore dans les prairies herbues, qui, abritées par de hautes collines, restent vertes en dépit des étés les plus secs. Plus loin, c'est l'industrie qui triomphe. Des rubans de fer couronnent le front des hauteurs, sur lesquelles courent de petits wagons chargés de minerai ou de charbon de terre, et qui sortent sans doute des bouches de la mine. Les collines, coupées, dénudées, tourmentées dans leurs escarpements, accusent en vigueur sur un fond brumeux les blessures qu'elles ont reçues de la main de l'homme! De tous

Esquiros, *Itinéraire descriptif et historique*, pp. 239–40, and *Black's* (Edinburgh: Adam and Charles Black, 1858), pp. 201–05.

les côtés de l'horizon, de longs tuyaux de brique font de la fumée dans du brouillard. Des bouffées de feu s'échappent à distance de sombres soupiraux, comme si c'était le sol lui-même qui brûlât. Le ciel en est noir; la campagne étouffe en quelque sorte dans un bain de vapeur. (p. 827)

[The scene outside changes: agriculture and industry seem to be fighting over the land. Little Welsh sheep, their wool blackened by the fog and factory smoke, still wandering in grassy fields that, sheltered by high hills, stay green despite the driest of summers. Further on, industry triumphs. Up above the fronts of the hills are crowned by ribbons of iron, with little wagons full of ore or coal running along them, probably coming from mine portals. The hills, cut, stripped, tormented in their steepness, bear active witness against a foggy backdrop to the wounds they have received from human hands! On the horizon on all sides, long brick chimneys smoke into the fog. In the distance, blasts of fire escape from dark basement windows, as if the earth itself were ablaze. It blackens the sky, while the countryside chokes, bathed in haze]

Human suffering also receives his attention and what Esquiros sees are martyrs to industry: 'L'industrie, religion des temps modernes, aurait-elle donc ses martyrs, comme l'indique le nom même de la ville?' (p. 831) [Does industry, the religion of modernity, have its martyrs then, as indicated in the name of the town?]. The workforce appears against an apocalyptic background of devastated nature (p. 833). This imagery, evoking an underworld, harks back to Romantic descriptions of the sublime, once again connecting the industrial to literary discourse, while also revealing Esquiros as a most politically engaged observer. What he sees, rather than the light and spectacle observed by La Villemarqué, is the devastating poverty of Merthyr Tydfil's people: 'une population pauvre et grossière' (p. 830) [a poor and unrefined population] with children playing half-naked in the mud like young ducks. The women are dressed like the men, wearing wooden shoes and carrying loads on their heads. Later he writes a description of the ironworks at night, a scene that had become a topos of writing about Merthyr Tydfil, but his account lacks the sense of excitement expressed by predecessors such as La Villemarqué, and speaks more of panic:

J'étais couché depuis quelques heures déjà lorsque je me sentis réveillé en sursaut par un éclat d'incendie. Je courus à ma fenêtre, vis le ciel rouge comme s'il eût été enflammé par une aurore boréale. J'étais sur le point de crier: au feu! Mais comme personne ne bougeait dans l'hôtel et que tout était tranquille dans le voisinage, je me rassurai, et bientôt je me souvins que je vivais cette nuit-là dans le pays des forges. La lueur sanglante qui empourprait les ténèbres était en effet une réverbération des *iron-works*. (p. 832)

[I had been in bed for a few hours when I was awoken bolt upright by a flash of fire. I ran to my window, saw the sky red as if ablaze with the Aurora Borealis. I was about to shout: 'Fire!' But as nobody was moving in the hotel and everything was quiet in the vicinity, I was reassured, and soon remembered that I was spending the night in the land of ironworks. The blood-like glow that reddened the gloom was in fact a reflection of the ironworks]

The human sacrifice is all too clear when the light of the forge becomes blood in the adjective 'sanglante' [bloody]. Esquiros is interested in the effects of industry on nature and people, but also displays pity for the Welsh culture and language. While he sees the 'blessures' [injuries] inflicted on the land, he seems equally aware that Welsh culture is being killed by industry: 'il [l'idiome] meurt au souffle contagieux du commerce, et dans les usines à fer au contact de l'industrie' (p. 825) [the language is dying from the contagious breath of commerce and, in the ironworks, on contact with industry]. His concern for the people of the industrial south, described as 'une race conquise' (p. 816) [a conquered race], causes him to scrutinize the behaviour of the English: 'Les Anglais – qu'il ne faut pas toujours croire sur parole quand il s'agit de la race celtique' (p. 811) [The English, who should not always be believed on the matter of the Celtic race], an accusation backed up by his remark that some English reporters at the *eisteddfod* are sniggering while watching the *gorsedd* (p. 818). However, he does not want to reverse this acculturation; rather he sees the Welsh language as unsuited to modern developments.

Esquiros, like so many French travellers, sees Wales through Brittany. This leads to a discussion of similarities of language and culture, and a broader exploration of Welsh culture. He hails the *eisteddfod* as the reason why Welsh culture has survived, providing a very detailed report of the Llandudno event of 1864, noting that he was 'curieux d'assister à une des scènes les plus émouvantes chez un peuple si sensible à la poésie' (p. 816) [curious to witness one of the most moving scenes among a people so sensitive to poetry], and including a detailed discussion of poetry, complete with erudite footnotes. Despite stating that he would like to learn some Welsh, Esquiros thinks that the language is doomed: English-medium schools are everywhere, trains are bringing in tourists and commerce, but the real problem, he reiterates, is that Welsh is not suited to modern life: 'cet idiome [...] n'a point du tout été fait pour une époque d'industrie, de commerce et de transactions pécunaires'

(p. 825) [this language (…) was not at all made for a time of industry, commerce and financial transactions]. Welsh, then, only works for rural life, religion and poetry. Furthermore, it makes little sense to blame the English for the demise of the language, as the English had nothing to gain by killing Welsh, he claims. Wales's links to Great Britain are so close that any dreams of secession are suicidal. At the recent *eisteddfod*, Shakespeare's *Hamlet* was the text for the Welsh translation competition, and Esquiros perceives this as an attempt to forge a link between the two races, 'les Bretons et les Anglo-Saxons' (p. 819) [the Bretons/Britons and the Anglo-Saxons]. The only 'patrie' the Welsh can have is 'Angleterre', and the most intelligent and active amongst them can see this. If the Welsh have been conquered, then at least they were conquered by liberty! Esquiros sees the loss of culture as the inevitable price for progress. Where Welsh culture and poetry is a story of decline, the fate of the factories is the opposite, as nobody is drunk on the past here: instead there is life and energy as the Welsh regenerate themselves by joining modernity. For Esquiros, the age of iron is the age of democracy. At this point he seems to have substituted positivist pro-industrial blind spots for those of Celtomania observed in Erny and Martin.

It comes as a surprise, then, when this text – like Michelet's – ends on a note of sadness, when Esquiros finds the situation surrounding the decline of Welsh cultural difference 'triste'. Following on from the description of a rasping harp, he stresses the 'tristesse' of the Welsh, whose identity is on its way out just as the *eisteddfod* speeches 's'éteignent dans le vide, ainsi que les derniers échos d'une nationalité expirante' (p. 842) [die out in the void, like the last echoes of an expiring nationality]. This melancholia seems surprising after his confidently positivist portrait, as does the poetic turn of phrase. There is perhaps an echo of Renan's lament for all things Celtic, as the latter imagines them 'expirant ainsi à l'horizon' [expiring on the horizon],[59] as if the sadness were the underside of the kind of positivism associated with contemporary philosopher Auguste Comte (1798–1857).

The final French visitor to south Wales in the 1860s to be considered here, Louis Simonin, must have read Esquiros's 1865 article before writing his own in the same year. As a professional miner – he was even dressed as a miner when he set out on 4 July 1862 to visit both Cornwall and Wales (p. 353) – his aim was to observe and record the progress of industry in south Wales. He opens by inserting his text in the lineage

59 Ernest Renan, 'La poésie des races celtiques', p. 377.

of French industrial writing by naming geologists, Léonce Élie de Beaumont (1798–1874) and Amédée Burat (1809–1883),[60] and engineers, Auguste Perdonnet (1801–1867)[61] and Frédéric Le Play (1806–1882),[62] and states that his own visit was inspired by hearing so much about their work. He also states that he has previously travelled the world to look at mines (p. 328), signalling to the reader that his will be an experienced, comparative and professional view. Simonin disagrees with Esquiros about Britain's pre-eminence in industry, as in his opinion England leads more by luck than judgement: 'La nature a seule préparé la situation' (p. 338) [Nature alone prepared the situation]. He is at pains to stress the mismanagement and poverty that he sees in Wales, and to imply the superiority of France. Like his predecessors, he is clearly conscious of industrial competition, and mentions that the Vivian factory fears spies when he and his companion, Breton artist Jean-Baptiste Henri Durand-Brager (1814–1878), are prevented from measuring machines here. This does not prevent him from publishing a highly technical description of them, however.

This is no cultural, Celtic traveller then; indeed, Simonin's discussions of culture have literally been borrowed from Esquiros. Simonin states in a matter-of-fact way that the Welsh language is dying as Wales moves closer to England, and then quotes Esquiros's account of the Llandudno *eisteddfod* (p. 332). The rest of his discussion of 'culture', including comments on Welsh grammar (p. 335), also seems to paraphrase or summarize Esquiros. He claims that the *eisteddfod* used to be about fighting the English enemy, and repeats the myth of mutual understanding between Bretons and Welsh. His argument on Welsh culture also follows that of Esquiros closely: the people will survive, they have integrated well into Britain, but the language will die, as it is suited to poetry and religion, not to modern life or business. However, as his itinerary in Britain has been dictated by mining interests, here

---

60   Amédée Burat, *Géologie appliquée, ou Traité de la recherche et de l'exploitation des minéraux utiles* (Paris: Langlois et Leclercq, 1843).

61   Dufrénoy and Beaumont, *Voyage Métallurgique*, pp. 429–38. The book reproduces extracts from the *Annales des Mines*, 1824–1827. The second edition with corrections (Paris: Bachelier, 1837–1839) bears the names of additional co-authors Auguste Perdonnet and Léon Coste.

62   Frédéric Le Play, *Description des procédés métallurgiques employés dans le pays de Galles pour la fabrication du cuivre, et recherches sur l'état actuel et sur l'avenir probable de la production et du commerce de ce métal* (Paris: Carilian-Goeury and V. Dalmont, 1848).

Simonin introduces a new element when he compares the situation in Wales with that in Cornwall (p. 336). His negative view of Welsh culture is in some part a reaction to the working conditions he observes. He is horrified by the state of workers in Swansea, particularly in comparison with those in Cornwall: 'Dans le pays de Galles, l'ouvrier est parfois couvert de haillons, le logis est des plus mal tenus, la famille grouille dans l'ordure' (p. 336) [In Wales the workers are sometimes in rags, the homes are the worst kept and the families crawl about in the dirt]. All travellers are struck by this, he claims, and conditions only worsen as he approaches Merthyr Tydfil, where he is appalled by the coexistence of such poverty with such prosperity, referring to a 'spectacle navrant' (p. 339) [distressing scene], a 'spectacle de la misère' (p. 336) [scene of destitution] and 'la misère galloise' (p. 339) [Welsh destitution]. Simonin's portrait of Merthyr Tydfil at night contains nothing of the drama of earlier examples discussed. The writing is restrained and remains factual. Even the 'immense incendie' (p. 337) [immense fire] is drained of its potential force, as there are no consequences, human or environmental. Where La Villemarqué had been panic-stricken, Simonin merely pays attention. As though working towards a deliberate toning down of a hysterical tradition, a later description of Merthyr Tydfil's suffering in the same text confines itself to words like 'triste' and 'navrant', nothing stronger (p. 339). It is a damning portrait, but largely painted in the restrained language of report writing. Simonin is nevertheless appalled by what he sees: 'Quelle misère écœurante, grand Dieu! Et se peut-il que dans un pays en apparence si riche, si industriel, il y ait des gens à ce point déshérités!' (p. 339) [What sickening destitution. Good God! And can it be possible that in a country so rich in appearance, so industrial, there be people this deprived!]. Gone is the wistful sadness of the Celticist travellers. What emerges is a sense of melancholy provoked by poverty which places the workers' material well-being above all else. Esquiros and Simonin redress the balance to some extent, repositioning Wales as a site of modernity which can move on from its Celtic heritage rather than relying on that heritage to enable development, as had been the Celtomaniac view. What both schools share, however, is the sense that Wales is changing.

By the end of the 1860s, a reading of Wales had been established in travel writing in French which revolved around the tense relationship between Welsh culture and the advance of modernity, and which was set against a background of French sociopolitical concerns relating to national identity, via the Celtic context of France's heritage as a

Gaulish nation and the centre-periphery relationship with Brittany. This reflected the broader debates in France around the concept of the Celtic 'other' which had shifted markedly over time and for some had come to focus on Breton identity itself. This shift is seen unusually clearly in the revised version of Michelet's Welsh passage from 1834, as the text's history bridges the 1830s and 1890s, illustrating in so doing the wholesale change that had come about by the second half of the nineteenth century. The original manuscript version, discussed earlier, was very much a private document. Michelet's second wife, Athénaïs, was frequently his literary collaborator but even she was not allowed access to the journal, and Michelet never envisaged publishing it. Having been granted sole rights to his papers on her husband's death in 1874, however, Athénaïs reworked the text to publish *Sur les chemins de l'Europe: Angleterre, Flandre, Hollande, Suisse, Lombardie, Tyrol* [On the Highways of Europe: England, Flanders, Holland, Switzerland, Lombardy, Tyrol] in 1893.[63] She made some significant cuts to the journal text, but her main aim seems to have been to enhance its literary value, just as Michelet himself had sought to do when reworking a text for publication.[64]

The revised version of the text, describing Michelet's journey in a stagecoach across north Wales, repays close attention as valuable evidence of evolving French perceptions of 'others', particularly the ambiguously domestic and exotic Celtic 'other'. Most notably, perhaps, Athénaïs reinforces the comparisons with Brittany that were already present in the text. Indeed, her amendments invariably foreground Wales's similarity to Brittany and dramatize the points of comparison. For example, she enhances the realization that Wales is similar to Brittany in two stark sentences that add a possessive for Brittany and confirmation of the name of the newly entered country: 'Je reconnais un coin de ma Bretagne. Nous entrons dans le pays de Galles' (pp. 72–73) [I recognize a corner of my Brittany. We are entering Wales]. She dramatizes the landscape by adding that slate – so typical in the north

63   Michelet's revised text on Wales was first published in *Sur les chemins de l'Europe: Angleterre, Flandre, Hollande, Suisse, Lombardie, Tyrol* (Paris: Marpon & Flammarion, 1893), pp. 71–78, then in its original form in Michelet, *Journal*, I: pp. 134–35.

64   This can be observed in Michelet's various writings on Brittany, passages that first appeared in his *Tableau de la France*, volume three of his *Histoire de France*, and *La Mer* (Paris: Hachette, 1861), and are collected in *Carnet de Bretagne*.

Walian landscape – is not merely present, but 'everywhere': 'Mais voici l'ardoise qui partout apparaît' (p. 72) [slate appears everywhere], and proceeds to add granite and imagined Druidic remains to the picture, again with the possessive: 'Ici et là, le granit se dresse sauvagement en pointes acérées. Je retrouve mon menhir Breton' (p. 75) [Here and there the granite rises up wildly into sharp tips. I recognize my Breton standing stone]. Athénaïs adds a paragraph in praise of Brittany's resilience: 'Elle résiste pourtant, notre vaillante presqu'île' (p. 74) [She resists, though, our valiant peninsula]. However, the pride shown here in Brittany is only of the paternalistic variety, as suggested by the rather telling use of the possessive: 'ma Bretagne' (p. 72) [my Brittany], 'mon menhir Breton' (p. 75) [my Breton standing stone], in the first person singular, whereas Michelet had only used the first person once, and only in the plural 'notre Bretagne' (p. 134) [our Brittany]. Michelet could claim possession of Brittany only in the sense that it 'belongs' to any Frenchman, for he was not Breton, but these textual details suggest an increasing sense of possession of Brittany over the course of the nineteenth century, from 'ours' (i.e. it belongs to all the French) to 'mine'. Though the Swiss point of comparison survives through the nineteenth century, at times coexisting with the Breton one in the same text, as it does in Athénaïs's 1893 version: 'une petite Suisse en miniature' (p. 75) [a little Switzerland in miniature], the Breton one comes to the fore and the Celticness of Wales becomes much clearer.

A positive appraisal of Celtic Wales was always central to Michelet's view. In his original text, he lauds Wales for being 'better' than Brittany, 'Le pays de Galles vaut mieux que notre Bretagne [...] Plus heureuse, la population semble moins affaissée et plus poétique' (p. 134) [Wales is worth more than our Brittany (...) Happier, the population seems less weighed down and more poetic]. Such praise for the foreign is perhaps surprising in a historian famed for his French nationalism. Yet this superiority is exaggerated further by Athénaïs, whose wording changes the message substantially. In the later version, Wales is described not only as happier and more poetic than Brittany, but when she changes the original plain, informative sentence on minerals, she implies that Wales has been more fortunate than Brittany in terms of mineral deposits, and furthermore seems to attribute Wales's superiority in this respect to the fact that it is part of Britain. For example, 'Il a de la houille, de la tourbe dans les parties basses' (p. 134) [it has coal and peat in its lowlands] in the original becomes the much more effusive 'Les parties basses [de la lande], chez nous donnent la tourbe. La riche Angleterre a de plus la houille' (p. 75) [At home the lowlands (of moorland) gives us peat. Rich England also has coal]. The editing that took place over half a century later reveals a heightened awareness of Britain as an industrial competitor of France. Where minerals were something to be listed in the text of 1834, in the style of an inventory or of topographical writing, by 1893 they function as shorthand for the industrial anxieties of competing nations.

The Industrial Revolution certainly concerned Michelet, and from his first day in London he had seen the acculturation, the effects of the rural exodus and workers transformed into objects. He was worried by what he saw in London because while he did not want France to become a rural backwater, economically dependent on Britain, neither did he want France to suffer culturally. Athénaïs's manipulation of his descriptions implies that Wales has got the balance just right in seeking to avoid either fate. Where the earlier text simply described the unexpected signs of industry in such a picturesque landscape ('Au milieu de ces campagnes pittoresques, dans ces forêts qu'on croirait vierges, on aperçoit des exploitations, des fourneaux, des mines' (p. 134) [Amid this picturesque countryside, in forests that seem virgin, we see exploitations, forges, mines]), and offered an economic explanation for it ('La cherté de la main-d'œuvre pousse ainsi l'industrie dans les lieux où le peuple est pauvre' (p. 134) [The high cost of manpower thus pushes industry into places where the people are poor]), the revised version omits this economic theory and stresses that Wales's industrial-natural balance, or 'harmonie', is visible in the way that the tops of the hills are a rural idyll of little black cows and 'melancholic' vegetation, while the lower parts of the hills show impressive signs of industry: 'fourneaux' [forges], 'puits des mines' [mine shafts], 'moulins' [mills] and feats of engineering (p. 73). Most striking among these are Telford's Menai Suspension Bridge and Pontcysyllte Aqueduct: 'Ces voies aériennes qui s'entre-croisent, ces arcades à travers lesquelles se joue la lumière, ennoblissent singulièrement la contrée' (p. 73) [These criss-crossing aerial ways, and the play of light on the arches, give a remarkable dignity to the area]. In emphasizing the harmonious coexistence of landscape and industry, Athénaïs echoes earlier narratives in seeing in Wales a site of inspiration, on this occasion with Brittany as backdrop.

Athénaïs Michelet's adaptation of her late husband's text shows that, with the consolidation of pan-Celtic ideas, the shift which had already occurred in early nineteenth-century discussions of French identity had intensified and for some writers had become about 'Celtic' identity or the role of Brittany in the construction of French identity. For the final group of travellers in this chapter, that cultural link was the explicit reason for their visit to Wales, as the relationship between Wales and Brittany in French-language travel accounts is further bolstered by a major event which epitomized the coming together of Welsh industry and culture, when Cardiff, the bastion of industry and export, hosted the 'pan-Celtic' National Eisteddfod in 1899. The myriad idealized views and optimistic visions of this event offered by Breton travellers provide a significant contrast with the 'tristesse' of visitors from earlier in the nineteenth century. This is typified by Anatole le Braz (1859–1926), the author and folklorist often referred to as *le barde breton* [the Bard of Brittany]. Le Braz evokes the migration of the original Bretons from Britain in the fifth century in order to envision a romanticized return to the Welsh cradle in 1899:

> Le chemin que sillonèrent dans leur exode leurs barques en peaux cousues, leurs currachs de cuir, nous le refaisons à rebours, pour aller saluer notre berceau, pour aller dire à nos cousins de Galles que nous sommes demeurés fidèles à nos origines et qu'elle parle en nous aussi haut que jamais, cette voix du sang qui fut toujours pour les Celtes, non un symbole, mais une réalité.[65]

> [The path traversed during their exodus by their small boats made of animal hides sewn together, their leather currachs, we are repeating it in reverse, in order to go and greet our cradle, to go and tell our cousins from Wales that we have stayed faithful to our origins, and that the call of blood, which has always been a reality rather than a symbol for the Celts, speaks louder in us than ever]

It was Le Braz's official invitation to attend the 1899 National Eisteddfod in Cardiff that inspired this declaration of fidelity to the Celtic family. The major annual national festival, celebrating literature and music through competitions and performances in the Welsh language, assumed a special significance in this year. Although representatives from Ireland, Scotland and the Isle of Man had been welcomed and honoured at previous festivals, the Cardiff *eisteddfod* was specifically designated as a pan-Celtic *eisteddfod* due to the presence of a sizeable delegation from Brittany.[66] Many of the twenty-five or so cultural figures and

65   Anatole Le Braz, 'Les Bretons de France au Pays de Galles', *La Revue des Revues* (July 1899), pp. 243–49 (p. 243).
66   M. Wynn Thomas argues that this designation responded to E.E. Fournier

political representatives who formed the Breton delegation were key players in the *Union régionaliste bretonne* [Breton Regionalist Union], including its president Le Braz. Prior to his journey he declared that the presence of the Breton delegation symbolized a point of departure for a new era for the Celtic nations.[67] The foundation in August 1898 of the *Union régionaliste bretonne*, a broadly conservative cultural and political organization dedicated to preserving Breton cultural identity and regional independence, was viewed by the wider pan-Celtic movement as a signal of the renewed strength and visibility of Breton culture, and an opportunity to welcome Brittany back into the Celtic fold.[68] Four Breton-speaking delegates were invested as bards and baptized with bardic names, and they were honoured with welcome ceremonies and official receptions. These Breton journeys to Wales represent an especially rich resource. Firstly, this is due to the amount of press coverage in Wales and France before the Breton delegation's visit, implying a significant sense of anticipation, as well as suspicion among some mainstream French newspapers, which viewed the invitation as an indication of a type of subversive pact.[69] Secondly, the occasion led to the publication of a multiplicity of accounts by members of the Breton delegation, which are still being uncovered and rediscovered.

Expectations amongst many of the delegates could hardly have been higher, akin to a journey to the land of a Celtic fairy tale with a happy-ever-after ending, with hopes that this particular model of Wales's past with its bardic tradition might provide a blueprint for Brittany's future. This idealized, late nineteenth-century perception of Wales as the more fortunate 'Celtic' cousin, and the belated construction of Wales

d'Albe's vision that the attempt to revive Celtic languages must lie at the heart of the pan-Celtic movement. Fournier (1868–1933) was the Honorary Secretary of the Irish Committee of the Pan-Celtic Congress. See Thomas, *The Nations of Wales*, pp. 180–81.

67   Le Braz, 'Les Bretons de France au Pays de Galles', p. 249. For an overview of the pan-Celtic movement, including the crucial role played by Ireland in its development, see Peter Berresford Ellis, *Celtic Dawn: The Dream of Celtic Unity* (Talybont: Y Lolfa, 1993). See also Daniel Williams, 'Pan-Celticism and the Limits of Post-Colonialism', pp. 1–29.

68   See the introduction to Anatole Le Braz, 'Une semaine au Pays de Galles: 17 au 22 juillet 1899', in *Voyage en Irlande, en Angleterre et au pays de Galles* (Rennes: Presses Universitaires de Rennes, 1999), pp. 299–320 (p. 299).

69   See Anatole Le Braz, 'Pèlerinage celtique', in *La Terre du passé* (Paris: Calmann Lévy, 1901), pp. 315–33 (p. 317).

as a utopian travel destination and a cultural model to be emulated by Brittany, was exemplified as we have seen by La Villemarqué in his correspondence, followed by Erny and Martin whose texts were influential for these later travellers. Writing on the eve of the 1899 *eisteddfod*, the Breton journalist, poet and art critic Jean le Fustec (1855–1910) hailed the 'triomphant exemple' [triumphant example] offered by the Welsh to their 'frères celtes' [Celtic brothers] in revitalizing their language and culture.[70] Echoing the notion of the Welsh 'perfect balance' between culture and industry praised by Erny and Martin in the 1860s, travel accounts by his fellow Breton-speaking delegates Le Braz and Charles Le Goffic (1863–1932) both begin by affirming their admiration for Wales's ability to adapt to modernity while preserving its traditions. Le Goffic asserts that

> elle présente ce phénomène unique d'une race qui, sans rien abandonner en apparence de son patrimoine de croyances, de langue et de mœurs, s'est pliée avec une admirable souplesse à toutes les conditions de la vie moderne.
>
> [Wales presents this unique phenomenon of a race which, to all appearances, without abandoning any of its heritage of beliefs, language and customs, has yielded with an admirable flexibility to all the conditions of modern life][71]

Similarly, Le Braz contends that

> De tous les peuples celtiques, celui qui a su se tailler au soleil la place la plus large et le mieux s'adapter aux conditions de la civilisation moderne, sans rien abdiquer des caractères originaux de la race, c'est assurément le peuple gallois.[72]
>
> [Of all the Celtic peoples, the one which has been able to achieve the most prominent position and adapt best to the conditions of modern civilization, without surrendering the original characteristics of the race at all, is without doubt the Welsh people]

---

70   Jean Le Fustec, 'Fêtes celtiques', *La Revue hebdomadaire*, 3:8 (July 1899), pp. 321–40 (p. 325).

71   Charles Le Goffic, 'Chez Taffy: quinze jours dans la Galles du Sud', in *L'Ame bretonne*, Vol. 2 (Paris: Champion, 1912), pp. 200–349 (p. 201). Originally published as 'Chez Taffy: quinze jours dans la Galles du sud', *La Revue hebdomadaire*, 5:6–7 (May 1901), pp. 448–68; (June 1901), pp. 22–50, 229–50, 369–95, 520–47.

72   Le Braz, 'Pèlerinage celtique', p. 315.

Such positivity offers a stark contrast with earlier nineteenth-century French travellers such as Simonin, who asserted that the Welsh nation's ties to its customs and language made it unsuited to modern life. The striking similarity between the optimistic opening of these two travel narratives could imply both an eagerness to pay homage, but also almost a reluctant initial lip service to a standard formula or politically acceptable pan-Celtic view of the Welsh success story. Both Le Braz and Le Goffic subsequently go on to present more critical views of the manifestations of Welsh tradition and modernity that they encounter during their visit, underlining the disjuncture between prior expectation and empirical experience. The case of Le Braz is particularly revelatory in this regard. The author published a laudatory account of his journey as part of his 1901 volume *La Terre du passé* [The Land of the Past], while his private travel notes, which remained unpublished until 1999,[73] offer a far more acerbic and critical perspective on his experience at the 1899 *eisteddfod*. The stark contrast between these public and private accounts of travel underline that Wales was by no means a cultural role model in the eyes of every Breton visitor. Yet the initial lofty expectations of some members of the Breton delegation regarding the Welsh ideal were met unequivocally. Following his journey to Cardiff, Le Fustec returned to Brittany affirmed in his belief in the unifying power of bardism following the model of the Welsh *gorsedd*. Le Fustec believed that 'au pays de Galles le seul bardisme parvient à grouper toute la nation, parce qu'il représente fidèlement la tradition et les inspirations de la race' [in Wales, only bardism is able to bring the whole nation together, because it faithfully represents the tradition and inspirations of the race].[74] Under the auspices of the Welsh *gorsedd*, he founded the Breton *goursez vreizh* the following year, becoming its first archdruid.

For the royalist *député* [member of parliament] Marquis Régis de l'Estourbeillon (1858–1946), Wales embodied a kind of haven as a result of the strength of its cultural nationalism, and at the close of his stay he writes that he feels as if he has spent many hours in an 'oasis de paix' [oasis of peace].[75] This representative of the aristocracy and the political establishment is impressed by the truly grandiose nature of

---

73   See Le Braz, 'Une semaine'.

74   Jean Le Fustec, 'La Musique chez les Gallois', *Revue hebdomadaire*, 8:7 (21 July 1900), pp. 376–90 (p. 387).

75   Alain de Botmelas (pseud. of Régis-Marie-Joseph de l'Estourbeillon de la Garnache), 'Les Bretons au pays de Galles', *Revue historique de l'Ouest*, 15

the 1899 *eisteddfod*, both in terms of the splendour and nature of the *eisteddfod* ceremonies (p. 3), which he describes, writing under the pseudonym Alain de Botmelas, as being attended by 15,000 fascinated spectators from all classes and social conditions, drawn there by a 'charme mystérieux' [mysterious charm].[76] L'Estourbeillon contends that the farewell banquet was held entirely in honour of the Breton delegation. It could be argued that he viewed this attention as a legitimization of the new visibility of Breton culture and the platform provided by the *Union régionaliste bretonne*, characterizing the event as a strong affirmation of the vitality of the Celtic race and an example to the world of high social morality.[77]

Several of the accounts suggest the reciprocal level of anticipation and excitement amongst the Welsh populace regarding their Breton visitors. Le Goffic hails the delegation's warm welcome on their arrival in Cardiff as proof of the fraternity between the Celtic peoples, and gives the impression of a happy family reunion. François Jaffrennou (1879–1956), known by his bardic name Taldir, notes the warmth of the reception accorded to the Breton delegation in particular during the *gorsedd* processions that took place each morning through the streets of Cardiff: 'Sur le parcours une foule énorme se pressait. Fréquemment des acclamations sympathiques accueillaient le passage des Bretons' [a large crowd thronged the route. The Bretons were frequently greeted with warm applause and cheers as they went by].[78] In his private travel notes Le Braz underlines that not all the delegates were treated equally, contending that subservience to the aristocracy meant that apart from the Marquis de l'Estourbeillon, the comte de Tressan and the Welsh-speaking Jaffrennou, the other Breton delegates were viewed as minor figures and insignificant small fry.[79] Moreover, in Le Goffic's

(30 November 1899); references here are to the pamphlet version *Les Bretons au Pays de Galles* (Redon: A. Bouteloup, 1899), p. 16.

76 Botmelas, 'Les Bretons', pp. 3–4.

77 Botmelas, 'Les Bretons', p. 11.

78 François Jaffrennou, 'Le Gorsedd de Cardiff', *La Résistance*, 29 July 1899, published in François Jaffrennou, *La Genèse d'un mouvement: articles, doctrines et discours 1898–1911* (Carhaix: Imprimerie-Librairie du Peuple, 1912), pp. 33–35 (p. 34).

79 Le Braz, 'Une semaine', p. 316. His fellow delegate the grammarian Frañsez Vallée had also learnt Welsh but is not mentioned by Le Braz at this juncture. Gilles Siche notes that Jaffrennou was already fairly well-known in Welsh-speaking circles prior to this occasion as a regular contributor to the popular children's

depiction the excitement generated by the arrival of the Breton delegation and the extent to which they were objects of curiosity is evident:

> C'était une véritable expédition que la nôtre et qui mettait en l'air toutes les têtes de Cardiff. On allait donc les voir, ces Bretons de Bretagne, qui sont les cousins des Gallois, qui parlent la même langue, qui chantent les mêmes airs ...[80]

> [Ours was a proper expedition, and everyone in Cardiff came out to witness it. They were actually going to see them, these Bretons of Brittany, who are the cousins of the Welsh, who speak the same language, sing the same tunes ...]

These accounts offer an insight into the complexity of relationships and power dynamics between speakers of minoritized languages in travel accounts. Le Goffic's collective indirect discourse and ellipsis implies a counter-narrative to his previous affirmations of Celtic kinship, a questioning of prevalent Welsh expectations of linguistic and cultural similarities that would subordinate and negate the distinctiveness of the Breton language.

Such a process of 'writing back' is also implied in several portrayals of the Welsh language. The use of the term 'writing back' is deliberate, as Le Braz constructs a colonial relationship, designating Wales as the metropolis and Brittany as a colony.[81] Such accounts offer a highly unusual perspective in travel literature on Wales by constructing Welsh as the major, dominant and oppressive language through its association with its chief representative in the texts, the forbidding figure of the Archdruid Hwfa Môn, the bardic name of Rowland Williams (1823–1905). Le Goffic's melodramatic 'terreur sacrée' [sacred terror] of the archdruid leads him and the other delegates to scrupulously observe the rituals of the ceremonies, conducted entirely in Welsh, like obedient schoolboys.[82] Le Braz goes further still in his private account, noting the archdruid's grimaces, shouts and malicious eyes.[83] Through the

---

magazine *Cymru'r Plant*; see Siche, 'Trois écrivains bretonnants au Pays de Galles', p. 36. See also Jaffrennou's two Welsh-language accounts of his journey to north Wales following the Cardiff *eisteddfod*: Taldir (François Jaffrennou), 'Tro yng Ngogledd Cymru', *Cymru*, 17 (1899), pp. 221–24 and 'Llanberis a Beddgelert. Fel y gwelodd Llydawr Hwynt', *Cymru*, 18 (1899), p. 41.

80   Le Goffic, 'Chez Taffy', p. 217.
81   Le Braz, 'Les Bretons de France au Pays de Galles', p. 244.
82   Le Goffic, 'Chez Taffy', p. 222.
83   Le Braz, 'Une semaine', p. 316.

figure of the archdruid, the head of the *gorsedd* and leader of official ceremonies, the Welsh language assumes animalistic, primitive qualities, echoing a longstanding tradition of associating Celts with animality.[84] His discourse during the investitures is almost described as a verbal assault:

> Debout sur la pierre du Destin, il haranguait en 'welsh' les délégations étrangères réunies sur les pelouses ombreuses de Carthays Park [*sic*]. Nous ne comprenions pas une syllabe de ce qu'il éructait, et ses rugissements nous émouvaient exactement comme eussent pu faire ceux d'un lamantin ou d'un auroch préhistorique.[85]

> [Standing on the Stone of Destiny, he harangued in Welsh the foreign delegations assembled on the shady lawns of Cathays Park. We did not understand a single word of what he was belching forth, and his roars moved us exactly as those of a sea cow or a prehistoric wild ox would have done]

Le Goffic thereby subverts the myth of Welsh-Breton linguistic mutual comprehension that was significant throughout the nineteenth century, especially in pan-Celtic circles, and of which La Villemarqué was a key exponent.[86] In addition to reinforcing this traveller's sense of alienation and disengagement, Le Goffic's rhetoric, and his choice of the deliberately archaic similes of the sea cow and the extinct prehistoric aurochs imply a view of the Welsh language as a cumbersome ancient relic, rather than a modern, dynamic vibrant force. Moreover, a similar emphasis on the wild, harsh sounds of the Welsh language as spoken by the archdruid can also be found in the much more sympathetic accounts, suggesting an element of Celticism in these Breton narratives, the Welsh becoming the savage and exotic Celtic 'other' whose words remain beyond translation. This lies in stark contrast to La Villemarqué's fake hybrid 'Welsh' language that would not even have required translation for its intended Breton audience.

84　For an Irish example of this association, see John Miller's 'R.M. Ballantyne and Mr G. O'Rilla: Apes, Irishmen and the 1861 Great Gorilla Controversy', in Paddy Lyons, Willy Maley and John Miller (eds), *Romantic Ireland from Tone to Gonne: Fresh Perspectives on Nineteenth-Century Ireland* (Newcastle upon Tyne: Cambridge Scholars Press, 2013), pp. 402–15.

85　Le Goffic, 'Chez Taffy', p. 221.

86　Le Braz also rejects this myth in his article written prior to his journey, and criticizes its proponents for showing a singular ignorance of linguistics. See Le Braz, 'Les Bretons de France au Pays de Galles', p. 246.

Many of the Breton delegates remained spectators on the margins due to the linguistic barrier, focusing their accounts on the visual spectacle, material objects, colours and symbolism. Le Goffic and Le Braz were unable to take the *gorsedd* seriously as custodians of a bardic tradition. On the one hand, Le Goffic seems to cling to the idea of the mystical Celtic fairy tale, referring to the *gorsedd* circle of twelve upright stones where the ceremonies are conducted as 'une sorte de cercle enchanté' [a sort of enchanted circle].[87] Yet he also offers a highly sardonic depiction of the *gorsedd* as comic figures of fun:

> La vérité est que ce costume, sauf pour les druides, témoigne d'un mauvais goût parfait. Bardes et ovates ont l'air d'avoir été surpris par quelque catastrophe nocturne et de s'être enveloppés précipitamment dans leurs rideaux de lit.[88]

> [The truth is that this costume, except when worn by the druids, shows perfect bad taste. Bards and ovates look as if they have been taken by surprise by some night-time catastrophe and have wrapped themselves up hurriedly in their bed curtains]

In his published account, Le Braz evokes an 'untoward' resemblance between his experience of being invested as a bard and the staging of an opera.[89] Privately he notes that the ceremony reminded him of the comedy-ballet *Le Malade Imaginaire* (1673) [The Hypochondriac] by Molière (1622–1673). He is perplexed by the costumes, which he likens to masquerade gowns and carnival rags.[90] He wonders whether they are in fact all engaging in an elaborate mockery of ancient druidism, and his conclusion that a great deal of irony underpins the ceremonies undermines the force and relevance of the Welsh cultural model.[91]

The choice of Cardiff, described by Le Goffic as the virtual capital of south Wales,[92] as the location of the 1899 *eisteddfod* is a further source of disillusionment. Le Goffic views this Anglicized and 'ill-defined' city as unrepresentative of the 'true Wales' (p. 225): 'Nos Bretons de France, qui y assistaient au nombre d'une vingtaine, si on ne les eût point avertis,

---

87   Le Goffic, 'Chez Taffy', p. 222.
88   Le Goffic, 'Chez Taffy', p. 221.
89   Le Braz, 'Pèlerinage celtique', p. 329.
90   Le Braz, 'Une semaine', p. 316.
91   Le Braz, 'Une semaine', p. 316.
92   Following a competition with other towns including Caernarfon and Aberystwyth, Cardiff was appointed the official capital of Wales in 1955.

se seraient crus toujours en pays anglais' [Our Bretons of France (…), if they had not been expressly told, would have believed that they were still in England].[93] Le Braz extends his critique from the city of Cardiff to the delegates of all Celtic nations due to their realpolitik and loyalty to the English crown, privately venting his disappointment that, 'Au fond, tous ces gens sont très anglais et ils ont raison, et ils ne sont nullement utopistes' [At heart, all these people are very English and they are right, and in no way are they utopians].[94]

Although Le Goffic may consider Cardiff an unsuitable location for the National Eisteddfod, his account expresses his admiration for the city's rapid industrial expansion, due mainly to the major development of the docks. In contrast to 'chez nous' in Brittany, the city is praised for not having destroyed its architectural past in pursuit of progress. Le Goffic highlights the volume of Welsh exports to France, observing the highly visible presence of French merchant ships, which carried 2,022,730 tonnes of coal to France and its colonies in 1898. Nevertheless, after his stay in Cardiff and visit to the Albion coal mine in Cilfynydd near Pontypridd, Le Goffic is relieved to reach the rural landscape of the Brecon Beacons: 'encadrée de grands massifs montagneux, – les Black Mountains, – dont les lignes harmonieuses n'étaient point déshonorées par les usines qui nous avaient gâté jusqu'alors le pays de Galles' (p. 287) [surrounded by a great massif – the Black Mountains – whose harmonious lines were not dishonoured by the factories which had hitherto spoiled Wales for us]. Le Goffic's ambivalent attitude towards Welsh industrialization can be read as continuing the perceptions of earlier travellers from Brittany and France.

Le Goffic is informed that a growing 'French colony' exists in Cardiff and goes in search of the French consul to express his disappointment at not finding any signs declaring 'ici on parle français' (p. 235) [French spoken here] in the shops. Le Goffic initially interprets the unnamed consul's conspicuous absence from any of the *eisteddfod* events as a sign of the French Ministry of Foreign Affairs' mistrust of Welsh-language culture. However, the consul himself expresses sincere admiration for recent Welsh achievements in industry, business affairs and educational provision, and in particular their ability to assimilate Anglo-Saxon migrants, observing:

93   Le Goffic, 'Chez Taffy', p. 219.
94   Le Braz, 'Une semaine', p. 316.

> Il faut vraiment que le Gallois, honni, persécuté comme il fut pendant plusieurs siècles, ait en lui une force d'assimilation toute spéciale pour avoir fini par conquérir ses propres adversaires. (p. 237)

> [The Welshman, reviled and persecuted as he has been for many centuries, must truly have a very special power of assimilation to have ended up conquering his own adversaries]

This French government representative also applauds the way Wales has gained an extraordinary confidence and self-assurance thanks to its prodigious economic development and industrial boom and wealth.

In stark contrast, having begun his account by celebrating Wales's ability to adapt to the conditions of modern life, Le Braz subsequently perceives the industrialized urban landscape as an Anglicized imposition which is incompatible with his vision of a return to the Celtic cradle. When travelling to visit the nearby seaside town of Penarth for the afternoon, Le Braz contends: 'Partout cependant la superposition de la vie anglaise à la vie galloise; un industrialisme effréné. Nous allons à travers un paysage de railways, de gares, d'usines, etc.' [Everywhere you see the superimposition of English life on Welsh life, a frantic industrialism. We travelled through a landscape of railways, stations, factories, etc.].[95] His portrayal of the 'tamed' seascape he visits at Penarth serves as a vehicle to assert Brittany's geographical distinctiveness, and implicitly perhaps its superior credentials as an 'authentic' Celtic landscape:

> Pen-Arth, avec sa grève fréquentée, ses aménagements, son sentier de mer solidement muré comme un quai, comme tout cela est loin de la côte bretonne, sauvage et naturelle![96]

> [Penarth, with its strand full of visitors, its facilities, its seaside footpath enclosed with solid walls like a quay, how far removed all that is from our wild and natural Breton coast!]

In his private diaries, Le Braz confides his longing to escape from the crowd-thronged ceremonies and his official duties as an *eisteddfod* delegate. This desire leads him to walk through Sophia Gardens to the leafy, quiet sanctuary of Llandaff parish and its cathedral, where he receives a warm welcome from a Breton sacristan. Le Braz finds the old tombstones in Llandaf's cemetery similar to those of Brittany, and the peaceful flow of the River Taff and the surrounding hills remind him of

95   Le Braz, 'Une semaine', p. 317.
96   Le Braz, 'Une semaine', p. 317.

Quimper's countryside.[97] In *La Terre du passé*, his journey to Wales is framed by the heading 'En Bretagne d'outre mer' [In Overseas Brittany], thus implying the impossibility of viewing the Welsh nation without recourse to the Breton prism.

The high point of the *eisteddfod* welcoming the return of the Bretons into the fold was a ceremony attended by a 'wildly enthusiastic' audience of up to 20,000 people on the evening of Tuesday 18 July.[98] The 1899 Cardiff *eisteddfod* was the first occasion the split swords ceremony between Welsh and Breton representatives had been held. The Welsh and Breton delegations entered from separate ends of the stage before conjoining two halves of a specially created sword, a symbol of peace and brotherhood to be brought together whenever Welsh and Breton bards were assembled.[99] The Breton half of the sword was carried by the Marquis de l'Estourbeillon in traditional costume, and the nineteen-year-old Jaffrennou's address to the assembly in Welsh was 'frénétiquement applaudi' [applauded frantically] by the audience.[100] The archdruid issued the proclamation of peace, 'a oes Heddwch?' [is there peace?], receiving the affirmation, 'Heddwch' [peace] from all those assembled. What happened next was highly charged and fraught with ambiguity, and is described most fully by journalist Rémy Saint-Maurice (1864–1918):

> Les vingt mille spectateurs sont debout, trépignant, hurlant: 'Brittany for ever! …' Les chapeaux s'agitent, les cannes aussi […] Un des lairds, levant sa toque, a crié: 'Vive la France! … la belle France!'
>
> Et tous ensemble ont repris le cri. Ce n'est plus la seule Armorique, c'est la France entière qu'on acclame! … Dans les yeux gallois, dans les yeux bretons, je vois des larmes prêtes à jaillir.[101]

97 Le Braz, 'Une semaine', pp. 313–14.
98 Le Braz, 'Pèlerinage celtique', p. 332.
99 The conceptualization of the sword ceremony was based on a poem written by Alphonse de Lamartine (1790–1869) for the 1838 Abergavenny *eisteddfod*. See Alphonse de Lamartine, 'Toast porté dans un banquet national des Gallois et des Bretons à Abergavenny, en Écosse [*sic*]', in *Recueillements poétiques* (Brussels. Jamar, 1839), pp. 95–99. After the establishment of the Breton *gorsedd* in 1900 it came to symbolize the unity of the two *gorseddau*. See the National Museum of Wales article 'Swords, Scrolls and Mystic Marks', https://museum.wales/articles/2010-07-25/Scrolls-swords-and-mystic-marks/ [accessed 7 June 2018].
100 Guillaume Corfec, *Indépendance Bretonne*, 22 July 1899, quoted in Jaffrennou, 'Le Gorsedd', p. 32.
101 Saint-Maurice in Botmelas, 'Les Bretons', p. 9.

[The twenty thousand spectators are standing, stamping their feet, shouting: 'Brittany forever!' (…) Hats and canes are waved aloft. One of the Scottish lairds, raising his cap, shouted: 'Long live France! Beautiful France!'

Everyone present took up this cry. It is no longer Armorica alone, but the whole of France that is being applauded! … In Welsh eyes, in Breton eyes, I see tears welling up]

This scene parallels the tense Anglo-Welsh relations at earlier *eisteddfod* events. Attention is shifted here from honouring the minoritized Breton culture to a celebration of its hegemonic universalist French oppressor. The applause ends abruptly on the signal of the archdruid, before the collective singing of the Welsh national anthem *Hen Wlad fy Nhadau* [Land of My Fathers] leads to what could be seen as a double silencing of Breton culture and Brittany. Conversely, Le Braz himself seems to express relief that the French language temporarily replaces the Welsh language, describing its presence in the Celtic 'cradle' in lyrical terms:

La salle entière est debout, applaudissant et trépignant. Un des lairds d'Ecosse crie: // Vive la France … la belle France! // Et soudain, les douces syllabes françaises volent de bouche en bouche, dominant l'âpreté des derniers hourrahs. Le plus sceptique en eût été remué jusqu'aux larmes.[102]

[Everyone in the room is standing, applauding and stamping their feet. One of the Scottish lairds shouts: 'Long live France … beautiful France! And suddenly, sweet French syllables fly from mouth to mouth, dominating the harshness of the final hurrahs (i.e. the word *heddwch*, 'peace'). The most sceptical person would have been moved to tears by this]

This episode suggests the extent to which encounters between peripheries remain within and become subsumed by the mediating framework of the relationship with the centre, as Bretons and Welsh negate their reciprocal cultural identities by designating the other as English and French.

After the mayoral banquet in their honour, ten of the Breton delegation made the hour-long journey by rail from Cardiff to Abergavenny, to stay at Llanover Hall on the invitation of Lady Augusta Charlotte Elizabeth Herbert (1824–1912). Characterized by L'Estourbeillon as a 'pieux pèlerinage' [pious pilgrimage],[103] the Breton delegates and their

102 Le Braz, 'Pèlerinage celtique', p. 332.
103 Botmelas, 'Les Bretons', p. 14.

patriotic hostess are all acutely aware that they are paying homage to their illustrious compatriots, including La Villemarqué, who were received at Llanover by Lady Herbert's mother Lady Augusta Hall in 1838. The grandeur, magnificence but also touching simplicity of Lady Herbert's reception in 1899 are compared with festivities worthy of the courts of Arthur or Llywelyn.[104] In his elegiac account of the delegation's visit to this Welsh enclave near the English border, François Jaffrennou asserts that the Llanover policy of only permitting Welsh-speaking tenants and servants offers a magnificent example to Breton lords and ladies.[105] The Breton travel accounts construct the family not only as exemplary patriots who serve as defenders and custodians of Welsh cultural traditions, but also of ties between Wales and Brittany. Llanover's opulent library houses an unrivalled collection of 'ancient' Welsh manuscripts and music, and specimens of indigenous art. Le Goffic pores feverishly through the epistolary correspondence between Lady Hall and historian Henri Martin, who was hosted at Llanover in 1862. Wales's significance for Brittany as a cultural role model is reaffirmed in the speech of appreciation given by L'Estourbeillon at the Llanover banquet. He asserted that the honour afforded the Breton delegation by their reception at Llanover would serve to further energise their patriotism, inspired by 'la foi ardente patriotique' [the ardent patriotic faith] of the Welsh.[106]

As was the case with La Villemarqué and other delegates to the 1838 *eisteddfod*, the myriad contemporary travel narratives in various different voices describing the 'pan-Celtic' *eisteddfod* of 1899 serve as vehicles to address hopes for the future and utopic visions for Brittany to their domestic readership. While the strength of the Welsh-Breton axis at the close of the nineteenth century represented a high point of inter-Celtic relations, it should be noted that the exemplary nature of Wales as a Celtic role model was not accepted unquestionably by every Breton traveller. It is clear that the rise of Celtic awareness in its dominant Renanian/Arnoldian form was accompanied by defeatist politics. As M. Wynn Thomas recently remarked on Arnold's brand of Celticism, the Welsh fell 'hook line and sinker for Arnold's propaganda, rarely noticing how they were disadvantaged by it'.[107] The French, no matter how

104 Jaffrennou, 'Le Gorsedd', pp. 36–37.
105 Jaffrennou, 'Le Gorsedd', p. 36.
106 Botmelas, 'Les Bretons', p. 16.
107 Thomas, *The Nations of Wales*, p. 147.

pro-Celtic they may seem, at this time always saw Wales and Brittany as 'petites patries' [little fatherlands]. It is not until the twentieth century that a real political awakening is seen in both Wales and Brittany, which leads to Bretons taking Wales as a radical role model, as well as a place of refuge following the Second World War.

CHAPTER THREE

Periphery, Modernity
and the Discovery of Wales in
Travel Writing in German
from 1790 to 1850

Writing in his *Briefe eines Verstorbenen: Ein fragmentarisches Tagebuch aus England, Wales, Irland und Frankreich* [Correspondence of a Dead Man: A Fragmentary Diary from England, Wales, Ireland and France], which was first published in 1830, Hermann von Pückler-Muskau (1785–1871), who travelled extensively around north Wales in 1829, noted that Wales was an unknown place, hidden between England and Ireland.[1] His observation is both accurate and misleading. For the German-speaking traveller in the nineteenth century, Wales was either a complete nonentity, merely an adjunct to England where a strange language was spoken or, increasingly as the century progressed, a specific destination for educated tourists, enthusiastic Celticists and industrial explorers. Travellers were drawn by the picturesque landscape, ancient bardic culture and the developing technology of the mining heartlands in the north and the south. At the very beginning of the century, however, Wales was at best an emerging destination on the travel itineraries of German travellers and was for many *terra incognita*. There had been a small number of travel texts covering Wales towards the end of the eighteenth century, notably Carl Gottlob Küttner's (1755–1805) *Beyträge zur Kenntniss vorzüglich des Innern*

---

1   Hermann von Pückler-Muskau, *Briefe eines Verstorbenen: Ein fragmentarisches Tagebuch aus England, Wales, Irland und Frankreich; geschrieben in den Jahren 1828 und 1829* (Stuttgart: Hallberger, 1836 [1830]), p. 122.

von England und seiner Einwohner (1791) [Contributions to the Knowledge of the Interior of England and its Inhabitants][2] and August Gottfried Ludwig Lentin's (1764–1823) *Briefe über die Insel Anglesea, vorzüglich über das dasige Kupfer-Bergwerk und die dazugehörigen Schmelzwerke und Fabriken* (1800) [Letters on the Island of Anglesey, in Particular its Copper Mines and the Allied Smelting Works and Factories],[3] but their impact on the broader understanding of Wales was limited.[4] This is partly due to the elision of Wales in the title of both texts with reference only to the hegemonic notion of the British Isles as 'England'[5] – very much 'das neue Reiseland des 18. Jahrhunderts' [very much the new travel destination of the eighteenth century][6] – or, conversely, the specifically local – the island of Anglesey – disconnected from its national context. This tendency would remain a feature into the next century. In the early part of the nineteenth century in particular, Wales is seldom mentioned by name in the titles of German-language travelogues and, even later, only rarely appears as the sole focus of a text.[7] This chapter will explore the extent to

2   Carl Gottlob Küttner, *Beyträge zur Kenntniss vorzüglich des Innern von England und seiner Einwohner*, 4 vols (Leipzig: Im Verlage der Dykischen Buchhandlung, 1791), I, pp. 53–60, 74–85; IV, pp. 3–8, 52–63.

3   August Gottfried Ludwig Lentin, *Briefe über die Insel Anglesea, vorzüglich über das dasige Kupfer-Bergwerk und die dazugehörigen Schmelzwerke und Fabriken* (Leipzig: Crusius, 1800).

4   Some English travel writing on Wales did appear in German translation but there was a marked tendency to focus on the factual. See Alison E. Martin, 'Celtic Censure: Representing Wales in Eighteenth-Century Germany', *Studies in Travel Writing*, 18 (2014), pp. 122–34.

5   For a discussion of the reception of England in German-language travel writing in the late eighteenth and early nineteenth century, see Robert Elsasser, *Über die politischen Bildungsreisen der Deutschen nach England vom Anfang des 18. Jahrhunderts bis 1815*, Heidelberger Abhandlungen zur mittleren und neueren Geschichte 51 (Heidelberg: Winter, 1917); Michael Maurer (ed.), *O Britannien, von deiner Freiheit einen Hut voll. Deutsche Reiseberichte des 18. Jahrhunderts* (Munich: Beck, 1992); Tilmann Fischer, *Reiseziel England: Ein Beitrag zur Poetik der Reisebeschreibung und zur Topik der Moderne (1830–1870)*, Philologische Studien und Quellen 184 (Berlin: Schmidt, 2004); Alison E. Martin, *Moving Scenes: The Aesthetics of German Travel Writing on England 1783–1830*, Studies in Comparative Literature 13 (London: Legenda, 2008).

6   Maurer, *Wales*, p. 7.

7   This tendency also characterizes the emerging guidebook market. See Dijkstra, 'Wales in Continental Guidebooks', (1850–2013).

which this textual invisibility dissipates gradually through the century as Wales becomes better known, and will examine how the nation's profile as a destination remains in constant tension with that of its near and dominant neighbour, England.

The absence of a profile for Wales at this time is to some extent at odds with the prevailing cultural trend. The Celtic world, with which one would automatically associate Wales today, was very much in vogue in the late eighteenth and nineteenth centuries. In the broader European context, the view of that world centred primarily on the Herderian enthusiasm for MacPherson's spurious bardic poem, *Ossian* (1765), and was later fed by the popular and increasingly voluminous works of Sir Walter Scott (1771–1832). For the German reader, the Celtic nations came to represent an exotic northern ideal. Filled with druidic mysticism and embodying the Herderian ideal of the *Volksgeist* [spirit of the people], they served, alongside Spain and the Nordic lands, as a peripheral other against which to measure the ongoing Romantic quest for cultural self-definition.[8] Following Herder, writers such as brothers Friedrich (1772–1829) and August Wilhelm Schlegel (1767–1845) and the Brothers Grimm, Jacob (1785–1863) and Wilhelm (1786–1859), sought paradigms of cultural authenticity on the periphery of Europe to help illustrate what they saw as the value of their own cultural heritage, itself threatened by a hegemonic neighbour, France.[9] In this context, the bardic values of *Ossian*, the Sagas and the Golden Age theatre of Calderón served as aspirational ideals for the development of a national literature.[10]

Yet, in the German mind, Wales was largely absent from the Celtic cultural landscape. This was caused in part by a tendency to view what one might term the Celtic nations of the British Isles as a cultural collective. Within this, whereas Scotland and Ireland were able to maintain an individual profile, Wales remained largely invisible. Although there was some awareness of Wales conceptually, there was no

8   See Howard Gaskill, 'Herder, Ossian and the Celtic', in Brown (ed.), *Celticism,* pp. 257–72; Howard Gaskill, 'Ossian, Herder and the Idea of Folk Song', in David Hill (ed.), *Literature of the Sturm und Drang* (Rochester, NY: Camden House, 2003), pp. 95–116.

9   See Carol Tully, *Creating a National Identity: A Comparative Study of German and Spanish Romanticism*, Stuttgarter Arbeiten zur Germanistik 347 (Stuttgart: Hans-Dieter Heinz, 1997).

10   See Dorota Masiakowska, *Vielfalt und Einheit im Europabild August Wilhelm Schlegels* (Frankfurt am Main: Peter Lang, 2002).

real appreciation of where it was and how it related to other parts of the British Isles.[11] To some extent, this reflected the position of Wales in the broader European context. Scotland had until relatively recently been an independent nation and boasted some of the oldest universities in Europe, while Ireland sat firmly on the European map as a stronghold of Christian tradition and was the scene of ongoing rebellion. In contrast, and despite clear Celtic credentials, for German-speaking readers, Wales lacked any major cities or seats of learning and was known at best as an adjunct to England with no real defined status. Consequently, German travellers arriving there were very much on a voyage of discovery, one resulting quite often in what Maurer describes explicitly as a 'Kulturschock' [culture shock].[12]

Many of the issues which would attract the attention of German travellers in the nineteenth century already begin to emerge in the few accounts of travel from the eighteenth century. Küttner, travelling through north and south Wales in 1784 on the way to and from Ireland, uses terms such as 'romantisch' (I, p. 53) [Romantic] and 'paradiesisch' (IV, p. 3) [paradisiacal] in his *Beyträge* to describe ancient buildings and the landscape but is generally critical of Welsh society and the lack of development. He notes that the mountains in the north lack the variety of the Alps and is in general less positive about the north than the south of Wales (I, p. 54). He finds the people in the north to be isolated and maintains that they see themselves as distinct from the English whereas the influence of England in the south is palpable on every level with evidence of far greater civilization (I, p. 54). Anglesey is singled out for particular criticism (I, p. 58), its landscape uninviting and its taverns the scene of cock fights and duels, abhorrent practices brought, he points out, by the large number of Irish travellers (I, pp. 60–61). Progress is not universally positive, however. Commenting on the south, he notes the negative impact of industry on the otherwise pleasant landscape (IV, p. 47). Küttner's comments draw out the key issues for future German-speaking travellers – the uneasy relationship with England, the backward nature of society, the sublime landscape – but he is also unusual in his positive bias towards the south which later German travellers will to a large extent ignore, preferring instead the majesty of the north Walian landscape.

11   See Carol Tully, 'The Celtic Misconnection: The German Romantics and Wales', *Angermion*, 2 (2009), pp. 127–41.
12   Maurer, *Wales*, p. 12.

The issue of Wales as a nation on the edge of modernity is the central focus of the Austrian Gottfried Wenzel von Purgstall's travel account of 1796 which was published posthumously in 1821.[13] Purgstall (1773–1812), who was married to Scottish noblewoman Johanna Anna Baroness of Cranstoun and knew Goethe, arrived in Wales via Somerset and left crossing the border at Chester. In so doing, he was conscious of entering Wales per se but treated it throughout as an extension of England. His narrative focuses on the sublime landscape, noting locations such as Devil's Bridge in mid-Wales, as well as the many Norman castles. He also provides a description of the emerging industrial landscape around Merthyr Tydfil and juxtaposes this with detailed descriptions of agricultural issues such as livestock pricing. Overall, however, his narrative gives an impression of Wales as a social backwater. His experience of travel via mail coach is particularly arduous and he complains about the lack of horses, poor inns and inadequate postal service, the latter leaving him without funds as repeated deliveries of money fail to materialize.

Another key issue which would later draw the attention of nineteenth-century travellers is that of Welsh culture and language. There is some evidence that information on Wales, its history and its culture was known to German-speaking travellers quite early on, gleaned most likely from general histories of the British Isles and translations into German of earlier travels such as *Bemerkungen auf einer Reise durch verschiedene Theile von England, Schottland und Wales* (1781) [Observations Made during a Tour through Parts of England, Scotland and Wales] by Richard Joseph Sullivan (1752–1806), translated from the English,[14] and *Nachrichten von Großbritannien und Irland* (1789) [Reports from Great Britain and Ireland] by Johan Meerman (1753–1815), which was translated from the Dutch.[15] This is the case, for example and perhaps

13   Gottfried Wenzel von Purgstall, 'Auszüge aus reisebeschreibenden Briefen des vorletzten Grafen von Purgstall', in Joseph von Hammer-Purgstall (ed.), *Denkmal auf das Grab der beyden letzten Grafen von Purgstall* (Vienna: Anton Strauß, 1821), pp. 98–141.

14   Richard Joseph Sullivan, *Bemerkungen auf einer Reise durch verschiedene Theile von England, Schottland und Wales; nebst einer Nebenreise in die Hölen von Ingleborough und Settle in Yorkshire. In Briefen. Aus dem Englischen, nebst einigen Anmerkungen des Uebersetzers* (Leipzig: Breitkopf, 1781); from *Observations made during a Tour through parts of England, Scotland and Wales in a series of letters* (London: T. Beckett, 1780).

15   Johan Meerman, *Nachrichten von Großbritannien und Irland* (Nürnberg

ironically, in Lentin's *Briefe über die Insel Anglesea*, a text which is primarily concerned with industrial practices. Travelling in north Wales towards the end of the 1790s to gather information on copper mining in order to improve practice at home, Lentin's otherwise hugely technical account is prefaced by a positive description of the north Walian landscape and, significantly, a detailed description of the history of the island of Anglesey and a narrative of the origins of the title Prince of Wales. He notes also the mistreatment of the Welsh by the English.

These first German narratives on Wales help set the scene in terms of identifying the issues which will be of interest to subsequent generations but they have little impact on the understanding of Wales in the German-speaking lands. They are very much initial forays, scoping out what Wales might be. The first nineteenth-century German travel text to deal with Wales in any great reflective detail and which tackles in more depth the issues first drawn out by Küttner, Lentin and Purgstall, is Christian August Gottlieb Goede's *England, Wales, Irland und Schottland. Erinnerungen an Natur und Kunst aus einer Reise in den Jahren 1802 und 1803* [England, Wales, Ireland and Scotland: Recollections of Nature and Art from a Journey in the Years 1802 and 1803], which was published in five volumes in Dresden from 1804 to 1805.[16] In presenting his narrative, Goede (1774–1812), a lawyer and professor of law at both Jena and Göttingen, provides the first detailed analysis in German of Wales, its culture and people, and, significantly, its relationship with its

and Altdorf: Monathischen Verlag, 1789); from *Eenige berichten omtrent Groot-Brittannien en Ierland* (The Hague: n.p., 1787).

16   Christian August Gottlieb Goede, *England, Wales, Irland und Schottland: Erinnerungen an Natur und Kunst aus einer Reise in den Jahren 1802 und 1803*, 5 vols (Dresden: Arnoldische Buch- und Kunsthandlung, 1804–1805), V, pp. 315–67. The travelogue was translated into English twice. The first translation was an abridged version, including only selected sections of Goede's Welsh narrative: *The Stranger in England or Travels in Great Britain from the German of C.A.G. Goede*, trans. anon, 3 vols (London: Mathews and Leigh, 1807); the second translation omitted the Welsh section entirely: *Memorials of Nature and Art, collected on a Journey in Great Britain during the years 1802 and 1803*, trans. Thomas Horne, 3 vols (London: Mawman, 1808); a second edition of Horne's translation appeared in 1821. Given the incomplete nature of the published translations, English versions have been provided. For a discussion of the translation history of Goede's text, see Carol Tully, '"Pride in their port, defiance in their eye": English translations of German Travel Writing on the British Isles in the Early Nineteenth Century', *Intralinea* (2013), http://www.intralinea.org/specials/article/pride_in_their_port_defiance_in_their_eye [accessed 3 January 2019].

dominant neighbour, England. Apparently unaware of earlier German narratives, Goede engages primarily with English-medium sources such as works by Thomas Pennant which, the latter's Welsh origins notwithstanding, provide an essentially Anglocentric view to which Goede responds in critical terms. Although Goede's work was not the first German-language account of travel in Wales, it is the first to reach a wider audience with a second edition and numerous translations into English, French and Dutch. As such, this text constitutes what one might term the foundation layer of the German narrative of Wales.

Goede addresses the issue of Wales's difference quite early in his narrative and in so doing shapes the debate on the relationship between centre and periphery, already alluded to in Küttner and Lentin, which will remain a feature of German writing on Wales throughout the nineteenth century. Perhaps unexpectedly, given the general enthusiasm in Germany for all things English at the time, Goede openly attacks the English government's treatment of this peripheral nation (pp. 360–61). His views are embedded in his own cultural context as a product of the early Romantic idealism prevailing at Jena. It is no coincidence that the opening lines of his first volume echo closely those of Novalis (Friedrich von Hardenberg, 1772–1801), whose seminal essay 'Die Christenheit oder Europa' (1799) [Christendom or Europe], which was not published in full until 1826, evokes the values of a bygone benevolent feudal era.[17] Goede's reading of what he sees as England's failings as a hegemonic power in relation to Wales is juxtaposed with this Romantic ideal.

Goede's understanding of Wales is tested immediately by the negative views expressed by his fellow English travellers. As they enter Llangollen, having crossed the Welsh border at Shrewsbury on the mail coach, they challenge him jokingly on his intentions to spend some time there:

> Nun, mein Herr, sagte die Dame zu mir, wollen Sie wirklich den romanhaften Entschluß ausführen, und in dieser Jahreszeit und bei diesem Wetter in Llangollen bleiben? Ich kann Ihnen, setzte der Offizier hinzu, alle Herrlichkeiten, die Sie hier finden werden, zum Voraus sagen: kahle Berge, häßliche Mädchen und schlechten Wein. Ja, freilich, sagte der dicke Engländer, eine sonderliche Berwirthung dürfen Sie sich in diesem elenden Orte nicht versprechen. (p. 313)

17 Friedrich von Hardenberg, *Novalis. Schriften*, III: *Das philosophische Werk II*, ed. Richard Samuel, Hans-Joachim Mahl and Gerhard Schulz, 2nd ed., 5 vols (Stuttgart: Kohlhammer, 1968), p. 507.

['Now, dear Sir', said the lady to me, 'are you really sure you wish to go through with this fanciful decision to remain in Llangollen at this time of year and in this weather?' 'I can tell you now', added the officer, 'what wonders await you: bare mountains, ugly young women and bad wine'. 'Yes, indeed', said the fat Englishman, 'you should not expect much in the way of hospitality in this miserable place']

Goede's references to Pennant notwithstanding, the English prism is established from the beginning of the text as his main source of information on Wales. His fellow travellers' comments suggest a negative English view of Wales which many subsequent German writers note and, in some cases, seek to challenge. Indeed, it is a view which Goede himself is happy to counter almost immediately, responding to the female passenger's concerns that he would regret his decision:

Ich freue mich sagen zu können, daß sie sich in ihrer Prophezeiung geirrt hat; den ich zähle die wenigen Tage, die ich zu Llangollen zubrachte, zu den heitersten und glücklichsten meines Lebens. (p. 314)

[I am pleased to be able to say that she was quite wrong in her prediction; for I count the few days I spent in Llangollen among the most cheerful and happy of my life]

Despite his enthusiasm, Goede does seek to present a realistic picture of what he finds in Llangollen, an approach which typifies his polarized reading of Wales throughout, juxtaposing the stark social reality with Romantic reverie on the sublime landscape and authentic culture. His opening description of the town sets the tone:

Llangollen liegt am Flusse Dee in einem schönen Thale, das von dem Städtchen den Namen führt. Es ist eine kleine, schmutzige Stadt. Die Häuser sind niedrig und schlecht gebaut, die Straßen eng und elend gepflastert. An der nordöstlichen Seite liegt eine lange Reihe kahler, grauer Kalkberge; da suchen sich die Einwohner Llangollens die Materialien, von denen die Häuser des Städtchens aufgeführt sind. Man hat aber zum Theil die Steine in ihrer rauhen, unbehauenen Form, wie man sie aufgelesen, zusammengefügt, und da die Wände nicht mit Kalk beworfen sind, so verstärkt diese kunstlose Bauart das ärmliche Ansehen des Ortes. (p. 316)

[Llangollen lies on the River Dee in a beautiful valley which takes its name from the little town. It is a small, dirty town. The houses are low and poorly built, the streets narrow and poorly laid. To the north-east lies a long bank of bare, grey chalk hills; it is from here that the inhabitants of Llangollen source the materials from which the houses of the little town are built. In some cases, the stones have, however, been used in their raw, unworked form, just as they were gathered up, and walls have not been rendered with lime so that the artless nature of this building style heightens the impoverished appearance of the place]

The town, although effectively embedded in the landscape by the prominent use of local materials, nevertheless fails to match the natural beauty of its surroundings. This stark, realistic description opens a discussion of the state of Wales and Welsh society when compared to England. Initially, the argument seems to condemn Wales as substandard:

> Ein Reisender, der von dieser Seite zuerst in Nordwales eintritt, bemerkt mit Erstaunen den wunderbaren Abstand äußerlicher Cultur, der noch so auffallend zwischen den Welschen und Englischen Volke nach einem so langen Vereine fortdauert. (p. 317)

> [A traveller who is entering Wales from this side notices with astonishment the amazing difference in terms of outward refinement which is still so striking between the Welsh and the English after such a long period of union]

This emphasizes both unity and disunity, suggesting both reticence (on the Welsh side) and failed influence (on the English), highlighting Wales's limited progress towards modernity. This polarized view results in a conflicted reading of Wales: Goede's words suggest that English refinement is yet to rub off on Wales, inferring therefore that Wales is in need of advancement, yet the lack of refinement is not necessarily negative. With the discourse of difference firmly established, the exotic, implicitly positive essence of Wales is soon foregrounded:

> Glaubte er nur in eine andere Provinz desselben Landes zu reisen, so sieht er sich mit Verwunderung unter einem fremden Volke, das sich ihm durch Sprache, äußeres Ansehen, Sitten und Lebensweise in einer ganz eigenthümlichen Verschiedenheit von dem Englischen darstellt. (p. 317)

> [If he thinks he is simply travelling to a province of the same country, then he will be astonished to find himself amongst a foreign people which differs quite peculiarly in language, physical appearance, customs and lifestyle from the English way]

Goede sees this difference as characterizing the lower and middle classes, not the wealthy, who are heavily Anglicized, if not actually of English extraction (p. 317). Overall, the impression given is of an economically and socially underdeveloped country which sits in stark contrast to the industrial boom being experienced across the border. At the same time, however, that contrast allows the survival of an alterity, the authenticity which accords Wales its Romantic edge. The emerging fear, as the century progresses, is that this alterity is under threat.

Such is the melancholic impact of his encounter with Llangollen and the negative contrast with England that Goede is driven to seek solace in the surrounding landscape and it is here that his affection for Wales begins to take root. The first encounter with what he goes on to extoll as the sublime Welsh landscape is on a walk to the ruined castle of Dinas Bran, which he praises highly, comparing the surrounding landscape, as many French counterparts do, to that encountered on an earlier visit to Switzerland (p. 319). He describes the scene in great detail and advises his reader on how to get the most from a visit in terms of appreciating the sublime aspect of the area. He is similiarly enthusiastic about Valle Crucis Abbey, emphasizing repeatedly the picturesque nature of what he finds there (p. 325). Drawing on this aesthetic in a visual context, Goede frames the landscape of Wales in terms which recall the work of his contemporary the artist Caspar David Friedrich (1774–1840), here pre-echoing the imagery of paintings such as *Abtei im Eichenwald* [Abbey in the Oak Forest], with their Romantic depiction of ruin and decay. This is supported by Maurer, who highlights in relation to Goede's text the fact that 'der genießende Blick des Reisenden der eines Malers ist' [the appreciative eye of the traveller is that of a painter] and notes that Goede's hosts in fact mistook him for such.[18] Although Friedrich's painting dates from 1809, Goede's 1805 description of the abbey stems from the same aesthetic, inspired by the work of Claude Lorrain (1600–1682) and other painters of the sublime, and speaks to the same values as those espoused by German Romantic artists, writers and thinkers. The ongoing emphasis on the landscape is interspersed with comment on the lack of industry and development, yet when Goede finally finds the latter in the shape of the Anglesey copper mines, he shows little interest (p. 357). The prevailing Romantic aesthetic of his native Germany therefore dominates his appreciation of Wales and sets the tone for many subsequent German narratives.

Goede's reading of Wales is further embedded in the broader Romantic cultural context in relation to the next site to be visited, the Pillar of Eliseg, near Llangollen. Here Goede encounters an English scholar who engages him in conversation about the need to record and preserve ancient Welsh culture, reflecting the ongoing cultural revival underway

18   Maurer, *Wales*, p. 16.

at the time led by figures such as Iolo Morganwg and societies such as the Cymmrodorion. In an attempt to place the debate in a broader context, Goede asks his new acquaintance if this interest in Welsh culture can be seen to relate to the widespread enthusiasm for MacPherson's *Ossian* (p. 328). The English scholar agrees that there is a clear link, but then goes on to place Welsh literature in a different, undoubtedly more exotic light. The underlying aesthetic fits with that expressed in the German Romantic reading of both northern and southern European cultures, epitomized in August Wilhelm Schlegel's essay 'Über das spanische Theater' [On Spanish Theatre], which appeared in his brother Friedrich's periodical, *Europa*, in 1803.[19] Goede's new companion, like Schlegel, presents the literature of southern Europe as one influenced by climate and the passionate character of its people and goes on to draw Wales into this as a northern parallel to the southern ideal:

> Es ist, sagte der Fremde, als wären die Welschen Lieder auf einem viel wärmeren Boden entstanden, und als hätte die Liebe in diesen Gegenden eine so feurige Sprache geführt, wie im Süden von Europa. (pp. 328–29)

> ['It is', said the stranger, 'as if the Welsh songs had sprung from a much warmer soil, and as if love in these parts spoke with a passion equal to that of southern Europe']

Echoing Goede's affinity with the work of Caspar David Friedrich and the broader Romantic aesthetic, this alignment of Welsh culture with the Schlegelian reading of the European periphery places Wales in a Romantic, exoticized context from the outset.

The views of the English scholar stand out as one of the few more positive English appraisals of Welsh culture to be recounted in German narratives, highlighted by Goede no doubt for its close correlation with his own cultural stance. The like-minded Englishman goes on to recommend other sites to visit, advice which Goede follows (p. 329). This is an interesting dynamic: the German traveller being guided by an English counterpart to sites which will enhance his understanding of Wales and its culture. Indeed, the Englishman goes on to give a view on

---

19 The essay would go on to form the basis for the apotheosis of Spanish Golden Age theatre which was at the heart of August Wilhelm Schlegel's *Wiener Vorlesungen* [Vienna Lectures] of 1809. See August Wilhelm Schlegel, 'Wiener Vorlesungen', 'Erster Theil (1809)' and 'Zweiter Theil (1809)', in Stefan Knödler (ed.), *Vorlesungen über dramatische Kunst und Literatur (1809–1811)*, I: Text (Paderborn: Ferdinand Schöningh, 2018), pp. 1–152, 153–270.

the relative safety of Wales as opposed to Ireland, Goede's next planned destination (p. 332). This places Wales in context as an unthreatening yet unknown territory – a kind of benign exotic – when compared to the bandit-ridden anarchy of Ireland. It seems almost impossible for Goede to escape the English gaze in his encounter with Wales, whether in the positive terms of the gentleman scholar or the negative views expressed by his fellow coach passengers at the beginning of his Welsh narrative. It would appear that the Celtic nations of the British Isles, as viewed through English eyes, are in general subject to a polarized reading, valued at best for their historical cultural interest, at worst condemned for their backward nature and social depravity.

Yet, from all of this, what stands out to Goede is the Romantic nature of what he has seen. As he prepares to leave Llangollen, he reflects that 'Drei Tage waren mir hier wie drei heitere Träume vorübergezogen' (p. 332) [Three days had passed over me here like three days in a blissful dream]. The area, despite, or perhaps even because of, the stark contrast between the town and its surroundings, is presented as an escape:

> In der schönen romantischen Gegend von Llangollen findet ein heiterer, phantasiereicher Geist so vielfältigen Genuß, daß er hier wohl leichter als an irgend einem anderen Orte bestimmt werden kann, dem übrigen bunten Schauspiele der Welt zu entsagen und sich in die Einsamkeit dieser freundlichen Natur zurückzuziehen. (p. 333)

> [A merry, imaginative spirit will find such varied enjoyment in the beautiful romantic area around Llangollen that he is more likely here than anywhere else to decide to forego the rest of the world's colourful spectacle and withdraw into the solitude of this friendly nature]

Landscape and society are here placed in direct juxtaposition, the former providing respite from the hustle and bustle of the latter in a manner which speaks to the broader contemporary fashion for health-promoting outdoor activity to overcome the negative impact of the emerging urban, industrial environment.[20] As if to underline this dichotomy, the enthusiasm for the unique restorative atmosphere of the Welsh landscape is tempered upon arrival in Corwen, where the poverty encountered is, according to Goede, only to be rivalled by that found in Ireland (p. 337). As well as underlining the value of the Welsh landscape, this further reinforces a more general negative view of society in the Celtic nations. This extends to the north as well as to the west: although the influence of

20 See Maurer, *Wales*, p. 9.

Scotland is presented positively in the same passage, with the narrative of Goede's encounter with a Scotsman on the mail coach whose sense of humour kept the other passengers merrily entertained, the author is at pains to note that this is 'ganz gegen den gewöhnlichen Charakter seiner Landsleute' (p. 339) [quite contrary to the normal character of his compatriots].

The focus on both Ireland and Scotland here shows the beginnings of the development in the German context of a Celtic hierarchy as the three larger Celtic nations of the British Isles are compared both to their hegemonic neighbour and to each other. In this, Scotland sits apart as a place where travellers encounter both the uncomfortable mix of the sublime and abject poverty – as they do in Wales and Ireland – but also the sophistication of developments such as Edinburgh's New Town and an intellectual life of European renown. Ireland, for its part, could offer an equally long-standing intellectual tradition based around Dublin and the seminaries of the Catholic Church to contrast with the verdant fields, harsh coastline and downtrodden rural population. For the German observer, the evidence of similar progress in Wales is harder to find. Instead, the overwhelming sense which emerges from comparison with its near neighbours is of Wales as a place of alterity with few familiar touchstones for the travelling European intellectual seeking a framework within which to place this peripheral nation.

The alterity of Wales is often embodied in the people themselves. In the area around Llanrwst, for example, Goede encounters a beggar girl on horseback. Wales and its people are exoticized through the unusual nature of this event – a beggar on horseback seems to contradict Goede's concept of need – the sense of foreignness underlined by the girl's poor command of English (p. 343). The uniqueness of Wales is further emphasized when, having travelled on via Conwy and Bangor, he finds himself stranded in Holyhead awaiting the ferry to Ireland due to bad weather. This enforced sojourn gives rise to further comment on the cultural and social alterity of Wales. He notes, for example, the prevalence of harpists in the hostelries of north Wales, describing them as 'Abkömmlinge der Barden' (p. 358) [descendants of the Bards]. This link to the culture of the past leads him to reflect once more on the general character of the Welsh, a character grounded in their inherent otherness:

> Es wird vieles vom Welschen Volke erzählt, was wunderbar scheint; wer aber auch nur einen Theil von Nordwales und einige Charakterzüge seiner

Bewohner kennen gelernt, wird sich geneigt fühlen, selbst auffallenden Berichten von ihren Eigenheiten Glauben beizumessen. (p. 359)

[Much is said of the Welsh people which seems wonderful; whoever comes to know only a part of north Wales and the characteristics of its inhabitants will feel compelled to lend credence to even the most remarkable reports of their peculiarities]

Goede is aware that this uniqueness is under threat from influences coming from England but nevertheless acknowledges 'der antike Nationalgeist' (p. 360) [the ancient national spirit] as something which persists in north Wales. This initially seems to suggest a negative isolation, describing a people bound to their ancient customs and entirely unsuited to the new industrial world, yet as he goes on to characterize their relationship with England the idea of tradition emerges as a positive, presenting a people defined by their modest character and aversion to ostentation which sets them at odds with their English neighbours:

Bei dieser Classe der Einwohner von Nordwales zeigt sich noch gegenwärtig eine fast unüberwindliche Scheu vor allem Fremden und eine Abneigung gegen die Engländer, die sie weniger beneiden (den das Welsche Volk ist sehr anspruchslos und genugsam) als wegen ihres Stolzes hassen. (pp. 359–60)

[Amongst this class of inhabitant of north Wales there is currently visible an almost insurmountable fear of everything foreign and an aversion to the English whom they do not so much envy (for the Welsh people are very undemanding and modest) but rather hate because of their pride]

England emerges as the negative pole in this comparison, leaving Wales to uphold its ancient ways as the positive defender of tradition. The resultant isolation of the Welsh is presented in part as a quasi-Herderian idyll where generations hold together bound by the ancient language and the ancient songs they sing (p. 360). For this reason, Goede argues, English culture has been unable to secure a foothold in many towns and villages. It is also the reason, he suggests, that Nonconformism, of which he has a very low opinion, has been able to take such a firm hold across the whole country, playing to the melancholic nature of the Welsh (p. 365). However, as Goede notes in highly critical terms, if the English government has an issue with this, then it is a problem of its own making:

Jeder aufmerksame Beobachter wird aber auch gestehen müssen, daß sich die Englische Regierung nicht gleichgültiger gegen die Cultivirung des Welschen Volkes hätte zeigen können, als es bis jetzt geschehen ist. Sind Schulen errichtet worden? Hat man für die Verbesserung des Volksunterrichtes durch gebildete und anständige Geistliche gesorgt? (pp. 360–61)

[Every alert observer will also have to agree, however, that the English government could not have been more disinterested in the cultivation of the Welsh people than it has been up to now. Have schools been built? Has anyone sought to improve the education of the people through the appointment of educated and decent clergy?]

Goede is at pains to note that this call for necessary improvement need not lead to the eradication of Welsh culture but should rather be aimed at enabling it to develop. Had the English attitude to Wales been different, then perhaps the spread of what he regards as the negative influence of the Chapel might have been stemmed. Instead, it has arrived to fill the void. Goede further questions the *laissez-faire* attitude of the English government to Wales and concludes that it is because of this approach, born of arrogance, that in Wales, but also in Ireland and the colonies, the English are regarded with such disdain. Instead of making an effort to build up a positive relationship between 'Sieger und Besiegten' (p. 361) [victor and vanquished] in these colonized nations, they have done little more than ride roughshod over indigenous cultures in an attempt to bring them into line with the English way. In the Welsh context, he cites the imposition of a legal system worded in English to govern whole areas where Welsh is the main and often only language understood (p. 364). Goede is the first, but not the last, to deploy such an overtly colonial, power-oriented discourse in describing the relationship between Wales and England. In so doing, ironically, he uses and cannot escape the English prism to garner his views on Wales but is nevertheless ultimately critical of the impact of English influence on its peripheral neighbour. England emerges as a threat to the exotic, Romantic Wales he has come to appreciate, flaws and all.

Goede's text lays the foundation for the German reading of Wales and is very much a product of its time. Its influence is evident in the work of subsequent travellers such as writer Wilhelm Benecke (1776–1837), whose letters written on a trip through Wales on the way to Ireland in 1816 were later published in *Wilhelm Benecke's Lebensskizze und Briefe* (1850) [Wilhelm Benecke's Biography and Letters].[21] Here, the Romantic reading

---

21   Levin Anton Wilhelm Benecke, *Wilhelm Benecke's Lebensskizze und Briefe*, ed. anon., 2 vols (Dresden: Druck der Teubner'schen Offizin, 1850), I, pp. 120–29.

dominates and shows how a narrative of Wales as a Romantic nation is gaining currency with a German-speaking readership. Referencing Goede's descriptions, Benecke is overcome by the beauty of the Vale of Llangollen and moved to tears at the sight of Valle Crucis Abbey (p. 122), before travelling on to the sublime landscape of Capel Curig and Snowdon (p. 125). For Benecke, who spent many years living in England, the Romantic tour of north Wales, set out by Goede for a German-speaking readership, would have been underpinned by the British Romantic reading of the same, in particular through key figures such as the poet William Wordsworth (1770–1850) and artist J.M.W. Turner (1775–1851). That reading is established in the German appreciation of the British Isles from this point onwards and remains a constant as the century progresses, one which leads ultimately to the mid-century tourist boom and associated concern on the part of many later German travellers for the survival of the Welsh language and culture.

Emerging in parallel to the development of the Romantic reading of Wales, another group of texts in this early period have a different emphasis, with detailed discussion of Wales as the site of industrial development. This approach draws out the second, to some degree contradictory, reading of Wales in the first half of the nineteenth century as a nation on the cusp of a much-needed shift towards modernity. Following on from Lentin's study of copper mining on Anglesey, Phillip Andreas Nemnich's *Neueste Reise durch England, Schottland und Ireland: Hauptsächlich in Bezug auf Produkte, Fabriken und Handlung* (1807) [Most Recent Journey through England, Scotland and Ireland: Mainly in Relation to Products, Factories and Methods] is indicative of this trend with its focus on the development of mining and commerce across Wales.[22] Nemnich (1764–1822) was an encylopaedist and lexicographer and accordingly displays a wealth of knowledge of the country he is visiting. Indeed, it is occasionally hard to distinguish what is gleaned first-hand and what is derived from other sources. The tone is largely devoid of personal comment, remaining factual throughout, providing a German readership with an impression of Wales as a site of imminent change, a development which can only be for the best in this backward location. Nemnich was widely read, but perhaps the most influential text of the period is Samuel Heinrich Spiker's *Reise durch England,*

---

22   Philipp Andreas Nemnich, *Neueste Reise durch England, Schottland und Ireland: Hauptsächlich in Bezug auf Produkte, Fabriken und Handlung* (Tübingen: J.G. Cotta, 1807), pp. 281–304.

Wales und Schottland im Jahre 1816 [A Journey through England, Wales and Scotland in the Year 1816], which was published in Leipzig in 1818 and soon translated into English as a notable example of how a foreign traveller appreciated British progress.[23]

Spiker (1786–1858) was a well-connected scholar and librarian to Friedrich Wilhelm II of Prussia who resided for a time in London in the years following the Napoleonic Wars. It was during this period that he travelled around the British Isles, publishing his narrative in two volumes with a dedication to his friends in England. Despite covering much of the same territory, he takes a different approach to Goede with a more practical, less aesthetic tone, more in line with the post-Napoleonic age in which he was writing. In so doing, his work reflects other changes in relation to the sociopolitical situation in the German-speaking lands, where, in the post-Napoleonic context, there was both an understandable desire for peace and order but also a drive for progress to ensure the re-establishment of stable government and a viable economy. As the various German-speaking states organized themselves to form the German Confederation following the Congress of Vienna in 1815, there remained an element of competition between them and paradigms of success were actively sought. One manifestation of this was a number of high-level, state-sponsored visits to the British Isles, some of which brought travellers to Wales as a site experiencing great change.

The emphasis of these post-Napoleonic texts is rarely cultural; difference of any sort is incidental to the discussion of progress. Arriving in Llangollen from the familiarity of England in 1816, Spiker was certainly aware that Wales was in some ways different and opens his narrative with a negative comparison between the standard of hotel rooms in Wales and their English counterparts (p. 25), while noting at the same time the generally welcoming nature of the Welsh people (p. 27). In general, however, the physical and cultural alterity of Wales in terms of landscape, heritage and customs is rarely discussed and there are, despite the explicit reference to Wales in the title, occasional conflations of Wales with England (p. 54). The main focus of Spiker's text is instead engineering and architecture, although his

---

23 Samuel Heinrich Spiker, *Reise durch England, Wales und Schottland im Jahre 1816*, 2 vols (Leipzig: Göschen, 1818), II, pp. 23–115. Translations are taken from: Samuel Heinrich Spiker, *Travels through England, Wales and Scotland in the Year 1816*, trans. anon., 2 vols (London: Lackington, Hughes, Harding, Mavor and Jones, 1820), II. For a discussion of the translation, see Tully, 'Pride in their Port'.

narrative remains couched in the contemporary aesthetic, in as much as he makes frequent passing references to the Romantic nature of the landscape, but this is muted. Descriptions are appreciative, but not effusive, the tone employed sufficient to highlight the grandeur of the scene without recourse to the hyperbole seen in Goede. Finding himself shrouded in mist in the highly Romantic surroundings of Llangollen, an experience which might have, in the hands of Goede or, later, Pückler-Muskau, illicited a Friedrich-esque reverie, Spiker's focus is instead on the practical implications for his plans to visit Valle Crucis Abbey, not the aesthetic impact of this essentially Romantic scene (p. 62). Indeed, earlier in his narrative, Spiker criticizes the excessive praise heaped on such Welsh sites in earlier accounts (p. 52). His sources as cited are primarly English, such as Pennant and George Nicholson (1760–1825),[24] but he also references Goede's description of the Pillar of Eliseg, which he does not have time to visit himself (p. 65 n.).

Like Goede, Spiker immediately points to the underdeveloped nature of Wales. Here, however, there is no positive side but rather an emphasis on the efforts then underway to improve infrastructure. Throughout Spiker pays a high level of attention to the act of travel itself, prompted by the fascination he shows for the work of Thomas Telford, whose efforts were by this time impacting hugely on the ease with which the traveller could explore north Wales.[25] In fact, at times Spiker's text becomes more about the impact of Telford on Wales than about Wales itself. He is the first German traveller to mention the Scottish engineer and even claims to know him personally (p. 66 n.). Later in his journey, Spiker comes across Telford's new road under construction along the banks of the River Llugwy. He describes the difficulties faced in detail and discusses the project with some of the workers, marvelling at the speed of construction (p. 53). Similarly appreciative detail is provided in relation to the Pontcysyllte Aqueduct, built by Telford and opened in 1805 (pp. 65–66). Spiker's normally reserved praise is cast aside when describing 'diesen talentvollen, kenntnissreichen und höchst liebens-würdigen Mann' (p. 66 n.) ['this most amiable gentleman, so well known for his great talents and scientific aquirements' (p. 51 n.)].

This marks the beginning of the adulation of the engineer which becomes a feature of German travel writing of the period until at least

---

24   The second edition of Nicholson's *The Cambrian Traveller's Guide and Pocket Companion* (London: Nicholson, 1813) had recently appeared.

25   See L.T.C. Rolt, *Thomas Telford* (Stroud: The History Press, 2008 [1958]).

the 1840s. Telford is presented as the architect of a modernization drive in Wales – albeit primarily for the benefit of English trade – bringing modernity to a recalcitrant, underdeveloped and passive country. His legacy, in particular the Menai Suspension Bridge and Pontcysyllte Aqueduct, is a repeated focus of interest. The Menai Suspension Bridge is met with particular enthusiasm as evidence of British technological prowess. The desirability of a bridge across the Menai Strait was raised in Küttner's 1791 text but soon discounted as an unlikely development as the English government would never pay for such a project (p. 57). The fact that the converse proved to be the case and that the bridge provided by Telford was so impressive was an awe-inspiring development for most German travellers to Wales, one which they often struggled to contextualize, placing the bridge somewhere between the Romantic and industrial. Early commentators, however, such as Johann Heinrich Meidinger (1792–1867), writing in his *Briefe von einer Reise durch England, Schottland und Irland im Frühjahr und Sommer, 1820* (1821) [Correspondence from a Journey through England, Scotland and Ireland in the Spring and Summer of 1820], centre primarily on the feat of construction itself.[26] Once opened in 1826, the bridge continued to astound. A writer known simply as Landbaumeister [Master Builder] Wedding noted in an article shortly afterwards that the bridge was an 'erstaunenswürdige Werk' [an astounding work], located, tellingly, 'in North Wales, England'.[27] Later writers, such as Johann Gottfried Kohl and Carl Carus, both writing in 1844,[28] go into great detail on the construction and social and economic impact of the bridge in particular. However, Spiker is unique amongst German travellers in claiming personal contact with Telford and his narrative is one of the few to capture the experience of road travel in north Wales in both the pre- and post-Telford eras.

Spiker's journey along the north Wales coast, although uncomfortable, enables a detailed commentary on the various small towns and sites he

---

26 Heinrich Meidinger, *Briefe von einer Reise durch England, Schottland und Irland im Frühjahr und Sommer, 1820* (Stuttgart and Tübingen: Cotta, 1821), pp. 194–98.

27 Landbaumeister Wedding, 'Die Kettenbrücken über die Meerenge Menai, die von Aber-Conwy und Hammersmith', *Verhandlungen des Vereins zur Beförderung des Gewerbefleißes in Preußen*, 7 (1828): II. 'Eigene Abhandlungen und Auszüge aus fremden Werken', pp. 234–43.

28 The work of Kohl and Carus will be discussed in more detail below.

travels through before finally arriving in Bangor from where he then makes his way by boat to Caernarfon along the Menai Strait. Once again, Wales is seen through the prism of England, supplemented by comparisons with the traveller's native land. Confronted with the enormity of Caernarfon Castle, Spiker attempts to contextualize Wales in relation to architecture in particular. A detailed description of both town and castle draws parallels with German architectural style and there are repeated comparisons with what he has seen in England. The emphasis on architecture is present throughout his account with detailed descriptions of country houses and churches, as well as the many castles he visits, although Spiker seems unaware that these are in fact English castles once built in order to contain the local population. Comparisons are made with English buildings and these are often negative. In relation to Bangor Cathedral, for example, he notes that: 'Der Thron des Bischofs ist an Pracht mit denen seiner englischen Amtsbrüder nicht im Entferntesten zu vergleichen' (II, pp. 47–48) ['The place appropriated for the Bishop is not to be compared for elegance in the remotest degree with those of his official brethren in England'; II, pp. 2–3]. The generally negative comparison of Wales with England and emphasis on engineering and the work of Telford point to an understanding of Wales as an underdeveloped opportunity, somewhere ripe for exploitation and modernization.

Spiker's views are echoed in a number of subsequent texts, many focusing almost exclusively on the development of Wales while all but ignoring its culture and language. For example, Johann von Österreich (1782–1859), travelling in the same year as Spiker, notes in his diary the desirability and impact of new canals and other infrastructure improvements,[29] while engineer Joseph von Baader (1763–1835), also travelling in 1816, makes much of the developing industrial railways and provides a detailed account of their construction and design for the benefit of readers at home.[30] A particularly notable comparative stance

---

29 Johann von Österreich, *'Ein Land, wo ich viel gesehen': Aus dem Tagebuch der England-Reise 1815/16*, ed. Alfred Ableitinger, Meinhard Brunner and Gerhard Dinacher (Graz: Selbstverlag der Historischen Landeskommission für Steiermark, 2010), pp. 232–34.

30 Joseph von Baader, 'Geschichte und Beschreibung der englischen Eisenbahnen – ihre Kosten – ihre Wirkung – ihre Vorzüge vor den gewöhnlichen Straßen und vor den schiffbaren Kanälen – ihre Mängel und Unbequemlichkeiten', *Polytechnisches Journal*, 7:1 (1822), pp. 1–52.

in the context of the Celtic nations emerges in the narrative provided by architect and artist Karl Friedrich Schinkel (1781–1841), who travelled through England, Scotland and Wales in 1826 and recorded his experiences in a journal and letters to family members which were eventually published in 1862.[31] Here, there is a marked difference in his appreciation of Scotland and Wales. In the case of the former, there is an effusive delight in the beauty of the landscape and the customs of the people. Schinkel was particularly taken with the landscape and atmosphere of the Northern Isles, recording his impressions in a series of starkly beautiful drawings. Yet his true enthusiasm is reserved not for the Scottish countryside, but later, during his visit to Wales, for Telford, the Scottish engineer whose two suspension bridges at Conwy and the Menai Strait had only recently opened. He is quite literally astounded, describing the Menai Suspension Bridge as 'ein bewunderungswürdiges Werk' ['a wonderful daring work'], taken aback by the 'die Colossalität des Gegenstandes' (p. 165) ['hugeness of the thing' (p. 188)]. His drawings of both suspension bridges are detailed and carefully executed but his broader understanding of their location is notable for its paucity. In contrast to his response to Scotland, Schinkel seems almost unaware of the existence of a different culture in Wales. No mention is made of the language and he refers throughout to his presence in 'England'. There is no evidence of any emotive response to his Welsh surroundings, his descriptions being often bland and concise. His narrative gives the impression that the march of industrialization through Wales is a force for the good, that Wales is a fitting blank canvas for exploitation by contemporaries such as Telford. Carl von Oeynhausen (1795–1865) and Heinrich von Dechen (1800–1889), travelling a decade later, provide a similar level of detail on the emerging passenger rail network in their *Ueber Schienenwege in England: Bemerkungen gesammelt auf einer Reise in den Jahren 1826 und 1827* (1829) [On the Railways of England: Observations Gathered on a Journey in the Years 1826 and 1827],[32] while

31   See Karl Friedrich Schinkel, *Die Reise nach Frankreich und England im Jahre 1826*, ed. Reinhard Wegener (Munich and Berlin: Deutscher Kunstverlag, 1990), p. 165. Translation taken from: *'The English Journey': Journal of a Visit to France and Britain in 1826*, trans. F. Gayna Walls, ed. David Bindman and Gottfried Riemann (New Haven and London: Yale University Press, 1993), p. 188.

32   Carl von Oeynhausen and Heinrich von Dechen, *Ueber Schienenwege in England: Bemerkungen gesammelt auf einer Reise in den Jahren 1826 und 1827* (Berlin: G. Reimer, 1829), pp. 125–27, 130–32, 145–50.

Johann Friedrich Ludwig Hausmann (1782–1859) focuses on factories and industrial sites in his diary in 1829.[33] Others show some awareness of the cultural context despite their focus on industry and engineering, but this still tends to place Wales in a negative light. In Meidinger's 1821 text, for example, the backward nature of Wales is emphasized through juxtaposition in his response to travelling back towards the English border 'und das alte, hoch cultivierte England mit seinen weiten Fluren, freundlichen Dörfern und schönen Menschen' (p. 198) [and the old, highly cultivated England with its wide meadows, friendly villages and handsome people], suggesting that Wales's landscape and society are, by contrast, to be avoided.

This negative reading of Wales as a place requiring modernization continues well into the 1830s and 1840s. Georg Dittler (1797–1835), travelling in 1830, notes the developments in the waterways in particular in his *Hydrotechnische Bemerkungen gesammelt auf einer Reise durch England, Holland, Nord- und Süddeutschland im Jahre 1830* (1835) [Hydrotechnical Observations Gathered on a Journey through England, Holland, and Northern and Southern Germany in the Year 1830].[34] In so doing, he presents the Welsh countryside as subservient to the modernizing force of Telford's engineering. Although appreciative of the landscape, he draws attention to the way in which it helps to enhance the impression of the technology placed within it:

> Indessen ist nicht zu verkennen, daß die Naturschönheiten des romantischen Deethals sehr viel zur Erhebung dieses Bauwerks [Pontcysyllte-Aquädukt] beigetragen, und daß es vielleicht seine allgemeine Berühmtheit – wenigstens gewiss ein Theil davon – eben so sehr seiner ausgezeichnet schönen Umgebung, welche von Reisenden aller Stände und Nationen besucht zu werden pflegt, als seiner sinnreichen, zweckmässigen und kühnen Konstruktion zu verdanken haben mag. (p. 114)

33   Johann Friedrich Ludwig Hausmann, 'Oxford, und die Englischen Fabrikdistricte, im Februar 1829', in *Aus dem Tagebuche einer Reise durch Holland, Belgien, Frankreich und England, in den Jahren 1828 und 1829. Kleinigkeiten in bunter Reihe. Bemerkungen und Betrachtungen über Gegenstände der Natur und Kunst*, 2 vols (Göttingen: Verlag der Dieterichschen Buchhandlung, 1859), II, pp. 353–70.

34   Georg Dittler, *Hydrotechnische Bemerkungen gesammelt auf einer Reise durch England, Holland, Nord- und Süddeutschland im Jahre 1830. Nebst einer kurzen Biographie des Verfassers* (Karlsruhe: n.p., 1835), pp. 111–27.

[In all of this, it cannot be denied that the natural beauty of the Dee Valley contributes a great deal to the exaltation of this structure [Pontcysyllte Aqueduct], and that perhaps its general fame – at least a part thereof – is due just as much to its notably beautiful surroundings, visited by travellers of all classes and nationalities, as it is to its useful, functional and clever construction]

The natural setting is seen to enhance the technical achievement of man, rather than dwarfing it, which was the more common Romantic reading found in Goede and later writers such as Pückler-Muskau. Joseph Russegger (1802–1863), writing in 1840, takes the appreciation of the industrial potential of Wales a step further, presenting the landscape of the south as a series of exploitable locations and elements:

> Man hat Kohlen im Ueberflusse und auf unabsehbare Zeit; man besitzt in einzelnen Oertlichkeiten das erforderliche Kraftwasser und Gefälle für Maschinen; gute Straßen durchziehen das Land; [...] zwischen den Schornsteinen der grossartigen Etablissements ragen die Masten der Briggs empor, in den Rauchwolken der Oefen schwellen sich die Segel, wehen die Flaggen; kurz der Continentbewohner erhält Eindrücke, von denen er sich in seinem Lande kaum träumen liess.[35]

> [There is coal in abundance and available for years to come; there are individual locations with adequate water and waterfalls for machinery; good roads traverse the countryside; (...) between the chimneys of the great factories you can see the masts of the ships rising up, the sails billowing, the flags fluttering in the clouds of smoke from the ovens; in short, the inhabitant of the Continent experiences things of which he would scarcely dream in his own country]

Notable, however, in both Dittler's and Russegger's texts is the emergence of a distinct poeticization of the industrial landscape which echoes that found in the narratives of French travellers to the area. By the mid-century, this aesthetic appreciation of Wales's shift towards modernity has developed to such an extent that Carl Klocke (dates unknown), writing in 1850, is able to recommend the Dowlais smelting works and the landscape around them as a tourist site in itself.[36]

---

35 Joseph Russegger, *Reisen in Europa, Asien und Afrika: Mit besonderer Rücksicht auf die naturwissenschaftlichen Verhältnisse der betreffenden Länder, unternommen in den Jahren 1835 bis 1841* (Stuttgart: Schweizbart, 1841), pp. 459–79, 492–500 (p. 460).
36 Carl Klocke, *Dawlais Works, die Eisen- und Schienen-Walzwerke des Hauses John Guest, in London* (Stettin: Druck v. H. u. R. Graßmann, 1850), pp. 12–13.

By the 1830s a narrative of Wales was beginning to emerge, centred on the parallel foci of the Romantic and the industrial, the peripheral and the advance of modernity. Subsequent narratives can be seen to negotiate a path between these polarized readings, often by combining both aspects. Perhaps the most significant early text to do so is the travel account by Hermann von Pückler-Muskau, the well-known eccentric aristocrat and landscape gardener[37] who published the record of his tour of the British Isles in 1828 and 1829, long before his death, under the rather morbid title *Briefe eines Verstorbenen* (1830) [Correspondence of a Dead Man].[38] The text draws on both Goede's overtly Romantic reading and the more utilitarian works by Spiker and others, with an emphasis on the workings of the many landed estates visited by the author. The text also makes explicit references to an emerging tourist industry with Pückler-Muskau contextualizing his action, itinerary and understanding of Wales within that frame. This is implicitly acknowledged by the author himself as he makes clear he is at pains not to fall into the trap 'eines Reisebeschreibers von Profession [...], der ennuyiren zu dürfen glaubt, wenn er unterrichtet' (p. 76) ['of a tour-writer by profession who thinks himself privileged to bore as he instructs' (p. 298)]. Yet this dismissal of travel writing is somewhat contrived. Pückler-Muskau is himself a highly self-conscious traveller whose narrative often focuses on the Romantic nature of the landscape, effectively using the places visited as a backdrop for his own idiosyncratic posturing and outrageous adventures. He consciously creates a version of these places to suit his own interests, noting of the scenes witnessed from his coach that 'erregen sie meine Fantasie bald Ernst, bald heiter, tragisch oder komisch, und mit grossem Vergnügen male ich dann in mir selbst die gegebenen Skizzen aus' (p. 14) ['they awaken fancies serious and gay, tragic and comic; and I find an intense pleasure in filling up the sketches thus presented to my eye' (p. 276)]. In this context, it is notable that his first reference to Wales is effusively positive:

37   See Peter James Bowman, *The Fortune Hunter: A German Prince in Regency England* (Oxford: Signal Books, 2010).

38   Translations are taken from the first volume of *A Tour in England, Ireland and France in the Years 1828 and 1829 with remarks on the manners and customs of the inhabitants, and anecdotes of distinguished public characters in a series of letters by a German Prince*, trans. Sarah Austin, 4 vols (Philadelphia: Carey and Lea, 1833).

Die schönste Wirklichkeit erwartete mich dagegen heute früh in Wales. Der Traum der Wolken schien mir im voraus die Herrlichkeit des Thales von Llangollen verkunden haben zu wollen, eine Gegend, die nach meinem Urtheil alle Schönheiten der Rheinländer weit übertrifft, und dabei eine ganz besondere Originalität in den ungewöhnlich geformten Spitzen und jähen Abhängen der Berge ausspricht. (p. 15)

[The most beautiful reality, however, awaited me this morning in Wales. The vision of clouds seemed to have been the harbinger of the magnificence of the vale of Llangollen, – a spot which, in my opinion, far surpasses all the beauties of the Rhine-Land, and has, moreover, a character quite its own, from the unusual form of the peaked tops and rugged declivities of its mountains (p. 277)]

This sets Wales apart from the outset as somewhere essentially different as the exotic is once more foregrounded alongside a positive comparison with his native German lands which, unusually, positions Wales as superior. Nature, ancient ruins, country houses and even industry combine to form what Pückler-Muskau sees as a unique environment, one he places immediately in a Romantic context with descriptions such as 'romantisch' [romantic], 'malerisch' [picturesque] and 'majestätisch' [majestic] peppering his narrative.

Pückler-Muskau is certainly aware of the cultural differences which surround him. There are lengthy, lively diatribes on contemporary social debates; the Welsh language is mentioned frequently and compared to the cawing of crows (p. 26); similarities are noted between the *eisteddfoddau* and the contests of the *Minnesänger* (p. 140); and there are some passing references to myths and legends, including a reprise of the history of the title 'Prince of Wales' (first narrated for a German audience by Lentin) (p. 75), a lengthy rendition of the legend of Beddgelert (pp. 120–22) and a brief mention of looking for specifically Arthurian locations (p. 114). All of this notwithstanding, there is no sense that Pückler-Muskau is deeply interested in the cultural alterity of Wales. Instead, he positions himself dramatically in the landscape like an actor on a stage, including episodes such as the drinking of champagne on the summit of Snowdon, an act of apparent arrogance which jars with the earlier descriptions of poverty in his narrative (p. 70). The emphasis throughout is on the theatricality of the Welsh landscape. Indeed, Pückler-Muskau explicitly uses the term 'Theaterdecoration' (p. 110) ['theatrical representation' (p. 308)]. This parallels his later treatment of the Irish landscape and culture in the same text. The default for his appreciation of Wales is thoroughly Romantic and he goes to some lengths to place himself in that context.

For example, relating his ascent of Snowdon, Pückler-Muskau describes the following scene which once again recalls the work of Caspar David Friedrich:

> Aussichten entschädigten mich nicht, den von Wolken ganz umschleiert, konnte ich kaum 20 Schritt weit vor mir sehen, und in diesem geheim-nißvollen clair obscur erreichte ich auch den ersehnten Gipfel, zu dem man über einen schmalen Felsenkamm gelangt. Ein Steinhaufen, in dessen Mitte eine hölzerne Säule steht, ist als Wahrzeichen aufgerichtet. Ich glaubte hier der Erscheinung meines Doppelgängers zu begegnen, als ein junger Mann aus dem Nebel hervortrat, der mir selbst völlig glich, NB. wie ich aussah, als ich vor 16 Jahren in den Schweizer-Alpen umherirrte. (p. 69)

> [I was not compensated for my sufferings by the view, for, shrouded as I was in clouds, I could hardly see twenty paces before me. In this mysterious 'clair obscur' I reached the wished for summit, the way to which lies over an irregular wall of rocks. A pile of stones, in the centre of which is a wooden pillar, marks the highest point. I thought I met my wraith, as a young man emerged from the mist who precisely resembled me, that is to say when I wandered over the Swiss Alps sixteen years ago (p. 295)]

The image of the traveller emerging from the mist evokes Friedrich's famous painting *Wanderer über dem Nebelmeer* (Wanderer above the Sea of Fog, c. 1818), and firmly ties the experience at the summit of Snowdon to the Romantic aesthetic in similar terms to those adopted by Goede some twenty-five years earlier. There is an implicit play also on the Romantic trope of the *Doppelgänger*, evoking both the author's double in the guise of the young man and Wales's double in the oft-repeated comparison with Switzerland. Further echoing Goede and his experiences in the countryside around Llangollen, Pückler-Muskau follows this with a description of a quasi-spiritual experience:

> Nach vollendeter Libation aber betete ich von Herzen. Es waren nicht Worte – aber innige Gefühle, unter denen der Wünsch lebhaft hervortrat, dass es doch Gottes Wille seyn möge, es Dir auf Erden gut ergehen zu lassen, und dann auch mir – if possible – und siehe! ein zierliches Lamm kamm durch die Wolkenschleier heran geklettert, und die Nebel theilten sich, und vor uns lag, in zuckenden Sonnenblitzen einen Moment lang klar die vergoldete Erde. (pp. 70–71)

> [After my libation was completed, the prayers I sent up were not words, but profound emotions; the most fervent amongst which was the wish,

that it might be Heaven's will to grant happiness on earth to you, and, if possible, to me; – and see, a pretty lamb sprang forth from the cloudy veil, and the mist opened and rolled away, and before us lay the earth suddenly gilded by a momentary gleam of sunshine (p. 296)]

This Romantic evocation of Wales as a spiritual haven sits in stark contrast to the social reality of life for the Welsh populace. The backward nature of both Welsh and Irish society is referenced throughout, highlighting once more a need for modernization and progress and reiterating the negative view of the socio-economic state of the Celtic nations. This is underlined by multiple references in the text to Telford's work. Although the engineer is not mentioned by name, reference is made to the Menai Suspension Bridge, the Pontcysyllte Aqueduct, the impressive new road to Holyhead and even the toll houses and distinctive sunburst design gates used along it. The positive impact of the road in particular is evident in the description of Llangollen, which offers notably better conditions than those described earlier by Goede (p. 16). Despite its role in bringing modernity to north Wales, Telford's work is nevertheless romanticized in Pückler-Muskau's text. The Menai Suspension Bridge is labelled 'das achte Wunder der Welt' (p. 91) [the eighth wonder of the world (p. 302)] and is described as blending with the scenery in a true, harmonious fusion of human endeavour and nature:

> Ich werde gleich Gelegenheit haben, sie Dir näher zu beschreiben, von hier sieht sie aus, als sey sie von Spinnen in die Luft gewebt. Hast Du bei diesem abentheuerlichen Anblick menschlichen Wirkens eine Zeit lang verweilt, so stellt sich, Dir gegenüber, eins der mannichfältigsten und grössten Schauspiele der Natur dar – die ganze Kette des Gebirges von Wales, das unmittelbar aus dem Wasser empor steigt, – hell und nahe genug, um Wälder, Dörfer und Schluchten deutlich zu unterscheiden, und in einer Lange von zehn deutschen Meilen sich ausbreitet. (pp. 91–92)

> [I shall have an opportunity hereafter of describing it more nearly; from this point it looked as if spiders had woven it from the air. After I had satisfied myself with gazing at this romantic specimen of human power and skill, I turned to one of the greatest and most varied works of nature; – the entire range of the Welsh mountains, which rises immediately from the water, distinct and near enough clearly to distinguish woods, villages, and valleys, and stretches along an extent of ten miles (p. 302)]

While the natural landscape clearly inspires Pückler-Muskau, the true focus of his professional interest is the many estates he visits and on which he provides a huge amount of detail. This draws him back to the influence of England with these estates and the aesthetic which shapes them forming part of a cultural dialogue foreign to the Welsh travellees he encounters on his travels. Pückler-Muskau comments on these estates as being essentially English in their operation and habits (p. 44), the refinement this suggests juxtaposed with regular references to the poverty found amongst the Welsh rural classes. This results in an ambivalent view of the English couched once more in colonial terms, referring to them pejoratively as 'fremde Eindringliche' (p. 72) ['foreign invaders' (p. 296)] and 'bankrotte Engländer' (p. 123) ['bankrupt Englishmen' (p. 392)] out to exploit Wales for their own benefit. Yet, despite this apparent criticism of English attempts to modernize Wales, there is a sense that Pückler-Muskau is a willing part of the civilizing force being brought to bear on the Welsh via the improvements in industry and infrastructure noted by many other travellers. This is highlighted by his lending of English-language novels to the Welsh girl serving at his hostelry in Caernarfon (p. 78). As this might suggest, like Goede, his response to Wales in relation to its hegemonic neighbour is conflicted. He is critical of the English ruling classes for their absentee landlord approach (p. 124), but then accuses the Welsh for their lack of ambition (p. 122). His attitude to them is often distanced. There is some interaction with the locals but, with few exceptions, this is aimed at facilitating his activities rather than finding anything out about them. In this respect, Pückler-Muskau is just as guilty of looking down on the Welsh, adopting without challenge the negative view which has begun to emerge in relation to their socio-economic ambition. Considering this in the context of his critique of English governmental shortcomings, it becomes clear that Pückler-Muskau, like many others, finds it hard to muster a consistent view of the Welsh-English dynamic. The resultant narrative displays once more the ambivalence already seen in Goede's work, with Wales presented at once both positively and negatively, as both culturally different and socially underdeveloped.

Similar views are found in the correspondence of Felix Mendelssohn (1809–1847).[39] The composer visited Wales in 1829 as part of his tour of the British Isles, including Scotland and, of course, the Hebrides, a visit which inspired his famous *Hebrides Overture* (1833). His response to the Celtic nations echoes that of Schinkel. Whereas Scotland is

---

39   Felix Mendelssohn Bartholdy, *Briefe*, ed. Rudolf Elvers (Frankfurt am Main: Fischer, 1984), pp. 85–91.

described as 'sehr unvergeßlich' (p. 89) [quite unforgettable], the reaction to Wales is decidedly ambivalent. Prompted by the efforts of the harpist playing at his inn, Mendelssohn's first letter from Wales, written from Llangollen in August 1829, begins with an attack on all 'Nationalmusik' [national music] and 'Volksthum' (p. 85) [folkishness], claiming that it gives him toothache. The humorous tone this suggests is typical of his letter writing which, although engaging, still reveals a degree of frustration with his Welsh surroundings: the weather is of particular note, Mendelssohn describing one particular day as 'ein guter Tag, d.h. ich wurde nur dreimal nass' (p. 87) [a good day, that is to say, I only got wet three times]. He is nevertheless impressed by the landscape and describes Wales as 'ein wunderschönes Land' [a wonderfully beautiful country], noting however that 'das Format ist so klein' (pp. 90–91) [the format is so small]. Much of his time is spent travelling, often in poorly equipped coaches, and his main concerns centre on travel onwards from Wales, efforts which are either thwarted by bad weather, like a sea crossing to Anglesey and on to Ireland, or are the source of great excitement, such as his adventures on the railway network around Chester, Liverpool and Manchester. His view of Scotland as 'sehr unvergeßlich' finds no parallel here and his level of actual engagement with the culture of Wales is limited. He acknowledges the language but finds cultural solace for the most part in the company of his English hosts, the mining engineer John Taylor (1779–1863) and his family, at their country residence, Coed Du Hall at Rhydymwyn, near Mold.

While Mendelssohn's views were confined to private letters, Pückler-Muskau's account was widely read and his influence is felt in the work of a number of travellers visiting Wales shortly after he did. He is cited in the effusive diary entries on north Wales written by publisher Heinrich Brockhaus (1804–1874) in 1836,[40] and echoed closely in the *Cartons aus der Reisemappe eines deutschen Touristen* [Sketches from the Travel Portfolio of a German Tourist] published by Karl von Hailbronner (1789–1864) in 1837.[41] The links to the 1838 account provided by fellow landscape garden enthusiast, Austrian general Franz Ludwig von Welden (1782–1853), are also clear with an emphasis on the landed estates of

---

40   Rudolf Brockhaus, *Aus den Tagebüchern von Heinrich Brockhaus*, 5 vols (Leipzig: F.A. Brockhaus, 1884), I, pp. 314–15, 327–28.

41   Karl von Hailbronner, *Cartons aus der Reisemappe eines deutschen Touristen*, 3 vols (Stuttgart and Tübingen: Cotta, 1837), I, pp. 224–29, 234–42.

north Wales,[42] and there is a clear affinity, perhaps surprisingly, with the work of Georg Varrentrap (1809–1886), travelling through Wales to visit various medical institutions.[43] As this suggests, Pückler-Muskau's text, like Goede's, is instrumental in establishing the German narrative of Wales in the first half of the century. By this point, the main concerns and attitudes have been established: the struggle between tradition and modernity, the relationship to England and the emergence of tourism. The next extensive treatment of Wales in German travel writing, Johann Georg Kohl's *Reisen in England und Wales* (1844) [Travels in England and Wales], draws these elements together more fully.[44]

Kohl (1808–1878) was a historian and geographer who made his way to Bangor from Liverpool by boat in 1842, viewing the north Wales landscape from the sea in the first instance. His text foregrounds the experience of travel and engages with Wales as a tourist destination more explicitly than previous narratives. This emerges early on when he describes the trade in cheap telescopes on the ferry from Liverpool to Bangor with which passengers can better view the north Wales coast (p. 197). Equally, his own itinerary is driven by the emerging tourist trail, his first goal the ascent of Snowdon. On arrival in Bangor, Kohl boards another ferry destined for Caernarfon. This short trip leaves an impression on him as it draws out a number of the key aspects of the traveller's engagement with north Wales, namely, the landscape, Telford's work and the slate mining industry. He admires the Menai Suspension Bridge as they pass below, noting that 'Die Verhältnisse dieser Brücke [...] sind so ungeheuer, daß man darüber staunen muss' (p. 201) [The dimensions of this bridge (...) are so enormous that one can only marvel at them]. Yet he sees its majesty dwarfed by the immensity of the landscape:

42 Franz Ludwig Freiherr von Welden, 'Ueber dekorirende Landschafts-Gartenkunst, Anlagen sogenannter Natur- oder englischer Gärten und Gebäude, im großen, wie im kleinsten Maßstabe; ganz vorzüglich für Deutschland und die wohlhabendere Mittelklasse berechnet: Beschreibung eines englischen Landhauses und seiner Umgebung', *Allgemeine Bauzeitung mit Abbildungen für Architekten, Ingeneurs, Dekorateurs, Bauprofessionisten, Oekonomen, Bauunternehmer und Alle, die an den Fortschritten und Leistungen der neuesten Zeit an der Baukunst und den dahin einschlagenden Fächern Antheil nehmen*, 4 (1839), pp. 91–103.

43 Georg Varrentrapp, *Tagebuch einer medizinischen Reise nach England, Holland und Belgien* (Frankfurt am Main: Varrentrapp, 1839), pp. 411–18.

44 Johann Georg Kohl, *Reisen in England und Wales* (Dresden: Arnold, 1844), pp. 196–259.

Die Berge von Wales, die weite Fläche von Anglesea, die lange Menai-Strasse auf der einen Seite, das breite Meer auf der anderen, sind so gross, daß die Größe des merkwürdigen Menschenwerks dabei verkleinert erscheint. Allein wenn man in die Nähe der Brücke kommt, wenn man hinüberfährt, noch mehr aber, wenn man darunter weg segelt, empfängt man wohl einen Eindruck, der mit der Größe, Genialität und Schwierigkeit der Arbeit correspondirt. (p. 202)

[The mountains of Wales, the wide plain of Anglesey, the long Menai Strait on the one side, the wide sea on the other, are so grand that the size of this noteworthy human construct appears diminished. Only when one comes close to the bridge, when one drives across it and, even more so, when one sails under it, does one truly gain an impression which accords with the dimensions, ingenuity and difficulty of the work]

This clear juxtaposition of nature and modernity is carried forward in Kohl's descriptions of slate mining, which, while detailed, maintain the sense of awe found in his appreciation of his natural surroundings, with the feeling that despite attempts to industrialize, the sublime nature of Wales and the Welsh landscape will continue to dominate. This is evidenced in his highlighting of the prevalence of ancient ruins in Wales (p. 209) which sits in stark juxtaposition with the industrial processes he also observes (p. 206). Making a direct link between the expansion of industry and the development of tourism, Kohl quotes from an unacknowledged English source which highlights the improvements to travel and hospitality that have emerged as a result of both (p. 204). Further evidence of progress, such as the development of a new quay at Caernarfon, is cited as evidence of this (p. 206). Here, the development of Wales in terms of infrastructure and social conditions urged by earlier travellers can be seen to be gradually taking shape. Equally, however, Kohl is aware of the impact this will have on the local culture and customs. He notes the presence of mapping and measuring equipment everywhere as Wales is brought into line with the rest of the country, effectively being standardized and to some extent de-exoticized (p. 228). It is as if he feels he is witnessing the last throes of Wales as an entity apart from England, the final acts of incorporation being experienced as he writes.

Echoing the critical colonial discourse of both Goede and Pückler-Muskau, Kohl is particularly incisive regarding the Welsh language and the fate of Welsh culture in general, conscious of the impact of what he terms 'englische Einwanderer' (p. 203) [English incomers]. He is aware also of the Anglicization of south Wales in contrast to the prevalence of

Welsh monolingualism in the north and makes an important comparison with Ireland and Scotland:

> Die wälsche Sprache scheint immer viel energischeren Widerstand gegen das Englische geleistet zu haben, als das Irische und Hochschottische. Es ist dieß um so merkwürdiger, da Wales nur als ein kleines Anghänsel von England erscheint und auf einer so langen Linie mit diesem Lande verbunden ist, während Schottland den Hauptcentralpuncten der Entwickelung der englischen Sprache so viel entfernter lag und Irland durch Meere ganz davon geschieden war. (pp. 214–15)

> [The Welsh language always seems to have resisted the English language more energetically than Irish or Scots Gaelic. This is all the more notable given that Wales appears to be but a tiny adjunct to England and linked to this land by such a long border, whereas Scotland lay so much further away from the main areas of development of the English language and Ireland was entirely separated from it by sea]

The impact of geography on the survival of indigenous languages is not as Kohl would expect to find it. Despite its long border with England, Wales has been able to retain a linguistic cultural identity for far longer than its Celtic cousins. This suggests a particular sense of the exotic in relation to Wales but, further underlining the conflicted reading identified in other texts, it also recalls Urbain's notion of the endotic: Wales, as an 'Anghänsel' [adjunct] of England, should be familiar and yet it is not; or at least, not yet. The exoticism this suggests, positively viewed or otherwise, is, according to Kohl, inevitably under threat:

> Die Ausbreitung des englischen Luxus, des Verkehrs, des Handels, der Industrie, auf die wir oben hindeuteten, insbesondere aber die Verbesserung der Schulen und der Volkserziehung, werden am Ende auch diesen Theil von England ganz mit dem Mutterlande verschmelzen lassen. In diesen Schulen, die jetzt überall errichtet werden, und zum Theil schon errichtet sind, wird zwar Alles in wälscher Sprache gelehrt; allein, da die englische Sprache, als überall im Reiche dominirend, so überwiegende Vortheile gewährt, so werden die Leute, wenn sie nur erst überhaupt mehr aufgeklärt und unterrichtet sind, natürlich die Kunstfertigkeiten des Lesens und Schreibens, die sie in ihrer Kindheit für das Wälsche erwarben, ganz auf das Englische verwenden, und das Wälsche wird durch diese Hebung der Culture ein immer mehr unbeackertes Feld werden. (p. 217)

> [The spread of English luxury, of transport, of trade, of industry, which we referred to above, but especially the improvement of schools and the

education of the populace, will in the end see this part of England merge entirely with the mother country. Everything in these schools, which are now being built everywhere, and in some cases are already built, is taught in Welsh; however, because the English language, dominant all through the land, offers so many overwhelming advantages, it is natural that the people, once they are generally better informed and educated, will shift to English in terms of the reading and writing skills they have acquired in Welsh in their childhood and Welsh will become an increasingly fallow field as a result of this improvement in culture]

These observations are highly attuned to the cultural landscape of mid-nineteenth-century Wales. The English language is presented as a cultural threat and, indeed, Kohl himself emphasizes this by framing Welsh as effectively linguistically subservient. He goes on to predict an inevitable cultural decline in the Welsh context (p. 217). The prescient assumption, pre-empting the notorious Blue Books reports of 1847, is that schooling will eventually be in English and that Wales is, its culture notwithstanding, effectively part of England and therefore ripe for exploitation by the English. Kohl is also eager to note that the Welsh are not indifferent to the erosion of their culture. Typically, he cites an unnamed English source on the subject:

Die Wälschen, verbunden wie sie immer im Unglück gewesen sind, fahren auch jetzt noch fort, einander geneigt und verbunden zu sein in einem außerordentlich hohen Grade. Obgleich sie unter der englischen Herrschaft leben, so sind sie doch sehr vorsichtig mit der Einführung und Zulassung englischer Gewohnheiten und Sitten, und außerordentlich mißtrauisch gegen Alles, was von ihren Eroberern und Unterdruckern kommt. (pp. 215–16)

[The Welsh, united as ever in their misfortune, continue to this day to be extraordinarily well-disposed towards each other and in alliance. Although they live under English rule, they are nevertheless careful in relation to the introduction and acceptance of English habits and customs, and are extraordinarily distrustful of everything which comes from their conquerors and oppressors]

Here Kohl places Wales in an explicitly colonial context, echoing and confirming comments found in both Goede and Pückler-Muskau. Interestingly, his unnamed travel companion is not content to accept this reading of Wales and seeks to place the Welsh independently in a broader Celtic context, linking them to the ancient Celtic Tyrol (pp. 217–18). This comment points to the emerging Celticist discourse in Europe which would result not only in the seminal works of Renan and Arnold, but in the development of Celtic studies as a major strength in German philological scholarship in the second half of the nineteenth century, the impact of which would be felt on German travel writing on Wales.

Kohl himself makes a direct comparison with the other Celtic nations, noting that where Scotland and Ireland have Ossian, Wales has Arthur, with all his associated locations and myths (p. 242). He then ventures into the overtly political with comparisons drawn between Robert the Bruce (1274–1389) and Owain Glyndŵr (c. 1359–1415), thus foregrounding the shared Celtic experience of an adversarial relationship with England (p. 242). The interface between the Celtic nations is a feature of Kohl's narrative throughout. Interestingly, in discussing Anglesey which, like Pückler-Muskau, he treats as a separate entity outwith the principality of Wales, he notes that Holyhead is a place of exchange of peoples and interaction between the Celtic nations (p. 257). His description makes it clear just how interconnected these nations are and he is one of the few travellers of the period to focus on this, along with French traveller Martin. His narrative overall is notable as a first attempt in German travel writing to really place Wales in its Celtic and European context while also dealing in detail with Wales's relationship as a minoritized nation with the hegemonic power of England.

The increase in tourist activity is closely linked to that colonial reading of Wales, both driving and driven by the need for information for the ever-increasing numbers visiting the various sites mentioned in travel accounts. The impact of this growing industry is highlighted in Kohl's often critical descriptions of his encounters with English tourists. His engagement provokes a rather sarcastic description of

> eine größere Gesellschaft von englischen 'sight seeing gentlemen', wie sie um diese Zeit Wales in allen Richtungen durchstreifen, um sich alle 'sights', d.h. Wasserfälle, Aussichten, die 126 Schloßruinen und Thäler des Landes, anzusehen. (p. 221)

> [a larger group of English 'sightseeing gentlemen', of the sort who are currently traversing Wales in all directions in order to see all the 'sights', such as waterfalls, views, the 126 ruined castles and valleys of the country]

Fortunately for Kohl, this particular group prove to be good company but he notes that this is not always the case, and indeed later writers such as Julius Rodenberg present quite scathing views on the new English tourist fashion.[45] This phenomenon is not restricted to Wales but affects the whole of the British Isles. The risk is one of homogenization and further colonization.

This dilution of Welsh identity is illustrated by a text written at the same time as Kohl's, also based on a journey in 1844, but with very little concept of Wales as an entity. Carl Gustav Carus (1789–1869), a physiologist and painter who studied under Caspar David Friedrich, published his *England und Schottland im Jahre 1844* [England and Scotland in the Year 1844] in 1845. It was translated into English almost immediately, no doubt as a result of the interest in Carus's travelling companion, the King of Saxony, Friedrich Wilhelm IV.[46] The text is one of many to include a narrative of Wales but which effectively elide the nation in the title of the volume. Ironically, then, it is one of the few travelogues of the period to encompass the whole of Wales, travelling from the south to north Wales via Aberystwyth. The absence of explicit reference to Wales in the title is telling. Despite the fullness of the itinerary, on which the king is met with enthusiastic applause at every turn, it is notable that Carus makes no mention of entering or leaving Wales and he refers to Wales as part of England throughout. Yet, despite this, he is very well informed on Welsh history and culture. The emphasis is broad, encompassing landscape, culture and industry, and the underlying aesthetic is once again Romantic, perhaps unsurprising given Carus's personal connection to the Romantic landscape artists. This is confirmed early on during a visit to Tintern Abbey where, describing the scene before him, he exclaims: 'Abermals müßte ich an Friedrich denken!' (p. 82) ['Again the recollection of Friedrich was pressed upon my mind!' (p. 229)], a first explicit reference to the painter whose influence had been implicitly present in earlier travelogues.

Echoing Kohl, the description of nature in Carus's text sits alongside that of industry as part of a sweeping integrated landscape. The depiction of Newport is typical, ranging from the Romantic castle walls to the industrious docks and back to the calm serenity of the church and view over the bay (pp. 85–86). Occasionally, this Romantic appreciation gives way to more explicit exoticization, including a comparison of

45   Rodenberg's work will be discussed more fully in Chapter 5.

46   Carl Gustav Carus, *England und Schottland im Jahre 1844*, 2 vols (Berlin: Verlag von Alexander Dunker, 1845), II, pp. 80–122. Translations are taken from: *The King of Saxony's Journey through England and Scotland in the Year 1844*, trans. S.C. Davison (London: Chapman and Hall, 1846).

the women   he sees with 'die Frau aus Unalaschka in Cooks Reisen' (p. 87) ['the women [*sic*] of Unalaska, mentioned in Cook's "Voyages"' (p. 231)]. Carus then moves back to a European context, comparing the view before him in Merthyr with 'die glühende Stadt des Dis im Dante' (p. 88) ['the blazing city of Dis, mentioned by Dante' (p. 231)], echoing the inferno analogy found in the work of several French writers. These observations stand out as very different to the stock Celtic comparators of most other texts, with Wales firmly exoticized on a global level rather than a Celtic one. Carus returns to the Dantean analogy later in the chapter with a highly stylized description of the industrial landscape which draws it explicitly into the Romantic context of his experience at Tintern:

> Jetzt in dieser dunkeln Nacht, hinter den glühenden Werken, die hohen, vulkanischen Kegeln vergleichbaren Schlackenberge, von rothem Flammenlicht wunderlich erleuchtet, – die Phantasie konnte sich bald eine glühende Festung, bald ein brennendes Schloß, bald die Flammen-Stadt des Dis aus dem Dante vorstellen – Welch ein Contrast, der heutige Abend mit seiner feurigen Lohe und seinem Lärm, und der gestrige mit seiner klaren romantischen Ruhe in Tintern Abbey! (p. 93)

> [While viewing in the dark night, behind these glowing works, the high volcanic looking cones of those mountains of dross which I have noticed, wonderfully illuminated by the red flames, one's fancy might easily represent, at one time a blazing fortress, at another a burning castle, at another the fiery city of Pluto, as represented by Dante. What contrast between this evening, with its fiery glow and its noise of steam and of melting iron, and yesterday evening, with its mild radiance and Tintern Abbey! (p. 234)]

The juxtaposition of nature and modernity takes on a different tone here, described in dramatic literary terms, with the modern industrial landscape given a threatening edge which is in contrast to the awe-inspired descriptions of the precise and highly controlled north Walian achievements of Telford found in Kohl and his predecessors. The Romantic peace of Tintern, with its sense of calm and historic continuity, albeit one in decline, jars with the quasi-Blakeian imagery of Merthyr at night.

Given the diversity of locations visited by Carus, it is clear that Wales has by now established a presence on tourist itineraries of the mid-century which is moving gradually towards a standard experience with key sites able to offer something to the traveller, whatever his or her interests might be. Indeed, like Kohl, Carus is very aware that he is travelling in what is now a tourist destination, noting of Dolgellau that it is 'einer der Mittelpunkte für Touristen von Wales' (p. 99) ['a central point for tourists in Wales' (p. 236)]. This is not necessarily a positive development, as becomes all too clear during the ascent of Snowdon where he notes the presence of many others engaged in the same activity and the poor quality of the inn on the mountainside (pp. 103–04). Further evidence of the gradual standardization of the experience of Wales is found in Carus's description of the Menai Suspension Bridge, which echoes almost verbatim the detail provided by Kohl (pp. 108–13). The facts provided about the bridge are not the only example of the layering of texts and sharing of sources. Indeed, much of Carus's text mirrors the detail found in Kohl. As both are writing at the same time, it appears they may have a common source or guide.

One key difference emerges, however, in Carus's reaction to the Menai Suspension Bridge which is at odds with every other traveller who records their impressions in German. Despite acknowledging the grandeur and engineering expertise and providing his own sketch of the structure, he finds it aesthetically dull and utilitarian, concluding that, in comparison with other examples, 'Diess bleibt immer nur eine große mathematische Figur' (p. 111) ['This is (…) and will always remain, (no more than) a great mathematical figure' (p. 243)]. This critical response could not be further removed from the amazement expressed by Kohl and others and is a first indication that the impact of Telford is beginning to fade as other innovations emerge. Just as Spiker records the early developments of the Telford era, Carus, like Kohl, draws attention to the arrival of the railways, firstly through his mention of the second bridge being planned across the Menai Strait (p. 113), but then subsequently through his direct referencing of the construction of the railway around Conwy (p. 120). For Carus, the arrival of the railways is a neutral act, a reflection perhaps of his own disengagement from the specifically Welsh context. The march of progress poses no threat simply because, in his view, there is nothing to threaten. Wales is simply another place on the king's itinerary with no particular added value. This view is at odds with his contemporary, Kohl, whose more positive appraisal of Wales and Welsh culture is echoed in that of another traveller in the 1840s, Franz Löher (1818–1892).

Löher's text, *Land und Leute in der alten und neuen Welt. Reiseskizzen* (1855) [Land and People in the Old and New World: Travel Sketches] is the narrative of a journey to Wales in 1846 as part of a trip to the United States embarking from Liverpool.[47] As such, this is the first text to place Wales in its Atlantic context although, in practice, the treatment of Wales in the narrative is self-contained with no contextualization beyond Europe. For Löher, Wales represents peace and solitude, its 'Gebirgsromantik' [mountain Romanticism] an antidote to the 'geräuschvollen Wochen' [noisy weeks] and 'Arbeitsgewühl' [working bustle] of London (p. 45). In fact, the opening paragraph of the narrative initially places both Wales and Scotland in positive juxtaposition to England, Löher noting that the sound of bagpipes being played on the Birkenhead ferry manages to shake off the 'englische Steifheit' [English stiffness] by being 'ächt gaelisch, kindisch und frech' [truly Gaelic, childish and cheeky] (p. 45). The Celtic nations emerge immediately as restorative and appealing when compared to England, but are at the same time infantilized, portrayed as perhaps less serious than their hegemonic neighbour.

The positive appraisal of Wales is further undermined, however, by Löher's focus on the dirt and poverty he finds, immediately placing Wales as subservient to England in terms of civilization and progress (p. 53). Löher is equally unimpressed with Welsh music when attending an *eisteddfod* in Caerwys, noting that 'der Geist der Musik scheint die Wälschen nicht zu seinen lieben Kindern zu zählen' (p. 55) [the spirit of music does not appear to count the Welsh amongst its dear children]. Even Nature, usually a reliably impressive aspect of the Welsh context, seems to let him down; the forests in north-east Wales are not what he had been hoping for (p. 56). The further west he travels, however, the more positive his narrative becomes, suggesting a westward drive for cultural authenticity, the more peripheral the better. Löher describes north Wales as a stronghold of ancient British culture and does so in quite heroic terms, noting that William the Conqueror was so impressed with the north Walian resistance that he encouraged his lords to marry into their families (p. 57). This sense of difference and resilience is drawn out in his discussion of the recent revival of Welsh culture which highlights the lack of unity between Wales and its hegemonic neighbour:

Die Wälschen waren in den beiden letzten Jahrhunderten ziemlich unbekannt, sie kümmerten sich nicht um England und dieses nicht um sie, nur ganz allmählich siedelte sich bei ihnen etwas Englisches an. In unsern Tagen aber erfrischen sich in allen Ländern die Nationalitäten,

47 Franz von Löher, *Land und Leute in der alten und neuen Welt: Reiseskizzen*, 2 vols (Göttingen: Georg H. Wigand, 1855), I, pp. 52–72.

andrerseits jedoch werden die geistig stärkeren von selbst eindringlicher, da sind den auch in Nordwales Sprache und Sitten der Vorvordern wieder mit Vorliebe gehegt und gefoerdert. (p. 57)

[The Welsh were relatively unknown in the last two centuries, they did not trouble themselves with England and the latter did the same, only very gradually did English influence take root amongst them. These days, however, the nationalities are reviving in every land; on the other hand, however, the intellectually stronger are becoming more forceful, therefore in north Wales too the language and customs of the forefathers are being cultivated and fostered with love]

This clearly places Wales and the revival of Welsh culture in the broader cultural context of the period. Noting the impact of this, including the establishment of Welsh presses and the ongoing *eisteddfod* revival (pp. 57–58), Löher is clearly influenced by German Celticist interests in identifying Welsh as a culture currently in resurgence rather than in decline. Interestingly, this is presented partly as a result of English neglect. At the same time, however, he notes how the interest of the world in Wales has grown with the expansion of industry, in particular mining, and that this is beginning to have an impact on the cultural and sociopolitical landscape (p. 58). The future for Welsh culture is, therefore, not as rosy as the present might suggest: 'Das Wälsche kann nicht mehr anders, als jährlich einbußen und muß sich endlich auf die versteckten Thäler zurückziehen' (p. 58) [Welsh can do nothing more than suffer every year and will eventually be forced to withdraw to the hidden valleys]. This results, as noted by most travellers since Goede, in a general mistrust of the English which sits in stark contrast to the otherwise positive and welcoming response of the Welsh to foreign visitors.

As Löher ventures further into north Wales, passing through Llanrwst along the River Conwy, the impact of the landscape begins to make itself felt positively. Like Pückler-Muskau, his response borders on the spiritual as he describes his walk:

Man versenkt sich da in das wunderbare Weben und Wirken der Natur und unbewusst gleitet unser Geist in ihre geheimen Tiefen. An solch einem einsamen Tage denkt und lernt man mehr, als wochenlang in den Städten. Man ist da nicht einsam, die grossen Geister der Natur wandern und rasten mit uns. Unsere Seele schafft fortwährend ernste und schöne Gebilde, und wie wir den Lauf des Wassers durch die Thäler und im Geiste seinen Ursprung in den Adern der Berge verfolgen, so dringen wir nachdenkend ein in die einfachen und erhabenen Gesetze des Weltalls. (p. 60)

[One immerses oneself in the wonderful weaving and workings of Nature and our spirit slides subconsciously into her secret depths. One thinks and learns more on such a solitary day than in many weeks in the towns. One is not lonely there, the great spirits of Nature wander and rest with us. Our souls create earnest and beautiful images over and over and, just as we follow the waters as they flow through the valleys and in spirit follow their source in the veins of the mountains, so we penetrate thoughtfully the simple and sublime laws of the universe]

The Welsh landscape provides Löher with a connection to a universal sense of well-being which represents a climax in the reception of Wales as a restorative location. There is a sense, however, that this is also under threat, mirroring the position of the Welsh language and culture. Ironically, the improvements called for by Goede, Spiker and Pückler-Muskau, and enabled by Telford's engineering feats, now threaten to engulf Wales altogether. North Wales in particular has become more accessible and more popular. Löher makes fun of the large numbers of tourists arriving to make use of the various hostelries which have sprung up prior to climbing Snowdon, equipped as if they were about to attempt an ascent in the Himalayas (p. 62). The scenery described explains the popularity of the location:

Man wird des Hinabschauens gar nicht müde, mit jedem Schritte, nach jeder Seite ändert sich die grossartige Bühne. Das Gebilde dieser Berge stellt sich etwa dar wie ein festgewordener Wellensturm des Oceans. Der Snowdon war der Gipfel der hochaufgethurmten Woge, hier brach sie zusammen und es bildeten sich nach der einen Seite der tiefe Bergkessel mit den Felsenzacken oben, und weiterhin die Berglinien, welche ich die Tage vorher überstiegen; auf dieser anderen Seite stromte die flüssige Masse in mehreren Zügen zurück, zwischen denen sich gleichsam grüner Meeresgrund aufdeckt. (p. 66)

[One does not tire at all of looking upwards, with every step, on every side the great stage changes. The shape of these mountains presents itself as if it were solidified surf in a storm. Snowdon was the crest of the high-reaching wave, it broke here and created on either side the deep corries with cliff peaks above, and further on the line of the mountains which I climbed over the days before; on this side the fluid mass streams back in several ranges, between which the equally green sea floor is visible]

Not for the first time, Wales and its landscape are presented as a stage setting, although this time the star is the landscape itself. The comparison made here with the rising waves further enhances the dramatic effect but also draws out the significance of the sea in the north Walian context. Löher further underlines this as he describes the combination of tourist- and slate-carrying vessels in the hectic scene at Caernarfon docks (p. 68), homing in on the two central mainstays of the north Wales economy already highlighted by Kohl. This is further enhanced by a description of the Menai Suspension Bridge, noting its delicacy and awe-inspiring size but also the way in which it was built to enable sea traffic from Caernarfon through to Beaumaris Bay, itself described as equal in beauty to that of Capri, echoing views expressed by some French travellers (p. 71).

As Löher makes his way back to Liverpool to prepare for his trip to America, he notes how the Welsh language has been gradually weakened by the influence of English (p. 69). This is symptomatic of the concerns he has expressed throughout and which culminate in the following dark passage:

> Ich nahm Abschied von ihm [Wales], von seiner finsteren Romantik und seinen blühenden Thälern. Nach wenigen Jahrzehnten wird das Naturvolk dieses Gebirges gründlich zersetz und von englischen Geist und Wesen bewältigt sein. Aber bis die Engländer soweit kamen, hat es die blutige, jahrhundertlange Kampfe gekostet. Die alten Nordwälschen haben manchen Engländer mit geschlagenem Schadel in ihren Bergen bestattet. Noch jetzt liegt etwas Unheimliches auf jenen Bergschluchten mit ihren schwarzen Seen. Es heisst, der finstere Geist des Gebirges sei zornig, daß jene Altäre nicht mehr rauchen, und fordere alljährlich ein junges Blut zum Opfer. (p. 70)

> [I took my leave (of Wales), of its dark Romanticism and its blooming valleys. In a few decades' time the indigenous population of these mountains will have been undermined and overcome by English spirit and being. But for the English to get this far has cost centuries of bloody conflict. The old north Walians have buried many an Englishman with a cracked skull in their mountains. Even now there is something uncanny about these mountain crevices with their dark lakes. They say that the dark spirit of the mountains is angry that smoke is no longer rising from these altars and is demanding fresh blood as a sacrifice each year]

This description speaks once again to a thoroughly Romantic reading of Wales, both explicitly through the reference to 'seine finstere Romantik' [its dark Romanticism] and in terms of the Enlightenment notion of the *Naturvolk* [indigenous people]. In this respect, the reading of Wales in the first half of the nineteenth century almost seems to have come full circle, back to Goede's Romantic reading of a peripheral nation set apart from its modern, hegemonic neighbour.

As the number of travelogues and other accounts increases during the first half of the nineteenth century, Wales, framed as a peripheral 'other', gradually emerges from the shadows to establish a presence in the German understanding of the British Isles. The early narratives highlight a conflicted reading with an exoticized, Romanticized but also colonized and threatened Wales as the focus of some travellers' attention, and encroaching modernity in the shape of industry and tourism at the centre of other works. As the century progresses, writers begin to adopt various prisms through which to read Wales, with clear evidence of the layering of texts and broadening of comparisons with other Celtic nations as the narrative of Wales consolidates. Increasingly Wales can be seen to gain importance as an actual destination with a distinct tourist trail rather than appearing as an aside to the greater narrative of England. That narrative is itself placed under scrutiny by the encounter with Wales. The British Isles, viewed from afar primarily as England, seemed to offer potential solutions in terms of paradigms of peace, stability and the sublime as well as providing examples of how to improve economically. Finding an 'integrated' part of Great Britain being dealt with negatively undermined the paradigm of English stability and of the value of constitutional monarchy. The developing struggle between Germanic north and south – Prussia and Austria – while not explicitly referred to, brought issues of hegemonic struggle into sharp focus for German-speaking travellers, with clear parallels in the case of Wales and its relationship to England which cannot have been lost on them, especially those from smaller German states. The spectre of German national identity would thus loom large over future travellers to Wales.

CHAPTER FOUR

Identity, Celtomania and the Narrative of Wales in Travel Writing in German from 1850 to 1905

The experience of Wales for German-speaking travellers in the first half of the nineteenth century is very much one of discovery, both of the landscape and the sociopolitical conditions. By the midway point of the century, however, the focus gradually begins to shift to see a greater, more detailed engagement with Welsh culture and the threats posed to it by the expansion of tourism. The concerns expressed by Kohl in his 1844 narrative are shared and felt more acutely by a number of later travellers, as the fragility of Welsh culture becomes a central theme. This reflects both the rise in the interest in Celtic studies in Germany and the debate around issues of national identity at play in the years leading up to German unification and the establishment of the Second Empire in 1871. German travellers in the first half of the century are equipped with a vague notion of Welsh cultural identity and make frequent references to local myth and legend without any real engagement with the language and literature which underpin them. Only very few, such as Goede, attempt to engage with Welsh culture in greater depth. This changes as the work of Celtic philologists in Germany becomes more widely known in the second half of the century.

The German interest in Celtic cultures fostered through the Herderian appreciation of *Ossian*, the works of Sir Walter Scott and the publication of the Grimms' *Irische Elfenmärchen* [Irish Elf Tales] in 1826 laid the foundations for the widely acknowledged Celtomania of the later century. Building on theories put forward in the late eighteenth century by Friedrich Gottlieb Klopstock (1724–1803), Herder and latterly August Wilhelm Schlegel, much of the debate centred on the presence or otherwise of the Celtic languages within the broader Indo-European linguistic landscape,[1] but interest also encompassed the folk and literary cultures of the Celtic nations. In this debate, Wales remained very much on the periphery until the early 1840s and the pioneering work of Albert Schulz (1802–1893), whose *Essay on the Influence of Welsh traditions on the literature of Germany, France and Scandinavia* was awarded the first prize at the Abergavenny Cymreigyddion *eisteddfod* in 1840 and went on to be published in Great Britain and Germany to great acclaim.[2] The 1842 German version of the essay was enhanced by Schulz's translation of three tales from Lady Charlotte Guest's translation into English of the *Mabinogion*,[3] the first instalment of which had appeared in 1841, thus providing German readers with their first glimpse of Welsh literary culture almost twenty years after Scott and the Brothers Grimm had done the same for Scotland and Ireland respectively. Schulz's work, which later included *Die Geschichte der wälschen Literatur* (1864) [The History of Welsh Literature], a translation of Thomas Stephens's 1849 *Literature of the Kymry*, marked the beginning of a fascination with Welsh language and culture within German-speaking scholarship which continues to the present day.[4]

---

1   See Erich Poppe, 'The Welsh Language in German Philology around 1850', in Bernhard Maier and Stefan Zimmer (eds), *150 Jahre Mabinogion – Deutsch-Walisische Kulturbeziehungen* (Tübingen: Max Niemeyer, 2001), pp. 203–21.

2   The essay was presented in German but published as *An Essay on the influence of Welsh tradition upon the literature of Germany, France, and Scandinavia, which obtained the prize of the Abergavenny Cymreigyddion Society, at the eisteddfod of 1840*, trans. Frances Berrington (Llandovery: William Rees; London: Longman, Williams, Hughes; Chester: Parry; Abergavenny: Morgan, 1841). See Edith Gruber, 'King Arthur and the Privy Councillor: Albert Schulz as a Cultural Mediator Between the Literary Fields of Nineteenth-Century Wales and Germany' (unpublished doctoral thesis, Bangor University, 2012).

3   The German version of Schulz's essay appeared as *Die Arthursage und die Märchen des rothen Buchs von Hergest*, Bibliothek der gesammten deutschen Nationalliteratur, section II, vol. 2 (Quedlinburg and Leipzig: Basse, 1842).

4   The work of Schulz notwithstanding, Celtic studies as a discipline in Germany is traditionally seen to begin with Johann Kaspar Zeuss's *Grammatica Celtica* (Leipzig: Weidmann, 1853), which set the benchmark for future studies of the Welsh language. Ferdinand Walter's *Das alte Wales* (Bonn: Adolph Marcus, 1859) provided a detailed account of medieval Welsh law and society.

This chapter will explore the extent to which this interest in the language and literatures of Wales soon became as significant for German travellers as their earlier enthusiasm for the landscape had been. Both aspects, perhaps ironically, added to the popularity of Wales as a destination and, ultimately, posed a threat to the very alterity which made the Celtic nation so attractive. Travel writers responded to this shift, and perhaps the key underlying theme of the second half of the nineteenth century for German-speaking travellers in Wales was the full-scale development of tourism, particularly from England, and its impact on Welsh culture. This adds to the complexity of the reading of Wales and its relationship to England, modern society and the march of progress. This tension was felt against a complex political background in the German-speaking lands themselves. For many, the post-Napoleonic quest for stability seemed to have failed as the Revolution of 1848 signalled the end of the restoration period and, to some degree, the German Confederation of 1815. The German states were experiencing unprecedented change. The 1834 *Zollverein* [Customs Union] and a process of rapid industrialization in the 1840s had undermined the conservative structure of German society, leading to a nervousness which manifested itself in the political tensions of the pre-revolutionary *Vormärz* [pre-March] period. Issues of national identity became increasingly acute as the German political elite, many of whom subscribed to the demands of a growing nationalist movement, debated the future of the Confederation in terms of *Klein-* [Lesser] versus *Grossdeutschland* [Greater Germany], the former leading to a Prussian-dominated alliance, the latter including Austria in a tense north-south power axis. After much political wrangling, the Confederation was eventually restored in 1851 with Austria on the outside, thus setting

---

Other notable studies included Franz Bopp's early essay 'Über die keltischen Sprachen vom Gesichtspunkt der vergleichenden Sprachforschung', *Abhandlungen und Sitzungsberichte der Preußischen Akademie der Wissenschaften* (1838), pp. 187–272; Nikolaus Sparschuh's *Keltische Studien* (Frankfurt am Main: Franz Varrentrapp, 1848); and Franz Josef Mone's *Celtische Forschungen zur Geschichte Mitteleuropas* (Freiburg: Herder, 1857). By 1901, the subject area had become part of the academic firmament with the establishment of a chair in Celtic Philology at the Friedrich-Wilhelms-Universität, the first incumbent of which was Celticist Heinrich Zimmer. See Bernhard Maier, 'Einleitung zur zweiten Sektion: Deutsch-walisische Kulturbeziehungen. Wales und Deutschland: Neun Jahrhunderte kulturellen Austauschs', in Maier and Zimmer (eds), *150 Jahre Mabinogion*, pp. 131–41 (pp. 133ff.).

the German-speaking states on a collision course for war, the ultimate outcome of which was Prussian domination of a united Germany under Bismarck in 1871. These developments at home are reflected in the travel writing on Wales with issues of national identity colouring a number of texts, writers empathizing with the struggle of this peripheral nation in the face of an increasingly dominant neighbour whose power was further bolstered by industry and empire.

In terms of its outward manifestation, this existential threat to Welsh identity was undoubtedly embodied, quite literally, in the large numbers of tourists making their way to Wales.[5] In some travel texts, the development of tourism is presented relatively neutrally. For example, Heinrich Karl Brandes (1798–1874), writing in his *Ausflug nach England im Sommer 1851* (1855) [Trip to England in the Summer of 1851], presents an unthreatening description of the tourist experience in the north as he interacts with other tourists and takes in the usual sites.[6] Equally, Malwida von Meysenbug (1816–1903) presents a genteel picture of upper-class outings around north Wales in 1852 in her *Memoiren einer Idealistin* (1900) [Memoirs of an Idealist].[7] The rapid expansion of the tourist industry is made clear by Wilhelm Heine (1827–1885) in his article 'Ein Sommerausflug nach Wales' (1871) [Summer Trip to Wales], which highlights the large numbers of tourists coming into Wales from Liverpool. This is presented positively, however, Heine noting that tourists in Wales seem better disposed towards each other than they do elsewhere, a consequence perhaps of the individual restorative effect of Wales noted in the narratives of the early century.[8] These texts are in the minority, however, with most travellers seeing the development of tourism as a threat.

On first reading, Ludwig Rellstab's *Sommermährchen in Reisebildern aus Deutschland, Belgien, Frankreich, England, Schottland im Jahr*

---

5   The general increase in tourist numbers in Great Britain was noted by a number of travellers. See for example Lukas Bauer, '"Sie durchziehen dieses Land in ganzen Schwärmen": Tourism as a Marker of Modernity in Heine's *Reisebilder*', *Monatshefte*, 110 (2018), pp. 487–508.

6   Heinrich Karl Brandes, *Ausflug nach England im Sommer 1851* (Lemgo: Meyer, 1855), pp. 50–57.

7   Malwida von Meysenbug, *Memoiren einer Idealistin*, 3 vols (Berlin: Schuster & Loeffler, 1900), II, pp. 34–62; III, pp. 122–30, 221–22, 248–49.

8   Wilhelm Heine, 'Ein Sommerausflug nach Wales', *Westermanns Jahrbuch der illustrierten deutschen Monatshefte*, 30:175 (April 1871), pp. 31–40; 30.176 (September 1871), pp. 155–61.

1851 (1852) [Summer Fairy Tales in Travel Sketches from Germany, Belgium, France, England and Scotland in the Year 1851] might also seem to present a neutral view of tourism but there is a more complex reading underlying his otherwise light-hearted narrative.[9] A poet and influential music critic[10] who had work set to music by Franz Schubert (1797–1828),[11] Rellstab (1799–1860) visited Wales in 1851 as part of a cultural tour of the British Isles. Despite not referring to Wales in the title of his volume, the Welsh section of his journey is described in great detail, especially the societal impact of improvements in infrastructure in the north. He notes immediately the effect that the Menai Suspension Bridge has had on his base, Bangor, which is by now full of hotels and well-equipped for the burgeoning tourist and general travel trade. The presentation of the impact of tourism is ostensibly positive but also notable is the lack of any sense of alterity. Rellstab is surprisingly disinterested, given his interest in music, in the language and culture of Wales. His initial description of the hustle and bustle of this small city could just as easily be of somewhere much larger such as Liverpool or Manchester. Yet there is a warmth to the welcome he receives which sets Bangor apart. The city is alive with businesses and he finds the locals extremely welcoming. The activity is down to one simple fact, emphasized throughout the narrative: the presence of the two bridges across the Menai Strait (referred to by Rellstab as the 'Bangor-Weltwundern' (p. 201) [Bangor Wonders of the World]), one complete, the other, the new Britannia Bridge, under construction as part of the ongoing expansion of the railway network.

The pleasing aspect of the natural surroundings and the enormity of the two bridges are the focus of an early description in the text which suggests an idyll of modernity and nature in harmony, echoing to some degree Pückler-Muskau's earlier description of the same location:

> Die Straße auf der wir dahinrollen, ist von beiden Seiten mit Gärten umgeben, die mit einzelnen Häusern wechseln; jedes Fleckchen ist

---

9   Ludwig Rellstab, *Sommermärchen in Reisebildern aus Deutschland, Belgien, Frankreich, England, Schottland im Jahr 1851*, 3 vols (Darmstadt: n.p., 1852), II, pp. 195–237.

10   See Wolfgang Franke, *Der Theaterkritiker Ludwig Rellstab* (Berlin: Colloquium, 1964).

11   The first songs of Schubert's *Schwanengesang* cycle of 1828 are by Rellstab, who was well-connected in the world of music through his father, the music publisher Johann Carl Friedrich Rellstab (1759–1813).

angebaut. Auch einige Hotels sind hier angelegt, die außer dem Vortheil einer herrlichen Lage und Aussicht, auch den haben, den berühmten Bauwerken um derretwillen Bangor besucht wird, noch ansehnlich näher zu liegen, als die Stadt, ohne dabei weiter vom Bahnhofe entfernt zu sein. (pp. 205–06)

[The road we drive along to get there is flanked on either side by gardens which alternate with small houses; every tiny bit of land is cultivated. There are even a few hotels situated here which, apart from the advantage of being located in a lovely place with lovely views, also have the advantage that they are markedly closer than the town to the famous constructions which draw visitors to Bangor, but without being further from the train station]

The road Rellstab refers to is undoubtedly that constructed some thirty years earlier by Telford, highlighting the impact of the improved infrastructure on the locality. This is an area on the up, a trajectory which is leading away from the traditions of the past, but oddly not at the expense of some aspects so highly valued in previous accounts. Wales remains a place of sanctuary. The sense of well-being evoked here marks the narrative, drawing out once more the restorative quasi-spiritual nature of the encounter with Wales, even in the heady bustle of a tourist destination of the sort described above. This positive description of modernity, including the trappings of tourist activity, very much foregrounds the needs of the traveller while largely overlooking the travellee, and places Wales and the Welsh landscape as a positive polar opposite to the more negative impression Rellstab has gained of England with its large, overwhelming cities (p. 205). There is an ethereal quality to this Welsh narrative as Rellstab seeks to place himself as a traveller recording his experiences as if inhabiting a world of fairy-tale wonder:

Die Seele erfüllt von den großartigen Eindrücken, das Gemüth erfrischt durch die herrlichen Morgenlufte und Dufte, durch den Glanz des blauen Himmels und der leuchtenden See, rollte der Sommermärchenschreiber, der wahrhaftig keine wunderbareren Mährchen zu erfinden wüsste, als er hier Wirklichkeiten vor sich sah und geschildert hat, den Weg nach Bangor auf dem leichten Wagen wieder zurück. (p. 226)

[The soul filled with the magnificent impressions, the spirit refreshed by the wonderful morning air and scents, by the brilliance of the blue sky and the shimmering sea, the summer fairy-tale writer, who truly could not imagine a more wonderful tale than that which he saw before him in reality and which he has described, made his way in the little coach back to Bangor]

Despite his own self-proclaimed role as the 'Sommermährchenschreiber' [summer fairy-tale writer], Rellstab's real interest is the bridges over the Menai Strait and his account is the first to deal with both in detail. The advance of modernity is felt here once more. Rellstab seems to appreciate Robert Stephenson (1803–1859), the engineer responsible for the original tubular design of the Britannia Bridge, above the previously exalted Telford whose feats have now been overtaken by new developments. Rellstab's description of the positioning of the sections of tubular tunnel used to create the carriageway of the Britannia Bridge is detailed and his amazement unfettered (pp. 206ff.). Nevertheless, he finds himself drawn time and time again to the impact of these wonders of construction on the Welsh landscape as he observes the excitement caused by the appearance of the second bridge:

> Jede Bergkuppe, jede Felsenklippe war mit Menschen bedeckt, auf jede hervorspringende Zunge der Küste drängten sich viele Tausende, so weit das Auge reichen konnte. Denken wir uns diese wunderherrliche Gegend, wo Meer, Gebirg, Fels, Wald, Gärten, Felder, Häuser, genug alles Schöne und Erhabene, was Natur und Cultur erzeugen, sich zu der grossartigen und reichsten Landschaft mischen, und die jetzt schon das Auge mit Staunen, die Seele mit erhebenden Gedanken erfüllt; von einer solchen Völkerwanderung belebt – in der ein lebendiges Interesse, ein gespannter Antheil glüht – wir würden nicht Worte zu finden wissen, um das mächtige Schauspiel zu schildern! (pp. 214–15)

> [Every hilltop, every cliff edge was covered in people, on every promontory along the coast, as far as the eye could see, there were people descending. Imagine this wonderful area, where sea, mountain, cliff, woods, gardens, fields, houses, all in all everything beautiful and sublime which Nature and Culture produce, and which now fills the eye with wonder, the soul with uplifting thoughts; enlivened by such an influx of people – in which a lively interest, a tense desire for involvement smoulders – we would be unable to find the words to describe this powerful piece of theatre]

Yet, despite this clear appreciation of the Welsh landscape and the complimentary impact of improvements to infrastructure, there remains a conflicted sense of place and, indeed, ownership which serves to foreground the fragility of Welsh identity as it is perceived in German travel writing. As the narrative progresses, it becomes clear that Rellstab is not entirely sure of the nation's status. He refers instead to the 'Grafschaft Caernarvon' (p. 214) [County of Caernarfon], thus eliding Wales completely, and like many before him, he sees Anglesey as a separate entity altogether. He also frequently conflates Wales with

England. This becomes particularly acute in his detailed description of the two bridges across the Menai Strait. The civilized environment surrounding Bangor is due, in Rellstab's view, to the presence of the bridges, but these are still essentially 'ein dauerndes Denkmal zum Rühme Englands' (p. 221) [a lasting monument to the fame of England]. The context is undoubtedly one of empire. The Britannia Bridge, as its name suggests, appears as a dominating English – that is to say, imperial British – force, flanked by lions and soon to carry a train, described by Rellstab as a fire-breathing dragon without any sense of the long-standing symbolic significance of the dragon in relation to Wales (p. 223). Similar rhetoric was not applied by earlier travellers to the Menai Suspension Bridge, a sign perhaps of the increasing significance of empire and industry on the German understanding of England as the hegemonic power and a cipher for Great Britain. Notable, too, is Rellstab's reference to the speed of travel, allowing only a brief glimpse of key scenes as Wales becomes part of the railway landscape rather than an entity in its own right (p. 230). This results in a sense of unease which is shared, as Tim Youngs highlights, by many other travellers adjusting to new modes of transport as they develop over time.[12]

The extent to which Wales is subsumed into the railway landscape is emphasized in a different way in the highly technical observations on the role of both bridges provided by Friedrich Kohl (1811–1876) which see Wales once more elided and decontextualized, nothing more than the passive site of engineering prowess.[13] The railway itself is positioned as a main link between the major cities of north-west England and the port of Holyhead and therefore Ireland. For Friedrich Kohl, Wales itself remains an incidental enabler rather than the true beneficiary, or indeed driver, of progress. The impact of the advance of the railways and the related infrastructure on the perceived identity of travellees illustrates further the ambivalent perception of the improvements being made. The locals encountered by Rellstab, for example, are incredibly proud of 'their' bridges (p. 227) but the author registers this as national, English

12   Tim Youngs, *The Cambridge Introduction to Travel Writing* (Cambridge: Cambridge University Press, 2013), pp. 68–70.

13   Friedrich Kohl, *Beschreibung der Göltzsch- und Elsterthal-Überbrückung im sächsischen Voightlande, sowie der Britannia-Röhrenbrücke und der über denselben Meeresarm führenden Kettenbrücke in England und der schiefen Ebene in Baiern. Vorangehend eine kurze Statistik deutscher und ausländischer Eisenbahnen* (Plauen: A. Schröter, 1854), pp. 41–72.

pride, eliding the local and underscoring the dominant voice of his narrative which pays little or no attention to Wales as an entity unless in the context of the natural environment. This is marked towards the end of his narrative, where he describes Wales in the following terms:

> Wales muß die reichste Ausbeute an Naturschönheiten geben, an wilden, pittoresken, wie an reizenden und sanften. Die blauen, zackigen Gipfel, wie die tiefgespaltenen Thalschluchten, über welche der Zug dahinbraust, geben die vollsten Andeutungen dafür. Aber auch das, woran wir nur im Eisenbahnflüge hinstreiften, gewährt schon eine reiche Ausbeute, belohnt die Reise im vollsten Masse. (p. 230)

> [Wales must offer the richest yield of natural beauties, wild and picturesque, as well as charming and delicate. The blue, craggy summits, as well as the deeply clefted crevices along which the train thunders, are the best illustration of this. But even that, where we only passed through at speed on the train, makes the journey worth it in the fullest sense]

Here, modernity enables a view of Wales but at speed, allowing only a superficial impression. There is a sense that one could go deeper but this is rendered impossible by the pace of travel. There is no time to stop and stare, yet the traveller has the tantalizing sense that, were he able to, he would be richly rewarded. The dichotomy present between the depiction of Wales itself and that of the advance of modernity in Wales is further reflected in Rellstab's reading of English and Welsh identity. The nomenclature here is significant as Rellstab oscillates between 'England' and 'Wales' depending on the aspect of the scene he is describing. In effect, when his text deals with the two bridges, the epitome of progress and modernity, the emphasis is on England (as a cipher for Great Britain and the empire); when the narrative shifts to landscape and nature, Wales (the local) comes to the fore. Rellstab's text, then, presents his readers with an appreciative but essentially destabilizing view of Wales, its language and culture overlooked in a narrative which foregrounds the relationship between landscape and modernity, the Welsh environment providing a fitting backdrop for the engineering feats of the age. In so doing, he demonstrates also how the expansion of the railways brings with it a tourist wave which threatens to homogenize culture while further enabling the ongoing hegemony.[14]

---

14 On the negative cultural effects of the railways and tourism on Wales, see Dot Jones, 'The Coming of the Railways and Language Change in North Wales 1850–1900', in Jenkins (ed.), *The Welsh Language,* pp. 131–49; David Llewelyn

The threats to Welsh identity presented implicitly in Rellstab's text are central to the narrative provided by Julius Rodenberg (1831–1914) in his *Ein Herbst in Wales. Land und Leute, Märchen und Lieder* (1858) [An Autumn in Wales: Land and People, Tales and Songs].[15] Rather than underplay Welsh culture, however, Rodenberg offers an alternative approach which sees him embedded in that culture, both physically and intellectually. His text relates his experiences as a traveller in north Wales in 1856 and is perhaps the first self-conscious example of *Keltomanie* in the German context. Earlier responses in travel writing to the Celticist debate do exist: the letters written by Carl von Bunsen (1791–1860) describing his engagement with a number of key figures involved in the 1839 Abergavenny *eisteddfod* give a flavour of the emerging Celticist trend,[16] while E. Soechting (dates unknown), writing in 1855, echoes Johann Georg Kohl in highlighting the cultural links between the Celtic nations and the culture of the Tyrol.[17] However, neither provide a detailed account or, indeed, celebration of Welsh culture in the way Rodenberg does. He was an enthusiast with a true love of literature and culture and is perhaps best known as the editor of the influential cultural magazine *Deutsche Rundschau* [German Review], which he founded in 1874 and which saw him occupy a position of influence at the heart of German intellectual life until his death.[18] Prior to his involvement with the magazine, and after studying at Heidelberg, Göttingen and Berlin, he undertook a series of tours in the 1850s and 1860s on which he visited

Jones and Robert Smith, 'Tourism and the Welsh Language in the Nineteenth Century', in Jenkins (ed.), *The Welsh Language*, pp. 151–75; Dylan Phillips, 'Pa Bris y Croeso? Effeithiau Twristiaeth ar y Gymraeg', in Geraint H. Jenkins and Mari A. Williams (eds), *'Eu hiaith a gadwant?': Y Gymraeg yn yr Ugeinfed Ganrif* (Cardiff: University of Wales Press, 2000), pp. 507–30.

15　Julius Rodenberg, *Ein Herbst in Wales: Land und Leute, Märchen und Lieder* (Hannover: C. Rümpler, 1858). Translations are taken from: *An Autumn in Wales (1856): Country and People, Tales and Songs*, trans. William Linnard (Cowbridge: D. Brown and Sons, 1985).

16　Frances Waddington Bunsen, *Christian Carl Josias Freiherr von Bunsen: aus seinen Briefen und nach eigener Erinnerung geschildert von seiner Witwe. Schweiz und England*, ed. Friedrich Nippold, 3 vols (Leipzig: F.A. Brockhaus, 1869), II, pp. 12–15, 29–33, 52, 72–81, 88–90.

17　E. Soechting, 'Kurze Mittheilungen von einer Reise in England und Schottland', *Zeitschrift für die gesamten Naturwissenschaften*, 5:11 (November 1855), pp. 378–99.

18　See Heinrich Spiero, *Julius Rodenberg. Sein Leben und seine Werke* (Berlin: Paetel, 1921).

various European countries including Wales, Ireland and England. These visits resulted in a series of travel narratives, including *Ein Herbst in Wales*, *Die Insel der Heiligen* (1860) [The Island of the Saints] and *Alltagsleben in London* (1860) [Daily Life in London].

Rodenberg's Welsh travel narrative is unusual in that it is one of very few to deal exclusively with Wales as the main destination. Equally unusual is his decision to stay not in local hostelries or with local gentry, as most other European travellers of the period did, but rather with a Welsh farming family of modest means in the village of Abergwyngregyn, a few miles east of Bangor. Rodenberg's narrative, developed from his travel diaries, is a hybrid text which, supported by wide reading of relevant sources, attempts to promote an understanding of Wales as a specifically Romantic nation: 'der Boden der Romantik' (p. 21) ['the ground of romance' (p. 9)], as he would have it. The volume incorporates not only Rodenberg's narrative but also a range of material collected to showcase Welsh folk culture, including poetry, legends and music. The actual travel narrative combines vignettes depicting life in the towns and villages of north Wales with a stylized account of his own relations with the Welsh farming community in which he finds himself. The text comprises eight chapters containing travel narrative, three with character portraits, four with background on Welsh history and culture and two lengthy sections with folk tales and poetry, accompanied at the end by four musical settings. Rodenberg also integrates numerous poems of his own which contribute to the core travel narrative as commentaries. These also enable the author to situate himself in and interact with the landscape, as was the case with Pückler-Muskau, very much in the manner of the Romantic artist. The result is a striking combination of travelogue, philology, creative writing and music which presents an image of Wales couched in German Romantic ideals but with notable elements of *Biedermeier* mannerist narrative typical of the mid-century.

The Welsh narrative is unique in Rodenberg's work in terms of its structure and approach. His Irish narrative, *Die Insel der Heiligen*, has some parallels with the Welsh text but also marked differences in the way Ireland and Irish culture are presented. Here, the focus is on factual information coupled with local vignettes, delivered for the most part as dialogues recounting encounters with various locals as Rodenberg makes his way through Ireland. Notable, too, is the emphatic description of the extreme poverty found in Ireland, the fault for which is laid squarely at the door of the English government. Rodenberg quotes from numerous sources to bolster his argument and heightens the sense of colonial tension already mooted in his Welsh narrative. Aesthetically, this text is also far closer to the *Biedermeier* than the Romantic in terms of its focus on customs and the drama of everyday contemporary life. This is underlined by the different way in which poetry is integrated into the text. Firstly, there are far fewer examples of Rodenberg's own verse. Instead he quotes extensively from anglophone Irish poets, Thomas Moore (1779–1852) in particular, and draws folk poetry into the text through the dialogue sections, rather than setting the verse aside in a separate chapter as he does in his Welsh narrative, notably using original Welsh-language texts. The effect is to present Ireland as having a Romantic side, reflected in the landscape and the inclusion, as the title suggests, of various legends of the Saints, rather than the land of romance as was the case with Wales.[19]

The paratextual material provided by Rodenberg for *Ein Herbst in Wales* gives some insight into his intentions for his Welsh volume. He clearly wants to present Wales in its best, Romantic light and is inspired to do so while in London on his way home to Germany in 1856. This is explained in detail in the dedication to Baroness Rothschild which precedes the main text. Echoing Johann Georg Kohl, Rodenberg's response to leaving the rural idyll of Wales is juxtaposed with his initially negative reaction to the metropolitan enormity of London (p. vii). It is this sense of longing combined with his conversations with the baroness, including a discussion of Thomas Moore's oriental romance, *Lalla Rookh* (1817), which inspires him to write his Welsh narrative (p. x). The preface thus succeeds in placing Wales in a Romantic, exoticized and poetic context before the narrative itself has even begun.

Rodenberg's Welsh narrative has two key elements: his memoirs and the cultural content. He deliberately combines these two elements in order to foreground the close correlation between his reading of Wales as a Romantic nation and his knowledge of Welsh language and culture. This dual focus is conveyed through two pairs of related themes which are woven through the narrative: firstly, national identity, emphasizing on the one hand the tense cultural relations between Wales and England and, on the other, the impact of travel on Rodenberg's own

19   The absence of what one might term more Romantic material in Rodenberg's Irish narrative should not be taken as an indication that he had no interest in it in the Irish context. He published a separate volume, *Die Harfe von Erin. Märchen und Dichtung in Irland* (Leipzig: Grünow, 1861), which included such material.

German identity; and secondly, the Romantic, with an emphasis both on Wales as a Romantic nation and on Rodenberg as a Romantic traveller. As a result, the text highlights the desire to understand and present a foreign culture and a high degree of self-reflection and stylization as self and other interact self-referentially in a symbiotic relationship of mutual affirmation. Rodenberg is able to confirm and consolidate his status as a Romantic, German traveller while Wales occupies centre stage for the first time in German travel writing as the sole subject of a volume.[20]

Throughout the text, issues of Welsh identity centre on the juxtaposition of Wales with neighbouring England. Rodenberg's own views are subjectively polarized, passing comment on contemporary England (the negative), while consistently emphasizing Wales's past (the positive). In so doing, his narrative suffers none of the ambiguity of previous accounts. His first view of Wales is as a majestic but mysterious other, clearly defined in his narrative as an essentially foreign land, one at the heart of his desires as a late Romantic (p. 12). The rationale for visiting the country is driven by the specific cultural curiosity of a traveller well-versed in the emerging German scholarship on Wales. Rodenberg has some preconceptions about what he is likely to find there, while at the same time expressing the feeling that he is on a journey 'in's Ungewiße' (p. 13) [into the unknown (p. 6)]. The fragility of the German reading of Wales as a site of difference and, therefore, of what Rodenberg perceives to be Wales's identity as a nation is made clear in the frequent references to the advance of tourism and the negative impact of mass travel on the sites visited. The negativity brought by specifically English travellers, arriving on their English-funded railway, is encapsulated in Rodenberg's caricature of three tourists from Birmingham. These travelling industrialists are presented as philistines unable to fully appreciate the land they have come to see:

> Der Meßerfabrikant schlief; aber jedesmal wenn er aufwachte, redete er mich an. – ‚Im Ganzen ein schönes Land, dieses Wales', äußerte er, ‚nur müßten die Berge nicht sein. Ich finde, daß sie die Aussicht verstören.' –, Und dem Verkehr sehr im Wege sind,' sagte der Materialist, der sich wieder eine Pfeife stopfte. (p. 256)

---

20   See Carol Tully, 'Nineteenth-Century German Travellers to Wales: Text, Translation and the Manipulation of Identity', in James Hodkinson and Ben Schofield (eds), *German in the World* (London: Boydell and Brewer, 2020), pp. 74–90.

[The knife manufacturer slept, but every time he woke up he spoke to me. 'A beautiful country on the whole, this Wales,' he said, 'apart from the mountains. I find that they spoil the view'. 'And greatly hinder the traffic', said the materialist, filling himself another pipe (p. 118)]

The adventures of these three men are woven into the narrative as a constant reminder of what Wales has to endure from its neighbours. The influx from the east is anything but beneficial. Indeed, it is not the new railway reaching into Wales from England but rather the more traditional mode of transport, the ships sailing from Caernarfon docks, which are presented as Wales's means of a positive engagement with the wider world (p. 265). This runs counter to Rellstab's earlier appreciation of the arrival of the railways as a symbol of progress and empire. Here, despite the fact that Rodenberg himself travels mostly by train, thus enabling his access to the majesty of Wales, the railway is not seen as a civilizing force but rather as a threat to the nation's cultural survival as it cowers in the face of advancing modernity. The persistence, in spite of this, of the Welsh language and local customs is seen as evidence of cultural tenacity, couched in the terms of Romantic nationalism. The advance of modernity, represented by the railway, is perceived by the rural Welsh as a constant threat to the quasi-mystical balance of nature and culture which were previously inextricably intertwined. Supporting this view, Rodenberg gives extensive background on the loss of Welsh political independence and presents critically the impact of English cultural domination and government policy, even going as far as to refer explicitly to the spread over the years of the English gentry into Wales as a process of colonization, gradually establishing 'englische Colonieen in Wales' (p. 54) ['English colonies in Wales' (p. 25)]. This is underlined in Rodenberg's narrative of a local wedding where the community elders bemoan the decline of ancient customs, complaining that 'Jetzt schämen sie sich's zu machen, wie's ihre Voreltern gemacht haben. Jetzt machen sie Alles den Engländern nach' (p. 306) ['Now they are ashamed to do it like their forefathers used to. Now they copy the English in everything!' (p. 145)]. Kohl's prediction, echoed by Löher, that Welsh culture and customs would be gradually eroded, seems on the verge of coming true.

Unlike Rellstab, however, who seemed to accept a homogenized 'English' Wales, Rodenberg is deeply disturbed and feels the effects of the assault on Welsh culture as a personal affront. The threat is existential, both in its impact on Wales and its analogous significance for Rodenberg himself. Just as Welsh identity is threatened by English interference, so Rodenberg's carefully crafted sense of self as a German is threatened by the potentially destabilizing effect of travel. Identity was an acute issue for Rodenberg, a German Jew. His surname was originally Levy but he changed it in 1854, choosing the name of the place he was born and for which he felt an enormous affinity, the village of Rodenberg in Hessen. He visited Wales two years later and on the very first page of his narrative, Rodenberg clearly defines his identity as a German and explicitly outlines his sense of affinity with his homeland:

> Wenn man die Heimat eben verlassen hat, ist das Herz noch weich, und wie jeden unangenehmen Eindruck einer ungewohnten Umgebung empfindet man auch den Blick und das Wort der Liebe, die ja überall dieselbe bleibt, unendlich tiefer. Und so, nach der Seite des Gemüthes, die der Deutsche stets am Schwersten überwindet, zufrieden gestellt, nimmt man allmälig auch an Allem, was uns bisher fremd war, gern seinen Antheil; man hat seine Freude daran wie an einem schönen Geisteswerk, das aus seiner Sprache in die unsere übersetzt worden ist. (p. 1)

> [Having just left home I was still soft, and perceived every unpleasant impression of an unaccustomed environment, but so too did I feel immeasurably more deeply the look and expression of love, which everywhere remains the same. And so, after my feelings had settled down, which is always the hardest thing for a German, I gradually took part in everything that was previously strange, enjoying it like a fine work of literature that has been translated into my own language (p. 1)]

That affinity is then put to the test as a result of his experience of travel. Using his own poetry within the narrative, Rodenberg is able to reflect on the emotions provoked by his visit to Wales as it distances him from home emotionally as well as physically. He then exploits this distance in order to reinforce his identity as a German and also to validate his native culture by emphasizing his role as an outsider in order to take a comparative stance when exploring various aspects of Wales and Welsh culture. The German more often than not emerges as superior but without denigrating the Welsh in the process. For example, his encounter with the Welsh musical form the *penillion*[21] draws him back to German *Lieder* and in comparing the two, he admires the Welsh

---

21   Rodenberg appears to be referring to *canu penillion*, or *cerdd dant* [string music], a particular way of setting poetry in counterpoint to an existing melody played on a harp. Traditionally, this is improvised by a solo singer. It is thought to have emerged as a musical form in the eighteenth century.

form greatly but concludes that the *Lied* is superior (pp. 243–44), thus the encounter with the foreign enables positive reinforcement of his own culture.

The focus on poetry and folk culture not only underpins notions of national and cultural identity but also sits at the heart of the Romanticization of Wales found in the text. The Romantic view of Wales is embedded in the narrative and is in part embellished by Rodenberg's self-representation as a travelling Romantic artist – Caspar David Friedrich's Romantic wanderer made flesh. Maurer also highlights this, referring to the emergence of 'das Selbstbild eines romantischen Deutschen, der stets ein Lied auf den Lippen hat' [the self-image of a Romantic German, always with a song on his lips].[22] Also critical here is the impact of the march of progress. Not only is it a threat to Welsh culture per se but also to Wales as a locus for the Romantic imagination. This is made clear early on in Rodenberg's narrative as his Romantic perception and expectations of Wales are contrasted with the modern experience of rail travel, here as he passes through the ramparts of Conwy Castle, echoing the views on the speed of travel by train expressed by Rellstab a few years earlier:

> Wenn man auf so raschen Fahrten zum Denken nur die Zeit hätte, so wäre gewiss kein Gedanke natürlicher gewesen, als der, die alten Ritter auf ihren Streitrossen in diesem Augenblick sich belebt vorzustellen und sich einzubilden, aus den dämmrigen Fenstern der Thürme grüßten schöne Frauen in den Burghof hinunter. Aber ein anderes Ross hat alle den morschen Staub unter seine Hufe getreten, das schnaubende Dampfross, das treibende Motiv, ja das Symbol unsrer Zeit; und alles Eisen der feudalen Zwingherrlichkeit scheint umgegoßen zu sein, um ihm den Weg zu bereiten, auf welchem es gradlinig, aller Romantik zum Hohne, dahingeht. (pp. 17–18)

> [If one only had the time to think on such rapid journeys, then certainly no thought would have been more natural at that moment than imagining and picturing the ancient knights on their war horses down in the castle courtyard, with beautiful ladies greeting them from the dusky windows of the towers. But another horse has trampled all the mouldering dust beneath its hooves, the snorting steam-horse, the driving power, the very symbol of our age; and all the iron of feudal tyranny seems to have been recast to prepare the way for it, on which it proceeds straight ahead, defying all romance (p. 8)]

22   Maurer, *Wales*, p. 21.

Here the railway emerges as an explicit threat with a clear reference to the oppression of the past being 'umgegoßen' [recast] to serve the advance of overbearing English modernity. This characterizes Rodenberg's view of the hegemonic power brought to bear on the Welsh, their identity under severe threat. The context is of course further complicated by the fact that the castle at Conwy is, like most of the surviving castles in Wales, an English construction. The Romantic view conjured up by Rodenberg is, then, a manifestation of the memory of previous hegemony, now pushed aside by a new wave from the east.

Despite the palpable sense of unease, what is clear from Rodenberg's text is that there is now an understanding of Wales in its own right with less requirement, ironically, to place it in the Celtic context. Wales is treated on a par with the other Celtic nations and attracts Rodenberg's attention as an entity in its own right. This emphasis on Welsh culture suggests that the emerging profile of Celtic studies in Germany through the work of Schulz and others, combined with the increasing number of travel narratives on Wales had, by the mid-nineteenth century, enabled a better understanding of Wales and the Welsh on their own terms. Further evidence of this is found in the steady stream of journal articles on Wales in the burgeoning periodical press from the late 1850s onwards. Many are published anonymously, but some named contributors produced several pieces over a period of years based on their travel experiences. One of the most prolific was revolutionary intellectual, Karl Blind (1826–1907), who travelled to Wales in 1862 with his wife, Frederike Cohen (dates unknown), and their children. Echoing Rodenberg, Blind presents Wales as a place apart and emphasizes the ancient nature of both the people and the Welsh language. In his article 'Erinnerungen aus Wales' [Recollections of Wales], which appeared in the Viennese *Neue Freie Presse* [New Free Press] in 1869,[23] he narrates an encounter with a landlady in Llandudno. His reaction to her comment that her husband spoke no English, a revelation which provokes a sense of otherworldliness, places Blind's Welsh encounter in an almost ethereal light:

> Die Worte übten auf uns eine fast komische Wirkung. Der im unterirdischen Geschosse hausende walisische Barbarossa dünkte uns ein drolliges Bild. Da saß er, ein lebendiges Alterthum, ein sonderbares Überbleibsel längst verschollene Geschichte. Seine 'Sprachlosigkeit' führte uns mit einem Ruck über die normännische Eroberung hinaus,

23 Karl Blind, 'Erinnerungen aus Wales', *Neue Freie Presse*, 19 March 1869, pp. 1–4.

hinter die angelsächsische Zeit zurück, mitten ins alte Britenthum hinein! Es wurde mir druidisch mispelhaft zu Muthe. Wäre die ehrenwerthe Wirthin nicht 'zwei Jahre in England gewesen', ich hätte mir sie als ein kymrisches Dornröschen vorstellen können, dem die Zeitenuhr stillsteht, während es in der Hecke schläft und die Ankunft des Erretters wartet, der Alles noch lebendig machen wird. (p. 1)

[The words had an almost humorous effect upon us. The image of the Welsh Barbarossa living in the chamber underground seemed peculiar to us. There he sat, a living ancient, a strange relic of long-forgotten history. His 'speechlessness' took us with one jolt back beyond the Norman Conquest, to before the Anglo-Saxon period, right into the midst of the Brythonic age! I came over all druid-like. Had the good lady not 'spent two years in England', I would have been able to picture her as a Welsh Sleeping Beauty for whom time had stood still as she slept in the hedge and waited for the arrival of her saviour who would bring everything to life again]

This description has a doubly alienating effect. Firstly, Blind's reference to the Welshman's 'Sprachlosigkeit' [speechlessness], albeit presented in parenthesis, has the effect of devaluing the Welsh language by suggesting it lacks currency because it is not English and therefore not readily understood. Secondly, he effectively distances Wales from its geographical, political and, to some extent, cultural context by emphasizing its difference from England – he notes that the Welsh see the English as foreigners (p. 1) – and by setting his reading of Wales in a frame bound only by ancient history. This is further underlined by the allusion to the German version of the 'Sleeping Beauty' tale, *Dornröschen*, made famous by the Brothers Grimm, which serves to broaden the cultural context further to a European setting but one embedded in the Romantic appreciation of ancient folk culture. Culturally and linguistically, Wales is presented as somewhere apart: ancient and asleep.

The interest in the role of language in setting Wales apart from its near neighbour and the placing of Welsh culture in a broader European context is taken a step further in the work of linguist Hugo Schuchardt (1842–1927), who narrates his experiences travelling along the north coast of Wales from Chester in 1875 in his *Keltische Briefe* [Celtic Letters], published in 1886.[24] Schuchardt is best remembered for his

24 Hugo Schuchardt, 'Keltische Briefe', in *Romanisches und Keltisches: Gesammelte Aufsätze von Hugo Schuchardt* (Strassburg: Karl J. Trübner, 1886), pp. 317–86.

work on the Basque language but the range of his linguistic interests
was vast and he developed a keen interest in the fate of Welsh and
what he saw as the cultural struggle with English.[25] Consequently, in
his narrative, Schuchardt places Wales in positive comparison with its
hegemonic neighbour from the outset, noting that 'Von Chester an
wurde es angenehmer; von beiden Seiten rückten Meer und Berge näher
und näher heran, und die englische Steifheit schien in der frischeren
Luft geschmeidig zu werden' (p. 319) [From Chester onwards, it became
more agreeable; on both sides the sea and the mountains came closer and
closer and the English stiffness seemed to soften in the fresh air]. While
the restorative impact of the Welsh landscape emerges here once more,
given his scholarly background, it is hardly surprising to find Schuchardt
soon firmly focused on Welsh culture. He notes the rhetorical skills of
the Welsh – those which find expression in the Chapel – and describes
these as a Celtic but more specifically 'kymrisch' (p. 323) [Cymric] trait.
He pays particular attention to the impact of Nonconformism and is
unsettled by what he observes. However, echoing Goede, he blames
the prevalence of such 'Sekten' (p. 324) [sects] on a negative influence
from England which has found fertile ground in a culture which has
in common with other Celtic nations, he claims, a tendency to overtly
expressed religious beliefs, citing the devout Catholicism in Ireland and
equally stout Calvinism of Scotland as equivalents (p. 325).

It is not, however, the religious practices of the Welsh which
command Schuchardt's attention most, but rather the Welsh language
itself. As a linguist, Schuchardt was himself a proficient Welsh speaker
and published in the Welsh press.[26] He uses this ability to frame his
experiences as a traveller – a scholar at large – and makes much of the
positive response of those he meets to this German who can speak Welsh
but no English (p. 326). The latter point is somewhat disingenuous as he
is clearly able to make himself understood in English when required, but
it all forms part of the self-stylization which he shares as a strategy with
Pückler-Muskau and Rodenberg. His own 'invented' self sits ironically
alongside his observations on what he sees as being a partly invented
Welsh tradition, noting that much of what he sees at the Pwllheli

25 See David Thorne, 'Hugo Schuchardt (1842–1927)', *Y Traethodydd*, 138
(1983), pp. 91–100.
26 Schuchardt's Welsh-language publications included versions of his *Keltische
Briefe*; see, for example, 'Ymweliad â Chymru', *Yr Herald Cymraeg* (20 August and
3 September 1875), p. 8.

eisteddfod is 'gefälscht oder höchst unzuverlässig' (p. 329) [fake or highly unreliable].[27] This is not to say, however, that he does not support the event or its content, but like Goede before him, who was unable to escape the English gaze as a means to access Wales, Schuchardt finds himself – perhaps unwittingly – in the default position of hegemonic observer, adopting the superior stance of a German scholar assessing the culture he has come to observe.[28] In so doing, he sees the occasion, and indeed the *eisteddfod* phenomenon in general, as a unifying force, bringing together the various aspects of Welsh culture under a national identity most ably expressed in the language itself (p. 331).

Schuchardt's particular self-stylization, rather like that of Rodenberg, does nevertheless enable a close engagement with the travellee culture. As well as socializing and interacting with the general populace, Schuchardt actively involves himself in intellectual debate. This marks a culmination of what can be seen as the gradual deepening of engagement of German travellers with their Welsh hosts and is further evidence of the impact of German Celtic philology on that relationship. Schuchardt even manages to appear on the *eisteddfod* field as an honorary bard, the 'Celtydd o'r Almaen' (p. 338) [the Celticist from Germany], a far cry from Goede's reliance on an English scholar for opinion on the context of Welsh literature. Indeed, the fact that Schuchardt can write and speak Welsh with scholarly authority is in itself an indication of the extent of the 'discovery' of Wales in the German-speaking context at this time. Here there is a view of Welsh culture as one which, for the first time, requires no improvement. In fact, for Schuchardt, the *eisteddfod* is the very manifestation of Welsh superiority:

> Nein, im Ernste zu reden, man vergleiche doch einmal ein englisches Volksfest mit einem kymrischen! Auf welcher Seite mehr Anstand, Bildung und Geschmack? Man suche doch in England die Partisane zu diesen Handwerken welche, voll geistiger Strebsamkeit, ihre Sprache rein und richtig schreiben und sich, fast ohne Anleitung, zu Dichtern und Sängern ausgebildet haben? Wird man wohl etwas Anderes finden als *savages with a turn for piety and mechanics*, wie einst ein Fremder die Engländer insgesammt bezeichnet hat? (p. 347)

> [No, to be serious, try comparing an English festival with a Welsh one! Which shows more decorum, education and taste? Try looking in

---

27   Schuchardt pre-empts the argument about Wales's invented tradition put forward by Prys Morgan in 'From Death to a View'.

28   See Tully, 'Nineteenth-Century German Travellers to Wales', pp. 83–84.

England for the partisans of these skills, full of intellectual drive, their language pure and correctly written who have, almost without guidance, taught themselves to write poetry and to sing? Would one find anything other than 'savages with a turn for piety and mechanics', as a foreigner once described the English as a whole?]

This apotheosis of the Welsh at the expense of the English is tempered to some degree by Schuchardt's observations on daily life, bemoaning the lack of public entertainment in Caernarfon (p. 347), but the reader is nevertheless presented with what is essentially a Herderian ideal: *Volkspoesie* [folk poetry] in action. This is not the only trace of the early Romantic reading of Wales to be found in Schuchardt's text. He also echoes Goede's Schlegelian approach in drawing parallels with the poetry of southern Europe and, reflecting his own academic interests, places Wales just as readily in its non-Celtic European context:

Die Penillion, meist vierzeilige Strophen, lassen sich mit den süddeutschen Schnaderhüpfeln und besser noch mit den Ritornellen und Rispetten der Italiener und den Coplas der Spanier vergleichen. Wenn auch die keltische und die südromanische Dichtung sonst durch die ganze Weite des Himmels getrennt sind, so kann es doch nicht Wunder nehmen daß hier, im unbefangensten Ausdruck der allgemeinsten menschlichen Regungen, besonders der Liebe, sich einander annähern. (p. 363)

[The *penillion*, mostly four-line verses, can be compared to the south German *Schnaderhüpfeln* and even more so with the *ritornelli* and *rispetti* of the Italians and the *coplas* of the Spaniards. Even if the Celtic and the Romance poetry of the south are separated by the great expanse of the sky, it cannot be anything other than a marvel that here, in the most unpretentious expression of the most general human actions, especially love, they come together]

Schuchardt's role as professor of Romance philology must have informed this stance. He will certainly have been aware of Schlegel's seminal text of 1803 'Über die spanische Poesie' and the subsequent apotheosis of Golden Age Spanish poetry and theatre. This clearly places Welsh culture once more in a European comparative context as an independent culture of value, as Schuchardt effectively shifts the focus from Wales's relationship to other Celtic cultures and to England and places it on the wider European stage. Welsh culture is treated as equal to others and the English prism is no longer necessary.

The need to appreciate Welsh culture on its own terms is further highlighted in Schuchardt's metacritical stance in relation to travel writing on Wales. By the time he was writing in the 1870s, this had become quite substantial with a narrative of Wales beginning to emerge which consisted of certain key elements garnered from previous accounts. As a Celticist, for Schuchardt the key thing was to establish what he considered to be the authentic Wales. The issue at stake is that of national identity with a clear sense that the main obstruction to gaining a real understanding of Wales is the view of the nation peddled by the English periodical press:

> Kein Urtheil kann ungerechter und unverständiger sein als das der Engländer über alles was kymrisch ist [...] Hauptsächlich die Zeitungsschreiber sind dem armen Taffy sehr aufsässig. Wenn sie nur nicht in so komische Irrthümer verfielen! Man kann z. B. in der *Times* lesen dass in Wales gaelisch gesprochen wird [...] Uebrigens kommt es den Engländern ungemein spasshaft vor Kymrisch reden zu hören; den sie sind überzeugt dass eine wirkliche Verständigung in einer so wunderlichen Sprache unmöglich ist. Wie kann man überhaupt sich in einer andern Sprache verständlich machen als in der englischen! (pp. 345–46)

> [No prejudice can be less just and less understandable than that held by the English in relation to everything Welsh (...) Journalists are particularly harsh on the poor Taffy. If they could only refrain from making such funny mistakes! *The Times*, for example, claims that Gaelic is spoken in Wales! (...) Furthermore, the English find it really funny to hear Welsh being spoken; they are convinced that it is not possible to communicate in such a strange language. In fact, how can anyone communicate in any other language than English!]

Not only does Schuchardt demonstrate his understanding of the differences between the Celtic languages here – noting *The Times*'s error in assuming that Gaelic, spoken in different forms in Scotland and Ireland, is the same as Welsh – but he also highlights the broader linguistic dominance of English and the attitude of the English themselves to speakers of any language other than their own. Once again, the context is that of empire with a side swipe at the arrogance of a people whose culture had by the late nineteenth century reached across the world. Here, however, the victims of this cultural dominance are very much on England's doorstep.

If Schuchardt's critique of the negative English view of Wales is perhaps to be expected, it is more surprising to find his overall criticism extends even to those who have presented Wales in a positive light. Introducing his narrative, he launches almost immediately into an attack on Rodenberg's 1858 work (pp. 319–20), claiming that, while it is an agreeable book, it is too poetic, with questionable accuracy and large sections derived, if not actually plagiarized from *Cambrian Popular Antiquities* published by Peter Roberts (c. 1760–1819) in 1815. Later in the text, Schuchardt returns to his criticism of Rodenberg, seeking to undermine the depiction of Welsh life which his predecessor had presented (p. 362). In all of this, the problem, it would seem, is that neither the positive German view nor the negative English view of Wales is really accurate. In Schuchardt's opinion, the peripheral land remains unknown, despite the efforts of various writers to make it familiar, their work drawing heavily on myth and stereotype. He points explicitly to the existence of a type of 'Keltomanie', one at odds with the so-called Anglomania of the early century and still prevalent in many travel works of the period. He picks up on the influential work of English traveller and scholar George Borrow (1803–1881) and criticizes him for his overly Romantic view of Wales, noting that his *Wild Wales* (1862) is just a bit too wild and should only be read by those who already know Wales, not by those seeking to understand this Celtic nation (pp. 391–93). Indeed, he cites Borrow's work as an exemplar of the type of travel writing which has come to shape but has also been shaped by expectations, not only of Wales, but of lesser known destinations in general:

> Es gibt Schriftsteller welche, nachdem sie in einem Lande vierundzwanzig Stunden auf der Eisenbahn hin- und hergerollt sind, in zwei oder drei Restaurationen gut gespeist und aus einer einflussreichen Persönlichkeit deren ganze politische und nationalökonomische Weisheit herausgelockt haben, in festen Zügen und mit frischen Farben uns ein Bild dieses Landes entwerfen [...] Manchmal kann man sich bei ihnen des Verdachtes nicht erwehren dass sie ein schon fertiges Manuskript auf die Reise mitgenommen haben, um einige an Ort und Stelle gepflückte Blumen – kleine Alibibeweise – hineinzustreuen. (p. 391)

> [There are writers who, once they have ridden up and down the railway line in a country for twenty-four hours, eaten in two or three restaurants and extracted a considered opinion on politics and socio-economics from some influential person or another, put together a fixed and freshly coloured image of the country in question (...) Sometimes one cannot help but suspect that they have taken a preprepared manuscript on their travels in order to scatter in one or two flowers picked on the spot as little pieces of evidence]

Schuchardt's comments highlight critically the impact of travel writing on the way in which later travellers record their experiences, driven by a set of expectations and textual paradigms which shape the accounts they produce, as well as their quality. He notes also how rail travel and mobility in general have begun to impact upon the way in which travel narratives are created, presaging to some degree the more derivative accounts of the later century. Despite this insight, however, Schuchardt himself ends up on a well-worn path as he focuses inevitably on what had by then become the standard topics in travel writing, reiterating the now established narrative of Wales. He discusses Nonconformism and the resulting puritanical lifestyle of the Welsh (p. 324), he covers the survival of the Welsh language and the *eisteddfod* phenomenon (p. 331) and he notes how hospitable the Welsh are (p. 325). He notes also the use of Welsh in Sunday schools as opposed to English which was the medium for state education (p. 349) and, like Goede and others, he makes the link to *Ossian* (p. 352). This suggests that the impact of previous narratives had, despite his best intentions, guided Schuchardt to specific topics and specific places as it had many travellers before him. However, Schuchardt's work, with its lack of reference to other well-known texts, such as those by Goede, Pückler-Muskau, or Kohl, also shows how the identity and influence of individual writers is undermined as they vanish from view.

The invisibility of previous generations of writers becomes a feature of the late century. By the 1880s, Wales had moved into focus in the burgeoning high-end book market, these volumes notable for their high-quality embossed covers and detailed etched prints. This commercial interest shows how the narrative of Wales had become part of the reading landscape of the aspirational middle classes and might suggest that the discovery of Wales was complete as it shifted from a peripheral Celtic nation to a standard site in the German consciousness along with many other nations. Key examples of this genre are *Nordland-Fahrten* (1881) [Journeys through Northern Lands], edited by Adolf Brennecke (1841–1892), Franz Brömel (1829–1904), Richard Oberländer (1832–1891) and Adolf Rosenberg (1850–1906),[29] and Adolf Brennecke's *Alt-England. Eine Studienreise durch London und die Grafschaften zwischen Kanal und Piktenwall. Gänzliche Neuarbeitung der 2. und 3. Abteilung der Nordlandfahrten* (1888) [Old England: A Study Tour through London and the Counties between the Channel and the Picts' Wall. Complete Reworking of the Second and Third Parts of the

29   Adolf Brennecke, Franz Brömel, Richard Oberländer and Adolf Rosenberg, *Nordland-Fahrten. Zweite Abteilung. Malerische Wanderungen durch England und die Kanalinseln: Mit besonderer Berücksichtigung von Sage und Geschichte, Literatur und Kunst* (Leipzig: Hirt, 1882); the section on Wales: pp. 177–238.

Journeys through Northern Lands].[30] The editors of *Nordland-Fahrten* say the following in their foreword, expressing a view which seems to confirm the culmination of the narrative of Wales:

> Diesem [...] Kapitel folgt zum Schluß eine Wanderung durch die Grafschaft Wales, sagen- und sangesvoll wie wohl kein Land Europas; wir wollen aber der Leselust unserer Wandersgenossen nicht vorgreifen, sie dürften zumeist einstimmen in das Bekenntniß, welches uns selbst entschlüpfte beim Empfang der von Francis Brömel an Ort und Stelle entworfenen Schilderungen, daß auch sie wenig wußten von der Existenz eines so eigenthümlichen Landes und Volks wie das der Waliser. (p. vi)

> [This (...) chapter is followed by a wander through the county of Wales, filled with legend and song like no other land in Europe; we do not however wish to pre-empt the reading pleasure of our fellow wanderers, they should at least agree with the confession which we ourselves attested when reading Francis Brömel's descriptions recorded there and then, that they also knew very little of the existence of a land and people so unique as the Welsh]

Here, Wales is once more exoticized and presented as a hidden nation, yet the nomenclature is confused for it is described as both a 'Grafschaft' [county] and a 'Land' [country]. Notable, too, is the lack of the English prism: Wales is placed again in a European context, eschewing even the Celtic. Perhaps surprising, however, and echoing Schuchardt, is the claim that this nation is undiscovered. By now, there were copious travel narratives, as well as a broad range of guidebooks typified by those of the well-known publishing house Baedeker,[31] yet none of these are referred to in the account by Brömel. His text is divided into three sections covering north, west and south Wales. The logic of the routes covered is often rather odd, suggesting the text may be an amalgam of Brömel's own travel experiences and other unacknowledged sources with an emphasis on landscape and legend but little detail on towns and society. By eschewing reference to any sources, Brömel's text effectively denies its own heritage as the product of a layering of accounts and an increased awareness of Wales and Welsh culture. Instead, it provides an assured account of a nation with

---

30   Adolf Brennecke, 'Wales und die Insel Man', in *Alt-England. Eine Studienreise durch London und die Grafschaften zwischen Kanal und Piktenwall* (Leipzig: Ferdinand Hirt & Sohn, 1888), pp. 151–65.

31   See Dijkstra, in particular the chapter '1850–1900: Wales – Aesthetically Pleasing, Yet Culturally Indistinct', pp. 113–62.

an established and unquestioned narrative, part of which, ironically, is that it remains unknown: both familiar and unfamiliar; recognizable and misunderstood. Important, too, is the emphasis throughout on placing Wales in a broader historical and geographical context with references to immigrant influences and numerous global points of comparison, including the links between Welsh and Sanskrit (p. 230), a set of observations which suggest a reliance on the work of Borrow, who devoted an entire chapter to the topic in his volume *Wild Wales*. The interaction with England remains important but not overbearing as it had been in earlier accounts. This reflects a shift in relation to the issue of national identity in these later texts, a result perhaps of the consolidation and security of German national identity following unification in 1871. Indeed, there is an echo of a Wagnerian ideal in the presentation of Wales which speaks to a strong national narrative of the type aspired to in the context of the Second Empire. Brömel's hyperbolic opening paragraph on north Wales sets such a tone for the rest of the narrative:

> Wales ist eine steinerne Ilias! Jede himmelanstrebende Höhe hat ein Heldengedicht geboren; in jedem seiner Ströme floß das Blut von Helden und jedes seiner Felder war irgend einmal ein Schlachtfeld und jede Ruine eine Feste dereinst, um deren Besitz im vorigen und in diesem Jahrhundert gerungen und gestritten wurde. Manches Schieferfeld bot unvergängliche Grabstätten für Könige und Fürsten, deren Namen und Thaten in Rhapsodien auf der Harfe bis auf die heute lebenden Nachkommen vererbt wurden. (p. 177)

> [Wales is a stone Ilias! Every summit which reaches for the sky gave birth to an epic poem; in every one of its rivers the blood of heroes flowed and every one of its fields was once a battlefield and every ruin once a stronghold, the possession of which was struggled for and fought over in the previous century and in this one. Many a slate quarry provided immortal graves for kings and princes whose names and deeds are handed down in harp rhapsodies to their ancestors living today]

Much of the historical background alluded to here revolved around the interaction with England, either political or industrial, yet England remains unnamed in an ironic reversal of the dominant trend. Instead, the Celtic context is foregrounded as the reason for Welsh survival:

> Nur weil seine alte Sprache niemals über seine Berge reichte, hörte die Welt nur wenig von diesen nordischen Heldenkämpfen, farbenreicher, gewältiger und wahrhaftiger als Macpherson in seinem Ossian für die

schottischen Hochlande erfand oder aus Fragmenten von Volkstradition aufbaute. (pp. 177–78)

[Only because their old language never reached beyond its mountains has the world heard little of these northern heroic battles, colourful, powerful and more truthful than that created or constructed from fragments of folk tradition by Macpherson for the Scottish highlands in his Ossian]

The emphasis on Wales as a hidden land of bards and princes persists here. Notable, too, is the superlative comparison of Welsh legend with that of Ossian, the authentic pitted against the spurious to the benefit of Wales and its ancient culture. Central to Brömel's reading of Wales are, rather oddly, the nation's ancient physical credentials. He claims that the very land of Wales has geographical precedence over both England and France, which, he suggests, remained under the seabed far longer (p. 194), thus allowing Wales to emerge as proud, independent and, ultimately, insular:

ein Volk, das ernst, arbeitsam und häuslich, [das] sich bis heute nimmer entschließen konnte, auszuwandern nach einem neuen Glück, sondern in allen Generationen daheim bleibt, wo seine Vorfahren Jahrhunderte gewohnt. (p. 178)

[a people which is serious, hardworking and homely, (which) has been unable to decide to this very day, to wander forth in search of better luck, but rather remained at home with every generation, where their forefathers have lived for centuries]

This echoes Blind's more humorous take on the ancient people of Wales, presented here as solidly part of the nation and its landscape. It is this domestic stability which has, in Brömel's view, led to the survival of the language when compared to Scots Gaelic, which has suffered the ravages of mass emigration (p. 228). Wales instead remains tightly bound to its ancient myths and culture, which in turn are intertwined with the landscape. Interestingly, too, this has ensured the survival of the culture in the face of English tourists, whose presence is noted but who appear much less of a cultural threat than in previous narratives. Brömel observes, in fact, that although the Welsh language had been driven out of the south-east by English, the rail network, so often seen as the vehicle for further cultural decline, has actually enabled the revival of interest in Welsh language and culture in the south by making the movement of people easier and thus facilitating the *eisteddfod* phenomenon (p. 228). The implicit parallel here with the impact of industrialization in enabling the unification of Germany and the development of the *Gründerzeit* [Founding Years] under Kaiser Wilhelm I and Bismarck is clear. As with the French-language authors discussed in the second chapter, modernity and tradition are seen to feed off each other in a mutually beneficial relationship, the outcome of which is strengthened national pride and stability.

Further echoes of the situation in Brömel's native Germany can be seen in his reading of Wales as part of Great Britain. Unlike most other observers, Brömel sees the relationship with England and the English as one which has improved over the years, the two 'längst eine Nation geworden' [long since a single nation] with 'nur hier und da tiefgewurzelte provinzielle Abneigungen' [only occasional deep-rooted provincial aversions] (p. 179). This once again suggests a sense of national unity in relation to the author's own national context, one built on more solid political and emotional foundations than that of Rodenberg some thirty years previously. The national here – like the newly emerged Germany – is essentially federal. Consequently, in describing the landscape, Brömel is often at pains to show how Wales sits in relation to the rest of the British Isles, as is the case in describing the view from the top of Snowdon, which affords a glimpse of 'alle drei Königreichen' (p. 190) [all three kingdoms]. This outward-looking perspective places Wales on a par with the other nations in a way not previously encountered. Whereas earlier commentators tended to either denigrate or praise Wales and Welsh culture in comparison to its near neighbours, Brömel treats the various nations relatively even-handedly. He echoes others in noting that the Welsh are generally more approachable than the English and comments on a slower pace of life, especially in relation to the railways (p. 202), but there is also a sense that, in many respects, Wales has somehow caught up with the rest of the country, evidenced not least by being the preferred residence of the British prime minister William Gladstone (1809–1898), whose love of his north Walian Hawarden estate is discussed at length (p. 191). There are no more than passing references to major sites such as the Menai Suspension Bridge and the Pontcysyllte Aqueduct, neither of which is mentioned by name. Instead, the presence of major engineering feats or industrial sites is taken for granted as it might be elsewhere. In relation to rural life, Wales is even seen to be in a better position than Ireland and some areas of England with accommodation maintained to a higher standard 'da Wales nach allen Richtungen von Touristen durchforscht wird' (p. 200) [now that Wales is being explored from all directions by tourists]. There is no longer the acute sense of Wales being a backwater requiring improvement. Instead, the focus is on the ancient Wales which lies beneath this modern landscape. In unearthing that ancient aspect, Brömel finds himself on a well-trodden cultural path with references to the Romantics (specifically Wordsworth and Novalis in relation to Tintern Abbey) (pp. 217–18) and mention of a range of Welsh myths and legends found in numerous previous narratives. Like others, he also draws on the unexpected aesthetic power of the industrial landscape but this in turn is grounded in its ancient geographical context, once more underlining the solid foundations upon which Welsh modernity is able to flourish.

Brömel's view of Wales as a nation with an independent role to play is echoed in another article by Blind, published in 1881 in the *Neue Freie Presse* with the title 'Eine Barden- und Volksversammlung in Wales' [A Bardic and Folk Gathering in Wales].[32] The article repeats many of the anecdotes in Blind's 1869 article, typifying the increasingly derivative nature of texts on Wales as the century progresses, but is significant for the way in which the author sets Wales apart as a Celtic nation in its own right. In so doing, he notes a shift in perspective from the English press which would suggest a change from Schuchardt's day:

> Heute ist das Alles ganz anders. Nicht länger gießt die Times mehr wohlfeilen Spott über das tüchtige, obwohl religiös noch etwas muckerisch aufgelegte Waliser Volk aus, das in politischen Fragen fest zur liberalen Partei steht. Nicht länger auch kommt keltische Leidenschaftlichkeit gegen England auf den Druiden- und Bardenversammlungen mehr zum Wort, trotzdem daß Wales weitaus keltischer ist als Irland. (p. 1)

> [Today it is all quite different. *The Times* no longer pours trite scorn on the upstanding, albeit religiously still somewhat obsequious Welsh people, who in matters of politics stand firmly with the Liberal party. No longer does one hear Celtic passion being voiced against the English at gatherings of druids and bards, even though the Welsh are far more Celtic than the Irish]

Like Bromel, Blind sees the Welsh relationship to England as one of mutual respect after many years of suspicion and misunderstanding. The Welsh are now framed as a political entity – one with expressly Liberal leanings – not just a cultural curiosity, their culture confident

---

32 Karl Blind, 'Eine Barden und Volksversammlung in Wales', *Neue Freie Presse*, 14 September 1881, pp. 1–3.

and well-defined. With Brömel and Blind, then, it would appear that the narrative of Wales in German travel writing had finally reached a level of stable maturity, the nation established as an entity in its own right in the reader's mind following many years of (re)discovery, interpretation and scholarly attention. Such is the fragility of that narrative, however, that only a few years later, a text claiming to be closely connected to *Nordland-Fahrten* set the narrative back to the stock debates around the tense relationship with England and the precarious position of Welsh culture in an ever-modernizing world.

Adolf Brennecke's *Alt-England* is rather misleading in citing a close relationship to the earlier *Nordland-Fahrten* volume. The two texts are only related in as much as the publishers, Hirt, wanted to publish further high-end volumes on 'England' and Brennecke was himself inspired to travel to Wales by Brömel's account. The text is essentially a combination of fact and hearsay but does claim to be based on the author's own travels. There is, however, no real sense of a traveller's voice in the narrative. Chapter sixteen of the volume is dedicated to Wales and the Isle of Man, the latter making a rare appearance in the context of the Celtic nations. Wales is again explicitly presented as a place apart, occupying 'eine scharf ausgeprägte Sonderstellung' (p. 151) [an acutely defined special position] and the problematic relationship with England is immediately foregrounded in terms which once again portray English influence in a negative way, here with a focus on the borderlands:

> Die Flussthäler bilden zumeist die Grenzen der 12 Grafschaften von Wales, sie weisen auch der von Osten vordringenden Civilisation die Bahnen, auf welchen Alt-England einst mit Heereszügen, heute mit einem Netze von Eisenbahnen dies Land der Berge und der Freiheit überzogen hat. (p. 153)

> [The river valleys make up the majority of the borders of the 12 counties of Wales. They also indicate the path to the expanding civilization coming from the east along which old England once advanced with its marching armies and now covers this land of mountains and freedom with a network of railway lines]

This echoes earlier texts which highlighted the colonial relationship between Wales and its hegemonic neighbour, but the imagery of conquest is more vivid. Here Wales's very freedom, seen as an essential characteristic in Brennecke's view of the nation, is found to be at risk, yet what threatens to engulf it is civilization itself. This complex and contradictory view epitomizes the narrative of Wales as it has developed by the end of the century. Brennecke goes on to discuss the history of the Welsh people, presenting them as heroic, their language as difficult and in decline (p. 153). He draws explicit links, unusually for a German traveller, with Brittany, and draws this into his discussion of Bardic culture (p. 153). The geographical reach of his text covers the whole of Wales with little comment, suggesting a reliance on the layering of texts which has gone before. The evidence of this is clear with information on mining, legends and key sites such as Bangor, Conwy and Tintern Abbey all suggesting a reliance on previous texts. Indeed, as the century ends, travellers seem to revert to the Romantic reading provided by the likes of Rodenberg and Blind. Nowhere is this more apparent than in the journal articles published by Adolf Heine (dates unknown) in *Prager Tagblatt* [Prague Daily] from the 1880s to the turn of the century. Two articles in particular, 'Eine Hochzeit im Walliser Land' (1891) [A Wedding in Wales] and 'Eine Maifahrt in die Englische Schweiz' (1896) [A May Outing to the English Switzerland], illustrate both the derivative nature of late-century accounts and also the ongoing heavily Romanticized reading of Wales.[33] Heine's texts are in fact largely plagiarized from Rodenberg's 1858 account, a fact made all the more outrageous by the former's explicit instruction, 'Nachdruck verboten' [reproduction not permitted]. The focus of both of Heine's articles is the representation of Wales as a land of language, bards, castles and pastoral idyll, with the notable reappearance of Switzerland as a point of comparison. This thematic combination is, according to Maurer, the end point of a century of development which sees Wales shift in the eyes of German travellers from a '*Natur*landschaft' [natural landscape] at the beginning of the century to a '*Geschichts*landschaft' [historical landscape] by its end.[34]

The final flurry of interest in Wales in the long nineteenth century, which resulted in a new but short-lived interest in Welsh culture, revolved around the 1904–1905 Revival. As well as the many French observers, a number of German believers also travelled to Wales. Although there were fewer of them, historian Noel Gibbard characterizes German interest in the Revival as 'quite strong' by the beginning of 1905, and notes

---

33   Adolf Heine, 'Eine Hochzeit im Walliser Land', *Prager Tagblatt*, 12 July 1891, pp. 1–4; 'Eine Maifahrt in die Englische Schweiz', *Prager Blatt*, 31 May 1896, pp. 1–4.
34   Maurer, *Wales*, p. 12. Original emphasis.

that many Germans made visits between February and August 1905.[35] Some of these travellers were mentioned by name in Welsh newspaper reports,[36] including prominent evangelist Johannes Seitz (1839–1922) and numerous lesser-known figures. The parties from Germany also included some prominent women, such as Eva von Tiele-Winckler (1866–1930) and Countess Schimmelmann (1847–1921), who attended an underground service in a colliery in Pontypridd. However, the German observers seem to have left far fewer textual traces of their visits than the French, both in terms of quantity and length, and the phenomenon seems to have received far less coverage in German newspapers at the time. Amongst the rare travel accounts in German are those by Seitz, who described the Welsh Revival in *Auf der Warte* [On Watch] in February and March 1905, and Tiele-Winckler, who was profoundly affected by her attendance of revivalist meetings in Cardiff, Neath and London.[37] Tiele-Winckler characterized her experiences in Wales as a 'Gnaden-Heimsuchung' [a visitation of grace] and was deeply moved by the contributions of lay preachers, the willingness of the congregation to make sacrifices for the cause and the communal singing and praying. She returned to Friedenshort in Germany determined to spread the spirit of the Revival and began holding revivalist meetings. In addition, under her direct influence a visiting party was formed and set out from Germany to Wales in September 1905. Yet, despite this evident interest on the part of some travellers, the impact of the Revival in Germany itself seems to have been geographically isolated, with a few revivalist meetings and conferences held in towns including Friedenwalde, Wandsbeck, Charlottenburg and Blankenburg, and on an individualized level rather than a national movement.[38]

35   Gibbard, *On the Wings of the Dove*, pp. 36–37. Dieter Lange also provides a brief description of German visits to Wales and the influence of the Revival in Germany in *Eine Bewegung bricht sich Bahn* (Giessen: Brunnen Verlag, 1979), p. 162.

36   'Pontycymer', *Y Tyst*, 16 August 1905; 'Y Diwygiad', *Y Gwyliedydd*, 8 June 1905, p. 5.

37   Eva von Tiele-Winckler, *Denkstein des lebendigen Gottes* (Giessen: Brunnen, 1970); details of her visit to Wales are on pp. 34–43. For a study of Eva von Tiele-Winckler's life and work, see Barbara Plathow-Holl, *Eva von Tiele-Wincklers Leben und Werk: Fachwissentschaftliche Überlegungen und fachdidaktische Konsequenzen* (Berlin: Lit Verlag, 2006).

38   For details of these meetings, see Gibbard, *On the Wings of the Dove*, pp. 39–47.

The limited travel writing which emerged from this period does not mark any particular shift in the perception of Wales, unlike the French writing of the same era. It is, however, embedded in the broader narrative of discovery which characterizes the development of writing on Wales from the late eighteenth century onwards.

By the end of the nineteenth century, a discernible if somewhat fragile narrative of Wales had emerged in German-language travel writing. As the accessibility of Wales improved with innovations such as Telford's coach road and the spread of industrialization westwards, the 'visibility' of Wales also began to improve. A number of sites, historical events and key figures, as well as topics such as Nonconformism and the Welsh language are gradually foregrounded to create an image of Wales which drives the expectations of travellers arriving there. Writing at the beginning of the century, Goede had no major German sources to rely on and therefore drew primarily on a Romantic reading of English-language sources such as Pennant. As noted, Goede effectively created the first layer of German narrative which others such as Pückler-Muskau, Kohl, Carus and Rodenberg then built on. By the late century, the impact of this textual layering has established a narrative of Wales which remains quasi-Romantic, informed by the flourishing interest in Celtic philology and, in some cases, highly stylized. As this develops, however, the nation is very rarely treated on its own terms. Instead, it is either viewed through a prism relating it to England or one relating it to its Celtic neighbours. This dual prism, via both hegemony and periphery, leads to a double-dilution, placing Wales in a constant comparative context with little opportunity for the establishment of a firm identity of its own. This in turn sees the emergence of a Celtic hierarchy which eventually settles on a ranking of Scotland, Ireland and Wales, all 'below' England, which sits, predictably, as the dominant force in the dynamic of the British Isles as understood by the German traveller.

A clear development is visible from the more personal accounts of the early century to the mass-produced, often largely identical, derivative accounts of the 1880s. The focus from a German perspective is firmly on north Wales simply because that is the area which attracts most attention and speaks roundly to the generally Romantic German reading of Wales, centred primarily on landscape and culture, which dominates the century with only few exceptions. Although that reading of Wales shifts occasionally from Romantic ideal to a focus on industry, the image which prevails by the end of the century is one of a nation of bards and princes embedded in a sublime and dominant landscape, but always with an eye to the hegemonic and not necessarily positive force of England. What emerges also is the vulnerability of the emerging narrative of Wales, both in the context of its own development and in the context of the legacy of the work of individual travellers. Although there is clear evidence of a layering of texts and influences, many writers who visit Wales and record their experiences are then themselves overlooked by the next generation of travellers who claim to 'discover' Wales anew. Despite this, the narrative of Wales which emerges is largely consistent throughout and characterized by a set of common themes, cultural references and physical locations. This complex cycle of intertext, discovery and rediscovery underpins the German narrative of Wales from its very inception in the early nineteenth century.

CHAPTER FIVE

Safe Haven, Literary Paradise and Present-Day Adventureland

Wales in Travel Writing in Breton, French and German from 1945 to 2018

Returning to Wales in the summer of 1955 following a previous year-long residence in the country, Swiss traveller Robert Schneebeli (dates unknown) diagnosed the disappearance of Wales from the European tourist map, even claiming that it had never been a desired tourist destination for the Continental traveller:

> Wales ist ein dem Kontinentaleuropäer wenig bekanntes Land. Er weiß von einem Prinzen von Wales, er weiß von Kohlengruben, aber wenige kennen das Land selbst. Es ist abseits vom europäischen Touristenverkehr, wie es immer abseits gelegen hat.[1]

> [Wales is a country which is hardly known to the Continental European. He knows about a Prince of Wales, he knows about coal mines, but few know the country itself. It is away from the European tourist traffic, just as it has always been off the beaten track]

Having been 'discovered' by Continental travellers in the nineteenth century, in the years following the First World War it would appear that Wales became lost once more, with the textual responses of previous travel writers leaving few traces. Especially in the case of German travellers, who found themselves less welcome than had previously been

---

1   Robert Schneebeli, 'Schule, Gesang und Kohlengruben: Kulturgeschichtliche Skizzen aus Wales', *Schweizer Monatshefte: Zeitschrift für Politik, Wirtschaft und Kultur*, 36:8 (1956), pp. 606–10 (p. 606).

the case, the number of accounts of journeys to Wales dwindled significantly in this period, before a new wave of interest emerged towards the end of the twentieth century.

The possible reasons for this decline include travel restrictions resulting from the two world wars as well as the economic downturn in Weimar Germany and 1930s France which led to a decrease in travel abroad. In the years following German division in 1949, East Germans faced further travel restrictions.[2] Elsewhere, travellers began to be attracted by new types of destination as the development of mass tourism and the package holiday led to the popularization of Mediterranean coastal resorts. French travel writers favoured remote travel to former colonies and the Far East, or reimagined the 'Home Tour', undertaking 'deep' or 'slow' travel around France.[3] The development of these new travel trends saw Wales once more confined to the periphery with very few published narratives. Those texts which did emerge from the end of the First World War onwards were often authored by specific types of traveller who found themselves in Wales as a result of sociopolitical events rather than of their own volition. It was not until the 1980s that the nation began to resurface in earnest as a regular destination in what one might term mainstream travel writing from the Continent. This chapter offers, as a prelude, a snapshot of the 'lost decades' of the interwar and post-war years, before examining closely the new interpretative frameworks offered by travel narratives in French, Breton and German published between the late 1980s and the present day. In the latter part of the twentieth century, differences between French and German cultural representations of Wales receded, which has allowed for a comparative analysis of their similar loci of interest and new interpretative frameworks for envisioning the nation. These include a sensory or physical 'consumption' of Wales, the 'internationalization' of Wales for a global visitor and a shift away from engagement with

2   Nevertheless, journeys from the GDR to Wales were produced by writers such as Günter Kunert (1929–), who travelled to Barmouth and Bangor in the winter of 1975, and Klaus Königsberger (dates unknown). See Günter Kunert, *Ein englisches Tagebuch* (Berlin: Aufbau Verlag, 1978); Klaus Königsberger, 'Durch König Artus' Land: Briefe aus Wales', *Ankunft und Abschied: Reisen auf 3 Kontinenten* (Leipzig: Brockhaus, 1986), pp. 133–80.

3   See Charles Forsdick, *Travel in Twentieth-Century French and Francophone Cultures* (Oxford: Oxford University Press, 2005).

the Welsh language and its cultures, leading to their neutralization and dilution.

In the early and mid-twentieth century, however, many of the more Romantic tropes which emerged through the nineteenth century persisted as Wales became a haven, a site of exile for those seeking refuge from a war-torn Continental Europe. To take one prominent example, more than four thousand Belgians sought refuge in Wales during the First World War, particularly in north Wales. Amongst them were the families of artists Valerius de Saedeleer (1867–1941), George Minne (1866–1941) and Gustave van de Woestyne (1881–1947), who were offered asylum in Wales by David (1880–1944), Gwendoline (1882–1951) and Margaret (1884–1963) Davies, patrons of the arts and grandchildren of the industrialist David Davies Llandinam (1818–1890);[4] Saedeleer and Minne lived for a number of years near Aberystwyth, where they exhibited their paintings of local views. Despite the large numbers involved, there are relatively few written accounts of Wales by refugees and exiles from this early twentieth-century period, as they have tended to leave visual rather than textual traces behind of their host nation. In her article 'Out of Europe' (2014), Carol Tully analyses diverse texts dealing with the experience of exile travel to Wales in the mid-twentieth century. Tully juxtaposes the isolated, parallel existence of Basque Republican children escaping the Spanish Civil War with the more negative experience of integration and estrangement of Jewish children fleeing Nazi Germany as part of the *Kindertransport*, as found in texts by Susi Bechhöfer (1936–2018), Ellen Davis (1929–) and Edith Milton (1932–). By contrast, the adult memoirs of renowned Polish artist Josef Herman (1911–2000), who made his home in Ystradgynlais between 1944 and 1955, and the letters of the German-Czech Jewish writer H.G. Adler (1910–1988) and his wife Bettina Gross (1913–1993) portray almost wholly positive experiences of Wales as a welcoming place of refuge. Tully argues that the ensuing image of Wales oscillates between 'the benign solidity of community, tradition and security and the dark, uncompromising location of myth and religious restraint'.[5]

This juxtaposition is reflected in the responses of a number of Allied military personnel who had escaped to Great Britain during the Second World War and for whom Wales subsequently served as a training

---

4 Moira Vincentelli, 'The Davies Family and the Belgian Refugee Artists and Musicians in Wales', *National Library of Wales Journal*, 22:2 (1981), pp. 226–33.
5 Tully, 'Out of Europe', p. 184.

ground and military base. From July 1940 onwards, for example, the seaside resort of Tenby became the main base for exiled Belgian airmen. Some of the testimonies collected in the volume *L'Heure du choix* (1985) [The Time to Choose][6] by Guy Weber (1921–2004) offer a negative assessment of the town in spite of its Romantic geographical location, and bemoan its latent 'English' austerity, especially on Sundays:

> TOUT EST MORT. Le paysage ne manque pas de romantisme mais rien ne prête à l'enthousiasme: ni le climat, ni le tempérament des habitants, ni les nouvelles diffusées par les communiqués de la B.B.C. (p. 43)

> [EVERYTHING IS DEAD. The landscape does not lack Romanticism but nothing gives rise to enthusiasm: neither the climate, nor the temperament of the inhabitants, nor the news broadcast by the BBC reports]

Most striking here is the use of a colonial paradigm ('bled') to describe the town and the 'impossible' Welsh 'dialect' spoken by its rural neighbours:

> L'intérieur des terres est constitué par des pâturages gallois séparés par des murs de pierre, des fermes isolées dont les habitants parlent un dialecte impossible. En deux mots: 'un bled' sur lequel il pleut beaucoup. (p. 43)

> [The country's interior consists of Welsh pastureland separated by stone walls, isolated farms whose inhabitants speak an impossible dialect. In a nutshell: 'a dump' on which it rains a lot]

In contrast, Chaplain Eugène Dethise (dates unknown) views Tenby's medieval architecture through the prism of familiar Flemish comparisons: 'Des restants de murailles moyenâgeuses, des petites rues enchevêtrées et, de ci, de là, des maisons à architecture familière (car, ce sont des Flamands qui, jadis, sont venus fonder la ville)' (pp. 57–58) [Remnants of medieval walls, small winding streets and, here and there, houses with familiar architecture (because it was the Flemish who came to found the town long ago)]. Tenby becomes a haven, its natural tranquility juxtaposed with the miserable state of the soldiers: 'Le soleil sur la plage, le profil rocailleux de l'île de Caldey. Et, pour contraster avec cette sérénité, une poignée de soldats déguenillés, blessés pour la plupart et surtout terriblement désemparés' (p. 58) [The sun on the beach, the rocky profile of Caldey Island. And, in contrast with this serenity, a handful of ragged soldiers, mostly wounded and above all terribly lost]. In addition,

6 Guy Weber, *L'Heure du choix ou les séquelles du drame belge de 1940* (Brussels: Éditions Louis Musin, 1985); chapter entitled 'Tenby', pp. 43–59.

Axis prisoners of war, such as the Italian Vittorio Bonucci (1920–) and the German Siegfried Kugies (1926–), also produced accounts of their internment in Wales, though their perspectives also remained 'hidden' for decades after the war. Bonucci's 1985 internment narrative *POW: Quasi Una Fantasia* [POW: Almost a Fantasy] details his life in Henllan prison camp from October 1942 to August 1944, noting the general kindness and solidarity with which the Welsh population treated the Italian POWs who worked on local farms.[7] In his 2010 memoir Kugies depicts his arrival in the same camp in 1946, undertaking the farm work previously done by Italian POWs, and serving as a translator.[8] His account praises the generosity and sensitivity of local Welsh inhabitants who ensured that German traditions and carols were incorporated into their celebration of Christmas in 1946.

Following the end of the Second World War, Wales became a site of refuge for several exiled Breton nationalists, including François 'Taldir' Jaffrennou, who had been part of the Breton delegation to the 1899 National Eisteddfod. The post-war exile memoirs of Breton nationalist Yann Fouéré (1910–2011), published as *La Maison du Connemara* (1995) [The House in Connemara],[9] are initially characterized by a myopic view of Wales.[10] Following his conviction *in absentia* for acts of wartime collaboration in March 1946, having served as the general secretary of the Vichy-authorized *Comité Consultatif de Bretagne* [Breton Consultative Committee],[11] and founded and edited the Vichy-authorized[12] daily newspaper *La Bretagne* [Brittany], Fouéré

7   Vittorio Bonucci, *POW: Quasi Una Fantasia* (Viterbo: Edizioni Cultura, 1985).

8   Siegfried Kugies, *Der ostpreussische Eisenbahner und die Amerikaner* (Trebur: self-published, 2010). Siegfried Kugies's online video testimonial account of his period as a prisoner of war in Wales can be viewed at https://www.zeitzeugen-portal.de/personen/zeitzeuge/siegfried_kugies [accessed 16 June 2018].

9   Yann Fouéré, *La Maison de Connemara: l'histoire d'un Breton* (Spézet: Coop Breizh, 1995), translated into English by his daughter Rozenn Fouéré as *'La Maison' in Connemara: The History of a Breton* (Oldchapel, Oughterard: Oldchapel Press, 2011), available at http://fondationyannfouere.org/english/translation-of-la-maison-du-connemara/ [accessed 1 July 2017]. All translations are taken from this online edition.

10   For his detailed biography, see the Fondation Yann Fouéré website, http://fondationyannfouere.org/english/hello-world/ [accessed 1 July 2017].

11   An advisory body on regional matters.

12   The newspaper was financed by the industrialist Jacques Guillemot and the *Propaganda-Abteilung* [propaganda division] of the Nazi occupied zone of France,

travelled to Wales on a false passport under the assumed name of Dr Jean Moger in July 1946. He began a new life in exile in Wales thanks to the support of contacts from the Celtic Congress and Plaid Cymru, the Welsh Nationalist party. Fouéré was hosted by prominent Welsh nationalist leaders Gwenallt Jones (1899–1968), Gwynfor Evans (1912–2005) and D.J. Williams (1885–1970), among others. Welsh nationalists formed the Welsh Breton Committee to help coordinate and support the exile to Wales of Breton nationalists. Fouéré observes that: 'Cette solidarité que je rencontrais parmi les militants gallois me réconfortait. Moralement et materiellement j'en avais besoin' (p. 77) ['This solidarity among Welsh activists was a great comfort to me. Morally and materially, I needed it']. Nevertheless, the power dynamic of Welsh host and Breton exile also leads to some tensions in his account.

During the first period of his exile, Fouéré seems oblivious to his new surroundings, and reluctant to view the Welsh landscape through the prism of Brittany; it is almost as if this aesthetic comparison with his lost homeland would be too painful to countenance. He reminds his readers that he is not visiting Wales as a tourist, and that he had 'guère le temps et encore moins les moyens de faire du tourisme' (p. 38) ['very little time and even less funds to do any tourism']. Instead his gaze remains directed within, on Breton nationalism and the fate of its activists. Having been asked by Plaid Cymru to write a brochure explaining the current situation of Breton nationalism, he scarcely seems to raise his head as he busies himself with this task in the quiet sanctuary of Aberystwyth University Library, while being hosted by Gwenallt Jones.

When Fouéré arrives in Swansea, where he has obtained a teaching post in Swansea University's French Department under Professor Mary Williams (1883–1977), who was unaware of his true identity, his gaze also remains circumscribed. Swansea's city centre, having been 'pratiquement rasé par les bombardements de la guerre' ['virtually razed to the ground by the bombings of the war'], is described as a void: 'il n'était guère encore qu'un espace vide et un champ de ruines déblayées' (p. 35) ['it was still only an empty space and clearing site of ruins']. His portrayal of Swansea is centred on depictions of his lodgings in St Helen's, 'triste à mourir, sombre [...] dans une petite venelle mal soignée et malodorante' (p. 36) ['very bleak, dark (...) off an unkempt bad smelling little laneway'], and mapping the route he takes

which included Brittany. Like all authorized publications of the period, it published Nazi and Vichy communiqués.

to and from the university. Swansea serves as a blank canvas where he can act out his new identity and attempt to preserve his anonymity, and his bleak lodgings are invaluable in securing an address, allowing him to act as a lynchpin for the 'petit groupe disparate de réfugiés que nous formions et dont je continuai d'être le centre à Swansea' (p. 52) ['our small ill-assorted group of refugees, centralised around myself in Swansea'].

As the number of Breton exiles in Wales increases, the narrator's gaze can be seen to widen; topographical comparisons with Brittany become more frequent, and the portrayal of Wales as a peaceful haven becomes more prominent. He describes a scene of rural idyll:

> L'endroit était agreste et le paysage bucolique. Des collines vertes, aux contours harmonieux, en partie boisées dominaient la rivière près de laquelle se cachait la maison d'habitation et les bâtiments qui l'entouraient. (p. 52)

> [It was a rustic spot in a pastoral setting. The harmonious outline of green, partly wooded hills overlooked the river, alongside where the house and the buildings around it were nestled]

Fouéré was joined by his wife and three children in March 1947. They were hosted by Gwynfor and Rhiannon (1920–2006) Evans on their farm at Wernellyn near Llangadog, which he describes as 'agreste et reposant' (p. 72) ['rustic and restful']. He begins to recognize similarities between Welsh and Breton place names, which he terms 'témoins de la communauté d'origine de nos deux peuples. Malgré l'environnement différent, je n'étais pas dépaysé' (p. 82) ['a testimony to the common origins of our people. In spite of the different environment, I was not disorientated']. The exile's account is predicated more on the safety of stasis rather than the danger of movement, noting that 'nous nous déplacions peu les uns et les autres, désireux de ne pas trop attirer l'attention' (p. 85) ['most of us moved around very little, not wanting to draw too much attention to ourselves'].[13]

---

13   The French embassy became aware of Fouéré's true identity in the course of 1947, and Swansea University was forced to terminate his contract. At the start of 1948, Fouéré received the order to leave British territory; he departed for Ireland at the beginning of March, a return to France being out of the question. On his return from Ireland to Brittany in 1955, Fouéré's retrial acquitted him of all charges, and he went on to play a major role in the post-war development of Breton nationalism and European federalism.

In addition to the presence of Continental prisoners and exiles in Wales, the early post-war years also saw the proliferation of journeys of education written in French. The *bourses Zellidja* [Zellidja grants], founded in 1939 by architect Jean Walter (1883–1957) and subsequently run by the *Académie française*, funded individual study trips for sixteen- to twenty-year-old French students. These month-long educational journeys on a topic of the traveller's own choosing produced a cluster of twelve unpublished travelogues on Wales between 1947 and 1971, which are now held in the *Bibliothèque nationale de France*. Although the young travellers were obliged to live on limited finances, these travelogues focus on tropes which are noticeably similar to those found in many nineteenth-century texts, highlighting Wales as a site of industrial progress and a still-flourishing Welsh-language culture. Studies of coal and slate mines and steelworks, Norman castles, and national and international *eisteddfodau* still feature heavily in these accounts, from Claude Moal's (dates unknown) rather naïve perceptions of a Wales under rationing in 1947 to Claude-François Courseau's (1954–) more complex interrogation of 'Cymru '71' [Wales '71] and its continued 'Celtic' traditions.[14] André le Sauce (1943–unknown), who stayed in Llangollen in 1961, observed the transformative effects of the advent of the international *eisteddfod* on the town and its inhabitants:

> Llangollen offre à tous ses visiteurs un accueil chaleureux, et, quand arrive la grande semaine, la petite ville est complètement transformée; car il faut dire que cet *Eisteddfod*, s'il a réclamé pour sa réalisation des transformations matérielles profondes, est aussi cause d'effets psychologiques. Les habitants ne sont plus les mêmes; plus souriants, plus hospitaliers, ils respectent cette tradition plus que jamais. (p. 32)[15]

> [Llangollen offers all its visitors a warm welcome, and when the big week arrives, the little town is completely transformed; because it must be said that whereas this *eisteddfod* required a major material transformation for its staging, it has also produced psychological effects. The inhabitants are no longer the same; they are more smiling, more hospitable and they respect this tradition more than ever]

14   Claude Moal, *En Galles*, 1947. Rapports de premier voyage Zellidja jusqu'en 1974; 135. Bibliothèque nationale de France, Paris. MS; Claude-François Courseau, *Les Survivances Celtes au Pays de Galles*, 1971, Rapports de premier voyage Zellidja jusqu'en 1974; 4814. Bibliothèque nationale de France, Paris. MS.

15   André le Sauce, *Les Eisteddfod du nord du Pays de Galles*, 1961. Rapports de premier voyage Zellidja jusqu'en 1974; 3011. Bibliothèque nationale de France, Paris. MS, p. 32.

Le Sauce enjoys the festival's 'ambiance de kermesse' (p. 54) [village fête atmosphere], and even acquires a degree of fame; after serving as an interpreter for a Senegalese dance group and appearing in the *Western Mail* newspaper, on several occasions he is asked for his autograph. While working as a steward at the National Eisteddfod in Rhosllanerchrugog, his experience of attending the chairing of the bard ceremony is portrayed in rhapsodic terms, as he is overcome with emotion: 'Je n'étais pas dans mon état normal, heureux d'être si près au milieu de coutumes étranges, privilégié, pourrait-on dire. J'étais pris d'une certaine angoisse' (p. 96) [I was not in my normal state, happy to be so close to the centre of strange customs, privileged, one could say. I was seized with some anxiety]. Le Sauce diligently records detailed descriptions of eisteddfodic competitions and ceremonies, yet by the end of the week tires of the linguistic barrier in place due to the 'official' embargo on the use of English.[16]

Conversely, Claude-François Courseau's account of the 1971 Bangor National Eisteddfod demonstrates greater political awareness and a more nuanced understanding of Welsh history. When visiting Conwy Castle, rather than focusing on its architecture, he calls it an 'immense batisse construite par les Normands pour pacifier les irréductibles Gallois' (p. 18) [huge building constructed by the Normans to pacify the irreducible Welsh], and further underlines its oppressive purpose and Welsh resistance by stating that Edward I was the country's 'pacifier' and hated by the Welsh.[17] This traveller is highly attuned to visual markers of Welsh nationalism, such as Welsh flags and 'CYM' car stickers (short for Cymru, meaning Wales), and buys the newly published *The Welsh Extremist* (1971), by activist and cultural commentator Ned Thomas (1936–). During an extended stay in Bangor, he is keenly aware of the city's great excitement at the start of the National Eisteddfod: 'La ville est prête à cet événement et ne vit que par lui. Partout paraissent des petits drapeaux gallois, des livres gallois, des manuels de vocabulaire Anglais-Gallois. Les Celtes arrivent' (p. 35) [The city is ready for this event and lives by it alone. Welsh flags, Welsh books, English-Welsh vocabulary books appear everywhere. The Celts are coming]. His account of the Welsh 'contact

---

16   The *Rheol Gymraeg* [Welsh rule] was established at the 1950 National Eisteddfod in Caerphilly, and decreed that Welsh was the only language which could be used on the *eisteddfod* stage.

17   Courseau, *Les Survivances Celtes*.

zone' is tinged with a frisson of danger, as he excitedly tells the reader that he spent a night with 'Welsh extremists' in a Welsh-language campsite at the *eisteddfod* (p. 36). His guitar-playing host explains the campers' Welsh nationalist background, and the traveller is kept awake through the night by their nationalist songs:

> Chemin faisant il m'expliquait qu'ils étaient tous du mouvement 'Plaid Cymru', un mouvement d'indépendance assez important. Je ne dormis pas la nuit mais toute la nuit j'entendis les chansons nationalistes des campeurs. (p. 36)

> [On the way he explained to me that they were all from the 'Plaid Cymru' movement, a fairly large independence movement. I did not sleep that night but all night long I heard the campers' nationalist songs]

In contrast to Courseau's enthralled elegy to Welsh nationalism, the Breton-language travelogue 'Un dro-vale' [A Ramble] by Erwan Kervella (1949–1984), which also appeared in 1971, offers a more critical assessment.[18] Kervella represents his experiences of hitchhiking around Wales in a series of comic vignettes and sardonic observations. A poet, humourist and artist who became a teacher at one of the first Breton-medium schools in Lannion, Kervella visited Wales on several occasions before his untimely death at the age of thirty-five and is commemorated in the song 'Erwan' by leading Welsh folk singer Meic Stevens (1942–).[19] On his arrival, Kervella initially offers a critical portrayal of Wales's perceived uniformity and lack of distinctiveness:

> Evit traoù 'zo, ret eo lavarout, Kembreiz n'int ket leun a ijin. Pa seller ouzh an tiez, heñvel int e pep lec'h. E Skos, Kembre pe Kent. Ar boued ivez a zo unton. N'eus ket a 'spécialités locales' pe neuze int dianav deomp.
> Ar c'hêrioù kennebeut n'o deus ket kalz a bersonelezh. Daoust dezho bezañ dedennus a-wechoù. Caerdydd a zo meur a dra da zizoloiñ enni, daoust m'hon eus graet ni nemet ruzañ kêr, o vont eus ur 'Wimpy' d'ur stal bennak. (p. 33)

> [It has to be said concerning these things that the Welsh are not full of inventiveness. When you look at the houses, they all look the same, in Scotland, Wales or Kent. The food is also monotonous. There are no local specialities, or at least we did not come across them.
> The towns do not have much personality either, though some are occasionally interesting. There are several things to discover in Cardiff,

---

18   Erwan Kervella, 'Un dro-vale', *Al Liamm*, 144 (1971), pp. 31–40.
19   Stevens's song 'Erwan' appeared on his 1985 album, *Lapis Lazuli*.

though we just wandered around the town, going from a Wimpy (burger bar) to some shop or other]

For Kervella, Wales's alterity lies in its inhabitants: 'Met an diforc'h brasañ a verzer eo en ur sellout ouzh an dud. Kembreiz n'int ket Saozon! Gwelet e vez diwar o emzalc'h' (p. 33) [But the greatest difference that you notice is looking at the people. The Welsh are not English! You can see that in their behaviour]. The travelogue focuses on the sounds of the Welsh people, underlining their loquacity, friendliness and fondness for loud communal singing and teasing the young Breton traveller.

While Kervella does visit the National Eisteddfod, he underplays the cultural significance of its competitions in favour of its social importance for young Bretons, the stands and local pubs becoming privileged sites for interaction and the formation of inter-Celtic friendships. In this convivial atmosphere, he reports that 'Sur e kavfet ur c'hembread hag a zo bet e Breizh – e Foujera peurvuiañ – hag a grogo da baeañ deoc'h pintadoù "cwrw" forzh pegement' (p. 32) [If you find a Welshman who has been to Brittany – usually to Fougères – he will start to buy you several pints of *cwrw* (beer)]. Kervella's travelogue can be situated within the framework of ethnic tourism, with an emphasis on immersion in contemporary Welsh-language culture. A portrayal emerges of Welsh linguistic vitality and a language which is part of the fabric of everyday life, in cafés, pubs and campsites. This appreciation does not, however, play to the myth of mutual understanding in cultural and linguistic terms. Kervella criticizes the enduring image left by previous Breton travellers to Wales, the Breton onion-sellers known as the 'Sioni Winwns' ('Johnny Onions'). He claims that this figure has led to widespread Welsh perceptions of Brittany as composed entirely of onion fields. Though Kervella highlights the notion of Celtic kinship and takes advantage of his Breton identity to some extent, the underlying tension in this travelogue is revealed after Kervella encounters some of the two hundred or so young people staying at a Welsh-language summer camp. While praising their openness and frankness, he despairs of their ignorance about Brittany:

> E Breizh pep emsaver yaouank en deus klevet komz eus Kembre. Du-hont ar reaouank ne ouzont ket petra eo Breizh. 'Llydaw'. Ret deomp deskiñ dezho ar ger kembraek zoken. An darn vrasañ eus Kembreiz a bled gant o aferioù ha ne deont ket da sellout e aferioù ar re all [...] M'hon eus ni ezhomm da gemer skouer war Gembreiz, int a zlefe ober kemend-all koulskoude. Breizhiz a gav mat pep tra a ra Kembreiz [...] Ar Breizhad en deus perzhioù prizius dianav e Kembre. (p. 35)

[In Brittany every young activist has heard of Wales. Over there, the young do not know what Brittany is. 'Llydaw'. We even had to teach them the Welsh word for it. Most of the Welsh tend to their own affairs and do not concern themselves with the affairs of others (...) However, if we need to follow the example of the Welsh, they should also do the same. The Bretons like the Welsh very much (...) The Bretons have precious qualities which are unknown in Wales]

When comparing Brittany and Wales, Kervalla notes from the outset that what he discovers is not difference, but rather a gulf (p. 31). Therefore, while recognizing the notion of Wales as a positive example for Brittany, he also calls for the relationship between the two nations to be based on a more equal and reciprocal basis. This is notably less idealistic than his nineteenth-century forebearers.

Whereas significant thematic continuities with previous travelogues on Wales can be found in these accounts published by the post-war generation, the cluster of texts which has emerged since the late 1980s offer new interpretative frameworks in their analyses of Wales. The selection of travel narratives analysed in the remainder of this chapter reflect significant and novel discursive frameworks. Not only have narratives increased in number and frequency of publication, but also in length, with the appearance of book-length travelogues on Wales, in French, such as Jean-Yves Le Disez's (1959–) *Une aventure galloise: portrait d'une petite nation solidaire* (2006) [A Welsh Adventure: Portrait of a Small Solidary Nation],[20] and in particular in German with Michael Bengel's (1946–) *Der Ritter mit der Web-Adresse: Walisische Panoramen* (2012) [The Knight with a Web Address: Welsh Panoramas],[21] Birgit Jürschik-Busbach and Peter Busbach's (1960–) *ARAF-Slow: Auf der Suche nach dem walisischen Herzschlag* (2012) [Slow-Slow: In Search of the Heartbeat of Wales][22] and Doris (1960–) and David (1969–) Lindner's *Traumzeit in Wales: Ein Reiseverführer* (2013) [Dreamtime in Wales: A Seductive Guide].[23] As this selection suggests, far more texts

20   Jean-Yves Le Disez, *Une aventure galloise: portrait d'une petite nation solidaire* (Spézet: Coop Breizh, 2006).

21   Michael Bengel, *Der Ritter mit der Web-Adresse: Walisische Panoramen* (Vienna: Picus, 2006).

22   Birgit Jürschik-Busbach and Peter Busbach, *ARAF-Slow: Auf der Suche nach dem walisischen Herzschlag* (Leverkusen: Drachenmond Verlag, 2012).

23   Doris and David Lindner, *Traumzeit in Wales: Ein Reiseverführer* (Battweiler: Traumzeit-Verlag, 2013).

have been published in German than in French (for example, articles on travel to Wales have appeared on a fairly regular basis in *Die Zeit* (Time), and the travel magazine *Merian* has devoted a special issue to Wales), thereby suggesting a greater readership and resonance amongst German-speaking travellers.

France and in particular Germany remain two of the most important overseas holiday markets for Wales and are the focus of much of Visit Wales's overseas marketing.[24] Improvements to inter-Continental transport infrastructures, such as the inauguration of the Channel Tunnel in 1994 and the expansion of Cardiff's commercial international airport, have undoubtedly facilitated a rise in visitor numbers to Wales. Dijkstra's study of guidebooks on Wales in Dutch, French and German demonstrates that this renewed interest in Wales goes hand in hand with a rise in guidebooks on Wales. The 1980s and 1990s also saw the emergence of guidebooks that focus solely on Wales, rather than viewing it within a British framework.[25] The greater variety of travellers to Wales following the popularization and democratization of travel is also reflected in the types of travel account they produce. As Carl Thompson has observed: 'Travel writing today probably accommodates a greater range of voices and divergent perspectives than at any point in its history'.[26] Contemporary travellers come to Wales in search of both spiritual or sensual experiences and adrenalin-fuelled adventures, and recount their journeys in travelogues, photobooks and blogs. Yet these recent authors have rarely shown awareness of their predecessors, and

---

24   Visit Britain, *Trends in Visits to Different Areas in Britain*, Foresight, 127 (2014), pp. 6–7. In 2015, Visit Wales invested one and a half million pounds in a campaign to promote Wales in Germany, as this country was identified as one of the three most promising target markets for the Welsh tourism sector (together with Ireland and the USA). Welsh Government, 'News and Alerts: Visit Wales Germany Marketing Campaign', http://content.govdelivery.com/accounts/UKWALES/bulletins/e8odd2 [accessed 16 March 2016]. Germany continues to be a key target market for Visit Wales.

25   Dijkstra's study reveals that guidebooks to Great Britain and Wales proliferated during the 1980s and 1990s, peaking in the 1990s with sixty-eight works in German, and in the 2000s with forty works in French. The total number of German-language titles is significantly higher than those published in Dutch or French. See Dijkstra, p. 18. Guidebooks fall outside the focus of the present work, which analyses narrative accounts of travel to Wales.

26   Carl Thompson, 'Travel Writing Now, 1950 to the Present Day', in Thompson (ed.), *The Routledge Companion to Travel Writing*), pp. 196–213 (p. 197).

the textual tradition and homogenized narratives that had formed by the late nineteenth century have been lost to a great extent.[27] The trope of a hidden, undiscovered and unknown Wales has proven to be surprisingly persistent, with the continued common portrayal of Wales as a quasi-invisible unknown quantity. Once again, Wales finds itself depicted as a site of inspiration and alterity.

The most extreme case of non-recognition occurs in journalist Pierre Delannoy's (1949–) travel article 'Pays de Galles: la tentation océane' (1991) [Wales: The Ocean Temptation], which even questions Wales's existence and identity, stating: 'on a du mal à comprendre en quoi on est bien au pays de Galles' (p. 126) [it is hard to understand in what sense we really are in Wales].[28] Perhaps surprisingly for a text published as late as 1991, Delannoy repeatedly questions Wales's essence and distinctiveness, in contrast to those of French regions:

> Où est le pays de Galles? L'insidieuse question ne me lâchera pas un instant du voyage. Parce que, enfin, il y a bien une Provence, une Bretagne, une Gascogne, des provinces immédiatement différentes, avec leurs villages, leurs couleurs, leurs odeurs. Là, excepté ce bilinguisme suraffiché, rien. (p. 128)

> [Where is Wales? The leading question will not leave me for a moment during this journey. Because at the end of the day, a Provence, a Brittany, a Gascony do exist, provinces which are immediately different, with their villages, their colours, their smells. There, except for this excessive bilingualism, nothing]

Framing his account in terms of a neocolonial relationship, he contends that present-day Wales is above all an outdoor playground for England, subject to social and economic exploitation by English holiday homeowners, and on viewing the 'atrocious' caravan parks housing holidaymakers, he declares that the English invasion is undeniable (p. 130). For Delannoy, Wales ultimately only exists in its inhabitants' loquaciousness, yet in his article only one travellee, his occasional female guide Llin, is given a voice. Wales is a land stuck

---

27 A rare example occurs in Julia Grosse's article 'Die Ladies von Llangollen', published in *Merian*, 10 (20 September 2012), pp. 88–91, in which she cites Pückler-Muskau's *Briefe eines Verstorbenen* (1830).

28 Pierre Delannoy, 'Pays de Galles: la tentation océane'; photographs by Richard Manin/Sipa Press, *Grands Reportages: Le Magazine de l'Aventure et du Voyage*, 109 (January 1991), pp. 122–34.

in time, where the kitsch décor of the 1950s still prevails: 'A bien des égards, Wales se résume à une collection de scènes tranquilles pour scénario immobile' (p. 129) [In many ways, Wales comes down to a collection of quiet scenes for a motionless scenario].

By contrast, Le Disez's *Une aventure galloise* offers an optimistic portrayal of post-devolution Wales as a dynamic model of collectivism and 'ce rêve communaliste' (p. 236) [this communitarian dream].[29] The narrator begins and ends his account by highlighting Wales's adventurous and determined attitude, declaring: 'Impossible n'est pas gallois' (pp. 10, 238) [there is no such word as impossible in Welsh]. He implies that Wales is no longer invisible and that a new, broader awareness of its existence and achievements has now emerged: 'Or tout le monde a maintenant entendu parler de ce grand petit pays' (p. 238) [But everyone has now heard about this great little country]. The voices and viewpoints of the Welsh travellees resonate and are placed at the heart of the travelogue. Le Disez's journey is thereby constructed in relational rather than spatial terms, and his itinerary is determined by the locations of his interviewees, who are mostly experts on Welsh affairs, members of the Welsh(-speaking) intelligentsia and his Welsh 'heroes', such as the crowned bard and musician Twm Morys (1961–), the painter Mary Lloyd Jones (1934–), the journalist Ned Thomas and, above all others, miners' leader Tyrone O'Sullivan (1945–), renowned for leading the coal miners' buyout of the Tower Colliery in 1995. Le Disez's work represents an exception amongst travel narratives in French in terms of the comprehensiveness and linearity of his journey, yet he avoids the country's main tourist and heritage attractions, privileging instead a type of political and cultural tourism which includes the dark legacies of Wales's industrial heritage, epitomized through a pilgrimage to the south Wales coal mining town of Aberfan, a central *lieu de mémoire* in Welsh collective memories: 'Je pensais qu'il était temps que je me rende sur les lieux où s'est déroulée cette épouvantable tragédie qui a si profondément marquée le pays et les consciences' (p. 37) [I thought that it was time

29 For an analysis of post-devolution Wales in travel writing in French, see Kathryn N. Jones, 'Locating "Pays de Galles" in the Twenty-First Century: Dynamic Model or Forgotten World?', *Studies in Travel Writing*, 18 (2014), pp. 187–98.

for me to go to the site where this terrible tragedy took place, which has marked the country and minds so deeply].[30]

The Welsh landscape can also serve as a backdrop to emotional trauma experienced by the travellers themselves, and ultimately offers catharsis. Writing in 2017 in a travelogue commissioned by the AHRC-funded 'European Travellers to Wales' project, German author Jörg Bernig (1964–) presents Wales as a periphery which serves as respite from the heightened political context in 'Mitte Europas' [Central Europe]:

> Mit einem solchen Reisegepäck also hinaus und hinweg an den Rand, nach Wales! Vielleicht, daß es dort und im Angesicht des Meeres etwas Ruhe und Sammlung gäbe? Was empfiehlt Christopher Logue[31] einem Freund auf der Suche nach ländlicher Abgeschiedenheit? 'When all else fails, // Try Wales'.[32]

> [With baggage such as this outwards and away to the edge, to Wales! Perhaps there and facing the sea some peace and composure can be found? What was it that Christopher Logue recommended to a friend, who was in search of rural solitude? 'When all else fails, / Try Wales' (p. 85)]

Surveying Worm's Head on the Gower coastline, Bernig summons the words of Swansea poet Vernon Watkins (1906–1967), 'the world's very verge', and the title of the travelogue 'Am Rand des Randes' [On the Edge of the Edge] constructs Wales on the outer edge of Europe. His journey to Wales affords him a fresh perspective on 'Mitte Europas': 'ich sehe sie vor mir, diese Mitte Europas, von hier aus, vom Rand, der, und sei es nur in mir, mit dieser Mitte doch zusammenhängt' (p. 68) ['And I see it before me, this centre of Europe, from here, from the edge which, even if it is only within me, is still connected to this centre' (p. 96)].

---

30   One hundred and sixteen children and twenty-eight adults died in the disaster in Aberfan on 21 October 1966, when a colliery spoil heap collapsed onto homes and a primary school.

31   Christopher Logue (1926–2011) was an English poet and pacifist.

32   Jörg Bernig, 'Am Rand des Randes. Reisemitschriften' (2017) in *Perthyn i Gymru / Belonging to Wales* (e-book: 2019), pp. 54–68 (p. 56); translation into English by Alyce von Rothkirch, pp. 83–96; available at: http://etw.bangor.ac.uk/downloads [accessed 28 February 2019]. Similar themes emerge in Bernig's novel *Weder Ebbe noch Flut* (Halle: Mitteldeutscher Verlag, 2007). For an analysis of the representation of Wales in the text, see Les, 'Space beyond Place'.

Whereas some accounts of travel to Wales continue to be constructed along a centre (England/Western Europe) and periphery (Wales/Celtic nations) axis, many demonstrate that Wales's increasing visibility has also led to the fragmentation of visions of Wales. Paradoxically, Wales's increasing accessibility, through the proliferation of dedicated guidebooks and travel websites and improvements to its travel infrastructure, has led to the atomization of representations of Wales and modes of experiencing the nation. Tensions arise between the greater accessibility of Wales, its greater prominence in terms of book-length travelogues and guidebooks devoted solely to Wales, and the absence of a sense of a Wales as a geographical entity in the ensuing textual accounts by travellers, who consume and represent the country in a piecemeal fashion. For example, in Doris and David Lindner's *Traumzeit in Wales*, geographical sites and tourist sights are located precisely, but also partially, which means that the connections between places recede. The volume recounts four separate journeys which take place over three years, and an absence of linearity predominates, with no sense of the travel undertaken between places and the connections between different sites. The focus shifts away from describing places and towards the exploration of themes, such as waterfalls, beaches, gardens, food, tranquillity. An emphasis on tempting others to follow in their footstep occurs throughout the narrative; techno-logical advances mean exact GPS locations can be given for many of their photographs, enticing others to share in the discovery of 'secret' sites of natural beauty. Indeed, the popularization and greater affordability of individual modes of travel such as the car, has led to travellers choosing more idiosyncratic, customized itineraries around Wales.

Jürschik-Busbach and Busbach's *ARAF-Slow* advocates decelerated modes of travel and a slower rhythm of life in order to appreciate a land which remains in the past:

> Das Erste, was einem ins Auge springt, sobald man England verlassen und Wales erreicht hat, ist 'ARAF'. ARAF heißt es an Straßenkreuzungen, an Bushaltestellen und vor Ampeln. ARAF bedeutet 'langsam' und nichts beschreibt *unser* Wales besser als diese vier Buchstaben. ARAF, langsam. In Wales scheinen die Uhren anders zu gehen. (p. 9; original emphasis)

> [The first thing that catches your eye as soon as you leave England and reach Wales is 'ARAF'. It says ARAF at junctions, bus stops and traffic lights. ARAF means 'slow' and nothing describes *our* Wales better than these four letters. ARAF, slow. In Wales, the clocks seem to work differently]

ARAF-Slow does not recount a linear journey, but rather a fragmented series of visual, atmospheric and humoristic encounters with Wales in the summer of 2012. A leisurely pace is necessary for the traveller to truly understand Wales, and stasis is to be admired rather than construed as regressive: 'ARAF – langsam. Wer den Herzschlag von Wales spüren möchte, sollte diesen freundlichen, hügeligen Westzipfel des Inselreichs im ARAF-Modus bereisen' (p. 9) [ARAF – slow. If you want to feel the heartbeat of Wales, you should visit this friendly, hilly western tip of the island kingdom in ARAF mode].[33] Similarly, seasoned visitor to Wales Le Disez chooses to travel only by public transport, such as the cross-Wales Trawscambria bus, as part of a deliberate strategy of defamiliarization and a search for alternative means of perception.

In order to counter presumed perceptions of Wales as a hidden nation, several travellers begin their narratives by attempting to categorize their 'unknown' destination. For Bengel, Wales's chief defining characteristic is the notion of difference, which he maintains serves as its corporate identity:

> *Wales is different*: Das ist die erste Lektion für Besucher. Die Eigentümelei als *corporate identity* des kleinen, selbstbewussten Landes am keltischen Westrand der Insel begegnet jedem Reisenden schon auf dem ersten Straßenschild. (p. 10)

> [Wales is different: this is the first lesson for visitors. The small, self-confident country on the Celtic western edge of the island takes ownership of difference as a corporate identity which every traveller encounters even on the first street sign]

This difference is firstly constructed in opposition to the more familiar English south-western counties of Devon and Cornwall; Wales's beaches are longer, and its hills occupied by a million sheep. Wales's alterity is also underlined in relation to other Celtic nations; unlike the Scots, with their moors, caber tossing and haggis,

> die Waliser, deren festes Land im Wesentlichen aus grünen Bergen und Schafen besteht mit einem harten Klöppelrand aus Klippen, essen *bara lawr*, *laverbread*, stundenlang gekochte Algen, und haben ihr *coasteering* [...] Eben *different*. (p. 10)

---

33   Similarly, in the final chapter of *Traumzeit in Wales*, Lindner and Lindner note that their main memories of Wales will be of 'Stille // Freundlichkeit // Entschleunigung' (p. 235) [tranquility // friendliness // deceleration].

[The Welsh, whose solid land consists essentially of green mountains and sheep with a hard hammer edge of cliffs, eat *bara lawr* (laverbread), which is seaweed boiled for hours, and have their *coasteering* (...) Just *different*]

Difference also corresponds to Welsh eccentricities or even madness:

Most different ist Wales indes in seinem zutiefst englischen Grundzug, der Liebe zum Spleen: Wo käme man wohl sonst auf die Idee, durch Schlamm zu schnorcheln, Querfeldein-Wettrennen zwischen Pferden und Menschen zu veranstalten oder ausgerechnet an Klippen das Klettern zu üben! (p. 10)

[Wales is, however, most different in its deeply English basic trait, the love of eccentricity: where else would one have the idea of snorkeling through mud, organizing cross-country races between horses and humans or practising climbing on cliffs of all places!]

However, while the eccentric is undoubtedly linked here to the excentric or peripheral, it is unclear whether the author is conflating *englisch* with Welsh or British at this point. By contrast, Bengel's travelogue on Cardigan represents an unusual reversal of the prevalent peripheral discourse: 'Cardigan, wie fast alle Hafenorte hier im Westen, war das Tor zur Ferne. Im Osten war die Welt, zumindest Wales, durch unwirtliches Bergland zugestellt' (p. 41) [Cardigan, like almost all harbour towns here in the west, was the gateway to distant destinations. In the east, the world was, at least for Wales, blocked by inhospitable mountains]. The western coast of Wales becomes a place of departure, and the east is reinvented as the hinterland.

For Lindner and Lindner, Wales cannot be easily categorized or fully described, and they underline its unknowable quality:

Wir fanden, Wales passt nicht in Genregruppen. Es passt nicht mal in Worte – viel zu zart und wild, zu duftend und bewegend ist seine Schönheit. Worte sind nicht in der Lage, es wirklich zu beschreiben. (p. 9)

[We discovered that Wales does not fit into generic groups. It does not even fit into words – its beauty is far too tender and wild, too fragrant and moving. Words are not able to truly describe it]

As Wales defies verbal descriptors, it becomes instead an emotion felt by those who encounter it, 'ein Ort, tief in deinem Herzen' (p. 9) [a place deep in your heart]. Wales's dramatic landscapes serve as worthy theatrical settings for Gothic novels: 'Das Land ist vollgestopft mit potenziellen Kulissen für romantische Schauerliteratur. Die Natur wuchert sattgrün und die Wolkengebilde, die sich über den walisischen Himmel schieben sind dramatisch' (p. 9) [The country is replete with potential backdrops for romantic Gothic literature. Nature grows lush green and the cloudscape that slides across the Welsh skies is dramatic]. Defying their preconceptions of Wales solely as a country of castles and history, the travellers are seduced by Wales's unexpected natural beauty:

> Wales verführt uns, wir sind willenlos. Burgen und Geschichte? Wunderbar, das erwartet jeder bei Wales. Doch Buchten, Strände, Klippen, klares Wasser, Sonnenschein – das glaubt uns zu Hause keiner. Wir treten den Beweis an. Wales, eine Art Fantasieland für Romantiker. Nur voll echt. (p. 24)

> [Wales seduces us, we are helpless. Castles and history? Wonderful, everyone expects them in Wales. But bays, beaches, cliffs, clear water, sunshine – nobody believes us at home. We can offer the evidence. Wales, a kind of fantasy land for romantics. Only completely genuine]

The suggestion of a new Romanticism as a filter for perceiving Wales is borne out by the remainder of the text. Through a series of compound nouns, the travellers fuse with the 'unbearably beautiful' Welsh coastline: 'Wir sind Im-Sand-Rumsitzer. Wellenwindriecher. Buchtenkletterer. Höhlengucker, Schöne-Steine-in-die-Hand-Nehmer, Bis-zum-Knie-Reingeher' (p. 25) [We are sitters-around-in-the-sand. Waves-and-wind-sensors. Bay-climbers. Cave-peepers, beautiful-stones-in-the-hand-takers, up-to-the-knee-goers-in].

The natural landscape also dominates Breton author Alexis Gloaguen's perceptions of Wales. In 'Galles Noires' (1989) [Black Wales], Gloaguen (1950–) deploys a highly poetic style to evoke a depopulated and anonymized Welsh countryside, depicting his encounters with local bird and animal life.[34] North of Machynlleth, he observes 'un couple de colverts se perd sur le grand lac. Des bergeronnettes printanières l'effleurent [...] Un garenne peu enclin à s'enfuir me surveille d'un regard égyptien' (p. 15) [A couple of mallards are lost on the large lake. Springtime wagtails brush over it (...) A wild rabbit disinclined to flee casts a sidelong glance at me]. While much of this travelogue is akin to literary nature writing, Gloaguen also romanticizes the few human inhabitants he encounters. When he is given a lift by a forester,

---

34 Alexis Gloaguen, 'Galles Noires', in *Traques Passagères* (Quimper: Calligrammes, 1989), pp. 11–18.

the traveller deems him to be a beautiful and erudite figure in a Welsh tradition, 'une personne de grande beauté masculine, ayant le visage d'André Breton,[35] les cheveux gris lissés en arrière [...] C'est un forestier au sens gallois, c'est-à-dire un savant' (p. 15) [a person of great masculine beauty, with the face of André Breton, his grey hair smoothed back (...) He is a forester in the Welsh sense, namely a wise man]. Here, the Romantic Wales found in so many nineteenth-century texts comes to the surface in a twentieth-century context with the nation's bardic heritage fused with the modern rural economy.

Though Wales's richly diverse and sublime natural beauty has continued to appeal to travellers, the late twentieth and early twenty-first century have seen the development of urban tourism, most evidently through the emergence of Cardiff as a 'happening place' ['in Cardiff kann man es erleben'], in Bengel's words.[36] Its prominence can be attributed partly to its status as Wales's capital city since 1955, and the seat of the devolved Welsh government since 1999, leading to what could be termed the 'Cardiffization' of Wales in travel narratives, as writers echo the guidebook custom of characterizing countries through their capitals. Its increased popularity can also be linked to improvements in travel infrastructure; Cardiff can be reached directly from the Continent by air since the opening of Cardiff International Airport in 1952. Yet perhaps above all it is the changing face of Cardiff, its post-industrial transformation in the past three decades, that accounts for its new prominence in travel narratives in French and German. Indeed, in these accounts Cardiff functions as a prism through which to view Wales's post-industrial society as a prosperous and progressive force, replacing the more prevalent English and Breton perspectives found in other narratives. Cardiff Bay serves as the locus of the city's reinvention, and the travel accounts frame its regeneration in terms of narratives of salvation and resurrection.

Although Le Disez ironically characterizes himself as 'reporter en enfer' (p. 11) [a reporter in hell], Wales, and especially the nation's vibrant cosmopolitan capital of Cardiff, appear as a type of paradise in his travel narrative extolling Wales's progress. In *Une aventure galloise* there is a clear element of idealization as he marvels at the new-look modern Wales, and he asserts: 'On a véritablement l'impression qu'une nouvelle capitale,

---

35   André Breton (1896–1966), French writer, poet and co-founder of the Surrealist movement.
36   Bengel, *Der Ritter mit der Web-Adresse*, p. 48.

pour ne pas dire un nouveau pays, est en train de sortir de terre' (p. 65) [You really get the impression that a new capital, even a new country, is rising from the ground]. When visiting Cardiff Bay, he describes the Wales Millennium Centre as an 'immense palais des arts à la gloire de la confiance retrouvée du pays et certainement de son bilinguisme' (p. 64) [enormous palace of the arts celebrating the country's new confidence and certainly its bilingualism]. The new Welsh Assembly building designed by Richard Rogers (1933–), 'une extension futuriste, face à la mer' (p. 65) [a futurist extension facing the sea], is also highly praised. However, it is not only the modern architecture of Cardiff Bay that is applauded, but also 'la naissance d'une démocratie d'un genre nouveau' (p. 65) [the birth of a new type of democracy] in the Assembly.[37]

Bengel's portrayal of the transformation of the multicultural dock area of Cardiff, Tiger Bay, begins by visualizing the harbour's industrial heyday as a major international port, when 'coal was king' and the global price of coal was determined in the Coal Exchange, now a newly refurbished entertainment venue. *Der Ritter mit der Web-Adresse* is unusual in that it repeatedly highlights the presence of Welsh guide figures, such as long-term resident Bill, who shows the author around Tiger Bay. Bengel praises the aura of authenticity preserved in the Roald Dahl Plass,[38] the oval basin where ships once queued to be loaded, yet also underlines the modern architecture symbolizing the city's resurrection, observing:

> die neuen Wahrzeichen der Stadt, das Millennium Centre mit der neuen gigantischen Oper, in deren bronzener Fassade sogar die Steinen singen, zweisprachig, wie alles in Wales, und gleich daneben der neue Sitz der Welsh Assembly, das Parlamentsgebäude, das neben dem monströsen Rundling wie eine südenglische Hopfendarre wirkt. Mit den Scharen von Besuchern in den kleinen water buses, sieht die Tiger Bay ein wenig wie ein postmodernes Disneyland am Wasser aus. (p. 49)

37   Some of the notable features of this 'new type of democracy' (in particular in the British context) include the introduction of a hybrid electoral system incorporating both first-past-the-post constituency elections and proportional representation; the equal and prominent use of the Welsh language in the written and spoken conduct of official Assembly business; and measures to ensure a high level of representation of women in the Assembly.

38   The author Roald Dahl (1916–1990) was born in Llandaff, Cardiff. The square named after him sits at the centre of the Cardiff Bay development, alongside the National Assembly for Wales and the Millennium Centre.

[the new landmarks of the city, the Millennium Centre with the new gigantic opera house, in its bronze facade even the stones sing, bilingually, like everything in Wales, and next to it the new seat of the Welsh Assembly, the Parliament building, which next to the monstrous oval resembles a southern English hops kiln. With the crowds of visitors in the small water buses, Tiger Bay looks a bit like a postmodern Disneyland on the water]

The 'postmodernes Disneyland' simile can be interpreted as accentuating Cardiff Bay's global appeal to visitors, but also suggests the eclectic and artificial nature of its new constructions. Where Cardiff Bay was once characterized by a continual flow of maritime transport, with each tide bringing more ships to export Wales's coal across the world, its new post-industrial facade now symbolizes stasis, due to the high-tech barrage securing the artificial azure lagoon.

The post-industrial prism remains present when travellers venture inland to visit Cardiff's castle and civic centre, albeit through a more critical viewpoint. Bengel admires the imperial civic centre, made of Portland stone, yet diminishes the size and significance of Wales as a country, deeming that the civic centre 'einer größeren Hauptstadt als der eines Drei-Millionen-Ländchens zur Zierde gereichte' (p. 58) [could adorn a capital larger than that of a small country of three million]. In Charlotte von Saurma's 2012 exploration of Cardiff for the travel magazine *Merian*, Cardiff's industrial heyday is represented as both golden and dark:

> Auch das Civic Centre ganz in der Nähe der Burg ist noch ein Relikt der goldenen Jahre. Schon von weitem leuchtet das 'Weiße Haus' der Stadt. Die imperiale, historische Selbstdarstellung mit Justiz-, Verwaltungs-, Universitäts- und Kunstgebäuden ist die helle, saubere Zuckerbäcker-Antwort auf das viele Geld, das man in dieser Zeit mit dreckig schwarzer Kohle gemacht hatte.[39]

[Even the Civic Centre very near the castle is also a relic of the golden years. The city's 'White House' gleams from far away. The imperial, historicist self-portrayal with judicial, administrative, university and art buildings is the bright, clean icing sugar answer to the vast wealth that was made from dirty black coal in that period]

39   Charlotte von Saurma, 'Cardiff', *Merian*, 10 (20 September 2012), pp. 30–38; online version cited: https://www.merian.de/europa/wales/cardiff/artikel/stadtrundgang-durch-cardiff [accessed 7 October 2016].

Unusually in contemporary travel accounts, Saurma (dates unknown) also draws attention to the new service industries which have replaced heavy industry, underlining the broader economic shifts which are also part of Cardiff's transformation: 'Cardiff ist wieder auferstanden. In den postindustriellen Unternehmen, in Verwaltungen, Versicherungen, in Callcentern und Universitäten muss sich heute keiner mehr die Hände dreckig machen' [Cardiff has risen again. In the post-industrial enterprises, in administration, insurance companies, call centres and universities, no one needs to get their hands dirty nowadays]. Nevertheless, Saurma's account also constructs a clear opposition between a cosmopolitan Cardiff and the rest of Wales. She maintains that Cardiff only feels properly 'Welsh' on the days of international rugby matches, when filled with supporters from the nearby valleys:

> Wenn Wales gegen England Rugby spielt, ist die Hauptstadt für ein paar Stunden zutiefst walisisch. Am nächsten Tag aber kommt sie wieder gewohnt kosmopolitisch daher, englischer, reicher. Dann wird es wieder deutlich: Cardiff ist anders als der Rest von Wales. Eine richtige Stadt, wenn auch erst seit 1905. Die erste Hauptstadt von Wales, wenn auch erst seit 1955.

> [When Wales plays rugby against England, the capital is deeply Welsh for a few hours. The next day, however, it returns to its usual cosmopolitan mood, more English, richer. Then it becomes clear again: Cardiff is different to the rest of Wales. A real city, even if only since 1905. The first capital of Wales, even if only since 1955]

Saurma portrays the 'true' Cardiff as a bustling cosmopolitan city, more self-confident yet whose inhabitants are also astonished that tourists actually travel there, mingling with the already multi-ethnic populace of the capital: 'In der Queen Street [...] wimmelt es nur so von Menschen aus aller Welt: Pakistani, Italiener, Somalier, Iren – eine internationale Stadt, ein New York en miniature' [Queen Street (...) is teeming with people from all over the world: Pakistani, Italian, Somali, Irish – an international city, a New York in miniature]. In stark contrast to Le Disez's account, which emphasized Wales's sense of self-confidence, initiative and agency (pp. 10, 238), in Saurma's portrayal this new vibrancy is not 'Welsh', suggesting that the 'true' Wales beyond Cardiff remains a land in the past, poorer, less confident and less developed. The question of what is 'authentically' Welsh is therefore still as pertinent for today's travellers as it was for many travellers in the nineteenth century.

In addition to an increased interest in urban tourism, contemporary travellers have discovered new modes of experiencing Wales. In recent years John Urry's 'tourist gaze' has been complemented by other sensory experiences, and this expansion of the senses is also reflected in the field of travel writing studies.[40] Several contemporary travel accounts portray Wales's emergence as a destination to be savoured. Challenging the negative preconceptions of their German readers regarding Great Britain's reputation for serving truly dreadful food (p. 2), Doris and David Lindner repeatedly vaunt the high quality of Welsh cuisine (p. 70), whose chefs transform home-grown and locally produced fresh produce into original dishes (p. 72). In Harlech they find themselves in Wales's 'ice cream heaven', chatting with the owners of Hufenfa'r Castell [Castle Ice Cream Shop], and they offer a detailed description of the sensory experience of tasting their award-winning elderflower ice cream: '[Ein] zartes Blütenaroma wird durch all die Cremigkeit und Süße dieses Milchspeiseeises transportiert […] blumig, wie ein sanfter Kuss' (p. 196) [a delicate floral aroma is transported through all of the creaminess and sweetness of this milk ice cream (…) flowery, like a gentle kiss]. At the Penderyn distillery in the Brecon Beacons, they deem that the excellent quality of the whiskey stems from the botanical environment, as they can taste the Welsh peat and plants (p. 100). In Cardiff's indoor market, Bernhard Hüttenegger (1948–) enjoys the down-to-earth fare which he perceives as the typical produce of the country: faggots, cockles served in a bag and laverbread: 'die größte kulinarische Originalität […] es ist Tang, stundenlang gesiedet, der pure Geschmack des Meeres und nahrhaft obendrein' (p. 92) [the most original culinary offering […] it is seaweed, simmered for hours, the pure taste of the sea and nutritious into the bargain].[41] By contrast, Marie Darrieussecq (1969–), one of the most eminent and acclaimed authors of contemporary France, views cuisine as symbolic of Swansea's multiculturalism as she encounters:

> plusieurs de ces voyageurs qu'on appelle les migrants. La cuisine, délicieuse, était faite par une jeune femme pakistanaise, et j'ai discuté longuement avec un ivoirien. Le monde entier était au Volcano Theatre.[42]

40   See, for example, Alasdair Pettinger and Tim Youngs (eds), *The Routledge Research Companion to Travel Writing* (London and New York: Routledge, 2019), whose third part, 'Sensuous Geographies', not only includes a chapter on 'Seeing', but also 'Hearing', 'Touching', 'Tasting' and 'Smelling'.

41   Bernhard Hüttenegger, 'Wales und England', in *Weg von Allem: Reisen und Schreiben* (Klagenfurt: Kitab Verlag, 2006), pp. 91–126 (p. 92).

42   Marie Darrieussecq, 'Les Fantômes du Pays de Galles' (2017), in *Perthyn i*

[several of those travellers known as migrants. The delicious food was made by a young Pakistani woman, and I had a long talk with an Ivorian. The whole world was at the Volcano Theatre (p. 39)]

The cosmopolitan aspects of Wales may have emerged more prominently in the travel writing of recent years, but the predominance of the Welsh landscape persists nonetheless. Perhaps due to the vast improvements to Wales's transport infrastructure leading to far smoother journeys, travellers who valorize physical travail are instead in search of new ways of pitting themselves against the Welsh terrain. While mountaineering remains a popular means of experiencing the sublime through physical endeavour, especially in Snowdonia,[43] developments in adventure tourism mean that recent travel accounts echo new ways of discovering the Welsh landscape through aerial, underwater and underground perspectives. Other tourism developments are also reflected in contemporary travel writing, including the launch of the Welsh National Coastal Path in 2012, making Wales the first country to have a dedicated footpath around its entire coastline. The ongoing marketing campaign by Visit Wales, exhorting tourists to 'Find Your Epic' (2016–), can be interpreted as resonating strongly with Continental visitors, in particular from Germany. Above all, it is coasteering, repeatedly claimed in several travel narratives to have been invented in Wales, that has captured the imagination of recent adventure tourists and acted as a magnet. Bengel contends that Wales has the ideal coastal terrain for the sport, which requires 'steile Klippen und exzentrische Bewohner' [steep cliffs and eccentric inhabitants], and 'die abgedrehte Rocky-Horror-Klippen-Show' (p. 10) [the crazy Rocky-Horror-Cliff-Show] has been staged in Wales since 1986. In his 2012 account of coasteering, journalist

Gymru / Belonging to Wales (e-book: 2019), pp. 29–33 (p. 30); translation into English by Kathryn N. Jones, pp. 38–42; available at: http://etw.bangor.ac.uk/ downloads [accessed 28 February 2019].

43   See, for example, Jean-Charles Duquesne, 'Voyages. Au pays de Galles, la nature est reine', *La Croix*, 26 May 1997, p. 18; Christophe de Chenay, 'Les montagnards du Pays de Galles', *Le Monde*, 20 October 2004, https:// www.lemonde.fr/archives/article/2004/10/20/les-montagnards-du-pays-de-galles_383729_1819218.html?xtmc=pays_de_galles&xtcr=1 [accessed 5 July 2011]; Peter Linden, 'In fremden Betten', *Die Zeit*, 23, 28 May 2003, https://www. zeit.de/2003/23/Hotel_Pen_y_Gwryd/komplettansicht [accessed 19 November 2016]; Bene Benedikt, 'Snowdon Gipfeltour in Wales', *Der Spiegel*, 1 May 2013, http://www.spiegel.de/reise/europa/snowdon-hoechster-berg-von-wales-a-895067. html [accessed 20 September 2013].

Julius Schophoff (1979–) presents himself as a self-deprecating warrior figure, but he also underlines an element of danger: 'Dann kommen wir, Krieger mit Plastikhelmen und nassen Turnschuhen, und mischen uns ein in diesen Kampf der Elemente. Die Irische See versteht keinen Spaß' [Then we come, warriors with plastic helmets and wet trainers, and get involved in this battle of the elements. The Irish Sea cannot take a joke].[44] In addition to triggering adrenalin, coasteering also allows privileged access to the different rhythms of an underwater natural world. At Porth Dafarch near Holyhead, Schophoff recounts that 'Seegras und Fingertang wogen im Rhythmus des Meeres, im Dickicht des Unterwasserwalds lauert regungslos ein Pollack' [Seaweed and oarweed swayed to the rhythm of the sea, and in the thicket of the underwater forest a pollock lurks motionless].

While coasteering turns Wales's natural environment into a tourist attraction, other new adventure pursuits have been part of the process of regenerating Wales's post-industrial landscape. Penrhyn Slate Quarry, located near Bethesda in north Wales, was the world's largest slate quarry at the end of the nineteenth century and, as such, was visited by numerous Continental travellers. Since 2013, however, it has been home to 'Zip World Velocity 2', the fastest zip line in the world, which allows visitors to descend over the quarry at over one hundred miles per hour. Following their landing, the visitors are encouraged to immerse themselves in the history of the quarry on a truck tour around the site, thereby combining adventure tourism and industrial heritage. Similarly, the 'Surf Snowdonia' adventure park offers the world's first inland surf lagoon, using cutting-edge technology on the site of a former aluminium factory at Dolgarrog. The attraction is portrayed as being in harmony with its natural surroundings; for example, the French daily newspaper *Le Monde* has observed that 'le bassin peut se fondre dans le paysage, comme c'est le cas à Conwy Valley dans le nord du Pays de Galles, au pied des montagnes de Snowdonia' [the pool can blend into the landscape, like at Conwy Valley in north Wales at the foot of the Snowdonia mountains].[45] Likewise, the Llechwedd slate mine at Blaenau Ffestiniog has been given a new life as an 'unterirdische Riesenspielplatz'

---

44   Julius Schophoff, 'Auf der Klippe', *Die Zeit*, 22, 5 June 2012, p. 61.

45   'La plus longue vague artificielle du monde déferle au Pays de Galles', *Le Monde*, 31 July 2015, https://www.lemonde.fr/sports-de-glisse/article/2015/07/31/surf-la-plus-longue-vague-artificielle-du-monde-deferle-au-pays-de-galles_4706388_1616666.html [accessed 25 September 2015].

[giant underground playground].[46] German journalist Christine Dohler's (1981–) experience of underground trampolining there in 2015 reminded the author of the surreal fantasy world of a computer game: 'Unter mir geht es mehr als 50 Meter in die Tiefe, wo spitze Felsen zu erahnen sind. Über mir und ringsum dräuen düstere Höhlenwände, angeblitzt von Neonlicht' [More than fifty metres below me sharp rocks are lurking. Above and around me dark cave walls loom, streaked with neon light]. Dohler deems 'das Ganze eine super Recycling-Idee für ausgediente Industrieorte' [the whole thing is a great recycling idea for disused industrial places]. Yet the industrial past itself is not neglected in her account, which concludes by undertaking a tour around the 'stockfinster' [pitch black] and 'totenstill' [deathly quiet] slate mine, and Dohler evokes the dangerous and difficult working conditions faced by the miners, including children. Such former industrial sites demonstrate that the amalgamation of natural landscape, post-industry and cutting-edge technology can bring new visitors to Wales and contribute to its portrayal in contemporary Continental travelogues as a vibrant destination.

Nevertheless, Wales's tranquillity and rural calm also remain important reasons for travel, as is borne out by its reputation since the 1970s as a 'Dorado für Alternative' [El Dorado for counterculturalists].[47] A recent variant on the excentric 'western fringe' paradigm used to represent Wales can be found in accounts of pilgrimages to Ynys Enlli (Bardsey Island), now a national nature reserve off the Llŷn Peninsula, and St David's in the far west of the Pembrokeshire Peninsula. Almost entirely absent from the itineraries of nineteenth- and early twentieth-century travellers, these sacred destinations appear for the first time in late twentieth-century and twenty-first-century travel accounts. An early example is provided by Bettina Hürlimann (1909–1983) in her 'Craig y Môr oder Erinnerungen an eine Reise nach Süd-Wales' (1979) [Craig y Môr or Recollections of a Journey to South Wales],[48] which recounts her extended stay in a rented cottage near St David's in 1959, and contains detailed descriptions of the city and its cathedral. Although

46   Christine Dohler, 'Untergrund Bewegung', *Die Zeit*, 9 June 2015, p. 60.

47   Petra Juling, *Wales, DuMont Reise-Taschenbuch* (Cologne: DuMont Buchverlag, 2000), p. 35.

48   Bettina Hürlimann, 'Craig y Môr oder Erinnerungen an eine Reise nach Süd-Wales', in *Zwischenfall in Lerida und andere Texte* (Zürich and Freiburg im Breisgau: Atlantis Verlag, 1979), pp. 67–84.

greater accessibility through improvements in travel infrastructure and the arrival of the car as travellers' main mode of transport could explain the recent popularity of these destinations, in fact the first pilgrims to Ynys Enlli were pre-Roman Celts, followed by Christians, and the island became a major centre of pilgrimage in the Middle Ages. In the thirteenth century, when the largest and last Augustinian abbey was built on the island, three pilgrimages to Ynys Enlli were accorded the equivalent value of one pilgrimage to Rome. The most detailed contemporary travel account on Ynys Enlli is provided in Bengel's chapter 'Zwanzigtausend Heilige und eine Insel' (p. 101) [Twenty Thousand Saints and an Island]. He characterizes the island as a sacred place of religion and nature: 'Ynys Enlli, der Treffpunkt der Gezeiten, wurde zum Hafen der toten Seelen und zum Sehnsuchtsort der Gläubigen' (p. 103) [Ynys Enlli, the meeting place of the tides, became the haven of dead souls and the place of worship of the faithful]. The remoteness of the island and its dependence on the capriciousness of the tides and weather are emphasized throughout the account; Bengel is hyper-aware of the risk of being cut off and unable to leave the island, and Ynys Enlli is presented as a beautiful, yet perilous destination. A temporal shift occurs through the traveller's conscious act of journeying in the footsteps of pilgrims past, giving the landscape a timeless quality:

> Wir kommen wie die Pilger kamen: zu Fuß, durch Farnkraut und Granit, dem höchsten Berg der Halbinsel entgegen, zuletzt hinab ans Meer, wo sich der Berg als Insel zu erkennen gibt, die wie ein riesenhafter Wal im Wasser liegt: Für uns ein Ausflugsziel für einen Tag, für die Pilger einst das Ende ihrer Fahrt, für ungezählte Tausende das Grab, das Tor zum Himmel, die Pforte in ihr Paradies. Den Namen 'Island of the twenty thousand Saints' hat sich Bardsey Island wohlverdient. (p. 101)

> [We come as the pilgrims came: on foot, through ferns and granite, towards the highest mountain of the peninsula, finally down to the sea, where the mountain reveals itself as an island, which lies like a gigantic whale in the water: for us a destination for a day's excursion, for pilgrims of long ago the end of their journey, for untold thousands the tomb, the gateway to heaven, the gate to their paradise. Bardsey Island has truly earned the name 'Island of the Twenty Thousand Saints']

Ynys Enlli is thus portrayed as a portal to the afterlife, the final destination of a life's journey. Bengel's account initially centres on a focalization of the pilgrims' aspirations as they waited for the chance to make the hazardous crossing to the island:

Hier haben sie gewartet auf den rechten Augenblick, da die Gezeiten günstig waren, die Strudel und die Strömungen erträglich, dass sie die Überfahrt zur Insel wagen konnten, zwei Meilen nur, und doch auch immer mal für Tage oder Wochen abgeschnitten. (p. 101)

[Here they waited for the right moment when the tides were favourable, and the whirlpools and the currents were bearable, so that they could venture to cross over to the island, only two miles, and yet every now and then cut off for days or weeks]

Not having travelled there to demonstrate religious faith, Bengel's views of Ynys Enlli upon his arrival are focused on its importance as a nature reserve, providing refuge and a resting place not for pilgrims but for an abundance of marine wildlife and birds.

Writing in 1997, German travel writer Peter Linden (1959–) juxtaposes the romantic reputation of Ynys Enlli with his journey to the island: 'Bardsey Island, vielfach als romantischste Insel Großbritanniens gerühmt, erreicht man in dreißig gänzlich unromantischen Minuten per Boot von Porth Meudwy aus. // Dann herrscht Ruhe, eine unfaßbare Ruhe' [Bardsey Island, often praised as the most romantic island in Britain, can be reached by boat from Porth Meudwy in thirty totally unromantic minutes. // Then there is silence, an incomprehensible calm].[49] Linden's concern is not with tracing the steps of former pilgrims, but rather gently mocking the exploits of visitors drawn to the island to seek affirmation of their mystical and mythological beliefs. He asserts that following the publication of Chris Barber and David Pykitt's *Journey to Avalon* in 1993, which claims that Ynys Enlli is in fact the legendary Avalon, the island in the mist to which the wounded King Arthur withdrew, tourists have flocked to the island to verify the claims for themselves, and even spent the night in the cave reported to be Merlin's grave.

Therefore it can be seen that rather than an enactment of religious devotion, modern-day travellers to Ynys Enlli come for mystical motives and leisure purposes. A similar transformation can be viewed in recent travel accounts on St David's. Following the start of its cathedral's construction in 1181 the city became a major medieval pilgrim destination, with Pope Calixtus II issuing a decree that two pilgrimages to St David's

---

49   Peter Linden, 'Drei Träume von Wales', *Die Zeit*, 25, 13 June 1997, https://www.zeit.de/1997/25/Drei_Traeume_von_Wales/komplettansicht [accessed 24 April 2016].

were as good as one to Rome. For Jürschik-Busbach, the city is characterized by its peripherality as 'das westlichste Örtchen in Wales' (p. 122)
[the westernmost village in Wales], its renown built simultaneously on
both its superlative and diminutive nature:

> Es ist die weltweit kleinste Stadt, die eine Kathedrale besitzt [...] Sie ist die
> liebenswerteste Kathedrale der Welt. Andere mögen größer oder schöner
> sein, aber keine passt so leichtfüßig in diese Landschaft oder erinnert so
> intensiv an den einfachen Glauben, der sie erbauen ließ. (p. 122)

> [It is the world's smallest city that owns a cathedral (...) It is the loveliest
> cathedral in the world. Others may be taller or more beautiful, but none
> fits so lithely into this landscape, or is so intensely reminiscent of the
> simple faith that built it]

In this account, the modest position of the cathedral, tucked away in a
hollow and protected, shows a symbiotic relationship with the religious
devotion of its founders and pilgrims.

Doris and David Lindner's numerous travels to Wales offer them a
deeper, quasi-spiritual experience:

> Diese Reise, sie führt in ein altes Land namens Wales. Doch wie jede
> Reise, die man mit dem Herzen macht, führt sie uns tiefer. Sie führt uns
> an einen noch älteren Ort, tief ins Herz der Sehnsucht. Sie führt dich
> heim. Heim zu dir ... (p. 2)

> [This journey leads to an old country called Wales. But like every journey
> one makes with the heart, it leads us deeper. It leads us to an even older place,
> deep into the heart of longing. It leads you home. Home to yourself ...]

In their observations on visiting the 'Bilderbuchörtchen' (p. 28) [little
picture book place] of St David's, they use a decidedly twenty-first-
century simile to frame their encounter in terms of relaxation rather
than religion:

> Spätnachmittaglich die Sonne. Sie bemalt den Friedhof, der aussieht
> wie ein Meditationsgarten in Goldgrün [...] Gesang fließt durch die
> schon abendlich duftende Luft. Als würde jemand einen Soundtrack
> zu unserer Ortsbesichtigung spielen, tauchen wir ein in diese Sinfonie
> von Geschichte und Natur, Endlichkeit und Lobpreisung, Urlaub und
> Einkehr. (p. 79)

> [The late afternoon sun paints the cemetery, which looks like a meditation
> garden in golden green (...) Singing flows through the air with its evening
> aroma. As if someone were playing a soundtrack to our site visit, we

immerse ourselves in this symphony of history and nature, finiteness and praise, holidays and retreats]

In this account the pilgrim destination of St David's is thus transformed into a countercultural twenty-first-century Mecca, which even orchestrates its visitors' aural experiences of the site.

The St David's coastline serves as a tragic backdrop for Marie Darrieussecq, who visited Swansea, Rhossili and Tenby in May 2017. Her subsequent travel narrative 'Les Fantômes du Pays de Galles' (2017) [The Ghosts of Wales] was commissioned by the AHRC-funded 'European Travellers to Wales' project. Darrieussecq is haunted by Wales after her return to France:

> On va quelque part et le pays vous suit, quand vous rentrez chez vous [...] J'ai vu le Pays de Galles un peu partout, à mon retour [...] J'essaie de raconter comme le Pays de Galles s'est mis à me suivre, de façon inattendue, à mon retour en France, comme un fantôme. (p. 30)

> [You go somewhere, and the country follows you when you come home (...) I saw Wales all over the place when I came back (...) I am trying to tell how Wales began to follow me, in an unexpected way, when I returned to France, like a ghost (p. 40)]

This haunting occurs after the death of her friend the prominent translator Bernard Hoepffner (1946–2017), who got into difficulties in the sea off St David's Head on 6 May 2017, and whose body was found on Tywyn beach in north Wales a month later. This long-cherished spot on the Pembrokeshire coastline is constructed as Hoepffner's true home. Darrieussecq was speaking in Swansea on 12 May 2017, and only learnt of her friend's disappearance after her return to Paris. The list of maritime accidents she read on the coastguard's noticeboard at Worm's Head on the Gower coast acquires new significance retrospectively, as she imagines the lives of each individual affected:

> Un tableau, sous la cabine des sauveteurs, avertissait des dangers des falaises, des vagues et des marées, et faisait la liste de tous les accidents recensés depuis des années. Chutes, suicides, noyades, disparus. (p. 30)

> [A board under the coastguard's hut warned of the dangers of cliffs, waves and tides, and listed all the accidents recorded over the years. Falls, suicides, drownings, disappearances (pp. 39–40)]

Darrieussecq draws on Dylan Thomas (1914–1953) in her final tribute to Hoepffner:

Il est parti en nous laissant ce cadeau que nous font les morts: ils nous rappellent que nous sommes vivants. Ils nous soufflent, de là où ils sont: Vis. Vis. Vis chaque seconde. Ne te lamente pas, et vis. Mais aussi, comme écrit Dylan Thomas:
Rage, rage against the dying of the light. (p. 33)

[He left us with this gift that the dead give us: they remind us that we are alive. They whisper to us from where they are: Live. Live. Live every second. Do not weep, and live. But also, as Dylan Thomas writes:
'*Rage, rage against the dying of the light*' (p. 42)]

Indeed, the life and literary works of one of the most world-renowned Welshmen of the twentieth century have become a key feature of recent travel accounts of Wales in French and in particular in German, as travellers delight in retracing the homes and haunts of Dylan Thomas.[50] The accounts confirm the poet's boathouse in Laugharne as a major new destination for contemporary Continental travellers, and very rarely do they fail to at least mention Thomas. There are numerous instances of what Lucas Tromly has termed 'echotourism', as travellers follow in the poet's footsteps on the Dylan Thomas trail, and visit one of his dwellings.[51] This keen interest dates from a relatively early period. For example, in her 1959 travelogue, six years after the poet's death, Bettina Hürlimann seeks out Laugharne and praises its aesthetic qualities, drawing attention to the inspiration provided by its inhabitants for the characters of Thomas's best-known radio play, *Under Milk Wood* (1953) (pp. 78–79). In the photobook *Wales* (1992), by German photographer Horst Zielske (1946–), the sole texts interspersed with his stark images of a depopulated Welsh hinterland are German translations of Thomas's works, thereby framing Wales through his words alone, appropriated in the German language.[52] Details of his colourful personal life and heavy drinking are as frequent as quotations from his works, such as in the volume *Dylan*

---

50 Dylan Thomas also features in fiction in the short story 'Nicht Morgen, nicht Gestern' (1999) by German author Uwe Timm (1940–), which appeared in a collection of the same title. For an analysis of the story in its Welsh context, see Les, 'Space beyond Place'.

51 Lucas Tromly, 'Echotourism and Women's Travel Writing', unpublished lecture, Freie Universität Berlin, 27 October 2017. The term 'echotourism' refers to the recent trend of 'footstep journeys', when travel writers consciously reconstruct journeys undertaken by illustrious predecessors.

52 Horst Zielske, *Wales: Mit Texten des walisischen Schriftstellers Dylan Thomas* (Dortmund: Harenberg Edition, 1992).

Thomas: Waliser, Dichter, Trinker (2011) [Dylan Thomas: Welshman, Poet, Drunkard] by journalist Elke Heidenreich (1943–) and photographer Thomas Krausz (1951–).[53] For Heidenreich, a journey to Wales is a necessity in order to gain a better understanding of the poet and the landscape that shaped him: 'Wales ist zerklüftet, wild, von herber Schönheit. Man landet in der Hauptstadt Cardiff, Dylan Thomas' Wortkaskaden im Kopf' (p. 24) [Wales is rugged, wild and of a harsh beauty. You arrive in the capital, Cardiff, with Dylan Thomas's word cascades sounding in your head]; 'Diese Landschaft hat ihn geprägt, hierher kam er immer wieder zurück, nach Wales, seiner Sprache, seinen Menschen hatte er immer Heimweh' (p. 24) [This landscape shaped him, he returned here again and again, to Wales, his language, he was always homesick for his people]. Heidenreich is pictured trying to outstare the statue of Dylan Thomas which stands next to Swansea marina, which she contends looks nothing like the poet; yet the shine on his bronze knee showing the trace of where so many visitors' hands have leant on him implies his continued popularity, and his expression suggests 'als würde er noch immer lauschen, was geredet wird' (p. 72) [as if he is still listening to what is being said]. She concludes that Thomas's presence can still be found all around Wales in terms of its landscape and habits, when the traveller learns to look beyond outer appearances:

> wenn man nicht nach Äußerlichkeiten sucht, findet man ihn in Wales überall – in der grauen Tristesse der Arbeiterstädte, in der Melancholie der unwirtlichen Strände, im Kreischen der Möwen und natürlich in den zahllosen Pubs, in denen die Männer versunken in ihre Biergläser starren wie damals auch er. (p. 32)

> [if you do not look for outward appearances, you find him everywhere in Wales – in the grey dreariness of the working-class towns, in the melancholy of the inhospitable beaches, in the screeching of seagulls and of course in the countless pubs where the men stare into their beer glasses, lost in reflection as he too was in those days]

Many of the recent accounts of pilgrimages to the poet's boathouse in Laugharne share a common trope, as the travellers construct an acute awareness of his continued presence. Doris and David Lindner's journey in his footsteps is emblematic of many similar experiences:

53   Elke Heidenreich and Thomas Krausz, *Dylan Thomas: Waliser, Dichter, Trinker* (Munich: Knesebeck, 2011).

Zur linken sein Schreibhüttchen, traumhaft über der Bucht thronend. Seine Jacke hängt noch da. Ah, die Flaschen sind leer. Dylan trinkt zu viel. Zerknülltes Papier auf dem Boden, hat wohl eine Schreibblockade. Wir blicken die Bucht entlang. Kommt er gerade vom Pub zurück? Wir suchen ihn. Finden auf dem Friedhof, am Eingang des Ortes, ein einfaches Holzkreuz. Es behauptet, wir seien zu spät gekommen. (p. 107)[54]

[To the left is the little writing cabin, wonderfully enthroned over the bay. His jacket is still hanging there. Ah, the bottles are empty. Dylan drinks too much. Crumpled paper on the floor – probably has writer's block. We look along the bay. Is he just coming back from the pub? We look for him. At the entrance to the cemetery we find a simple wooden cross. It suggests we have arrived too late]

Narrating Thomas's actions in the present tense, it is implied that he has only just left this quasi-sacred creative space, and the travellers have narrowly missed an encounter with the poet himself.

Renaud Camus's (1946–) work *Demeures de l'esprit. Grande-Bretagne I* (2008) [Residences of the Spirit: Great Britain Vol. I] offers a fragmented itinerary around southern England and Wales, portraying a selection of notable sites with strong intellectual and cultural connections.[55] Unusually, Camus's representation of Dylan Thomas's reception in Wales is highly critical, as he implies that the local Welsh community does not pay sufficient attention to the poet's legacy in terms of preserving its sites in Laugharne. In a highly indignant tone, Camus hastens to record his visit to the boathouse, contending that what makes it 'unique' and 'wondrous' will inevitably have been irreparably lost by the time his book appears (p. 201):

Le *boathouse* de Dylan Thomas [...] est une des plus séduisantes demeures qui soient au monde [...] ce n'est pas à cause de son architecture, qui n'a rien d'extraordinaire, mais de son admirable isolement [...] La maison de Dylan Thomas tenait toute sa magie de sa solitude et de lui. (pp. 202–03)

---

54   Other examples include Hüttenegger, 'Wales und England', pp. 97–105; Bengel, *Der Ritter mit der Web Adresse*, pp. 74 77; Bernadette Conrad, 'Dorfdichter von Welt', *Die Zeit*, 45, 30 October 2014, p. 61.

55   Renaud Camus, *Demeures de l'esprit Grande-Bretagne. I, Angleterre sud & centre, Pays de Galles* (Paris: Fayard, 2008). Only three out of sixty-two chapters in this volume deal with Welsh sites. In addition to the chapter on Dylan Thomas's boathouse in Laugharne, the other two chapters are devoted to Tŷ Mawr, y Wybrnant, home of William Morgan (1545–1604), who was the first to translate the Bible into Welsh in 1588, and Plas Newydd, home of the 'Ladies of Llangollen'.

[Dylan Thomas's boathouse (...) is one of the most attractive homes in the world (...) it is not because of its architecture, which has nothing extraordinary about it, but because of its admirable isolation (...) All the magic of Dylan Thomas's house emanated from its loneliness and from him]

Camus rails against the 'stupidity' of local planning authorities who permitted the 'evil' of a millionaire's conspicuous villa to be built in close proximity to Thomas's former home, elegiacally lamenting the 'destruction' of a site of timeless perfection, intact beauty and poetic force. In this instance, the traveller's prior expectations clash with his empirical experience when visiting the site, and it offers a rare narrative of disappointment and disillusionment amongst the late twentieth-century and early twenty-first-century travelogues on Wales.

The parallel narrative frameworks of Wales's topographical periph-erality or excentricity and its exoticism or eccentricity are blended harmoniously in the portrayal of Hay-on-Wye, a major new destination on Welsh tourist trails. Declared the world's first 'town of books' in 1977, this remote town on the Welsh-English border has global appeal. Writing in *Le Monde* in 2002, French journalist Danielle Tramard (dates unknown) underlines its peripheral location and singular nature:

Aujourd'hui, les amoureux de livres et d'estampes viennent en majorité d'Oxford, de Bristol ou de Birmingham, mais aussi d'Europe et d'au-delà des mers. Ils découvrent une ville singulière. Car la cité galloise, frontalière avec l'Angleterre, est unique. De Cardiff, on y parvient après avoir traversé les Brecon Beacons, les montagnes Noires, rondes et solitaires, éblouissantes.[56]

[Nowadays book and print enthusiasts mainly come from Oxford, Bristol or Birmingham, but also from Europe and overseas. They discover a singular town. Because this Welsh town on the border with England is unique. Travelling from Cardiff, you reach it after traversing the Brecon Beacons, the Black Mountains, round and solitary, splendid]

The town is predominantly defined by its remoteness and isolation due to the surrounding mountainous terrain, which leads in turn to a deceleration valued by several travellers. German journalist Julia Grosse (1976–) underlines that 'der zelebrierte Unwille zur Hektik scheint den

---

56   Danielle Tramard, 'Hay-on-Wye, le livre aux champs', *Le Monde*, 25 April 2002, https://www.lemonde.fr/archives/article/2002/04/25/hay-on-wye-le-livre-aux-champs_4238294_1819218.html?xtmc=&xtcr=20 [accessed 24 January 2016].

Bewohnern in jeder Pore zu stecken' [the celebrated resistance to the frantic pace of life seems to be present in the inhabitants' every pore].[57] Tramard is transported to foreign lands while reading in the back rooms of bookshops, the passage of time marked only by the tick-tock rhythm of the clock's pendulum. For early German visitor Elmar Schenkel (1953–), who travelled to Hay after traversing the border country of Offa's Dyke in 1980, a pilgrimage to the town of books resembles an otherworldly journey to a labyrinthine mythological ideal: 'Schon lange hatte ich von diesen Orten geträumt, Orte, an denen sich die Welt in Bücher verwandelt, Städte zu Labyrinthen aus Gedrucktem werden' [I have long dreamed of such places; places in which the world is transformed into books, and towns turn into labyrinths made from printed materials].[58]

In several travel accounts the portrayal of Hay-on-Wye's eccentricity centres on the figure of bibliophile and bookseller Richard Booth (1938–2019), the founder of Hay's first bookshop in 1961 and self-proclaimed 'King of Hay' who declared its independence as a 'kingdom of books' in 1977. The eccentricity also extends to the practice of displaying books on shelves nestled in the castle's walls, exposed to the elements and relying on a quaint honesty box for payment.[59] Now welcoming around half a million visitors a year and home to some two million books, the town is an established international literary destination thanks to its annual Hay Festival of Literature and the Arts, described by Julia Grosse as the literary equivalent of the Venice carnival, and its events like an Oscars for bookworms. Indeed, amongst Continental travellers to Wales interested in cultural tourism, the town and its predominantly Anglo-centric festival feature far more prominently in their accounts as reasons to visit Wales than the Welsh-language *eisteddfodau*.

On the whole, it can be seen that interest in the Welsh language and cultural events has waned in the travelogues published in the past three decades. Certainly in comparison with nineteenth- to mid-twentieth-century travellers, the Welsh language and culture do not feature

57   Julia Grosse, 'Im Königreich der Bücher', *Merian*, 10 (20 September 2012), pp. 60–66.

58   Elmar Schenkel, 'Paradies für Büchernarren: Das Städtchen Hay ist Pilgerziel für Literarische Wanderer', *Die Zeit*, 33, 8 August 1980, p. 46.

59   See, for example, Tramard, 'Hay-on-Wye'; also Bengel, *Der Ritter mit der Web-Adresse*, p. 65.

strongly in most contemporary visitors' motivations for coming to Wales. In the 2013 travelogue *Traumzeit in Wales*, the representation of the Welsh language is mainly confined to a practical guidebook-style entry, reassuring the reader that it is not imperative to learn the Welsh language before travelling there, and advising them not to worry unduly about it. Lindner and Lindner's depiction of their initial encounter with Welsh on bilingual road signs straight after they cross the border into Wales is tantamount to a denial of its status as a language and its speakers' agency: 'eine scheinbar wirre Ansammlung von Buchstaben. Unmöglich, dass es sich um eine Sprache handelt, denkt man erst einmal. Vielleicht ist das so etwas wie eine Stenoschrift' (p. 175) [A seemingly confused collection of letters. At first you think it is impossible that it is a language. Perhaps it is something like a stenographical script].

In Bengel's *Der Ritter mit der Web-Adresse*, the Welsh language itself becomes a commodity that can be 'experienced' by the traveller. While staying in the former quarrymen's cottages at Nant Gwrtheyrn, a Welsh language and heritage centre opened in 1982 which has since taught Welsh to more than 25,000 adults, he observes: 'Auch wer Walisisch eher als Erlebnis denn als Sprache anstrebt, kann die Cottages für Tage oder Wochen mieten' (pp. 98–99) [Even those who seek Welsh more as an experience than as a language can rent the cottages for days or weeks]. The author outlines the official recognition of Welsh in the Welsh Language Acts of 1967 and then 1993, but questions the expense of mounting translation costs that followed: 'Das geht wohl mit der Zeit ins Geld, aber es sichert den inneren Frieden' (p. 98) [This will probably cost a pretty penny over the course of time, but it secures internal peace]. Nant Gwrtheyrn's dramatic setting is ultimately of utmost interest rather than the Celtic language it seeks to sustain, and the following description continues the theatrical metaphors which pervade several contemporary Continental depictions of the Welsh landscape:

> Wie ein griechisches Theatr liegt die Stätte da in einem Halbkreis von Granit, die Wände künstlich überhöht vom Abraum, die Hänge steiler als in der Natur. Die Bühne ist das Meer mit seinem täglichen Programm des Sonnenuntergangs. (p. 96)

> [The site is like a Greek theatre situated in a semicircle of granite, the walls artificially elevated by the overburden, the slopes steeper than in nature. The stage is the sea with the sunset as its daily programme]

In his 1997 exploration of north-west Wales, Linden deploys the dual narrative framework of excentricity and eccentricity to situate his portrayal of the Welsh language. In this travel account, the north-west peninsula's geographical isolation has led to it becoming a bastion for the Welsh language, a 'Refugium keltischer Sprache und Tradition' [refuge for Celtic language and tradition], a relic from the past which is flourishing in this region alone: 'Hier gibt es kein Post Office, sondern ein Llythyrdy. Hier heißen die Ortschaften Pwllheli, Chwilog, Llangwnnadl. Wer ins Pub geht [...] erlebt eine Sprache aus der Vergangenheit in voller Blüte' [There is no post office here, but a *llythyrdy*. Here the towns are called Pwllheli, Chwilog, Llangwnnadl. People who go to the pub (...) experience a language from the past in full bloom]. Linden suggests that this linguistic stronghold has attracted a certain type of resilient Welsh eccentric: 'Kein Wunder, daß es die letzten Idealisten hierher nach Lleyn verschlagen hat. Sprachrebellen zum Beispiel, Fanatiker' [No wonder the last idealists came here to Llŷn. Language rebels, for example, fanatics]. Nevertheless, this traveller ultimately shifts his narrative gaze from the exotic to the endotic, underlining that throughout its history Wales has been a 'Schmelztiegel' [melting pot], and that its strange language in fact has familiar European roots: 'Die Sprache, so fremd sie klingen mag, ist voll von griechischen und lateinischen Wurzeln, hat Anleihen aus dem Irischen genommen, englische Wörter adaptiert' [The language, strange as it may sound, is full of Greek and Latin roots, borrowing from the Irish, adapting English words].

Jürschik-Busbach and Busbach's *ARAF-Slow* stands out from other travelogues in German by mounting a strong defence of the Welsh language and the rights of its speakers. Jürschik-Busbach asserts that rumours of the demise of the Welsh language have been highly exaggerated, and that Welsh has probably seen more comebacks than Frank Sinatra and Tom Jones put together (p. 89). Echoing Schuchardt over a century earlier, Jürschik-Busbach criticizes the perceived English inability or unwillingness to accept and normalize the status of the language, rather than viewing it as a threat:

> Es scheint ihnen unbegreiflich zu sein, dass Walisisch einfach die Sprache ist, in der sie sich gern unterhalten, in der sie Klatsch über die Nachbarn austauschen. Es ist die Sprache, mit der sie einkaufen gehen – es ist – besonders im Norden – ihre Alltagssprache. (p. 89)

> [It seems incomprehensible to them that Welsh is simply the language in which they like to talk, exchanging gossip about their neighbours. It is

the language in which they go shopping – it is their everyday language, especially in the north]

This traveller's perception of the minoritized status of Welsh language speakers appeals to her German readers' awareness of more globally renowned oppressed peoples in order to situate Wales in a similar sociopolitical context:

> Diese Menschen wollen einfach nur in ihrer Muttersprache kommunizieren, in der einzigen Art, die sie kennen. Wie die Tibeter fühlen sich viele Waliser als Fremde im eigenen Land, in einer Art internem Exil. (p. 89)

> [These people just want to communicate in their native language, in the only way they know. Like the Tibetans, many Welsh feel like foreigners in their own country, in a kind of internal exile]

By contrast, the issue of the minoritization of the Welsh language is filtered through a far more positive prism in accounts by contemporary Breton travel writers, who testify to the enduring significance of Wales as a cultural example for Brittany in particular and a model for minoritized nations in general. In Le Disez's polyphonic narrative *Une aventure galloise*, the voices and viewpoints of the Welsh resonate and are placed at the heart of the work. Many of their discussions are centred on the effects of devolution and the situation of the Welsh language. For Le Disez, the terms of the language debate have progressed to a far more advanced state in Wales than in Brittany:

> Comme la question de la langue galloise a évolué en un quart de siècle! Ce qui est en jeu ici est quelque chose de vital. Au risque de choquer, je dirais qu'en Bretagne nous pensons encore cette question de la langue dans un paradigme que je qualifierai de 'colonialiste-honteux'. Le pays de Galles, lui, est entré résolument dans l'ère non seulement post-coloniale mais post-colonialiste. (p. 162)

> [The issue of the Welsh language has evolved so much in a quarter of a century! Something vital is at stake here. At the risk of shocking (you), I'd say that in Brittany we still consider this language issue using a paradigm that I would describe as 'shameful-colonialist'. As for Wales, it has resolutely entered not only the postcolonial but also the postcolonialist era]

Nevertheless, to a certain extent the travelogue negates the suggestion that Brittany could adopt the Welsh model of language revitalization:

> Comparaison n'est pas raison: le modèle gallois n'est pas transférable en Bretagne. Il y a au moins deux grandes différences essentielles entre les deux situations linguistiques: la première est que le gallois est encore dans de nombreuses régions […] une langue de communication, que l'on entend à la poste, au pub, dans la rue, parlée par toutes les générations; la deuxième est que le gallois est, de longue date, une langue à la fois populaire et savante. (p. 163)

> [Comparison is no proof: the Welsh model cannot be transferred to Brittany. There are at least two significant essential differences between the situations of the two languages; the first is that in many regions (…) Welsh is still a language of communication that is heard at the post office, in the pub, on the streets, spoken by all generations; the second difference is that Welsh has long been a language that is both vernacular and scholarly]

Conversely, *Une aventure galloise* emphasizes an inclusive, civic understanding of nationalism, which draws attention to numerous individuals who have learned and adopted Welsh as their first language. Le Disez points to a decisive shift in attitudes towards the desirability of learning Welsh and bilingualism:

> Et peut-être peut-on quand même oser une comparaison: la région où le gallois progresse le plus est le Sud, et notamment Cardiff. Or Cardiff, il y a encore dix ans, n'était pas plus galloisante que la Bretagne actuelle n'est bretonnante. Ici, on n'apprend pas le gallois parce qu'on l'a toujours parlé. On apprend le gallois parce que le vent a tourné. (p. 165)

> [And perhaps one comparison can be ventured all the same: the region where Welsh is making the most progress is the south, notably Cardiff. But Cardiff, even ten years ago, was no more Welsh-speaking than today's Brittany is Breton-speaking. Here, you don't learn Welsh because it has always been spoken. You learn Welsh because the wind has changed]

Therefore, in spite of the key differences between the respective situations of the two languages, the travelogue ultimately deploys the Welsh example in order to offer a hopeful message for other lesser-used languages such as Breton. Wales is perceived as a positive role model to be emulated and a source of hope for other small and oppressed nations: 'Si impossible n'est pas gallois, il n'est peut-être pas davantage français, ni breton, ni tchétchène, ni palestinien, ni …' (p. 238) [If there is no such word as impossible in Welsh, perhaps there isn't in French either, nor Breton, nor Chechen, nor Palestinian, nor …].

This sense of optimism and new possibilities also extends to Le Disez's own 'complex' relationship with the Breton language, which was not passed on to him by his parents, and which he therefore learnt as an adult. Following a chance encounter with Breton-speaking crowned bard and musician Twm Morys and his friend Gorwel Roberts, the narrator finds a new confidence: 'C'est ainsi que je me suis retrouvé à parler breton pendant une bonne demi-heure, moi qui n'ose presque jamais le faire en Bretagne' (p. 154) [This is how I found myself speaking Breton for a good half hour; me, who hardly ever dares to speak it in Brittany]; 'Voici au moment que je l'attendais le moins, je parle breton, avec une aisance qui étonne mon interlocuteur et m'étonne moi-même, ici au Pays de Galles' (p. 154) [When I was least expecting it, here I am speaking Breton with an ease that surprises my interlocutor and myself, too, here in Wales]. Wales is therefore portrayed as a privileged space for linguistic revival both on an individual and collective basis, and the narrator, echoing La Tocnaye, depicts the encounter as a return to Breton's linguistic origins: 'C'est un peu comme si douze siècles, ceux qui nous séparent de l'immigration galloise en Bretagne étaient abolis' (p. 155) [It is as if the twelve centuries that separate us from the Welsh migration to Brittany had vanished]. In his romanticized reimagining, Twm Morys is depicted as a near contemporary of the sixth-century Brythonic poet Taliesin (534–599), and the narrator himself is likened to 'un traducteur itinérant allant de minuscule cour princière en cour princière, de ferme en ferme plutôt, à la recherche de textes à traduire, à importer, à diffuser' (p. 155) [a travelling translator wandering from one tiny princely court to another, or rather from one farm to another, searching for texts to translate, import, share].

Self-styled modern-day Breton troubadour Samuel Allo (1978–) has undertaken a series of journeys to Celtic nations to collect traditional tales, which are recounted in his book *Au fil des contes: Voyages dans les pays celtes* [Tracing Tales: Journeys to Celtic Countries] and his Breton-language blog, both published in 2014.[60] Resolving not to pay for accommodation or travel, seeking 'hospitality' for the night by knocking on doors, this traveller's accounts focus on his hosts and on the Welsh-medium schools he visits. Throughout his travels Allo is struck by

60   Samuel Allo, *Au fil des contes: voyages dans les pays celtes* (Saint-Brieuc: Imprimerie Jacq, 2014); Samuel Allo, 'Tour des pays celtes', http://samuelallo.com/index.php?option=com_content&view=article&id=150:bro-iwerzhon-irlande-ireland&catid=3:autres-projets&Itemid=30 [accessed 3 July 2017].

the visual markers of bilingualism he encounters, such as in shop aisles marked 'bara', bread, which is the same word in Breton. In a similar vein to Le Disez, Allo learnt Breton as an adult, and during his journey Wales becomes a performative space to perfect his Breton, this time in the form of a blog. The blog also features sound recordings of travellees recounting myths, thus decentring his narrative and allowing their voices to occupy a central space in his account. Thus in this contact zone, the emphasis on cultural transfer between Welsh and Breton cultures is established within a framework of equality and exchange. In Machynlleth, he is permitted to enter the classroom of a secondary school, and he observes:

> Lorsque je chante la chanson des korrigans 'dilun dimeurzh dimerec'h …', ils me regardent tous avec de grands yeux étonnés […] Ils ont compris les jours de la semaine dans la chanson […] Ma joie est intense. Le breton est donc plus qu'une langue régionale et peut permettre à deux personnes de pays différents de communiquer, de se comprendre. Les élèves me chantent une belle mélodie du Pays de Galles. Le moment est beau. (pp. 50–51)

> [When I sing the korrigans' song 'Dilun dimeurzh dimerec'h',[61] they all stare at me wide-eyed in amazement (…) They have understood the days of the week in the song. (…) My joy is intense. Breton is therefore more than a regional language and can enable two people from different countries to communicate, to understand each other. The pupils sing me a beautiful melody from Wales. It's a beautiful moment]

The next day, pupils in nearby Taliesin primary school proudly recount to Allo the tale of the bard Taliesin and discuss the *Mabinogi* tales with ease. These myths and legends will be shared virtually and in person, when Allo returns to Brittany and narrates them to a number of schools. The cultural frameworks and linguistic approaches favoured by Le Disez and Allo thereby suggest a vision of Wales as a repository of a mythology that is very much alive to its inhabitants, and a haven for minoritized languages. Their portrayal of linguistic revival and visions of vitality and agency in Wales provide an indication of some of the original viewpoints that can be opened up by examining the narratives of travellers from minoritized cultures, and the importance of investigating travel between peripheries.

By the second decade of the twenty-first century, Wales is very much viewed on its own terms by travellers writing in French, Breton and

---

61 In Welsh, Dydd Llun (Monday), Dydd Mawrth (Tuesday), Dydd Mercher (Wednesday).

German, and as an entity and often a country in its own right. Whereas eighteenth- and nineteenth-century visitors travelled westwards through Wales often en route to Ireland, by the late twentieth century western Wales in particular had shifted from being a transit zone to a stated destination. Comparisons with Switzerland have disappeared entirely from recent narratives; parallels with Brittany as a prism for viewing Wales have also abated, now only occurring in Breton-authored texts and some French guidebooks. Conversely, such views of Wales as an autonomous destination have gone hand in hand with an increasing peripheralization which occurs in different forms and guises. In the accounts by Lindner and Lindner, Bernig and Le Disez, Wales continues to be represented as a country on the outer reaches of Europe, an excentric place of refuge and respite where the traveller can get away from it all, often in an attempt to reconnect with the self and to broaden the mind – a modern-day version of the gentleman scholar on tour. In this fresh appreciation of Wales, new towns and destinations have emerged on the tourist map, and Wales is now 'read' through Dylan Thomas's Laugharne, the 'book town' of Hay-on-Wye, the sites of pilgrimage of Ynys Enlli and St David's, and perhaps above all through its capital city Cardiff. Appreciative accounts of Welsh-language culture have largely made way for narratives focusing on famous producers of Welsh writing in English. Interest in the bards has been replaced by a fascination with Dylan Thomas, and the Hay Festival, an Anglo-centric meeting place for international cultures, attracts far more attention than the National Eisteddfod. Nevertheless, in Breton accounts Wales continues to serve as a cultural and political role model for Brittany. Such portrayals of the Welsh language as a point of interest rather than a living, everyday language also proliferate in contemporary English-language travelogues. In his investigation of journeys by majority-English-language travellers through the territories of endangered or minority languages, Michael Cronin asserts that such accounts construct minority-language speakers as fixed in time, and that:

> The axiomatic inclusion of language as a feature of culture, comparable to a local cheese or a distinctive wine, means that the speakers are almost invariably deprived of agency as there is no structural analysis in the present moment as to what it is they can do apart from withering away in their picturesque surroundings.[62]

---

62   Michael Cronin, 'Speech Acts: Language, Mobility and Place', in Forsdick, Fowler and Kostova (eds), *Travel and Ethics*, pp. 16–30 (p. 26).

Though some commonalities exist with previous modes of perception of Wales, such as admiration of its mountainous landscape, others have been transformed. Wales may no longer be perceived as a paragon of modernization and industrial progress, but its post-industrial heritage is attracting new visitors, and leading perhaps to more multilayered travel accounts. It is also possible to argue that a new Romanticism has emerged, most notably in relation to a fresh focus on Wales's coastal landscape and beaches, in particular by German-language travellers in search of what is different to or largely missing from their domestic landscapes. Indeed, in many recent travel accounts, Wales is portrayed to a certain extent as a flexible blank canvas for the traveller's own desires and dreams, a backdrop which can be altered to accommodate the weight of the traveller's expectations.

Conclusion

The Narrative of Wales:
From Blind Spot to Blank Canvas

The profile of Wales as a destination for Continental travellers has undergone substantial shifts over the course of the last two and a half centuries, with periods of heightened interest in the Celtic nation and others where it disappeared almost entirely from view. Although the English 'Home Tour' of Wales was an established genre by the 1780s, outside of Britain Wales was still hardly known at all, or else dismissed as a rainy and barren land. Starting out from tiny numbers in the eighteenth century, the genre of the Continental travelogue on Wales grew and enjoyed its golden age around the middle of the nineteenth century, when railway lines opened up travel possibilities in unprecedented ways. By the end of the century a narrative of Wales had clearly been established in both French and German, with texts becoming increasingly derivative, many written by 'belated travellers', often walking in the footsteps of predecessors both in terms of itinerary and discourse.[1] Yet there were nevertheless multiple readings of Wales emanating from different interest groups and nationalities as the nation was viewed through numerous distorting prisms, always reflecting the home culture, whether it be France's need to reconnect with her Celtic ancestry following the trauma of the Revolution or the German speaking lands' anxieties about their own slow democratic and industrial advance. The travel accounts demonstrate how the depiction of a nation by a visiting traveller in fact reflects the issues, concerns and reality of

---

1   See Ali Behadad, *Belated Travelers: Orientalism in the Age of Colonial Dissolution* (Durham, NC: Duke University Press, 1994).

that traveller's home environment, as the contact zone is used as an area for reflection, cultural self-understanding and appreciation. It is only really in the twentieth century that Wales is treated on its own terms in travel writing, beginning with the French narratives of the 1904–1905 religious revival. Yet, even here, the purpose of travel was the quest for a potential paradigm to influence practice back home in France. A narrowing of the field for travellers, primarily due to the two world wars, then left Wales ripe for rediscovery by new travellers towards the end of the twentieth century, but now with little reference to the work of their predecessors. The narrative of Wales which emerges from these complex textual and empirical interactions is essentially consistent but undoubtedly multifaceted. Hard-won as it may have been by the end of the nineteenth century through decades of textual layering, forgetting and reappraisal, that narrative then vanished from view for the best part of the following century, only to remerge in new garb at the dawn of the twenty-first: Wales as haven, a modern peripheral nation with a capital city rich in attractions and a boundless range of opportunity for the outward-looking traveller with a taste for adventure. Thus Wales is discovered, lost and rediscovered and shifts in and out of view, from blind spot to blank canvas.

Initial contact with Wales for many travellers was made through the English-language sources of the home tour, such as Gilpin, Pennant, Nicholson and Borrow. There are, however, fewer references to these texts in French and German sources than one might expect given the now canonical status of these seminal English texts. They remain a shadow-like influence, often mentioned in passing comments and footnotes but only seldom the subject of critical engagement. Another shadow source for travellers is the guidebook genre which grew in importance over the course of the nineteenth century – mirroring the expansion of the railway network – to become a channel for the indirect mediation of emerging key themes such as the impact of tourism and the advance and value of modernity. Their influence is undoubtedly greater than the travel writers seem willing to admit, and material from English-language guidebooks can be found unacknowledged in travelogues such as Alfred Erny's 'Voyage dans le pays de Galles' (1867).[2] The

2   It seems likely, based on the analysis of his detailed description of Welsh dress in this text, that Erny used sources that he does not name, such as Mr S.C. and Mrs Hall's widely read *The Book of South Wales, the Wye, and the Coast* (London: Virtue and Co., 1861). Similarly, Erny's descriptions of Taliesin's grave and of a

underplayed recourse to such sources is an understandable tactic for the traveller trying to position themself in a new context. Indeed, it has long been acknowledged that travellers are often 'travel liars', making use of the work and experiences of others to narrate their impressions of a new environment.[3] However, as Carl Thompson notes, the long-standing association between travellers and liars 'is not just a consequence of the many hoaxes and deceptions practised by travellers over the years' but is derived from a perennial predicament: 'the fact that these people and places may be so far beyond the ken of the audience, and may appear so strange and exotic, that they beggar belief back home'.[4] The unexpected nature of Wales for many Continental travellers places them in danger of falling into this category as they seek ways to contextualize the 'other' culture in which they find themselves: that place called Wales, often unexpectedly different from the 'England' most of them had come to see. This is often achieved by explicit reference to literary sources, hence the frequent references to *Ossian* or Scott, with the implications of Celticness which that entails. Exilic writing, such as that by La Tocnaye, Penhouët and Fouéré, also has a role to play but clearly has no equivalent in English-language sources. Yet the importance of Wales as a haven constitutes a significant trope in Continental travel writing from the French Revolution onwards. Other political exiles followed in the wake of political upheavals throughout the nineteenth century, the First World War brought thousands of Belgians to Wales, and yet others fled the Spanish Civil War, Nazi Germany and Nazi-occupied Europe. These experiences of involuntary travel to Wales are an important part of the multifaceted picture, and detailed work remains to be done on these particular travellers. By the twenty-first century, the construction of Wales as a haven had become depoliticized, a refuge which could be chosen by a traveller in search of temporary respite.

To some extent, the representation of Wales in any given text is dependent upon which part of the country the traveller is describing; the awe-inspiring landscape of the north provokes a very different

---

graveyard in Briton Ferry are extremely close to the relevant passages in *Black's Picturesque Tourist of England and Wales*, in several editions from the 1840s onwards.

3 See Percy G. Adams, *Travelers and Travel Liars 1660–1800* (Berkeley: University of California Press, 1962).

4 Carl Thompson, *Travel Writing* (London and New York: Routledge, 2011), pp. 65–66.

response to the industrial advances of the south, for example. The regional differences could also be attributed to the patterns and beaten tracks established in previous texts. Pennant, despite the title of his work *A Tour in Wales*, only writes about north Wales, and Gilpin, author of the other seminal text on the Welsh landscape, leaves out mid-Wales. This geographical emphasis is reflected in the works of Continental travellers. The nineteenth-century German focus is firmly on north Wales largely because that is the area which speaks most to the generally Romantic reading of Wales, centred on landscape and culture, which dominates the century with only few exceptions. A greater balance between north and south can be found in the nineteenth-century French examples examined here, with visitors attracted by the mountainous north, the Arthurian south, the industries of both north and south, and linguistic, cultural and religious activities held in both north and south such as *eisteddfodau* and the 1904–1905 Revival. In the late twentieth and early twenty-first centuries, south Wales emerged as the focal point of most accounts due to growing interest in Cardiff as the capital city, the 'book kingdom' of Hay-on-Wye and sites associated with Dylan Thomas such as Swansea and Laugharne. However, for the first time, travellers were also drawn towards Wales's western extremities, most notably St David's and Ynys Enlli (Bardsay Island), suggesting a westward drive for cultural authenticity and spiritual retreat, the more peripheral the better. Although Wales is coming into closer focus in more recent texts, paradoxically it also remains peripheral: the traveller's desire for escape impels the discovery of ever new 'havens'.

Another more practical reason for the geographically polarized view of Wales is that the main points of entry into the country are in the north and south: Holyhead and Telford's A5 (taking travellers from Shrewsbury, via Llangollen into the heart of north Wales) in particular is responsible for many of the texts that the European Travellers to Wales project has uncovered, and most of the south Wales tours enter Wales via Chepstow and Raglan. None of the travellers land in Cardigan Bay, and surprisingly few come through Kington in the marches, via Pumlumon,[5] which is unexpected given that English tours do take this route.[6]

5   Some of the exceptions to this are discussed in Heather Williams, 'Views of Mid-Wales by Artists, Exiles and Royals from Europe', *Ceredigion*, 18:2 (2019), pp. 27–53.
6   The omission of mid-Wales is also borne out in English-language tours.

Following the advent of the car, and despite the customization of travel and greater accessibility of destinations which lie beyond the familiar routes of the coaches and trains, mid-Wales remains something of a blank spot in more recent travel accounts. Exceptions to this trend can be found in Breton narratives, perhaps due to their interest in Welsh-language culture, for example by Jean-Yves Le Disez and Samuel Allo, who visit the towns of Aberystwyth, Machynlleth and Dolgellau.

Arriving in Wales does not always immediately translate to a feeling of 'being there'. The place or moment when different travellers believe themselves to have reached 'Wales proper' shows the importance of cultural as well as geographical measures. It also suggests the growth of clichés of 'Welshness', but is equally symptomatic of a persistent level of confusion as to 'where' Wales is. In his account of his visit to Wales in August 1862, for example, Alfred Erny draws the Welsh border somewhere between Newport and Cardiff, and does not believe he is truly in Wales if the Welsh language is not in evidence: 'Ce fut à Cardiff que j'entendis pour la première fois parler le gallois' (p. 262) [It was in Cardiff that I heard Welsh spoken for the first time]. His travel companion Henri Martin points out that in Cardiff you might not realize you were in Wales were it not for the shop signs, and he feels that he is in real Wales only once he has left the town.[7] Simonin, travelling around the same time, claims that 'real' Wales begins in Swansea.[8] This local confusion is overlaid by the ongoing conflation, which continues to the present day, of England and Wales in the nomenclature adopted by Continental travellers to describe their destination. The pervasive issues of the location and categorization of Wales remain integral features of contemporary travel accounts, which would suggest that Wales's identity and image remain fluid and have not yet solidified in European eyes. For a twenty-first-century Breton traveller, the border is topographical rather than linguistic. As he crosses the Severn Bridge in July 2005, Jean-Yves Le Disez underlines the way in which geographical alterity immediately marks the traveller's entry into a new country:

As Elizabeth Edwards has observed: 'Comparatively few visitors to Wales left accounts that cover the whole of the country: trips to either the north or south, or along the Wye Valley are more common', "A Kind of Geological Novel", p. 143.

7   Martin, *Études d'archéologie celtique*, pp. 33–34.

8   Simonin, 'Une Visite aux grandes usines du pays de Galles', p. 331.

Alors que je vois se profiler au loin les premiers contreforts des Brecon Beacons, je m'étonne pour la énième fois que le pays de Galles soit, aussitôt passé la 'frontière' physiquement si différent de sa voisine anglaise. (p. 18)

[As I glimpse the outline of the first foothills of the Brecon Beacons in the distance, I am taken aback for the umpteenth time that Wales, as soon as you have crossed the 'border', is physically so different to her English neighbour]

For Birgit Jürschik-Busbach, in her 2012 narrative *ARAF-Slow*, crossing the Welsh border entails an induction into decelerated modes of travel, which in her view is the only way to feel the true 'Herzschlag' (p. 9) [heartbeat] of Wales. However, in most recent travel narratives, the fragmented itineraries and piecemeal consumption of Wales means that there is frequently no sense at all of travellers crossing the border and entering Wales.

Once arrived, writers adopt a variety of prisms through which they seek to understand and contextualize the country in which they find themselves: Celtic, Breton, English, sublime, Romantic, industrial, modern, touristic, colonial – all contributing to the narrative as it emerges by the end of the nineteenth century. In terms of the landscape, informed primarily by notions of the sublime and the Romantic, Switzerland is the dominant point of comparison for Welsh scenery in the earliest accounts, as it is in English tours of the time. It is found in Bombelles and Penhouët, as well as much later works, including those by Swiss travellers such as Arthur d'Arcis (dates unknown).[9] German writers such as Goede and Pückler-Muskau draw similar comparisons. The sublime theatricality of the Welsh landscape is another significant trope which bridges many of the works written across the centuries, from Pückler-Muskau in 1829 to Bengel in 2012. In the representation of Wales and its landscape as a stage setting, the nation resembles a blank canvas onto which the traveller's own aspirations and fantasies can be projected.

To some extent, the Romantic valorization of mountains by Continental travellers simply reinforces what was known from the English sources, but this is not the case in other domains. Most notably, industrial development in Wales is viewed both in French and German from the perspective of a rival, with frictions increasingly evident

---

9 Arthur d'Arcis, 'Voyage au nord du pays de Galles', *Le Globe: Journal géographique, Bulletin*, 6 (1887), pp. 34–51.

in mutual paranoia about spying as well as brutal criticisms of the environmental, social and cultural damage done by industry. Travellers' perceptions of the mediation between landscape, industry and culture play a central role in determining the representation of both modern advances and the preservation of cultural traditions in Wales. Comments on the impact of industry on the landscape, noted particularly by French travellers in south Wales, and the threat to Welsh-language culture posed by the growing number of tourists brought by the developing rail network, which is a key area of concern in German accounts, draw out the dangers presented by modernity in the Welsh context, often directly contradicting the calls by many travellers to see Wales brought into the modern world. The reading of Wales as backward and in need of modernization sits uneasily with the parallel reading of the nation as a paradigm of progress worthy of the attention of industrial spies. This conflicted reading is typical of the complexity found in the travel writing of the period. The differing priorities of individual travellers are foregrounded over time as the narrative of Wales gradually emerges.

Another key element in this process, and one which further differentiates the Continental material from the home tours, is criticism of the British government in London. Nineteenth-century German travellers in particular are faced with a quasi-colonial scenario which cuts across their understanding of British democracy and development. This in turn impacts on their self-understanding as travellers from a fragmented set of German-speaking lands. Seeking a positive paradigm in 'England' against which to measure their own slow democratic and industrial advance, they find themselves confronted with an equally fragmented British Isles with many issues still to resolve. It becomes clear to many German travellers that they are visiting a country not only with different cultures but with differing experiences of the advance of modernity which are in turn shaped by both perceptions of character and sociopolitical forces. Within this, Wales once again occupies a conflicted role. On the one hand, the nation and its people are viewed negatively as backward and recalcitrant; on the other, they find themselves and their landscape lauded as ideals of cultural tenacity and natural beauty.

Perhaps the most significant and enduring prism through which Wales is understood, however, is the 'Celtic' – and alongside it, from a French perspective, the 'Breton'. Like the genre of travel writing, the notion of the Celtic also enjoyed a golden age in the nineteenth century. The growth of interest in the Celts in both France and Germany, for different reasons, is reflected in travel accounts of Wales. There are some constants amongst the obscuring filters; for instance, comparisons with Switzerland are still being drawn in the 1890s, before declining in the twentieth century. Conversely, the Celtomaniac comparison with Brittany goes from being non-existent to dominating views of Wales from the post-revolutionary period onwards. This has lasted to the present day, with a contemporary French guidebook, *Angleterre, Pays de Galles (Le Routard,* 2013 edition) [England, Wales], heading its section on Welsh history 'Le pays de Galles à l'origine de la Bretagne' [Wales at the origins of Brittany], and seeing the Welsh 'à l'image des Bretons' [in the image of the Bretons].[10] The emergence of the Breton prism also made the French more likely to notice that Wales was different from England in the first place. If in the work of Genlis the notion of 'Celticness' was only just emerging, and might be described as confused, comparison of the two versions of Michelet's *Journal* shows to what extent the Celtic point of comparison had become standard by the end of the nineteenth century. It could be argued that Michelet, for instance, might not have 'seen' Wales at all had it not been for Brittany. Celtomania also, significantly, spread beyond the Bretons to those thinkers who were engaged in the France-wide project of rediscovering a Celtic, or Gaulish, past, as seen in the work of Michelet and especially Henri Martin. For the Celtomaniacs, describing Wales was all about seeing France in its Gaulish past. They saw in Wales what France had lost, and increasingly as time goes on they saw that Wales had held onto this past more successfully than their own Brittany had. Likewise, in Germany the Celtic regions came to represent an exotic northern ideal, and to embody the Herderian ideal of the *Volksgeist* [Spirit of the people]. While in the first half of the nineteenth century those Germans who engaged with Welsh culture and the Welsh language were relatively few, this changed as the work of Celtic philologists in Germany became more widely known. In terms of the reading of Wales, however, this Celtic appreciation was firmly tied to a Romantic world view with Wales's Celtic heritage and sublime landscape emerging as a battle-ground for the survival of tradition in the face of advancing modernity in the dual guise of industrialization and developing tourism.

By the early twentieth century, Wales became 'lost' again as the field of 'travellers' narrowed, primarily due to the two world wars. It was discovered afresh towards the end of the twentieth century by new

10   *Angleterre, Pays de Galles (sans Londres)* (Paris: Hachette Tourisme, 2012), pp. 507–08.

travellers largely unaware of the writing produced by their predecessors. From this period onwards, for the most part, there are fundamentally different frameworks of interpretation and loci of interest with a shift away from Welsh language and culture to a more sensory and physical 'consumption' of Wales, at which point the differences between French and German cultural spheres recede. However, some commonalities with previous modes of perception persist; in particular, Wales continues to serve as a cultural and political role model for Brittany, and the Romantic evocation of Wales as a spiritual haven finds a counterpart in the twenty-first century. As was the case with the nineteenth-century German reception, tensions emerge between the greater accessibility of Wales and the impact this has on its reception by writers. There is certainly notable visibility in terms of book-length travelogues being devoted solely to Wales from the start of the twenty-first century, but this also exhibits a tendency to atomization and fragmentation with a lack of a sense of a geographical entity as, unlike the largely linear narratives of the nineteenth century, the destination is consumed piecemeal as a place of adventure, freedom and literary connection. As contemporary narratives become increasingly diverse and individu-alized, further research will be necessary in order to gain a more detailed understanding of what M. Wynn Thomas terms 'the particular nexus of complexities that make Wales distinct'.[11]

Analysis of these European textual responses to Wales, in particular those written towards the end of the twentieth century and in the first decades of the twenty-first, has provided an opportunity to observe dynamics both between major and minor cultures and also between minor cultures. Being a cultural 'minority' is a predicament largely generated by the nation state, a concept that is now being questioned with the development of transnationalism and transnational studies. Although postcolonial studies have unlocked opportunities for 'minorities' and have made them visible, they are also part of the problem in confining debate to a centre-periphery binary, in fields including travel writing. As a result, the minoritized culture's struggle is only examined in relation to its dominant neighbour or colonizer, and periphery-periphery relations are occluded. In other words, focusing on the cause of a culture's minor status amounts to framing the cultural battle 'vertically', and obscuring the 'lateral networks' that may hold between minoritized cultures.[12] The

11   Thomas, 'Studying Wales Today: A Microcosmopolitan Approach', p. 3.
12   Shu-mei Shih and Françoise Lionnet, 'Introduction: Thinking through the

analyses in this study demonstrate the value of travel writing as a means to interrogate 'lateral', periphery-periphery relations, which deserves to be explored further in other contexts and nations.

The traveller's own agenda, and the negotiation between pre-travel expectation and empirical experience, play a central role in determining whether the 'minoritized' becomes visible in the traveller's account. Furthermore, the traveller's own understanding of 'minority' cultures is instrumental in filtering their perceptions of Wales, and this understanding evolves in the light of the specific socio-historical context. To take one example, it would be difficult to describe the Welsh heard by the Romantic-era gentleman traveller in Wales as a 'minority' language (because it would have been spoken by the majority at that time); however, it would be correct to describe this language as oppressed. Furthermore, said traveller is likely to have described it as a vestige, a fascinating cultural artefact belonging to the past. In the nineteenth century, French travellers to Wales were more likely to think that they were getting a view of another branch of the origins of France, namely close cousins to the Bretons; they were perhaps conscious that they were contemplating a language that was in inevitable decline, but was not perceived as having been minoritized by oppressive forces. On the other hand, some nineteenth-century travellers to Wales saw nothing minor in it, but rather glimpsed the future of Europe in the feats of engineering and industrial architecture that dominated the landscape or saw it as a paradigm of cultural tenacity.

The significance of Brittany in travel writing on Wales in French, which serves here as a case study, highlights a key question around the extent to which a 'minoritized' culture can bypass the hegemonic cultures in its interactions with other minoritized or peripheral cultures, or whether mediation by the mainstream or 'centre' is inevitable for the 'minority' culture. In the course of this volume a further type of traveller has emerged who seeks cross-national solidarity, or a model for their own 'minority' culture to follow, as is the case for numerous Bretons in Wales. Penhouët's account of his visit in 1796 demonstrates that peripheral cultures can and do interact with other peripheral cultures

Minor, Transnationally', *Minor Transnationalism* (Durham, NC and London: Duke University Press, 2005), pp. 1–23 (p. 1). They sum up the paradox of the centre's role in their claim that their personal 'minor orientations would have remained invisible to each other' had they not met at an academic conference in a major metropolis (p. 1).

from an early date. Penhouët's experience of being in Wales connects a Breton traveller with his cultural identity, which foreshadows many twentieth- and twenty-first-century Breton travel accounts, such as Le Disez's new-found ease with conversing in Breton while visiting Wales in 2005.

These texts offer illuminating insights into the complexity of centre-periphery and periphery-periphery relationships and power dynamics between speakers of minoritized languages in travelogues. Writing in 1862, historian Henri Martin maintained that Wales had far more in common with France than England, due to their common 'Keltic' origins.[13] Conversely, at the end of the nineteenth century, the cluster of texts written about the 1899 Cardiff *eisteddfod* highlight the French view that Brittany should be seen as an obedient 'petite patrie' [little fatherland], always subordinated to the 'grande patrie' [big fatherland]. This concept was extended and applied to Wales by the Breton delegates to the 1899 *eisteddfod*, thereby subsuming encounters between peripheries within the mediating framework of the relationship with the centre, as Bretons and Welsh negate their reciprocal cultural identities by designating the other as English and French. Nevertheless, the analyses in the final chapter demonstrate that in some cases it is possible for travellers to circumvent the centre in their accounts of travel to minoritized nations and cultures. Those narratives written in Breton, and which postdate the political awakening of the Bretonist movement in the 1920s, are different in tone from those written by nineteenth-century Celticists. The fact that several of these later texts are written in Breton (rather than French) suggests on the face of it a more direct and 'lateral' relationship between minoritized cultures and small nations.

Conversely, the German travellers do not gaze at Wales through the prism of any such 'petite patrie' movement, nor do they lay claim to a shared cultural or linguistic heritage. The analyses in chapters three, four and five have shown that travellers writing in German do not tend to evoke their own minorities in response to the Welsh, nor have recourse to minoritized languages or cultures. Instead, as the nineteenth century progresses, there is some evidence of an understanding of Wales as part of a 'national' federal construct not dissimilar to that emerging in the Second Empire, but viewed nonetheless from the privileged position of cultural hegemony, underscored by the erudition of German scholars examining Celtic culture from afar.

13   NLW MS 947 A, unpaginated.

This study has explored the portrayal of Wales in travel writing in French, German and Breton; much work remains to be done on Welsh travel writing beyond the British Isles. Detailed analyses of travelogues in Welsh and English would not only hold a mirror up to the images of Wales which have been projected to the world in travel writing by Welsh authors, but may also reveal new insights into relations between minoritized cultures.[14] Moreover, the vast majority of this Continental textual traffic since 1780 has been in a single direction, and works on Wales have not travelled far. Very few of the Continental travel texts examined here were translated during the period of their publication, making it difficult to measure reader reception in Wales amongst the travellees the works depict.[15] Such linguistic barriers precluded the possibility of travellees 'writing back', and the hidden nature of the texts also compounded this difficulty. The 'Journey to the Past: Wales in Historic Travel Writing from France and Germany' research project[16] has begun the translation process for texts from the eighteenth and nineteenth centuries; more recent works from the twentieth and twenty-first centuries also need to reach a broader audience in order to enhance understandings of the ways in which Wales is also constructed in imagological terms, namely the study of cross-national perceptions and images as expressed in literary discourse. Moreover, whilst the present study has examined textual responses to Wales, future research could usefully focus on visual cultures, including landscape painting, photography, film and television.[17]

14   Heather Williams, 'Travelling Ideas between Wales and Brittany', *VTU Review: Studies in the Humanities and Social Sciences*, 2:1 (2018), pp. 47–54. Williams's article examines travel writing in Welsh on Brittany in O.M. Edwards's *Tro yn Llydaw* (1888) [A Tour in Brittany], Ambrose Bebb's *Llydaw* (1929) [Brittany] and *Pererindodau* (1941) [Pilgrimages], and Dyfnallt's *O Ben Tir Llydaw* (1934) [From the Headland of Brittany].

15   Amongst the few exceptions are Hermann von Pückler-Muskau, whose *Briefe eines Verstorbenen* (1830) was published in English in 1833, and François 'Taldir' Jaffrennou, who published accounts of his visit to the 1899 Cardiff Eisteddfod in Welsh in the journal *Cymru*.

16   See the project website, http://footsteps.bangor.ac.uk/en/, where extracts from key texts are translated into Welsh, English, French and German. 'Journey to the Past' is a follow-on project from the original 'European Travellers to Wales: 1750–2010' research project, and was also funded by the Arts and Humanities Research Council.

17   This research pathway was initiated through Rita Singer's article 'Through Wales in the Footsteps of William Gilpin', pp. 127–47.

The present volume demonstrates the case for the study of travel writing to challenge and move beyond centre-periphery binaries in order to reach a more nuanced understanding of other complex intercultural relationships. This work has focused on the Welsh-Breton paradigm, but to what extent might future research discover similar findings for other minor relationships portrayed in travel writing? For example, would a study of travel writing on Catalonia or in Catalan and Castilian Spanish reveal a comparable tendency to search for shared cultural and linguistic characteristics that pervades Breton and French travel writing on Wales? How might travel writers mediate the centre-periphery relationship between Spain and Catalonia, and further problematize notions of hegemony and identity within the genre of travel writing? Moreover, future research could look at transnational responses to ongoing changes in Wales's political and socio-economic status, and broaden the field of research to compare these with other devolved or semi-autonomous nations such as Scotland in order to bring the findings into further relief.

This work has perceived Wales through the prism of microcosmo-politanism, first explored with regard to Ireland by Michael Cronin and Wales by M. Wynn Thomas. As Cronin argues, microcosmopolitanism

> expresses the notion of a cultural complexity which remains constant from the micro to the macro scale. That is to say, the same degree of diversity is to be found at the level of entities judged to be small or insignificant as at the level of large entities.[18]

While the fifth chapter of our study presents traces of a new cosmopolitanism in the major urban centres of the south, Cronin's concept extends beyond evidence of multiculturalism and ethnic diversity in contemporary Wales. This research bears witness not only to the complexity of the rich and evolving narrative on Wales and the diversity of the Welsh nation itself, but also the diversity of the frameworks used to perceive it in multilingual textual responses. It shows that one cannot fully understand Wales in isolation. There has been much discussion in the last twenty years or so of the need to consider the two literatures of Wales, in English and Welsh, in parallel and in dialogue with each other for a full understanding of Wales,[19] but this study demonstrates

18 Cronin, 'Global Questions', p. 192.
19 See M. Wynn Thomas, *Corresponding Cultures: The Two Literatures of Wales* (Cardiff: University of Wales Press, 1999).

that other languages also demand to be taken into account, and that the multilingual process of recovering lost texts should continue within a framework of fully comparative research. This work has uncovered hidden texts and has prised open brand new perspectives on Wales for a non-francophone/germanophone readership, offering fresh insights into the construction of Wales's identities from external sources. In addition, these neglected texts constitute a new resource in the discipline of modern languages for investigating the evolving perception of the 'other', particularly the crucial Celtic 'other' in the French context.

The study concludes that new ways of thinking about intercultural relations and tensions are needed. This need is all the more pressing as it remains the case that work on these types of minoritized text is the least likely to be discussed in mainstream academic discourse, partly for reasons of linguistic skill, partly due to the issue of which works are available in print and accessible to researchers. Wales currently benefits from greater accessibility thanks to the affordability of transport and the plethora of travel accounts now available to Continental visitors through both traditional publishing and online blogs and vlogs. Conversely, this new-found visibility and possibilities for intercultural exchange could be perceived as endangered by falling numbers of modern language learners in Wales and the rest of the United Kingdom, and the constantly evolving British-European relations following the 2016 Brexit referendum and resulting concerns about insularity and isolationism. Travel writing remains a vital vehicle for exploring these evolving intercultural relations and a valuable medium in the interrogation of such shifting cultural and political landscapes.

Bibliography

'Aus dem Land der Barden und Druiden', *Rigasche Rundschau*, 20 August 1914.

'Cofnodau Cymdeithas Cymmreigyddion y Fenni', National Library of Wales MS 13858E.

'Description des mines de cuivre de l'île d'Anglesey, dans le pays de Galles: extraite et traduite du voyage de M. Pennant, intitulé: Tour in Wales. Londres, 1781, tome II, pag. 265', *Journal des mines* in Nivôse, of year 4, in the revolutionary calendar (or December–January 1795).

'Foreigners and the Revival', *The Western Mail*, 6 February 1905.

Gazette de France [report on Abergavenny *Eisteddfod*], 22 October 1838.

Hereford Times, Supplement on Abergavenny *Eisteddfod*, 20 October 1838.

'La plus longue vague artificielle du monde déferle au Pays de Galles', *Le Monde*, 31 July 2015, https://www.lemonde.fr/sports-de-glisse/article/2015/07/31/surf-la-plus-longue-vague-artificielle-du-monde-deferle-au-pays-de-galles_4706388_1616666.html [accessed 25 September 2015].

'Minningar úr ferð Söngskólakórsins til Wales í byrjun julí', *Alþýðublaðið Sunnudagsblað*, 146 (24 July 1977), pp. 3, 8.

'Pontycymer', *Y Tyst*, 16 August 1905.

'Swords, Scrolls and Mystic Marks', https://museum.wales/articles/2010-07-25/Scrolls-swords-and-mystic-marks/ [accessed 7 June 2018].

'Y Diwygiad', *Y Gwyliedydd*, 8 June 1905.

Aaron, Jane, and Chris Williams, *Postcolonial Wales* (Cardiff: University of Wales Press, 2005).

Adams, Percy G., *Travelers and Travel Liars 1660–1800* (Berkeley: University of California Press, 1962).

Allo, Samuel, *Au fil des contes: voyages dans les pays celtes* (Saint-Brieuc: Imprimerie Jacq, 2014).

Allo, Samuel, 'Tour des pays celtes', http://samuelallo.com/index.php?option=com_content&view=article&id=150:bro-iwerzhon-irlande-ireland&catid=3:autres-projets&Itemid=30 [accessed 3 July 2017].

Andrews, Malcolm, *The Search for the Picturesque* (Aldershot: Scholar Press, 1989).

Angleterre, Pays de Galles (sans Londres) (Paris: Hachette Tourisme, 2013).

Arcis, Arthur d', 'Voyage au nord du pays de Galles', *Le Globe: journal géographique, Bulletin*, 6 (1887), pp. 34–51.

Arnold, Matthew, *On the Study of Celtic Literature* (London: Smith, Elder & Co., 1867).

Atzori, Pamela, 'The International Effects of the Welsh Revival 1904–5: The Case of France' (unpublished master's thesis, Aberystwyth University, 2005).

Baader, Joseph von, 'Geschichte und Beschreibung der englischen Eisenbahnen – ihre Kosten – ihre Wirkung – ihre Vorzüge vor den gewöhnlichen Straßen und vor den schiffbaren Kanälen – ihre Mängel und Unbequemlichkeiten', *Polytechnisches Journal*, 7:1 (1822), pp. 1–52.

Bauer, Lukas, '"Sie durchziehen dieses Land in ganzen Schwärmen": Tourism as a Marker of Modernity in Heine's *Reisebilder*', *Monatshefte*, 110 (2018), pp. 487–508.

Bebb, Ambrose, *Pererindodau* (Llandysul: Y Clwb Llyfrau Cymreig, 1941).

Beddoe, Deirdre, *Out of the Shadows: A History of Women in Twentieth-Century Wales* (Cardiff: University of Wales Press, 2000).

Behadad, Ali, *Belated Travelers: Orientalism in the Age of Colonial Dissolution* (Durham, NC: Duke University Press, 1994).

Benecke, Levin Anton Wilhelm, *Wilhelm Benecke's Lebensskizze und Briefe*, Vol. 1, ed. anon. (Dresden: Druck der Teubner'schen Offizin, 1850).

Benedikt, Bene, 'Snowdon Gipfeltour in Wales', *Der Spiegel*, 1 May 2013, http://www.spiegel.de/reise/europa/snowdon-hoechster-berg-von-wales-a-895067.html [accessed 20 September 2013].

Bengel, Michael, *Der Ritter mit der Web-Adresse: Walisische Panoramen* (Vienna: Picus, 2006).

Bénichou, Paul, *Nerval et la chanson folklorique* (Paris: José Corti, 1970).

Bernig, Jörg, *Weder Ebbe noch Flut* (Halle: Mitteldeutscher Verlag, 2007).

Bernig, Jörg, 'Am Rand des Randes. Reisemitschriften' (2017), in *Perthyn i Gymru / Belonging to Wales* (e-book: 2019), pp. 54–68; translation into English by Alyce von Rothkirch, pp. 83–96, http://etw.bangor.ac.uk/downloads [accessed 28 February 2019].

Bertaud, Jacques, 'Madame de Genlis et l'Angleterre: la femme et l'œuvre de 1779 à 1792' (unpublished doctoral thesis, Paris III-Sorbonne, 1974).

Black, Adam, and Charles Black, *Black's Picturesque Tourist of England and Wales* (Edinburgh: Adam and Charles Black, 1858).

Blind, Karl, 'Erinnerungen aus Wales', *Neue Freie Presse*, 19 March 1869, pp. 1–4.

Blind, Karl, 'Eine Barden und Volksversammlung in Wales', *Neue Freie Presse*, 14 September 1881, pp. 1–3.

Bohata, Kirsti, *Postcolonialism Revisited* (Cardiff: University of Wales Press, 2004).

Bois, Henri, *Le Réveil au Pays de Galles* (Toulouse: Société des publications morales et religieuses, 1906).

Bombelles, Marc de, *Journal de voyage en Grande Bretagne et en Irlande 1784*, ed. Jacques Grury (Oxford: Voltaire Foundation, 1989).

Bonucci, Vittorio, *POW: Quasi Una Fantasia* (Viterbo: Edizioni Cultura, 1985).

Bopp, Franz, 'Über die celtischen Sprachen vom Gesichtspunkt der vergleichenden Sprachforschung', *Abhandlungen und Sitzungsberichte der Preußischen Akademie der Wissenschaften* (1838), pp. 187–272.

Botmelas, Alain de (pseud. of Régis-Marie-Joseph de l'Estourbeillon de la Garnache), 'Les Bretons au pays de Galles', *Revue historique de l'Ouest*, 15 (30 November 1899), also published in pamphlet form as *Les Bretons au Pays de Galles* (Redon: A. Bouteloup, 1899).

Bowe, Mary Camille, *François Rio: sa place dans le renouveau catholique en Europe (1797–1874)* (Paris: Boivin, 1938).

Bowman, Peter James, *The Fortune Hunter: A German Prince in Regency England* (Oxford: Signal Books, 2010).

Bracewell, Wendy, 'Europe', in Carl Thompson (ed.), *The Routledge Companion to Travel Writing* (New York: Routledge, 2015), pp. 341–50.

Bracewell, Wendy, and Alex Drace-Francis (eds), *A Bibliography of East European Travel Writing on Europe* (Budapest: CEU Press, 2008).

Bracewell, Wendy, and Alex Drace-Francis (eds), *Under Eastern Eyes: A Comparative Introduction to East European Travel Writing on Europe* (Budapest: CEU Press, 2008).

Bradley, Margaret, and Fernand Perrin, 'Charles Dupin's Study Visits to the British Isles, 1816–1824', *Technology and Culture*, 32:1 (1991), pp. 47–68.

Brandes, Heinrich Karl, *Ausflug nach England im Sommer 1851* (Lemgo: Meyer, 1855).

Brennecke, Adolf Wilhelm Herman, 'Wales und die Insel Man', in *Alt-England. Eine Studienreise durch London und die Grafschaften zwischen Kanal und Piktenwall* (Leipzig: Ferdinand Hirt & Sohn, 1888), pp. 151–65.

Brennecke, Adolf Wilhelm Herman, Franz Brömel, Richard Oberländer and Adolf Rosenberg, *Nordland-Fahrten. Zweite Abteilung. Malerische Wanderungen durch England und die Kanalinseln: Mit besonderer Berücksichtigung von Sage und Geschichte, Literatur und Kunst* (Leipzig: Hirt, 1882).

Brockhaus, Rudolf, *Aus den Tagebüchern von Heinrich Brockhaus*, 5 vols (Leipzig: F.A. Brockhaus, 1884).

Brooks, Simon, *Pam na fu Cymru? Methiant Cenedlaetholdeb Cymraeg* (Cardiff: University of Wales Press, 2015), subsequently published in English as *Why Wales Never Was: The Failure of Welsh Nationalism* (Cardiff: University of Wales Press, 2017).

Brown, Terence (ed.), *Celticism* (Amsterdam: Rodopi, 1996).

Bunsen, Frances Waddington, *Christian Carl Josias Freiherr von Bunsen: aus seinen Briefen und nach eigener Erinnerung geschildert von seiner Witwe. Schweiz und England*, ed. Friedrich Nippold, Vol. 2 (Leipzig: F.A. Brockhaus, 1869).

Burat, Amédée, *Géologie appliquée, ou Traité de la recherche et de l'exploitation des minéraux utiles* (Paris: Langlois and Leclercq, 1843).

Camus, Renaud, *Demeures de l'esprit Grande-Bretagne. I, Angleterre sud & centre, Pays de Galles* (Paris: Fayard, 2008).

Carroll, Clare, and Patricia King (eds), *Ireland and Postcolonial Theory* (Notre Dame: University of Notre Dame Press, 2003).

Carus, Carl Gustav, *England und Schottland im Jahre 1844*, 2 vols (Berlin: Verlag von Alexander Dunker, 1845).

Carus, Carl Gustav, *The King of Saxony's Journey through England and Scotland in the Year 1844*, trans. S.C. Davison (London: Chapman and Hall, 1846).

Chapman, Malcolm, *The Gaelic Vision in Scottish Culture* (London: Croom Helm, 1978).

Chapman, Malcolm, *The Celts: The Construction of a Myth* (London: Macmillan, 1992).

Chenay, Christophe de, 'Les montagnards du Pays de Galles', *Le Monde*, 21 October 2004, https://www.lemonde.fr/archives/article/2004/10/20/les-montagnards-du-pays-de-galles_383729_1819218.html?xtmc=pays_de_galles&xtcr=1 [accessed 5 July 2011].

Chr., M.M., 'Schetsen uit Noord-Wales: Uit de Reis-herinneringen eener jeugdige Hollandsche', *Het Leeskabinet*, 36:1 (1869), pp. 134–51.

Clark, Steve, 'Introduction', in Steve Clark (ed.), *Travel Writing and Empire: Postcolonial Theory in Transit* (London: Zed Books, 1999), pp. 1–28.

Colbert, Benjamin, 'Britain through Foreign Eyes: Early Nineteenth-Century Home Tourism in Translation', in Benjamin Colbert (ed.), *Travel Writing and Tourism in Britain and Ireland* (London: Palgrave Macmillan, 2012), pp. 68–84.

Conrad, Bernadette, 'Dorfdichter von Welt', *Die Zeit*, 45, 30 October 2014, p. 61.

Conroy, Jane, 'Time and the Traveller: The Case of Coquebert de Montbret', in Eamon Maher and Catherine Maingant (eds), *Franco-British Connections in Space and Time* (Oxford: Peter Lang, 2013), pp. 29–52.

Constantine, Mary-Ann, 'Ossian in Wales and Brittany', in Howard Gaskill (ed.), *The Reception of Ossian in Europe* (London: Thoemmes Continuum, 2004), pp. 67–90.

Constantine, Mary-Ann, 'Beauty Spot, Blind Spot: Romantic Wales', *Literature Compass*, 5:3 (2008), pp. 577–90.

Constantine, Mary-Ann, '"Impertinent structures": A Breton's Adventures in Neo-Gothic Wales', *Studies in Travel Writing*, 18:2 (2014), pp. 134–47.

Constantine, Mary-Ann, '"To trace thy country's glories to their source": Dangerous History in Thomas Pennant's *Tour in Wales*', in Porscha Fermanis and John Regan (eds), *Rethinking British Romantic History 1770–1845* (Oxford: Oxford University Press, 2014), pp. 121–43.

Constantine, Mary-Ann, 'La "sainte terre de Cambrie": La Villemarqué et le romantisme gallois', in Nelly Blanchard and Fañch Postic (eds), *Au-delà du Barzaz Breiz: Théodore Hersart de la Villemarqué* (Brest: CRBC, 2016), pp. 209–26.

Constantine, Mary-Ann, and Fañch Postic, '"C'est mon journal de voyage": La Villemarqué's Letters from Wales, 1838–1839', 2019, https://hal.univ-brest.fr/hal-02350747/document [accessed 1 April 2020].

Corfec, Guillaume, *Indépendance Bretonne*, 22 July 1899.

Courseau, Claude-François, *Les Survivances celtes au Pays de Galles* (1971), rapports de premier voyage Zellidja jusqu'en 1974; 4814. Bibliothèque nationale de France, Paris. MS.

Croisille, Christian, 'Michelet et les Gaulois; ou, Les séductions de la patrie celtique', in Paul Viallaneix and Jean Ehrard (eds), *Nos ancêtres les Gaulois: Actes du colloque international de Clermont-Ferrand* (Clermont-Ferrand: Association des publications de la Faculté des lettres et sciences humaines, 1982), pp. 195–201.

Cronin, Michael, *Across the Lines: Travel, Language, Translation* (Cork: Cork University Press, 2000).

Cronin, Michael, 'Global Questions and Local Visions: A Microcosmopolitan Perspective', in Alyce von Rothkirch and Daniel Williams (eds), *Beyond the Difference* (Cardiff: University of Wales Press, 2004), pp. 186–202.

Cronin, Michael, 'Home Truths: Language, Slowness, and Microspection', in Benjamin Colbert (ed.), *Travel Writing and Tourism in Britain and Ireland* (Basingstoke: Palgrave Macmillan, 2012), pp. 219–35.

Cronin, Michael, 'Speech Acts: Language, Mobility and Place', in Corinne Fowler, Charles Forsdick and Ludmilla Kostova (eds), *Travel and Ethics* (New York: Routledge, 2013), pp. 16–30.

Crossley, Ceri, *French Historians and Romanticism: Thierry, Guizot, the Saint-Simonians, Quinet, Michelet* (London: Routledge, 1993).

Darrieussecq, Marie, 'Les Fantômes du Pays de Galles' (2017), in *Perthyn i Gymru / Belonging to Wales* (e-book. 2019), pp. 29–33; translation into English by Kathryn N. Jones, pp. 38–42; available at: http://etw.bangor.ac.uk/downloads [accessed 28 February 2019].

Davies, Gaius, 'Evan Roberts: wedi ei ddifa gan y tân?', in Noel Gibbard (ed.), *Nefol Dân: Agweddau ar Ddiwygiad 1904–05* (Pen-y-bont ar Ogwr: Gwasg Bryntirion, 2004), pp. 157–67.

Davies, Hywel M., 'Wales in English Travel Writing 1791–8: The Welsh Critique of Theophilus Jones', *Welsh History Review*, 23:3 (2007), pp. 65–93.

Davies, J.H. (ed.), *The Letters of Lewis, Richard, William and John Morris, of Anglesey*, (Morrisiaid Mon), 1728–1765, 2 vols (Aberystwyth: Published privately by the editor and printed for him by Fox, Jones & Co., Oxford, 1907–1909).

Davies, John, *A History of Wales* (London: Penguin, 1997).

Davies, Mererid Puw, 'On (Not) Reading Wales in W.G. Sebald's *Austerlitz* (2001)', *Oxford German Studies*, 47:1 (2018), pp. 84–102.

Davies, R.R., *The First English Empire: Power and Identities in the British Isles, 1093–1343* (Oxford: Oxford University Press, 2000).

Davison, Rosena, 'Friend or Foe? French Émigrés Discover Britain', in Kathleen Doig and Dorothy Medlin (eds), *British-French Exchanges in the Eighteenth Century* (Newcastle: Cambridge Scholars Publishing, 2007), pp. 131–48.

Deans, Alex, and Nigel Leask, 'Curious Travellers: Thomas Pennant and the Welsh and Scottish Tour (1760–1820)', *Studies in Scottish Literature*, 42:2 (2016), pp. 164–72.

Delannoy, Pierre, 'Pays de Galles: la tentation océane'; photographs by Richard Manin/Sipa Press, *Grands Reportages: Le Magazine de l'Aventure et du Voyage*, 109 (January 1991), pp. 122–34.

Diderot, Denis, *Œuvres esthétiques*, ed. Paul Vernière (Paris: Garnier Frères, 1968).

Dijkstra, Anna-Lou, 'Wales in Continental Guidebooks (1850–2013): A Country on the Imaginative Periphery' (unpublished doctoral thesis, Swansea University, 2017).

Dittler, Georg, *Hydrotechnische Bemerkungen gesammelt auf einer Reise durch England, Holland, Nord- und Süddeutschland im Jahre 1830. Nebst einer kurzen Biographie des Verfassers* (Karlsruhe: n.p., 1835).

Dohler, Christine, 'Untergrund Bewegung', *Die Zeit*, 9 June 2015.

Dow, Gillian, 'Stéphanie-Félicité de Genlis and the French Historical Novel in Romantic Britain', *Women's Writing*, 19:3 (2012), pp. 273–92.

Doyle, William, *The Oxford History of the French Revolution* (Oxford: Oxford University Press, 2002).

Drace-Francis, Alex, *The Traditions of Invention: Romanian Ethnic and Social Stereotypes in Historical Context* (Leiden and Boston: Brill, 2013).

Dufrénoy, Pierre-Armand, and Léonce Élie de Beaumont, *Voyage Métallurgique en Angleterre: ou Recueil des Mémoires sur le gisement, l'exploitation et le traitement des Minerais d'étain, de cuivre, de plomb, de zinc et de fer, dans la Grande-Bretagne* (Paris: Bachelier, Libraire pour les sciences, 1827).

Dupin, Charles, *Mémoires sur la marine et les ponts et chaussées de France et d'Angleterre* (Paris: Bachelier, 1818).

Dupin, Charles, *Voyages dans la Grande-Bretagne V*, part of Vol. 1 of his *Force Commerciale de la Grande-Bretagne* (Paris: Bachelier, 1824).

Duquesne, Jean-Charles, 'Voyages. Au pays de Galles, la nature est reine', *La Croix*, 26 May 1997, p. 18.

Dutens, Joseph-Michel, *Mémoires sur les travaux publics de l'Angleterre* (Paris: Imprimerie royale, 1819).

Edwards, Elizabeth, 'Iniquity, Terror and Survival: Welsh Gothic, 1789–1804', *Journal for Eighteenth-Century Studies*, 35:1 (2012), pp. 119–33.

Edwards, Elizabeth, '"A Kind of Geological Novel": Wales and Travel Writing, 1783–1819', *Romanticism*, 24:2 (2018), pp. 134–47.

Edwards, Hywel Teifi, 'Eisteddfodau'r Cyngor 1858–1868', *Taliesin*, 14 (1967), pp. 82–93.

Edwards, Hywel Teifi, 'Eisteddfodau Cenedlaethol Chwe-degau'r Ganrif Ddiwethaf a'r Wasg Saesneg', *Ysgrifau Beirniadol*, 8 (1974), pp. 205–25.

Edwards, Hywel Teifi, *Gŵyl Gwalia: Yr Eisteddfod Genedlaethol yn Oes Aur Victoria 1858–1868* (Llandysul: Gomer, 1980).

Edwards, Hywel Teifi, 'The Welsh Language in the *Eisteddfod*', in Geraint H. Jenkins (ed.), *The Welsh Language and its Social Domains 1830–1911* (Cardiff: University of Wales Press, 2000), pp. 293–316.

Ellis, Peter Berresford, *Celtic Dawn: The Dream of Celtic Unity* (Talybont: Y Lolfa, 1993).

Elsasser, Robert, *Über die politischen Bildungsreisen der Deutschen nach England vom Anfang des 18. Jahrhunderts bis 1815*, Heidelberger Abhandlungen zur mittleren und neueren Geschichte 51 (Heidelberg: Winter, 1917).

Erny, Alfred, 'Voyage dans le pays de Galles', *Le Tour du Monde*, 15:1 (1867), pp. 257–88.

Esquiros, Alphonse, *Itinéraire descriptif et historique de la Grande-Bretagne et de l'Irlande* (Paris: Hachette, 1865).

Esquiros, Alphonse, 'Le Sud du pays de Galles et l'industrie du fer. Carmarthen, les Eisteddfodau et les Iron-Works de Merthyr Tydfil', *Revue des Deux Mondes*, 55 (1865), pp. 801–43.

Evans, Chris, and Göran Rydén (eds), *The Industrial Revolution in Iron: The Impact of British Coal Technology in Nineteenth-Century Europe* (Aldershot: Ashgate, 2005).

Evans, D. Ellis, 'Celticity, Celtic Awareness and Celtic Studies', *Zeitschrift für celtische Philologie*, 49–50 (1997), pp. 1–27.

Evans, Evan, *Some Specimens of the Poetry of the Antient Welsh Bards* (London: R. and J. Dodsley, 1764).

Evans, E. Vincent (ed.), *Cofnodion a Chyfansoddiadau Buddugol Eisteddfod Aberdar, 1885 / Transactions of the National Eisteddfod of Wales, Aberdare, 1885* (Cardiff: Duncan and Sons, 1887).

Evans, R. Paul, 'Thomas Pennant (1726–1798): The Father of Cambrian Tourists', *Welsh History Review*, 13:4 (1987), pp. 395–417.

Fabian, Johannes, *Time and the Other: How Anthropology Makes its Object* (New York: Columbia University Press, 1983).

Fer, Claudio Rodríguez, 'Que verde era o meu Gales', *Unión libre: Cadernos de vida e culturas*, 15, 'Meus amores celtas' (2010), pp. 75–80.

Ferner, Bengt, *Resa in Europa, en astronom, industriespion och teaterhabitue genom Denmark, Tyskland, Holland, England och Italien – 1758–1762*, ed. Sten G. Lindberg (Uppsala: Swedish Society for the History of Science, 1956).

Fischer, Tilmann, *Reiseziel England: Ein Beitrag zur Poetik der Reisebeschreibung und zur Topik der Moderne (1830–1870)*, Philologische Studien und Quellen 184 (Berlin: Schmidt, 2004).

Forsdick, Charles, *Travel in Twentieth-Century French and Francophone Cultures* (Oxford: Oxford University Press, 2005).

Forsdick, Charles, Corinne Fowler and Ludmilla Kostova, 'Introduction: Ethics on the Move', in *Travel and Ethics: Theory and Practice* (New York: Routledge, 2014), pp. 1–15.

Fouéré, Yann, *La Maison de Connemara: l'histoire d'un Breton* (Spézet: Coop Breizh, 1995), trans. Rozenn Fouéré, *'La Maison' in Connemara: The History of a Breton* (Oldchapel, Oughterard: Oldchapel Press, 2011), http://fondationyannfouere.org/english/translation-of-la-maison-du-connemara/ [accessed 1 July 2017].

France, Peter (ed.), *The Oxford Companion to French Literature* (Oxford: Oxford University Press, 1996).

Franke, Wolfgang, *Der Theaterkritiker Ludwig Rellstab* (Berlin: Colloquium, 1964).

Fursac, Joseph Rogues de, *Manuel de Psychiatrie* (Paris: Alcan, 1903).

Fursac, Joseph Rogues de, *Un mouvement mystique contemporain. Le réveil religieux du Pays de Galles (1904–1905)* (Paris: Alcan, 1907).

Gaskill, Howard, 'Herder, Ossian and the Celtic', in Terence Brown (ed.), *Celticism* (Amsterdam: Rodopi, 1996), pp. 257–72.

Gaskill, Howard, 'Ossian, Herder and the Idea of Folk Song', in David Hill (ed.), *Literature of the Sturm und Drang* (Rochester, NY: Camden House, 2003), pp. 95–116.

Gaskill, Howard, *The Reception of Ossian in Europe* (London: Thoemmes Continuum, 2004).

Gelléri, Gábor, 'Les "promenades" de La Tocnaye: exil, voyage, survie, transfert', in Augustin Lefebvre and Judit Maar (eds), *Exils et transfers culturels dans l'Europe moderne* (Paris: L'Harmattan, 2015), pp. 277–87.

Gelléri, Gábor, *Philosophies du voyage: visiter l'Angleterre aux 17e–18e siècles* (Oxford: Voltaire Foundation, 2016).

Gemie, Sharif, *Brittany, 1750–1950: The Invisible Nation* (Cardiff: University of Wales Press, 2007).

Genlis, Stéphanie-Félicité du Crest de Saint-Aubin, comtesse de, *Mémoires inédits de Madame la comtesse de Genlis, sur le dix-huitième siècle et la révolution française, depuis 1756 jusqu'à nos jours*, 8 vols (Paris: Ladvocat, 1825).

Gibbard, Noel, *On the Wings of the Dove: The International Effects of the 1904–05 Revival* (Pen-y-bont ar Ogwr: Gwasg Bryntirion, 2002).

Gibbard, Noel, *Fire on the Altar: A History and Evaluation of the 1904–05 Welsh Revival* (Pen-y-bont ar Ogwr: Gwasg Bryntirion, 2005).

Gilpin, William, *Observations on the River Wye and several parts of South Wales, &c. relative chiefly to picturesque beauty: made in the Summer of the year 1770* (London: R. Blamire, 1782).

Gilpin, William, *Observations pittoresques sur le cours de la Wye et sur différentes parties du pays de Galles, par M. William Gilpin*, trans. Baron de B*** [Blumenstein] (Breslau: G.T. Korn, 1800).

Gitre, Edward J., 'The 1904–05 Welsh Revival: Modernization, Technologies, and Techniques of the Self', *Church History*, 73:4 (2004), pp. 792–827.

Gloaguen, Alexis, 'Galles Noires', in *Traques Passagères* (Quimper: Calligrammes, 1989), pp. 11–18.

Goede, Christian August Gottlieb, *England, Wales, Irland und Schottland: Erinnerungen an Natur und Kunst aus einer Reise in den Jahren 1802 und 1803*, 5 vols (Dresden: Arnoldische Buch- und Kunsthandlung, 1804–1805).

Goede, Christian August Gottlieb, *The Stranger in England or Travels in Great Britain from the German of C.A.G. Goede*, trans. anon., 3 vols (London: Mathews and Leigh, 1807).

Goede, Christian August Gottlieb, *Memorials of Nature and Art, collected on a Journey in Great Britain during the years 1802 and 1803*, trans. Thomas Horne, 3 vols (London: Mawman, 1808).

Gosetti, Valentina, and Antonio Viselli, 'L'"autoexotisme" des poètes provinciaux: une ruse dix-neuviémiste? Le cas des *Amours jaunes* de Tristan Corbière', *Romantismes*, 181 (2018), pp. 47–61.

Gougaud, L., 'Alexis-François Rio et la Bretagne', *Annales de Bretagne*, 29:3 (1913), pp. 439–63.

Gougaud, L., 'La Société lettrée de Londres observée par un écrivain français en 1839: journal inédit de François Rio', *Revue d'histoire ecclésiastique*, 30:2 (1934), p. 297.

Gourvil, Francis, *Un Centenaire: l'Eisteddfod d'Abergavenny (Septembre 1838): et les relations spirituelles Bretagne-Galles* (Morlaix: Imprimerie nouvelle, no date), extract from *Bulletin de la Société d'études artistiques, littéraires et scientifiques du Finistère*, 1938.

Gourvil, Francis, *Théodore-Claude-Henri Hersart de la Villemarqué (1815–1895) et le 'Barzaz-Breiz'* (Rennes: Oberthur, 1960).

Gramich, Katie, 'Dehongli'r Diwygiad: Ymateb Awduron Cymreig i Ddiwygiad 1904–05', *Taliesin*, 128 (2006), pp. 12–28.

Gramich, Katie, '"Every Hill Has its History, Every Region its Romance": Travellers' Constructions of Wales, 1844–1913', in Benjamin Colbert (ed.), *Travel Writing and Tourism in Britain and Ireland* (Basingstoke: Palgrave Macmillan, 2012), pp. 147–63.

Griffiths, Miriam, 'Wider Empire for the Sight: Picturesque Scenery and the First Tourists', in William Tudeman (ed.), *The Welsh Connection* (Llandysul: Gomer, 1986), pp. 67–98.

Grosse, Julia, 'Die Ladies von Llangollen', *Merian*, 10 (20 September 2012), pp. 88–91.

Grosse, Julia, 'Im Königreich der Bücher', *Merian*, 10 (20 September 2012), pp. 60–66.

Gruber, Edith, 'King Arthur and the Privy Councillor: Albert Schulz as a Cultural Mediator Between the Literary Fields of Nineteenth-Century Wales and Germany' (unpublished doctoral thesis, Bangor University, 2012).

Guest, Revel, and Angela V. John, *Lady Charlotte Guest: An Extraordinary Life*, 2nd ed. (Stroud: Tempus, 2007).

Gurden-Williams, Celyn, 'Lady Llanover and the Creation of a Welsh Cultural Utopia' (unpublished doctoral thesis, Cardiff University, 2008).

Gurden-Williams, Celyn, *Pwy Oedd Arglwyddes Llanofer, Gwenynen Gwent? / Who Was Lady Llanover, The 'Bee of Gwent'?* (Coleford: Cymdeithas Gwenynen Gwent, 2016).

Gury, Jacques, 'Le Pays de Galles oublié', in *Le Voyage Outre-Manche. Anthologie de voyageurs français de Voltaire à Mac Orlan du XVIIIe au XXe siècle* (Paris: Robert Laffont, 1999), pp. 565–85.

Guskin, Phyllis, 'A French Tourist in Wales', *The Bulletin* (1995), pp. 3–4.

Hailbronner, Karl von, *Cartons aus der Reisemappe eines deutschen Touristen*, Vol. 1 (Stuttgart and Tübingen: Cotta, 1837).

Hale, Amy, and Philip Payton, 'Introduction', in Amy Hale and Philip Payton (eds), *New Directions in Celtic Studies* (Exeter: University of Exeter Press, 2000), pp. 1–14.

Hall, Mr S.C. and Mrs, *The Book of South Wales, the Wye, and the Coast* (London: Arthur Hall, Virtue and Co., 1861).

Hardenberg, Friedrich von, *Novalis. Schriften*, ed. Richard Samuel, Hans-Joachim Mahl and Gerhard Schulz, 2nd ed., 5 vols (Stuttgart: Kohlhammer, 1968).

Harris, John R., *Industrial Espionage and Technology Transfer: Britain and France in the Eighteenth Century* (Aldershot: Ashgate, 1998).

Harvey, Paul, and J.E. Heseltine (eds), *The Oxford Companion to French Literature* (Oxford: Oxford University Press, 1959).

Hausmann, Johann Friedrich Ludwig, 'Oxford, und die Englischen Fabrikdistricte, im Februar 1829', in *Aus dem Tagebuche einer Reise durch Holland, Belgien, Frankreich und England, in den Jahren 1828 und 1829. Kleinigkeiten in bunter Reihe. Bemerkungen und Betrachtungen über Gegenstände der Natur und Kunst*, Vol. 2 (Göttingen: Verlag der Dieterichschen Buchhandlung, 1859), pp. 305–76.

Hay, Malcolm, *Prince in Captivity: Based on the Memoirs and Unpublished Letters of Antoine Philippe d'Orléans Duc de Montpensier, 1775–1807* (London: Eyre & Spottiswoode, 1960).

Heidenreich, Elke, and Thomas Krausz, *Dylan Thomas: Waliser, Dichter, Trinker* (Munich: Knesebeck, 2011).

Heine, Adolf, 'Eine Hochzeit im Walliser Land', *Prager Tagblatt*, 12 July 1891, pp. 1–4.

Heine, Adolf, 'Eine Maifahrt in die englische Schweiz', *Prager Blatt*, 31 May 1896, pp. 1–4.

Heine, Wilhelm, 'Ein Sommerausflug nach Wales', *Westermanns Jahrbuch der illustrierten deutschen Monatshefte*, 30:175 (April 1871), pp. 31–40 and 30:176 (September 1871), pp. 155–61.

Holland, Patrick, and Graham Huggan, *Tourists with Typewriters: Critical Reflections on Contemporary Travel Writing* (Ann Arbor: University of Michigan Press, 1998).

Hughes, W.J., *Wales and the Welsh in English Literature from Shakespeare to Scott* (Wrexham: Hughes and Son, 1924).

Hürlimann, Bettina, 'Craig y Môr oder Erinnerungen an eine Reise nach Süd-Wales', in *Zwischenfall in Lerida und andere Texte* (Zürich and Freiburg im Breisgau: Atlantis Verlag, 1979), pp. 67–84.

Hüttenegger, Bernhard, 'Wales und England', in *Weg von Allem: Reisen und Schreiben* (Klagenfurt: Kitab Verlag, 2006), pp. 91–126.

Jaffrennou, François (Taldir), 'Llanberis a Beddgelert. Fel y gwelodd Llydawr Hwynt', *Cymru*, 18 (1899), p. 41.

Jaffrennou, François (Taldir), 'Tro yng Ngogledd Cymru', *Cymru*, 17 (1899), pp. 221–24.

Jaffrennou, François (Taldir), 'Le Gorsedd de Cardiff', *La Résistance*, 29 July 1899, published in François Jaffrennou, *La Genèse d'un mouvement: articles, doctrines et discours 1898–1911* (Carhaix: Imprimerie-Librairie du Peuple, 1912), pp. 33–35.

Jaffrennou, François (Taldir), *Eur wech e oa* (Morlaix: Armorica, 1944).

James, Simon, *The Atlantic Celts: Ancient People or Modern Invention?* (London: British Museum Press, 1999).

Jenkins, Bethan M., *Between Wales and England: Anglophone Welsh Writing of the Eighteenth Century* (Cardiff: University of Wales Press, 2017).

Jenkins, Geraint H., *The Foundations of Modern Wales 1642–1780* (Cardiff: University of Wales Press, 1987).

Jenkins, Geraint H. (ed.), *The Welsh Language and its Social Domains, 1801–1911* (Cardiff: University of Wales Press, 2000).

Jenkins, Geraint H., *Bard of Liberty: The Political Radicalism of Iolo Morganwg* (Cardiff: University of Wales Press, 2012).

Jenkins, Geraint H., Ffion Mair Jones and David Ceri Jones, *The Correspondence of Iolo Morganwg*, 3 vols (Cardiff: University of Wales Press, 2007).

John, S. Beynon, 'Alphonse Esquiros: A French Political Exile in Merthyr and Dowlais in 1864', *Merthyr Historian*, 3 (1980), pp. 12–23.

Jones, David Llewelyn, and Robert Smith, 'Tourism and the Welsh Language in the Nineteenth Century', in Geraint H. Jenkins (ed.), *The Welsh Language and its Social Domains, 1801–1911* (Cardiff: University of Wales Press, 2000), pp. 151–75.

Jones, Dot, 'The Coming of the Railways and Language Change in North Wales 1850–1900', in Geraint H. Jenkins (ed.), *The Welsh Language and its Social Domains* (Cardiff: University of Wales Press, 2000), pp. 131–49.

Jones, Ethel, *Les Voyageurs français en Angleterre de 1815 à 1830* (Paris: Boccard, 1930).

Jones, Kathryn N., 'Locating "Pays de Galles" in the Twenty-First Century: Dynamic Model or Forgotten World?', *Studies in Travel Writing*, 18 (2014), pp. 187–98.

Jones, R. Tudur, *Faith and the Crisis of a Nation: Wales 1890–1914* (Cardiff: University of Wales Press, 2004).

Jones, T.C., and R. Tombs, 'The French Left in Exile: *Quarante-huitards* and Communards in London, 1848–80', in Debra Kelly and Martyn Cornick (eds), *A History of the French in London: Liberty, Equality, Opportunity* (London: Institute of Historical Research, 2013), pp. 165–91.

Joppien, Rüdiger, *Philippe Jacques de Loutherbourg, RA 1740–1812* (London: Greater London Council, 1973).

Joppien, Rüdiger, 'A Visitor to a Ruined Churchyard: A Newly Discovered Painting by P.J. De Loutherbourg', *The Burlington Magazine*, 118:878 (1976), pp. 294–301.

Juling, Petra, *Wales, DuMont Reise-Taschenbuch* (Cologne: DuMont Buchverlag, 2000).

Jürschik-Busbach, Birgit, and Peter Busbach, *ARAF-Slow: Auf der Suche nach dem walisischen Herzschlag* (Leverkusen: Drachenmond Verlag, 2012).

Kaplan, Caren, *Questions of Travel: Postmodern Discourses of Displacement* (Durham, NC: Duke University, 1996).

Kervella, Erwan, 'Un dro-vale', *Al Liamm*, 144 (1971), pp. 31–40.

Klocke, Carl, *Dawlais Works, die Eisen- und Schienen-Walzwerke des Hauses John Guest, in London* (Stettin: Druck v. H. u. R. Graßmann, 1850).

Kohl, Friedrich, *Beschreibung der Göltzsch- und Elsterthal-Überbrückung im sächsischen Voightlande, sowie der Britannia-Röhrenbrücke und der über denselben Meeresarm führenden Kettenbrücke in England und der schiefen Ebene in Baiern. Vorangehend eine kurze Statistik deutscher und ausländischer Eisenbahnen* (Plauen: A. Schröter, 1854).

Kohl, Johann Georg, *Reisen in England und Wales* (Dresden: Arnold, 1844).

Königsberger, Klaus, 'Durch König Artus' Land: Briefe aus Wales', in *Ankunft und Abschied: Reisen auf 3 Kontinenten* (Leipzig: Brockhaus, 1986), pp. 133–80.

Kugies, Siegfried, *Der ostpreussische Eisenbahner und die Amerikaner* (Trebur: self-published, 2010).

Kunert, Günter, *Ein englisches Tagebuch* (Berlin: Aufbau Verlag, 1978).

Küttner, Carl Gottlob, *Beyträge zur Kenntniss vorzüglich des Innern von England und seiner Einwohner* (Leipzig: Im Verlage der Dykischen Buchhandlung, 1791).

La Tocnaye, Jacques-Louis de, *Promenade d'un Français dans l'Irlande*, 3 vols (Dublin: imprimé aux frais de l'auteur par Graisberry, 1797).

La Tocnaye, Jacques-Louis de, *Promenade autour de la Grande Bretagne; précédé de quelques détails sur la campagne du duc de Brunswick, par un officier français émigré* (Edinburgh: imprimé pour l'auteur par Jean Paterson, 1795), revised as *Promenade d'un Français dans la Grande-Bretagne* (Brunswick: P.F. Fauche et Compagnie, 1801).

La Villemarqué, Hersart de, NLW MS 964E, no. 308, Hersart de la Villemarqué to Thomas Stephens, 29 July 1861, in Knowledge Transfer and Social Networks Transcript, https://archives.library.wales/index.php/letters-534 [accessed October 2017].

La Villemarqué, Pierre de, *La Villemarqué sa vie et ses œuvres* (Paris: Champion, 1926).

Lamartine, Alphonse de, 'Toast porté dans un banquet national des Gallois et des Bretons à Abergavenny, en Écosse', in *Recueillements poétiques* (Brussels: Jamar, 1839), pp. 95–99.

Lange, Dieter, *Eine Bewegung bricht sich Bahn* (Giessen: Brunnen Verlag, 1979).

Le Braz, Anatole, 'Les Bretons de France au Pays de Galles', *La Revue des Revues* (July 1899), pp. 243–49.

Le Braz, Anatole, 'Pèlerinage celtique', in *La Terre du passé* (Paris: Calmann Lévy, 1901), pp. 315–33.

Le Braz, Anatole, 'Une semaine au Pays de Galles: 17 au 22 juillet 1899', in *Voyage en Irlande, en Angleterre et au pays de Galles* (Rennes: Presses Universitaires de Rennes, 1999), pp. 299–320.

Le Disez, Jean-Yves, *Une aventure galloise: portrait d'une petite nation solidaire* (Spézet: Coop Breizh, 2006).

Le Fustec, Jean, 'Fêtes celtiques', *La Revue hebdomadaire*, 3:8 (July 1899), pp. 321–40.

Le Fustec, Jean, 'La Musique chez les Gallois', *Revue hebdomadaire*, 8:7 (21 July 1900), pp. 376–90.

Le Goffic, Charles, 'Chez Taffy: quinze jours dans la Galles du Sud', in *L'Ame bretonne*, Vol. 2 (Paris: Champion, 1912), pp. 200–349; originally published as 'Chez Taffy: quinze jours dans la Galles du sud', *La Revue hebdomadaire*, 5:6–7 (May 1901), pp. 448–68; (June 1901) pp. 22–50, 229–50, 369–95, 520–47.

Le Mallier, Denise, *Le Roman des Dufaud* (La Charité-sur-Loire: Imprimerie Delayance, 1971).

Le Play, Frédéric, *Description des procédés métallurgiques employés dans le pays de Galles pour la fabrication du cuivre, et recherches sur l'état actuel et sur l'avenir probable de la production et du commerce de ce métal* (Paris: Carilian-Goeury and V. Dalmont, 1848).

Le Sauce, André, *Les Eisteddfod du nord du Pays de Galles*, 1961. Rapports de premier voyage Zellidja jusqu'en 1974; 3011. Bibliothèque nationale de France, Paris. MS.

Leigh, R.A. (ed.), *Correspondance complète de Jean-Jacques Rousseau*, 52 vols (Geneva: Institut et musée Voltaire, 1965–1998).

Lentin, August Gottfried Ludwig, *Briefe über die Insel Anglesea, vorzüglich über das dasige Kupfer-Bergwerk und die dazugehörigen Schmelzwerke und Fabriken* (Leipzig: Crusius, 1800).

Les, Christina, 'Space beyond Place: Welsh Settings in European Fiction, 1900–2010' (unpublished doctoral thesis, Bangor University, 2019).

Lichtenwalner, Shawna, *Claiming Cambria* (Newark: University of Delaware Press, 2008).

Linden, Peter, 'Drei Träume von Wales', *Die Zeit*, 25, 13 June 1997, https://www.zeit.de/1997/25/Drei_Traeume_von_Wales/komplettansicht [accessed 24 April 2016].

Linden, Peter, 'In fremden Betten', *Die Zeit*, 23, 28 May 2003, https://www.zeit.de/2003/23/Hotel_Pen_y_Gwryd/komplettansicht [accessed 19 November 2016].

Lindner, David, and Doris Lindner, *Traumzeit in Wales: Ein Reiseverführer* (Battweiler: Traumzeit-Verlag, 2013).

Lindsay, Claire, 'Beyond *Imperial Eyes*', in Justin D. Edwards and Rune Graulund (eds), *Postcolonial Travel Writing: Critical Explorations* (London: Palgrave Macmillan, 2011), pp. 17–35.

Linnard, William, 'A Swedish Visitor to Flintshire in 1760', *Flintshire Historical Society Journal*, 30 (1981–1982), pp. 145–49.

Löher, Franz von, *Land und Leute in der alten und neuen Welt: Reiseskizzen*, 2 vols (Göttingen: Georg H. Wigand, 1855).

Lord, Peter, 'Y Bardd: Celtiaeth a Chelfyddyd', *Cof Cenedl*, 7 (1992), pp. 99–131.

Lord, Peter, *The Visual Culture of Wales: Industrial Society* (Cardiff: University of Wales Press, 1998).

Loutherbourg, Philippe-Jacques de, *Romantic and Picturesque Scenery of England and Wales: From Drawings Made Expressly for this Undertaking by P.J. de Loutherbourg, Esq. R.A. with Historical and Descriptive Accounts of the Several Places of which Views are Given / Scènes romantiques et pittoresques, de l'Angleterre et du pays de Galles* (London: T. Bensley, 1805).

Loutherbourg, Philippe-Jacques de, *Sketches*, W6 DV 61 (4to), National Library of Wales, Aberystwyth. MS.

Maier, Bernhard, 'Einleitung zur zweiten Sektion: Deutsch-walisische Kulturbeziehungen. Wales und Deutschland: Neun Jahrhunderte kulturellen Austauschs', in Bernhard Maier and Stefan Zimmer (eds), *150 Jahre Mabinogion – Deutsch-Walisische Kulturbeziehungen* (Tübingen: Max Niemeyer, 2001), pp. 131–41.

Maier, Bernhard, and Stefan Zimmer (eds), *150 Jahre Mabinogion – Deutsch-Walisische Kulturbeziehungen* (Tübingen: Max Niemeyer, 2001).

du Marhallac'h, Auguste François Félix Du, 'Fête galloise d'Abergavenny', *Journal des débats politiques et littéraires*, 19 October 1838.

Martin, Alison E., *Moving Scenes: The Aesthetics of German Travel Writing on England 1783–1830*, Studies in Comparative Literature 13 (London: Legenda, 2008).

Martin, Alison E., 'Celtic Censure: Representing Wales in Eighteenth-Century Germany', *Studies in Travel Writing*, 18 (2014), pp. 122–34.

Martin, Henri, *Histoire de France depuis les temps les plus reculés jusqu'en 1789*, 19 vols (Paris: Furne, Jouvet, 1833–1854).

Martin, Henri, [*Eisteddfod* speech] *The Cardiff Times*, 23 August 1861.

Martin, Henri, [*Eisteddfod* speech] National Library of Wales MS 947A, unpaginated [1861].

Martin, Henri, letter to La Villemarque, 1861. Document numerise par le CRBC (LV21.034) et conserve aux Archives departementales du Finistere. Fonds Theodore Hersart de la Villemarque. 263 J. Fonds en cours de classement [collection currently being catalogued].

Martin, Henri, National Library of Wales MS 964E, no. 189, letter to Thomas Stephens, 1861, in Knowledge Transfer and Social Networks Transcript. https://archives.library.wales/index.php/letters-534 [accessed October 2017].

Martin, Henri, 'Le Pays de Galles: notes de voyage', *Le Siècle*, 17 December 1861, 27 December 1861 and 9 January 1862.

Martin, Henri, *Études d'archéologie celtique: notes de voyages dans les pays celtiques et scandinaves* (Paris: Didier, 1872).

Masiakowska, Dorota, *Vielfalt und Einheit im Europabild August Wilhelm Schlegels* (Frankfurt am Main: Peter Lang, 2002).

Maurer, Michael (ed.), *O Britannien, von deiner Freiheit einen Hut voll. Deutsche Reiseberichte des 18. Jahrhunderts* (Munich: Beck, 1992).

Maurer, Michael (ed.), *Wales: Die Entdeckung einer Landschaft und eines Volkes durch deutsche Reisende (1780–1860)*, Quellen und Forschungen zur europäischen Kulturgeschichte 3 (Frankfurt am Main: Peter Lang, 2014).

McCormack, W.J., *Ascendancy and Tradition in Anglo-Irish Literary History from 1789 to 1939* (Oxford: Clarendon Press, 1985).

Mee, Catharine, *Interpersonal Encounters in Contemporary Travel Writing: French and Italian Perspectives* (London and New York: Anthem Press, 2014).

Meerman, Johan, *Nachrichten von Großbritannien und Irland* (Nürnberg and Altdorf: Monathischen Verlag, 1789); from *Eenige berichten omtrent Groot-Brittannien en Ierland* (The Hague: n.p., 1787).

Meidinger, Heinrich, *Briefe von einer Reise durch England, Schottland und Irland im Frühjahr und Sommer, 1820* (Stuttgart and Tübingen: Cotta, 1821).

Mendelssohn Bartholdy, Felix, *Briefe*, ed. Rudolf Elvers (Frankfurt am Main: Fischer, 1984).

Meysenbug, Malwida von, *Memoiren einer Idealistin*, 3 vols (Berlin: Schuster & Loeffler, 1900).

Michelet, Jules, *Histoire de France*, 17 vols (Paris: Hachette, Chamerot, 1833–1841).

Michelet, Jules, *La Mer* (Paris: Hachette, 1861).

Michelet, Jules, *Sur les chemins de l'Europe: Angleterre, Flandre, Hollande, Suisse, Lombardie, Tyrol* (Paris: Marpon & Flammarion, 1893).

Michelet, Jules, *Journal*, ed. Paul Viallaneix, Vol. 1 (Paris: Gallimard, 1959).

Michelet, Jules, *Carnet de Bretagne: journal de Michelet en Bretagne (1831) suivi de la Bretagne dans 'Le Tableau de la France' (1833)* (Rennes: Terre de Brume, 1997).

Miles, Gareth, 'Y Diwygiad trwy lygad Ffrancwr', *Taliesin*, 124 (2005), pp. 22–26.

Miller, John, 'R.M. Ballantyne and Mr G. O'Rilla: Apes, Irishmen and the 1861 Great Gorilla Controversy', in Paddy Lyons, Willy Maley and John Miller (eds), *Romantic Ireland From Tone to Gonne: Fresh Perspectives on Nineteenth-Century Ireland* (Newcastle upon Tyne: Cambridge Scholars Press, 2013), pp. 402–15.

Moal, Claude, *En Galles*, 1947. Rapports de premier voyage Zellidja jusqu'en 1974; 135. Bibliothèque nationale de France, Paris. MS.

Mone, Franz Josef, *Celtische Forschungen zur Geschichte Mitteleuropas* (Freiburg im Breisgau: Herder, 1857).

Montbret, Charles Étienne Coquebert de, *Voyage de Paris à Dublin à travers la Normandie et l'Angleterre en 1789* (Lyon: Université Saint-Etienne, 1995).

Morgan, Nigel, and Annette Pritchard, 'Culture, Identity and Tourism Representation: Marketing Cymru or Wales?', *Tourism Management*, 22 (2001), pp. 167–79.

Morgan, Prys, *The Eighteenth-Century Renaissance* (Swansea: Christopher Davies, 1981).

Morgan, Prys, 'From Long Knives to Blue Books', in R.R. Davies, Ralph A. Griffiths, Ieuan Gwynedd Jones and Kenneth O. Morgan (eds), *Welsh Society and Nationhood: Historical Essays Presented to Glanmor Williams* (Cardiff: University of Wales Press, 1984), pp. 199–215.

Morgan, Prys, 'From a Death to a View: The Hunt for the Welsh Past in the Romantic Period', in Eric Hobsbawm and Terence Ranger (eds), *The Invention of Tradition* (Cambridge: Cambridge University Press, 1992), pp. 43–100.

Morgan, Prys, 'Wild Wales: Civilizing the Welsh from the Sixteenth to the Nineteenth Centuries', in Peter Burke, Brian Harrison and Paul Slack (eds), *Civil Histories: Essays in Honour of Keith Thomas* (Oxford: Oxford University Press, 2000).

Morgan, Prys, 'Lady Llanover (1802–1896), "Gwenynen Gwent"', *Transactions of the Honourable Society of Cymmrodorion*, new series 13 (2007), pp. 94–106.

Nemnich, Philipp Andreas, *Neueste Reise durch England, Schottland und Ireland: Hauptsächlich in Bezug auf Produkte, Fabriken und Handlung* (Tübingen: J.G. Cotta, 1807).

Nicholson, George, *The Cambrian Traveller's Guide and Pocket Companion*, 2nd ed. (London: Nicholson, 1813).

Oeynhausen, Carl von, and Heinrich von Dechen, *Ueber Schienenwege in England: Bemerkungen gesammelt auf seiner Reise in den Jahren 1826 und 1827* (Berlin: G. Reimer, 1829).

Österreich, Johann von, *'Ein Land, wo ich viel gesehen': Aus dem Tagebuch der England-Reise 1815/16*, ed. Alfred Ableitinger, Meinhard Brunner and Gerhard Dinacher (Graz: Selbstverlag der Historischen Landeskommission für Steiermark, 2010), pp. 232–34.

Penhouët, Armand-Louis-Bon Maudet de, *Letters Describing a Tour through Part of South Wales: by a Pedestrian Traveller. With Views, Designed and Etched by the Author* (London: T. Baylis, Greville-Street, 1797).

Pettinger, Alasdair, and Tim Youngs (eds), *The Routledge Research Companion to Travel Writing* (London and New York: Routledge, 2019).

Phillips, Dylan, 'Pa Bris y Croeso? Effeithiau Twristiaeth ar y Gymraeg', in Geraint H. Jenkins and Mari A. Williams (eds), *'Eu hiaith a gadwant?': Y Gymraeg yn yr Ugeinfed Ganrif* (Cardiff: University of Wales Press, 2000), pp. 507–30.

Pitchford, Susan, *Identity Tourism: Imaging and Imagining the Nation*, Tourism Social Science Series 10 (Bingley: Emerald, 2008).

Plathow-Holl, Barbara, *Eva von Tiele-Wincklers Leben und Werk: Fachwissentschaftliche Überlegungen und fachdidaktische Konsequenzen* (Berlin: Lit Verlag, 2006).

Poenaru, Petrache, 'Voyage en Angleterre', in N. Iorga (ed.), 'Contributii la istoria literaturii romane in veacul al XVIII-lea si al XIX-lea', *Analele Academiei Romane. Memoriile sectiunii literare*, 2nd series, 28 (1905–1906), pp. 255–57.

Poppe, Erich, 'The Welsh Language in German Philology around 1850', in Bernhard Maier and Stefan Zimmer (eds), *150 Jahre Mabinogion – Deutsch-Walisische Kulturbeziehungen* (Tübingen: Max Niemeyer, 2001), pp. 203–21.

Postic, Fañch, 'La Villemarqué et le pays de Galles (1837–1838)', *Triade I, Galles, Ecosse, Irlande* (Brest: CRBC, 1995), pp. 15–30.

Postic, Fañch, 'Le voyage de La Villemarqué au pays de Galles en 1838. Les premières relations interceltiques', *Ar Men*, 125 (November 2001), pp. 34–43.

Pratt, Mary Louise, *Imperial Eyes: Travel Writing and Transculturation*, 2nd ed. (London and New York: Routledge, 2008 [1992]).

Prescott, Sarah, *Eighteenth-Century Writing from Wales: Bards and Britons* (Cardiff: University of Wales Press, 2008).

Price, Angharad, *Ffarwél i Freiburg: Crwydriadau Cynnar T.H. Parry-Williams* (Llandysul: Gomer, 2013).

Pückler-Muskau, Hermann von, *A Tour in England, Ireland and France in the Years 1828 and 1829 with remarks on the manners and customs of the inhabitants, and anecdotes of distinguished public characters in a series of letters by a German Prince*, trans. Sarah Austin, 4 vols (Philadelphia: Carey and Lea, 1833).

Pückler-Muskau, Hermann von, *Briefe eines Verstorbenen: Ein fragmentarisches Tagebuch aus England, Wales, Irland und Frankreich; geschrieben in den Jahren 1828 und 1829* (Stuttgart: Hallberger, 1836).

Pulszky, Ferencz A., *Aus dem Tagebuche eines in Grossbritannien reisenden Ungarn* (Pesth: Gustav Heckenast, 1837).

Purgstall, Gottfried Wenzel von, 'Auszüge aus reisebeschreibenden Briefen des vorletzten Grafen von Purgstall', in Joseph von Hammer-Purgstall (ed.), *Denkmal auf das Grab der beyden letzten Grafen von Purgstall* (Vienna: Anton Strauß, 1821), pp. 98–141.

R., J.J. de, 'Naar Llandudno', *Voorwaarts: sociaal-democratisch dagblad*, 9 October 1930, n.pag.

Rearick, Charles, 'Henri Martin: From Druidic Traditions to Republican Politics', *Journal of Contemporary History*, 7:3 (1972), pp. 53–64.

Reclus, Élisée, *Nouvelle géographie universelle: la terre et les hommes*, Vol. 4 (Paris: Hachette, 1879).

Rellstab, Ludwig, *Sommermärchen in Reisebildern aus Deutschland, Belgien, Frankreich, England, Schottland im Jahr 1851*, 3 vols (Darmstadt: n.p., 1852).

Renan, Ernest, 'La poésie des races celtiques', in *Essais de morale et de critique* (Paris: Calmann-Lévy, 1928), pp. 375–456, first published in *Revue des Deux Mondes*, n.s. 5 (1854), pp. 473–504.

Rigney, Ann, 'Immemorial Routines: The Celts and their Resistance to History', in Terence Brown (ed.), *Celticism* (Amsterdam: Rodopi, 1996), pp. 159–82.

Roberts, Gwyneth Tyson, *The Language of the Blue Books: Wales and Colonial Prejudice* (Cardiff: University of Wales Press, 1998).

Rodenberg, Julius, *Ein Herbst in Wales: Land und Leute, Märchen und Lieder* (Hannover: C. Rümpler, 1858).

Rodenberg, Julius, *Die Harfe von Erin: Märchen und Dichtung in Irland* (Leipzig: Grunow, 1861).

Rodenberg, Julius, *An Autumn in Wales (1856): Country and People, Tales and Songs*, trans. William Linnard (Cowbridge: D. Brown and Sons, 1985).

Rogers, Shannon L., 'From Wasteland to Wonderland: Wales in the Imagination of the English Traveller, 1720–1895', *North American Journal of Welsh Studies*, 2:2 (2002), pp. 15–26.

Rojek, Chris, and John Urry, 'Introduction', in *Touring Cultures: Transformations of Travel and Theory* (London: Routledge, 1997), pp. 1–19.

Rolt, L.T.C., *Thomas Telford* (Stroud: The History Press, 2008 [1958]).

Russegger, Joseph, *Reisen in Europa, Asien und Afrika: Mit besonderer Rücksicht auf die naturwissenschaftlichen Verhältnisse der betreffenden Länder, unternommen in den Jahren 1835 bis 1841* (Stuttgart: Schweizbart, 1841).

Said, Edward W., *Orientalism* (London: Penguin, 1995 [1978]).

Saillens, Jeanne, *Le Réveil du Pays de Galles* (Valance: Ducros, 1905).

Saint-Germain-Leduc, Pierre-Etienne-Denis, *L'Angleterre, L'Ecosse et L'Irlande: relation d'un voyage récent dans les trois royaumes*, 4 vols (Paris: Levrault, 1838).

Saurma, Charlotte von, 'Cardiff', *Merian*, 10 (20 September 2012), pp. 30–38, https://www.merian.de/europa/wales/cardiff/artikel/stadtrundgang-durch-cardiff [accessed 7 October 2016].

Schenkel, Elmar, 'Paradies für Büchernarren: Das Städtchen Hay ist Pilgerziel für Literarische Wanderer', *Die Zeit*, 33, 8 August 1980, p. 46.

Schinkel, Karl Friedrich, *Die Reise nach Frankreich und England im Jahre 1826*, ed. Reinhard Wegener (Munich and Berlin: Deutscher Kunstverlag 1990).

Schinkel, Karl Friedrich, '*The English Journey': Journal of a Visit to France and Britain in 1826*, trans. F. Gayna Walls, ed. David Bindman and Gottfried Riemann (New Haven and London: Yale University Press, 1993).

Schlegel, August Wilhelm, 'Wiener Vorlesungen', 'Erster Theil (1809)' and 'Zweiter Theil (1809), in Stefan Knödler (ed.), *Vorlesungen über dramatische Kunst und Literatur (1809–1811)*, Vol. 1: *Text* (Paderborn: Ferdinand Schöningh, 2018), pp. 1–270.

Schneebeli, Robert, 'Schule, Gesang und Kohlengruben: Kulturgeschichtliche Skizzen aus Wales', *Schweizer Monatshefte: Zeitschrift für Politik, Wirtschaft und Kultur*, 36:8 (1956), pp. 606–10.

Schophoff, Julius, 'Auf der Klippe', *Die Zeit*, 22, 5 June 2012, p. 61.

Schuchardt, Hugo, 'Ymweliad â Chymru', *Yr Herald Cymraeg*, 20 August 1875, p. 8 and 3 September 1875, p. 8.

Schuchardt, Hugo, 'Keltische Briefe', in *Romanisches und Keltisches: Gesammelte Aufsätze von Hugo Schuchardt* (Strassburg: Karl J. Trübner, 1886), pp. 317–86.

Schulz, Albert, *An Essay on the influence of Welsh tradition upon the literature of Germany, France, and Scandinavia, which obtained the prize of the Abergavenny Cymreigyddion Society, at the eisteddfod of 1840*, trans. Frances Berrington (Llandovery: William Rees; London: Longman, Williams, Hughes; Chester: Parry; Abergavenny: Morgan, 1841).

Schulz, Albert, *Die Arthursage und die Märchen des rothen Buchs von Hergest*, Bibliothek der gesammten deutschen Nationalliteratur, Section II, Vol. 2 (Quedlinburg and Leipzig: Basse, 1842).

Shih, Shu-mei, and Françoise Lionnet, 'Introduction: Thinking through the Minor, Transnationally', in *Minor Transnationalism* (Durham, NC and London: Duke University Press, 2005), pp. 1–23.

Siche, Gilles, 'Trois écrivains bretonnants au Pays de Galles: Taldir Jaffrennou, Frañsez Vallée et Roparz Hemon', in *Parcours Pays de Galles–Bretagne* (Brest: CRBC, 1995), pp. 33–46.

Simond, Louis, *Journal of a Tour and Residence in Great Britain, during the Years 1810 to 1811, by a French Traveller: with Remarks on the Country, its Arts, Literature, and Politics, and on the Manners and Customs of its Inhabitants* (Edinburgh: Ramsay and Co., for Constable and Co., 1815).

Simond, Louis, *Voyage d'un Français en Angleterre pendant les années 1810 et 1811* (Paris: Treuttel et Würtz, 1816).

Simonin, Louis, 'Une Visite aux grandes usines du pays de Galles', *Le Tour du Monde*, 11 (1865), pp. 321–52.

Sims-Williams, Patrick, 'The Visionary Celt: The Construction of an Ethnic Preconception', *Cambrian Medieval Celtic Studies*, 11 (1986), pp. 71–96.

Sims-Williams, Patrick, 'The Invention of Celtic Nature Poetry', in Terence Brown (ed.), *Celticism* (Amsterdam: Rodopi, 1996), pp. 97–124.

Sims-Williams, Patrick, 'Celtomania and Celtoscepticism', *Cambrian Medieval Celtic Studies*, 36 (1998), pp. 1–34.

Sims-Williams, Patrick, 'How Are You Finding it Here?', *London Review of Books*, 28 October 1999, pp. 30–31.

Singer, Rita, 'Through Wales in the Footsteps of William Gilpin: Illustrated Travel Accounts by Early French Tourists, 1768–1810', *European Romantic Review*, 30:2 (2019), pp. 127–47.

Smyers, L., *Essai sur l'état actuel de l'industrie ardoisière en France et en Angleterre, suivi de quelques observations pratiques sur la formation du schiste ardoisier* (Paris: Poulet-Malassis, 1858).

Soechting, E., 'Kurze Mittheilungen von einer Reise in England und Schottland', *Zeitschrift für die gesamten Naturwissenschaften*, 5:11 (November 1855), pp. 378–99.

Solkin, David H., *Richard Wilson: The Landscape of Reaction* (London: Tate Gallery Publications Department, 1982).

Sparschuh, N., *Keltische Studien* (Frankfurt am Main: Varrentrapp, 1848).

Spiero, Heinrich, *Julius Rodenberg. Sein Leben und seine Werke* (Berlin: Paetel, 1921).

Spiker, Samuel Heinrich, *Reise durch England, Wales und Schottland im Jahre 1816*, 2 vols (Leipzig: Göschen, 1818).

Spiker, Samuel Heinrich, *Travels through England, Wales and Scotland in the Year 1816*, trans. anon., 2 vols (London: Lackington, Hughes, Harding, Mavor and Jones, 1820).

Stearns, Peter, 'British Industry through the Eyes of French Industrialists (1820–1848)', *The Journal of Modern History*, 37:1 (1965), pp. 50–61.

Suffren, Amélie de, *Voyage pittoresque dans le midi et le nord du pays de Galles, ou suite de 48 vues déssinées sur les lieux* (Paris: Gille, 1805).

Sullivan, Richard Joseph, *Bemerkungen auf einer Reise durch verschiedene Theile von England, Schottland und Wales; nebst einer Nebenreise in die Hölen von Ingleborough und Settle in Yorkshire. In Briefen. Aus dem Englischen, nebst einigen Anmerkungen des Uebersetzers* (Leipzig: Breitkopf, 1781); from *Observations made during a Tour through parts of England, Scotland and Wales in a series of letters* (London: T. Beckett, 1780).

Tanguy, Bernard, *Aux origines du nationalisme breton*, 2 vols (Paris: Union générale d'éditions, 1977).

Thiébault, Adolphe, *Voyage à pied dans le nord du pays de Galles*, Books 14.1–2 (1827), Thiébault Family mss., 1733–1872, bulk 1793–1872, Lilly Library, Indiana University Bloomington.

Thierry, Amédée, *Histoire des Gaulois*, 3 vols (Paris: Hachette, Hetzel, 1828, 1834, 1845).

Thierry, Augustin, *Histoire de la conquête de l'Angleterre par les Normands*, 3 vols (Paris: Firmin Didot, 1825).

Thomas, Mair Elvet, *Afiaith yng Ngwent* (Cardiff: University of Wales Press, 1978).

Thomas, M. Wynn, *Corresponding Cultures: The Two Literatures of Wales* (Cardiff: University of Wales Press, 1999).

Thomas, M. Wynn, *In the Shadow of the Pulpit: Literature and Nonconformist Wales* (Cardiff: University of Wales Press, 2010).

Thomas, M. Wynn, *The Nations of Wales 1890–1914* (Cardiff: University of Wales Press, 2016).

Thomas, M. Wynn, 'Introduction: Microcosmopolitan Wales', in *All that Is Wales: The Collected Essays of M. Wynn Thomas* (Cardiff: University of Wales Press, 2017), pp. 1–29.

Thomas, M. Wynn, 'Studying Wales Today: A Microcosmopolitan Approach', http://www.cymmrodorion.org/wp-content/uploads/2017/01/STUDYING-WALES-TODAY-M-W-THOMAS-6-DECEMBER-2016-compressed.pdf [accessed 27 January 2019].

Thompson, Carl, *Travel Writing* (London and New York: Routledge, 2011).

Thompson, Carl, 'Travel Writing Now, 1950 to the Present Day', in Carl Thompson (ed.), *The Routledge Companion to Travel Writing* (New York: Routledge, 2015), pp. 196–213.

Thompson, Christopher W., *French Romantic Travel Writing: Chateaubriand to Nerval* (Oxford: Oxford University Press, 2012).

Thorne, David, 'Hugo Schuchardt (1842–1927)', *Y Traethodydd*, 138 (1983), pp. 91–100.

Thuillier, Guy, *Georges Dufaud et les débuts du grand capitalisme dans la métallurgie, en Nivernais, au XIXe siècle* (Paris: SEVPEN, 1959).

Tiele-Winckler, Eva von, *Denkstein des lebendigen Gottes* (Giessen: Brunnen, 1970).

Timm, Uwe, 'Nicht Morgen, nicht Gestern', in *Nicht Morgen, nicht Gestern* (Cologne: Verlag Kiepenheuer & Witsch, 1999), pp. 25–46.

Trabaud, Pierre, 'Pays de Galles', in *D'Inverness à Brighton: notes et sentiments sur les Îles Britanniques* (London: Baillière, 1853).

Tramard, Danielle, 'Hay-on-Wye, le livre aux champs', *Le Monde*, 25 April 2002, https://www.lemonde.fr/archives/article/2002/04/25/hay-on-wye-le-livre-aux-champs_4238294_1819218.html?xtmc=&xtcr=20 [accessed 24 January 2016].

Tromly, Lucas, 'Echotourism and Women's Travel Writing', unpublished lecture, Freie Universität Berlin, 27 October 2017.

Tully, Carol, *Creating a National Identity: A Comparative Study of German and Spanish Romanticism*, Stuttgarter Arbeiten zur Germanistik 347 (Stuttgart: Hans-Dieter Heinz, 1997).

Tully, Carol, 'The Celtic Misconnection: The German Romantics and Wales', *Angermion*, 2 (2009), pp. 127–41.

Tully, Carol, '"Pride in their port, defiance in their eye": English Translations of German Travel Writing on the British Isles in the Early Nineteenth Century', *Intralinea* (2013), http://www.intralinea.org/specials/article/pride_in_their_port_defiance_in_their_eye [accessed 3 January 2019].

Tully, Carol, 'Out of Europe: Travel and Exile in Mid-Twentieth-Century Wales', *Studies in Travel Writing*, 18:2 (2014), pp. 174–86.

Tully, Carol, 'Nineteenth-Century German Travellers to Wales: Text, Translation and the Manipulation of Identity', in James Hodkinson and Ben Schofield (eds), *German in the World* (London: Boydell and Brewer, 2020), pp. 74–90.

Urbain, Jean-Didier, *Secrets de voyage: menteurs, imposteurs et autres voyageurs immédiats* (Paris: Payot, 1998).

Urry, John, *The Tourist Gaze: Leisure and Travel in Contemporary Societies* (London: Sage, 1990).

Urry, John, and Jonas Larsen, *The Tourist Gaze 3.0* (London: Sage, 2011).

Van Tieghem, Paul, *Ossian en France*, 2 vols (Geneva: Slatkine, 1967).

Varrentrapp, Georg, *Tagebuch einer medizinischen Reise nach England, Holland und Belgien* (Frankfurt am Main: Varrentrapp, 1839).

Vatout, Jean, *Notices historiques sur les tableaux de la Galerie de SAR, Mgr le Duc d'Orléans*, Vol. 4 (Paris: Gaultier-Laguionie, 1825–1826).

Vincentelli, Moira, 'The Davies Family and the Belgian Refugee Artists and Musicians in Wales', *National Library of Wales Journal*, 22:2 (1981), pp. 226–33.

Visit Britain, *Trends in Visits to Different Areas in Britain*, Foresight, 127 (2014), https://www.visitbritain.org/nation-region-county-data [accessed 21 August 2015].

Voogt, Gosewinus de, 'Per Grimsbylijn: Great-Central Ry. naar Wales', *Eigen Haard*, 34:34 (22 August 1908), pp. 534–38.

Wagstaffe, Brian, 'Welsh Ironworkers in France', *Glamorgan Family History Society*, 51 (1998), pp. 14–15.

Wahba, Magdi, 'Mme de Genlis in England', *Comparative Literature*, 13:3 (1961), pp. 221–38.

Walford Davies, Damian, *Presences that Disturb: Models of Romantic Identity in the Literature and Culture of the 1790s* (Cardiff: University of Wales Press, 2002).

Walford Davies, Damian, and Lynda Pratt (eds), *Wales and the Romantic Imagination* (Cardiff: University of Wales Press, 2007).

Walter, Ferdinand, *Das alte Wales* (Bonn: Marcus, 1859).

Warner, Rev. Richard, *A Walk through Wales in August 1797* (Bath: Cruttwell, 1798).

Watkins, John, 'Wales and France', *Transactions of the Honourable Society of Cymmrodorion*, 2 (1967), pp. 179–202.

Weber, Guy, 'Tenby', in *L'Heure du choix ou les séquelles du drame belge de 1940* (Brussels: Éditions Louis Musin, 1985), pp. 43–59.

Wedding, Landbaumeister, 'Die Kettenbrücken über die Meerenge Menai, die von Aber-Conwy und Hammersmith', *Verhandlungen des Vereins zur Beförderung des Gewerbefleißes in Preußen*, 7 (1828): II. Eigene Abhandlungen und Auszüge aus fremden Werken, pp. 234–43.

Welden, Franz Ludwig Freiherr von, 'Ueber dekorirende Landschafts-Gartenkunst, Anlagen sogenannter Natur- oder englischer Gärten und Gebäude, im großen, wie im kleinsten Maßstabe; ganz vorzüglich für Deutschland und die wohlhabendere Mittelklasse berechnet: Beschreibung eines englischen Landhauses und seiner Umgebung', *Allgemeine Bauzeitung mit Abbildungen für Architekten, Ingeneurs, Dekorateurs, Bauprofessionisten, Oekonomen, Bauunternehmer und Alle, die an den Fortschritten und Leistungen der neuesten Zeit an der Baukunst und den dahin einschlagenden Fächern Antheil nehmen*, 4 (1839), pp. 91–103.

Welsh Government, 'News and Alerts: Visit Wales Germany Marketing Campaign', http://content.govdelivery.com/accounts/UKWALES/bulletins/e8odd2 [accessed 16 March 2016].

Williams, Daniel, 'Pan-Celticism and the Limits of Post-Colonialism: W.B. Yeats, Ernest Rhys and Williams Sharp in the 1890s', in Tony Brown and Russell Stephens (eds), *Nations and Relations: Writing across the British Isles* (Cardiff: New Welsh Review, 2000), pp. 1–29.

Williams, Daniel, *Black Skin, Blue Books: African Americans and Wales, 1845–1945* (Cardiff: University of Wales Press, 2012).

Williams, Daniel, *Wales Unchained: Literature, Politics and Identity in the American Century* (Cardiff: University of Wales Press, 2015).

Williams, Gwyn Alf, *When Was Wales?* (Harmondsworth: Penguin, 1985).

Williams, Heather, 'Celtomania', in John T. Koch (ed.), *Celtic Culture: A Historical Encyclopedia*, Vol. 5 (Santa Barbara: ABC-CLIO, 2006), pp. 391–92.

Williams, Heather, *Postcolonial Brittany: Literature between Languages* (Oxford: Peter Lang, 2007).

Williams, Heather, 'Cymru trwy lygaid Rousseau (ac eraill)', *Y Traethodydd*, CLXVIII (2013), pp. 241–54.

Williams, Heather, 'Rousseau and Wales', in Mary-Ann Constantine and Dafydd Johnston (eds), *'Footsteps of Liberty and Revolt': Essays on Wales and the French Revolution* (Cardiff: University of Wales, 2013), pp. 35–51.

Williams, Heather, 'Rousseau and Romanticism in Wales', in Russell Goulbourne and David Higgins (eds), *Jean-Jacques Rousseau and British Romanticism* (London: Bloomsbury, 2017), pp. 75–90.

Williams, Heather, 'Travelling Ideas between Wales and Brittany', *VTU Review: Studies in the Humanities and Social Sciences*, 2:1 (2018), pp. 47–54.

Williams, Heather, 'La construction du Moyen Âge dans les récits de voyage français portant sur le pays de Galles', *Quel Moyen Âge? La recherche en question, Histoires des Bretagnes 6*, ed. Hélène Bouget and Magali Coumert (Brest: CRBC, 2019), pp. 65–81.

Williams, Heather, 'Views of Mid-Wales by Artists, Exiles and Royals from Europe', *Ceredigion*, 18:2 (2019), pp. 27–53.

Withey, Lynne, *Grand Tours and Cook's Tours: A History of Leisure Travel, 1750–1915* (London: Aurum Press, 1997).

Youngs, Tim, *The Cambridge Introduction to Travel Writing* (Cambridge: Cambridge University Press, 2013).

Zaring, Jane, 'The Romantic Face of Wales', *Annals of the Association of American Geographers*, 67:3 (1977), pp. 397–418.

Zeuss, Johann Kaspar, *Grammatica Celtica*, 2 vols (Leipzig: Weidmann, 1853).

Zielonka, Anthony, *Alphonse Esquiros (1812–76): A Study of his Works* (Paris: Champion, 1985).

Zielske, Horst, *Wales: Mit Texten des walisischen Schriftstellers Dylan Thomas* (Dortmund: Harenberg, 1992).

Websites

Bibliothèque patrimoniale numérique, Mines ParisTech, https://patrimoine.mines-paristech.fr/Journaux_de_voyage [accessed 22 February 2019].

'Journey to the Past: Wales in Historic Travel Writing from France and Germany', http://footsteps.bangor.ac.uk/en/ [accessed 27 April 2020].

Kugies, Siegfried, online video testimonial account of his period as a prisoner of war in Wales, https://www.zeitzeugen-portal.de/personen/zeitzeuge/siegfried_kugies [accessed 16 June 2018].

Teithwyr Ewropeaidd i Gymru/European Travellers to Wales, etw.bangor.ac.uk [accessed 7 August 2019].

Index

References to non-English terms have only been included when the term is used separately, as English translations have been provided throughout the book.

Author names only have been included in the index and not the titles of their works.